Educational Psychology:
Concepts, Research and Challenges

D1555825

Research in educational psychology has had a huge impact in terms of enhancing understanding and challenging thinking about teachers and learners. *Educational Psychology: Concepts, Research and Challenges* brings together the latest research across many areas of educational psychology, introducing and reporting on the most effective methodologies for studying teachers and learners and providing overviews of current debates within the field. With chapters from international authors, this academic text or advanced level textbook provides theoretical overviews and research findings from across the field including:

- Teaching and learning
- Research methods
- Motivation and instruction
- Curriculum – reading, writing, mathematics
- Cognition
- Special Educational Needs and behaviour management
- Sociocultural and socioemotional perspectives
- Assessment and evaluation.

Educational psychology has historically had a focus on students with particular learning needs. This book provides a discussion of the gradual movement toward inclusion and the possibility of developing a more cohesive and potentially more effective education system for all students. It also presents recent research into effective behaviour management and illustrates specific and valuable techniques employed in applied behaviour analysis. The contributors also deliver analysis on the motivation of students and how home and society in general can contribute towards constraining or enhancing student learning.

This book is a must-read for academics, researchers, undergraduate and graduate students who recognize the substantial contribution of educational psychology to increasing our understanding of students and their learning, teachers and their teaching.

Christine M. Rubie-Davies is currently Senior Lecturer in the Faculty of Education at the University of Auckland, New Zealand.

Educational Psychology: Concepts, Research and Challenges

Edited by
Christine M. Rubie-Davies

 Routledge
Taylor & Francis Group

LONDON AND NEW YORK

This first edition published 2011
by Routledge
2 Park Square, Milton Park, Abingdon, Oxon, OX14 4RN

Simultaneously published in the USA and Canada
by Routledge
270 Madison Avenue, New York, NY 10016

Routledge is an imprint of the Taylor & Francis Group, an informa business

Typeset in Galliard by Keystroke, Tettenhall, Wolverhampton
Printed and bound in Great Britain by
CPI Antony Rowe, Chippenham, Wiltshire

British Library Cataloguing in Publication Data
A catalogue record for this book is available from the British Library

Library of Congress Cataloging-in-Publication Data
Educational psychology : concepts, research and challenges / edited by
Christine Rubie-Davies.
p. cm.
Includes bibliographical references and index.
1. Educational psychology–Research. 2. Education–Research–
Methodology. I. Rubie-Davies, Christine M.
LB1051.E3616 2011
370.15–dc22
2010020809

ISBN13: 978–0–415–56263–8 (hbk)
ISBN13: 978–0–415–56264–5 (pbk)
ISBN13: 978–0–203–83888–4 (ebk)

Contents

Figures

Tables

Contributors

Angelika Anderson is a Senior Lecturer in the Faculty of Education at Monash University, Melbourne, Australia. She teaches in the areas of developmental and behavioural psychology. Her research interests include developmental disabilities, evidence-based practice and inclusive education with a focus on interventions in a behavioural paradigm.

Mere Berryman is a Senior Research Fellow in the Faculty of Education at the University of Waikato. Her role enables her to build on research aimed at supporting educators to work more effectively with Māori students and their families in a range of education settings.

Russell Bishop is foundation Professor for Māori Education at the University of Waikato, Hamilton. He is currently project director for Te Kotahitanga, a large New Zealand Ministry of Education project that seeks to improve the educational achievement of Māori students through the implementation of a culturally responsive pedagogy of relations.

Don Brown is Director of the Resource Teacher: Learning and Behaviour programme at Victoria University, Wellington. He was formerly Chief Psychologist and Director Special Education with the New Zealand Department of Education, and is a Fellow of the New Zealand Psychological Society. His research interests are in teacher professional development.

Gavin T.L. Brown is an Associate Professor and Associate Head of the Department of Psychological Studies at the Hong Kong Institute of Education. His research focuses on cross-cultural differences in teacher and student responses to and understandings of educational assessment.

John Church is a Senior Lecturer at the University of Canterbury. His research interests include the measurement of behaviour change, the experimental analysis of behaviour and behaviour change, instructional processes, origins of antisocial development and effective responses to behaviour problems and learning difficulties in children.

John A. Hattie is a Professor of Education at the University of Auckland. His research interests include research methodology, structural equation modelling, self-concept and models of teaching and learning. John is the Director of asTTle and of the Visible Learning Laboratories.

Putai Jin is a Senior Lecturer at the University of New South Wales. His research interests are self-regulated learning, stress and research methods. His publications appear in outlets such as *Psychological Bulletin, Journal of Educational Psychology*, and *Journal of Psychosomatic Research*.

Louise J. Keown is a Senior Lecturer in Child and Adolescent Development in the Faculty of Education, University of Auckland. She is a developmental psychologist whose research interests focus on the influence of parenting on young children's social and behavioural development, with particular emphasis on preschool behaviour problems.

Renae Low is a Senior Lecturer at the University of New South Wales. Her research interest is in educational psychology for learning and teaching. Her findings have been published in international academic journals such as the *Journal of Educational Psychology*.

Angus H. Macfarlane is Professor of Māori Research at the University of Canterbury. In 2003, he was awarded the inaugural Research Fellowship by the New Zealand Council for Educational Research, and the following year he received a Tohu Kairangi award, a citation for academic achievement in Māori education.

Stuart McNaughton is Professor of Education at the University of Auckland and Director of the Woolf Fisher Research Centre. His research focuses on literacy and language development including processes of education, socialization and culture, and on the design of effective instruction and educational programmes for culturally and linguistically diverse populations.

Dennis Moore is the Professor in Educational Psychology at Monash University. He is an educational psychologist with long-standing research interests in how we might better teach children with special needs, and how we can better support their parents and teachers. Dennis has published widely in these areas.

Tom W. Nicholson is a Professor of Education at Massey University, New Zealand, who specializes in literacy and child development. He advises the government on national standards and is a member of the International Reading Association Hall of Fame.

Judy M. Parr is an Associate Professor of Education at the University of Auckland, New Zealand. Her research interests focus on optimizing literacy development, particularly writing. Classroom practice, assessment and the nature of knowledge for teachers of writing are her areas of specialization.

Elizabeth R. Peterson is a Senior Lecturer in the Psychology Department at the University of Auckland. Her research interests include the psychology of individual differences, the development of educational beliefs and cognitive styles. Elizabeth mainly focuses on the factors and processes that lead to the development of successful well-rounded students.

Jane E. Prochnow is a Senior Lecturer in the School of Educational Studies at Massey University. Her research interests include learners' emotional and behavioural disorders, the problems associated with including learners with behavioural disorders in the classroom, and the relationship between reading and behavioural disorders.

Dennis Rose is a Principal Lecturer in the Faculty of Education, University of Auckland. His research is mostly concerned with children's learning and behaviour, usually within a behaviour analytic methodology. His most recent research is a series of studies on fluency.

Christine M. Rubie-Davies is a Senior Lecturer in the Faculty of Education at the University of Auckland with expertise in teacher expectations and the social psychology of the classroom. She is a recipient of a National Tertiary Teaching Award and is a Fellow of the Association for Psychological Science.

John Sweller is an Emeritus Professor of Education at the University of New South Wales. His research is associated with cognitive load theory. The theory is a contributor to both research and debate on issues associated with human cognition, its links to evolution by natural selection, and the instructional design consequences that follow.

Lottie Thomson is a Registered Psychologist and a Senior Lecturer in the Resource Teacher: Learning and Behaviour Programme at Victoria University of Wellington. Her research focus is teacher professional development, collaborative consultation and evidence based practice.

Helen S. Timperley is Professor of Education at the University of Auckland. Her research focuses on how to promote professional and leadership learning in schools. She has published numerous research articles in both these areas in international journals and has written five books on her specialty research areas.

Michael Townsend is Professor of Educational Psychology in the School of Education, Massey University (Auckland campus). His research interests in learning and instruction span cognitive, social and motivational dimensions of classrooms.

Thanh-Binh Tran is a Researcher in the Woolf Fisher Research Centre at the University of Auckland. She is also a Lecturer in educational and developmental psychology and pedagogy. Her research interests are early literacy, partnership with families, individual activity and shared activity.

William E. Tunmer is Distinguished Professor of Educational Psychology at Massey University. He received his PhD in Experimental Psychology from the

University of Texas at Austin in 1979. His research focuses on literacy development, reading difficulties, and intervention strategies. Professor Tunmer is currently Associate Editor of *Reading and Writing: An Interdisciplinary Journal.*

Jennifer M. Young-Loveridge is an Associate Professor in Mathematics Education and Human Development at the University of Waikato. She received her PhD in Applied Psychology from the University of Toronto in 1983. Her research interests include the development of mathematical thinking, teachers' mathematical pedagogical content, and learners' perspectives on mathematics learning.

Foreword

During my time as editor of the *British Journal of Educational Psychology* I had the opportunity to review over 500 submissions. Needless to say they were varied in content, approach and theoretical acumen. There were, during this period, submissions and reviews from researchers in New Zealand. I was introduced to new areas of work, impressed by the clarity of the thinking and intrigued by the ways in which the academics there used their particular contexts to address the issues that were central to educational psychology. So it gives me great pleasure to write a foreword for this creative and exciting collection of chapters grounded in research from New Zealand. This pleasure is enhanced by the opportunity I had to gain a deeper understanding of the New Zealand context, and research carried out, during a recent visit to Auckland.

There are many challenges for education in the twenty-first century. This collection, located within the discipline of educational psychology and informed by the unique experiences and opportunities afforded in the New Zealand context, provides a distinctive approach to some of these challenges. The chapters present studies and approaches to analyses that are relevant to researchers across the globe. There are three central premises which underpin this collection: (1) accessibility; (2) addressing current challenges in educational research; and (3) contextualizing learning and the learner.

In the past 100 or so years we have become skilled at assessing pupils' needs but are still challenged in creating successful learning environments. Effective teaching and learning are central to educational change, a key international objective. Central to effective teaching and learning is robust research in the field of educational psychology. Yet research by academics which is only considered by academics has limited impact for teachers and pupils in real-world settings. The research needs to be accessible to practitioners and students as well as the academic community. This collection aims to do exactly that. State of the art research is presented in an accessible way which should support the understanding of students as well as that of more experienced professionals.

Researchers in the field of educational psychology must also be prepared to tackle issues that have, for different reasons, not been consistently addressed. It is all too easy to follow a particular research trajectory and in so doing miss new and important challenges. Yet, if students are to learn effectively and efficiently, we need to address both ways to support learning and development and to identify potential barriers. The contributors to this volume have confronted this challenge. The book contains chapters that address issues relating to the reliability and validity of assessments, critical if we wish to use these to guide teaching and learning, motivation and thinking and reasoning.

To have ecological validity, research needs to be informed by different learning environments and different groups of learners. Students can be empowered in different ways. The New Zealand context offers a particular window on these issues and is addressed through the innovative work carried out with Māori students. Work of this kind can help us review our attitudes and practices towards minority groups.

I have learnt a significant amount from my contact with the researchers in New Zealand. I trust that by reading chapters in this book you will also gain from their expertise, and that this may help in further developing research in educational psychology.

Julie Dockrell
Professor of Psychology and Special Needs
Institute of Education, London

Introduction

Christine M. Rubie-Davies

This book was designed to bring together a range of fields within educational psychology, thus making them accessible to academics, graduate students and teachers (especially those returning to graduate study) within one volume. It is anticipated that this book will make a major contribution to the field of educational psychology since the reader can locate recent research and understandings in several theoretical areas rather than having to read through a large number of separate volumes on each topic. This is rare at the graduate level and above and so this volume will be welcomed by researchers, students and teachers alike.

The book provides a synthesis of educational psychology research across the various specialties. More advanced educational psychology books often have a narrow focus on a specific area, such as cognitive psychology or developmental psychology, or are based on specific educational theories such as goal theory. This book is intended to provide a broader coverage of educational domains than current books focused on classroom practice (e.g. those related to classroom management or the reflective teacher) or those with a specialized theoretical focus (e.g. cognitive dissonance theory). Because the book includes a wide range of educational psychology domains, it will challenge the thinking of readers across the various fields but can also provide a springboard for more intense study in particular areas or provide a quick reference point for current research across the broad spectrum of educational psychology. It may also provide an opportunity for readers to consider how theories in one educational psychology domain relate to theoretical understandings in another. Moreover, teachers will be encouraged to closely examine their instructional practices in light of the findings presented in this volume since most chapters skilfully link the research findings with classroom practice. Graduate students will be exposed to a range of potential topics for further research in the various fields of educational psychology because the book reveals the depth and breadth of topics within educational psychology that are available for further specialized study. In addition, because the chapters are written by leading academics in their respective areas, students can be guided to appropriate methodologies for their own future studies. For academics, the book brings together very recent research in several educational psychology fields and draws extensively on a broad range of international findings.

With increasing numbers of students enrolling in honours programmes, teachers returning to university to upgrade their qualifications, and students from varied backgrounds wanting to pursue educational psychology as their graduate field of study, there is an undeniable need for a book such as this that provides a broader overview of educational psychology at the graduate level than is currently available. The contributors to this book are all researchers with well-established international reputations. Most are New Zealanders and are internationally recognized in their specific fields but all have drawn extensively from the work of colleagues in the United Kingdom, the United States and Europe. Further, each chapter was peer-reviewed by other experts in the particular specializations. Hence the book provides leading research in most domains of the discipline of educational psychology.

Over the years, research in educational psychology has enhanced understanding and challenged thinking about teachers and learners. The most effective methodologies for studying teachers and learners are presented, along with current debates about teaching and learning. For example, while there has been much debate about a phonics versus whole language approach to reading, which has led to much greater understandings of how students learn to read, there has been little research related to how students learn to write and effective techniques for teaching writing. And in mathematics, what does the research tell us about developing particular mathematical skills, such as multiplicative thinking?

Another current debate relates to the climate of accountability and high stakes testing in many Western countries. This book shows that arguments about summative and formative assessment should move from debates about types of assessment (since each has specific uses) to debates about the reliability and validity of the assessments used in schools.

Educational psychology has also taught us much about how the mind functions and the most effective conditions under which students learn and understand concepts and ideas, and the book presents the latest research in this area. However, learning concerns not just cognition but also student motivation and so this book provides understandings about not just how students should be presented with materials but also the significance of student motivation for learning. There is also discussion on the importance of providing a stimulating socioemotional, as well as instructional, climate in classrooms, and on the importance of friendships for children and the role of fostering peer relationships in developing a classroom community.

Educational psychology has historically had a focus on students with special learning needs. This book provides a discussion about the gradual movement towards inclusion and the possibility of developing a more cohesive and potentially more effective education system for all students. It also provides recent research into effective behaviour management and proposes specific and valuable techniques employed in applied behaviour analysis. Further, within this book the emphasis is moved from exclusively focusing on the classroom to understanding atypical behaviour such as hyperactivity, to also examining parenting styles that potentially contribute to children's behaviour.

This leads to a final component of this book which demonstrates how the home and society in general can contribute to constraining or enhancing student learning. It calls for shifts in perceptions of deficit for some minority groups and offers exciting research demonstrating how changes in teacher practice and understandings have contributed to substantial learning gains for Māori students in New Zealand.

This book, then, is a must-read for researchers, graduate students and teachers who recognize the substantial contribution of educational psychology to increasing our understanding of students and their learning, teachers and their teaching.

Themes and chapters

The chapters within the book are organized so that they form themes which flow one from another. Chapter 1 by Lottie Thomson and Angelika Anderson begins by discussing the recent reforms in education in the United States that emphasize accountability and outcome-based activities and shows how this has encouraged not only a surge of research interest but has also spawned acrimonious and heated argument and debate. It is within this context that the chapter examines salient issues relating to research methods in educational psychology. The position is taken that research must not be confused with method or technique; appropriate method is a function of purpose and research questions should drive methodology. The disconnect between education research and practice is explored. The writers conclude by advocating that rigorous education research should seek out rather than reject diverse perspectives and alternative paradigms.

Chapters 2, 3, 4, and 5 focus on the contribution of educational psychology to our understanding of teaching and learning. While the positive effect of mastery goals on student learning is well documented, Chapter 2 by Helen S. Timperley and Judy M. Parr argues that relatively little attention has been given to the quality of mastery goals, how teachers convey them through lesson activities and how they are understood by students. It puts forward a study that shows how students' expressed understanding was closely related to how clearly the learning goals and mastery criteria were articulated by their teachers during lessons. The chapter concludes with implications for teaching and learning.

Chapter 3 by Tom W. Nicholson and William E. Tunmer is in three parts. First, a brief overview is provided of how two major theories of reading, top down and bottom up, have collided in the past four decades and how a lot of good has come from this. Second, the implications of the theoretical debates for the teaching of reading are discussed. Third, several practical and theoretical studies that have exciting implications for the teaching of reading over the next decades, are presented.

Writing is a cognitively complex social and cultural act of communication. It is a potentially dynamic act as the practices, uses and modes of writing change with new technologies. Chapter 4 by Judy M. Parr examines the links among research and writing assessment and pedagogy. It begins with the traditional view of writing whereby it is employed as a means of making evaluative judgements about knowledge or skill and moves to a consideration of pedagogy and assessment in writing more aligned with current theoretical conceptions.

Finally, in this curriculum-focused group of chapters, Chapter 5 by Jennifer M. Young-Loveridge focuses on what constitutes multiplicative thinking and reasoning, and how it differs from additive thinking. A variety of frameworks for the development of multiplicative thinking and reasoning are described, including the number framework of New Zealand's Numeracy Development Project. Data showing the effect of this project on children's multiplicative thinking, and on multiplicative thinking in classroom contexts are presented. The chapter concludes by reflecting on why educational psychology is important to mathematics educators, including some challenges for the future.

The next two chapters, Chapters 6 and 7, also relate to the instructional aspects of a teacher's role. The former presents recent understandings in relation to cognitive load theory while the latter focuses on assessment. Chapter 6 by Renae Low, Putai Jin, and John Sweller discusses the considerable implications our rapidly progressing knowledge of human cognitive architecture has for instructional design. Cognitive load theory uses this architecture to generate a large range of instructional effects concerned with procedures for reducing extraneous working memory load in order to facilitate the acquisition of knowledge in long-term memory. The chapter reviews the theory, summarizes some of the effects generated and indicates the instructional implications that flow from the theory.

Chapter 7 by John A. Hattie and Gavin T. L. Brown argues that the design of good assessment involves awareness of modern measurement theory and insights into user psychology. The New Zealand Ministry of Education has supplied (since 2003) the Assessment Tools for Teaching and Learning (asTTle) software to all New Zealand schools for self-managed improvement of student outcomes in reading, writing, and mathematics. This chapter outlines the research studies used in the development of the software and argues for greater attention in the user community to measurement principles and for greater attention in the test developer community to the usage of assessments as a criterion of validity.

Following the focus of the first half of the book on the instructional and academic components of the teacher's role, the next two chapters concentrate on consideration of social aspects of schooling. The emphasis in Chapter 8 is on how our theoretical and scientific knowledge about motivation can be applied to instruction in educational contexts. The author argues that motivation is a concept in crisis because of the complex array of concepts and theories that all claim to relate to 'motivation'. Further, the layman's use of 'motivation' in a positive sense with reference to a person who finds an interest in something, pursues it, and gains satisfaction in completing it is probably accurate. However, Michael Townsend contends that we cannot 'give' motivation to students described as lacking motivation. Such students are just not motivated by school activities. The real skill in teaching is to provide learning experiences that encourage students to develop adaptive motivational structures for learning.

An important component in promoting student motivation and learning is found in the socioemotional climate of the classroom. Chapter 9 by Christine M. Rubie-Davies and Elizabeth R. Peterson explores how teacher expectations can contribute to the socioemotional environment of the classroom. The authors argue that expectation research should focus on teachers who have high (or low) expectations for all students rather than on expectations for individual students. This is because expectations for a whole class affect a whole class whereas particular teacher behaviours towards individual students mostly affect only those individuals. Hence the implications for class-level expectations in terms of student learning are much greater than the implications for individuals. The authors show how the very different beliefs and practices of teachers who have high, versus those who have low, expectations for all their students lead teachers to structure the socioemotional environment of their classrooms quite differently. Implications for students and their learning are discussed.

The next two chapters are also concerned with a social aspect of the classroom: behaviour management. Chapter 10 by Jane E. Prochnow and Angus H. Macfarlane sets out research related to classroom management while Chapter 11 by Dennis Rose and John Church focuses on applied behaviour analysis and its use in classrooms. A major area of concern in education is skilful classroom management of learner behaviour. Thus, an aim of Chapter 10 is to examine evidence regarding quality classroom management on learner behaviour by discussing the theoretical background of positive behaviour management in the context of New Zealand schools. The chapter discusses the challenges for behaviour management as a result of changes in all Western countries from the adoption of an inclusive education system. The statistics in New Zealand and many other countries indicate that learners from minority cultural backgrounds are disproportionately removed from the classroom for challenging behaviours. Hence it is suggested that in addition to teacher practices, knowledge and dispositions affecting desired student outcomes, there is also reason to focus on the principles of culturally responsive practice.

Chapter 11 recognizes that applied behaviour analysis research remains a minority research endeavour in educational psychology. However, the chapter shows that in less than 40 years, behaviour analysts have made considerable progress in understanding the variables on which human learning depends. Further, the authors show that although applied behaviour analysis has received less attention in recent times, it is becoming influential once more in commissioned reports on children with severe behaviour problems and as best practice with children with autism.

Leading on from the chapter on applied behaviour analysis, the next chapter, Chapter 12 by Don Brown and Dennis Moore, is given over to educational psychology's contribution to special education. In this chapter the history of special education is reviewed and the New Zealand experience is related to trends in other developed countries. The authors consider the role educational psychology has played in the development of special education and they discuss the facilitators and barriers to progress. They also consider the need for a separate special education system within the inclusive education framework, while retaining special education skills and support for general education. The position taken in this chapter is that there is no special education pedagogy that is fundamentally different from what is effective for all students. Hence the argument is presented that no dichotomy of delivery of specialist services to a restricted population of identified students should exist.

The final four chapters consider student factors in relation to learning. Chapter 13 by Tom Nicholson and Michael Townsend highlights the research related to friends (real and imaginary) and friendships. The authors show that children spend a lot of time with other children because they want and need company as part of their social and emotional development. Children learn many social skills by interacting with their friends. Moreover, parents can help their children to make friends and teach them how to keep their friends. Also, while some parents worry about the peer group being a bad influence, most children choose friends who are similar to them and have the same values as them. The authors show that children need friends since not having friends is associated with loneliness, depression, aggression, and other negative outcomes. Hence the importance of having friends in childhood, adolescence, and in adulthood should not be underestimated.

Chapter 14 by Louise J. Keown reviews some of the recent work on the parenting correlates of hyperactivity during the preschool years. The review focuses on cross-sectional and prospective studies of high risk and clinical mother–child dyads. In addition, the chapter considers studies that examine whether parenting is linked to hyperactivity independently of conduct problems. The second aim of the chapter is to discuss the need to expand our understanding of the role of family relationships in the development of preschool children with hyperactivity from a primary focus on mothers to one that includes both fathers and mothers. Reasons we might expect fathers to play a significant role in the development of children with hyperactivity are extrapolated from developmental psychology studies that highlight the unique contribution made by fathers to children's social and behavioural development.

Chapter 15 by Thanh-Binh Tran, Stuart McNaughton and Judy M. Parr further emphasizes the significant role the family environment plays in children's intellectual and social development. There is a long history of optimism about how educational and developmental psychology might contribute to child rearing. This chapter focuses on one area of optimization: the reading of story books to children as a vehicle for promoting particular types of language skills. It includes a description of an intervention programme designed to enhance language development in a group of Vietnamese children before they start school, and shows how storybook reading can be used to enhance children's learning.

The penultimate chapter, Chapter 16 by Mere Berryman and Russell Bishop, considers the educational disparities of New Zealand's indigenous Māori, from both societal and cultural perspectives. It does this in relation to Te Kotahitanga, a research and development initiative designed to improve the educational outcomes of Māori students in a number of New Zealand secondary schools. The chapter begins by introducing some of the historical discourses and practices that continue to pathologize Māori, and which are associated with the more common societal view of the underachievement of Māori students in schools. It explains these from a sociological perspective associated with issues of power and control, and reflects on psychological viewpoints that are legitimized by these discourses. It then uses the Te Kotahitanga research to explore how the problems experienced by a minority ethnic people can be more effectively understood and responded to through the cultural lens of the students themselves, rather than by being externally theorized and imposed. Chapter 17 is the Conclusion.

The chapters in this book thus offer an eclectic mix of topics embedded in the discipline of educational psychology. Moreover, while the focus is on the international research evidence, the unique contribution made by New Zealand to the educational psychology literature is highlighted. The asTTle programme, developed by John Hattie, has had enormous effects not only on New Zealand assessment practices but also on the professional discussions encouraged by the evidence produced by the asTTle reports that teachers can create related to individual achievement, class achievement and achievement in relation to schools with similar populations. The Numeracy Development Project, a major Ministry of Education initiative in New Zealand, has had a significant effect on mathematics teaching. Chapter 10 on behaviour management highlights the disproportionate numbers of Māori students who are stood down from school, a problem that confronts all developed countries with large numbers of minority group students. That chapter, however, along with Chapter 16, calls for examination of teacher attitudes and practices towards minority group students. The Te Kotahitanga programme in New Zealand, discussed in Chapter 16, has had enormous success in enhancing the performance of Māori students and is presented in this book as a model that could potentially be used in many other countries that want to enhance the achievement of their indigenous and minority group students. But this is not the only chapter with potential for wide application. It is hoped that this book will make a major contribution to educational psychology that will show the way ahead in many of the other areas it places in the spotlight.

I would like to thank the authors for their contribution of leading international findings in their particular areas and for their thoughtful and considered writing. Every chapter underwent peer review and several revisions to meet the high standards expected for this book. I am extremely grateful to the reviewers for the generous donation of their time and for the calibre of their feedback. You know who you are! I would also like to offer special thanks to Janet Rivers who worked tirelessly in providing exceptional editorial assistance on this book. I really do not know how I would have managed without her help. Thanks also to Nesrin Kennedy who assisted in helping with editing and checking of chapters in the final stages.

Chapter 1

Research methods in education

Contemporary issues

Lottie Thomson and Angelika Anderson

In the United States, the emphasis in recent reforms in education on accountability and outcomes-based activities has encouraged a surge of research interest. An industry of task forces and research activity, variously described as a movement (Kratochwill and Shernoff 2004) or a bandwagon (Hoagwood and Johnson 2003), depending on one's perspective, has developed. Mandates within American legislation (the No Child Left Behind Act of 2002, in particular) are requiring educators to embrace and implement what has come to be known as evidence-based research, or evidence-based practice (Dirkx 2006; Kratochwill 2002; Gutkin 2002; Reschly 2004; Schaughency and Ervin 2006).

Although there is considerable disagreement about what constitutes evidence, or what it means to engage in evidence-based practice, there is general agreement that education needs to move towards evidence-based practice. 'Appropriate concern exists that investment in practices that lack adequate empirical support may drain limited resources and, in some cases, may result in the use of practices that are not in the best interest of children' (Horner *et al.* 2005: 176). Our modern world needs educated people. Young people who have been failed by schools have few prospects. It is obvious that education should be accountable to them. Yet so far education resists or at best avoids systemic reform and development informed by cycles of innovation, improvement and evaluation, and therefore still moves from fad to fad (Slavin 2002).

A dominant view (Shavelson and Towne 2002) is that the term 'evidence-based practice' refers to a body of scientific knowledge about a range of educational practices that denotes research-based, structured and manualized practices that have been tested by rigorous, systematic and objective methods via randomized trials in which experimental and control groups or conditions are used to establish causation and to assess the magnitude of effects – the 'gold standard' of research (Dirkx 2006; Hoagwood and Johnson 2003; Kratochwill and Shernoff 2004; Walker 2004).

Definitional and inclusion–exclusion criteria have been problematic and there is considerable disagreement on these issues among professionals (Dirkx 2006; Hoagwood 2003–04; Kratochwill and Hoagwood 2005; Walker 2004). The debate has been particularly heated, as the definitional issues strike at the heart of the nature of research and science itself. Legislation has been criticized as being more concerned with promoting political and ideological agendas than improving the education of children. These critics also see it as fostering retrograde science, negating or dismissing qualitative methodologies and alternative epistemologies that have developed and gained respectability over the past 30 years (St. Pierre 2006). 'The stakes are high, because the very nature of science and scientific evidence and therefore the nature of knowledge itself is being contested by scholars and researchers who think and work from different epistemological, ontological and methodological positions' (ibid.: 239). What constitutes evidence and evidence-based practice is a central and contentious issue (Waas 2002).

Some identify two components in evidence-based practice. Hargreaves, in a seminal lecture on the topic, defines 'evidence-based education' as operating on two levels; first, 'to utilize existing evidence from worldwide research and literature on education and related topics', and second, 'to establish sound evidence where existing evidence is lacking or of a questionable, uncertain, or weak nature' (Hargreaves, cited in Brusling 2005: 88). In practice, then, there might be two concurrent processes that practitioners are required to engage in: the process of drawing on the best available evidence to inform practice, on one hand (which requires knowledge about what counts as evidence), and the process of monitoring the effectiveness of one's own practice on the other (which requires a scientific and critical approach to one's practice). Some also suggest that the implementation of evidence-based practice is different at different levels. For policy-makers, decisions tend to be long-lasting and hard to change, and mistakes costly. Decisions made at this level therefore require more robust and generalizable evidence than the day-to-day decisions that teachers make. Teachers should perhaps be encouraged to draw on their own experience and expertise as well as existing evidence, and consider the specifics of a given context (Brusling 2005).

At the classroom level, evidence-based practice might be more about a particular way of practising teaching, incorporating ongoing monitoring of one's own effectiveness, essential in a context such as education where there is a dearth of high quality experimental studies, and where the specific context can have a powerful effect on the effectiveness of given strategies and treatments. Few educational studies can match the so-called gold standard. For example, Herman (2002), in describing the research on comprehensive school reform in the United States, reported that only one of 130 studies could meet this criterion. Perhaps the best approach is to bring the discussion back to a common denominator, and that is the desire to build knowledge and expertise.

In line with the above argument, a discussion on appropriate research methods to promote evidence-based practice in education needs to clearly identify the specific purpose of the research. There are then essentially two questions: first, what kind of research is sufficiently rigorous to count as evidence, such that it should inform practice?, and second, what kind of research methods are required, and are sufficiently rigorous to enable a practitioner to monitor and demonstrate their own effectiveness – that is, what are acceptable and appropriate research methods in education and educational psychology? It is questions such as these that might stimulate much needed research in this field at several levels.

It is unfortunate, therefore, and a distraction, that the paradigm wars and skirmishes of the past 20 years, which many thought had reached a truce as the legitimacy of the qualitative paradigm became more established (Guba and Lincoln 2005), have been reignited. A number of researchers have railed against the narrow definition of science as positivism and methodology as quantitative which they see as being strongly promoted through legislation (Berliner 2002; Erickson and Gutierrez 2002; Pellegrino and Goldman 2002; St Pierre 2002). Berliner (2002) goes so far as to say that 'evidence-based practices' and 'scientific research' are code words for positivistic methods. Science, however, is not synonymous with one particular method and indeed the positivistic approach is simply not feasible in many of the complex situations in education (Feuer *et al.* 2002; Reid and Robinson 1995).

Indeed, it can reasonably be argued that what we are experiencing at this time is a resurfacing of a long-standing methodological crisis in research in educational psychology – a crisis first identified at the end of the nineteenth century by Windelband (cited in Pajares 2007) – and not yet, according to Bruner (1996), successfully resolved. Psychologists have been pulled between the research methods of the physical sciences and those of the humanities – between nomothetic and idiographic epistemologies: that is, between the search for universal laws that could apply across contexts and the belief that phenomena can only be understood in relation to the situated, contextual factors that bind them. According to Bruner (1996), most psychologists have chosen to value the universal and to devalue the particular. Pajares (2007: 23) agrees: 'The quest for universal truths is not only prevalent but deeply entrenched in educational and psychological research.'

It can be argued that progress will not be made as long as we flounder in this quagmire of controversy and debate. The maintenance of polarized positions is a fundamental problem bedevilling educational and psychological research. Warring factions must step back from entrenched positions to examine the salient issues and develop an integrative approach that will assist us to ground policy and practise decisions in better evidence. So, let us bring the discussion back to basics and to a common denominator. The purpose of research is to generate knowledge. Research questions must guide researchers' selection of scientific methods, and different methodologies are needed to address different types of research question (Berliner 2002; Feuer *et al.* 2002; Odom *et al.* 2005; Shavelson and Towne 2002). Scientists and social philosophers as diverse as B. F. Skinner, John Dewey, and Jürgen Habermas have emphasized that the appropriate match between questions and methodology is an essential feature of scientific research (Odom *et al.* 2005). The question must drive the method. The merit or otherwise of any particular research method can only be judged by its ability to answer the identified research question. 'The overzealous adherence to the use of any given research design flies in the face of this fundamental principle' (Feuer *et al.* 2002: 8).

Research for the purpose of identifying 'what works' is quite specific. It needs to show beyond a reasonable doubt that a particular intervention is effective, or more effective, most of the time and under most circumstances, than no intervention or some other currently used practice. To find out what works requires true experiments. But there are other important questions which require a different approach.

For example, in the context of an entirely new field of enquiry (such as to explore the effect of student location in a classroom on student participation), exploratory, descriptive studies might first be designed to identify factors that may affect a situation or outcomes. Through direct classroom observations, one might notice that a relationship exists between the rate of participation of students and their physical location in a classroom (see, for example, Adams 1969).

A correlational study might then follow to reveal that in most classrooms students who sit at the rear of the room are asked fewer questions (see, for example, Dykman and Reis 1979). At present we still do not know why this is the case. To answer this question requires the experimental manipulation of different conditions (the same student sitting sometimes at the front and sometimes at the rear, for example) to establish if a functional relationship exists between variables. In our example, a well-conducted experiment might show that questioning rate is purely a function of location in the room, and not of some other student or teacher characteristic (e.g. Moore and Glynn 1984).

Even the simple example above illustrates some of the challenges, such as the importance of context. To what extent are the findings above valid or important in a classroom that is organized very differently? For example, if the teacher were to engage the class in cooperative group activities, say, 'numbered-heads-together' (Kagan 1994), student participation would increase no matter where the student was seated. Factors other than location would be important. In such a context we would need to ask entirely different research questions.

All quality research (exploratory, correlational, or experimental) should meet certain standards: our measurement systems need to be reliable and valid, and the general approach should be characterized by rigour, transparency, and accountability. Are we attempting to rule out biases, are we permitting even those answers to our questions that we are not looking for? Is the effect widely applicable? Does our work build meaningfully on the work of others? Is there enough thick description to satisfy a critical audience? Could a practitioner make use of the description to develop an equally effective intervention in their own setting, or are there enough and varied data to make the explanations credible?

Perhaps it is time to move the focus of discussion from the promotion of certain types of research design and data collection to the construction of appropriate research questions and the identification and application of rigorous research criteria. Research in educational psychology deals with a wide range of issues, thus producing a wide range of research questions. Many of the critical questions in this field cannot be settled by universal prescriptions (Pajares 2007). They require examination of contextual variations. Therefore, to answer the diversity of questions, a range of different methods will be required.

Feuer *et al.* (2002: 7), citing the National Research Council's report, identify a typology of commonly framed questions in educational and social research: 'What is happening (description); is there a systematic effect (cause); and why or how is it happening (process or mechanism)?' While each question can be answered by a range of methods, they point out that some methods are better than others for particular purposes. Randomized trials are usually the method of choice to answer causal questions while qualitative methods are usually needed to describe complex phenomena and processes. Problems related to identifying effective instructional methods are essentially causal questions – in the current jargon, what works? 'Clearly randomized experiments ought to play a central role in a research agenda designed to discover and disseminate effective new interventions for instructional improvement' (Raudenbush 2005: 28). However, educational psychology is an applied field. A salient interest is in identifying interventions, based on convincing evidence that will improve outcomes for students through improving teaching and learning. We do not only need to know 'what works?' but also 'in what circumstances?' and 'how do we make what works work in the range of diverse contexts such as our schooling systems?' Randomized experiments are a necessary but not sufficient element in achieving this.

There is an obvious and growing awareness that the focus of evidence-based research has been on outcomes rather than on the processes by which the outcomes are achieved; that the emphasis has been on product (an inventory of practices) rather than on the application of the understandings gained. This could be seen as a contributing factor to the oft-noted phenomenon in education – the disconnect between research and practice, known as the research to practice gap. While there exists a robust research base for effective educational interventions (Alton-Lee 2003; Forness *et al.* 1997; Gersten *et al.* 1997; Stanovich and Stanovich 1997; Stoiber and Kratochwill 2000; Swanson 2001), generalization to educational settings has frequently proved to be difficult. Nastasi and Truscott (2000: 118), citing Argyris and Schön, describe the phenomenon as a 'predictable and recurrent pattern when scientific inquiry meets practitioners' applications'. The real gap in the research base of educational psychology is not so much a lack of information on effective practices but rather a lack of information on how to promote the adoption and implementation of effective practices in the somewhat complex and diverse contexts of schools and classrooms.

It appears that practitioners' enthusiasm for research-based practices is limited. There is a schism between the availability of research information and its use in classroom practice (Carnine 1995; Fullan 1991; Gersten *et al.* 1997; Ysseldyke 2001). 'Research findings in education, as in other fields (e.g. health), are embraced by some, ignored by others and modified to suit the routines and preferences of still others' (Gersten *et al.* 1997: 466). Even when practices are shown unequivocally, to the satisfaction of the researchers, to produce positive outcomes for students, sustained use by practitioners is not guaranteed. Reflecting on his 25 years as an educational researcher, Ysseldyke identifies teachers' unwillingness to put into practice well-researched methods as a phenomenon encountered early in his research career. He identifies monitoring student progress as a case in point. Despite overwhelming evidence that this practice improves outcomes for students, teachers have not incorporated it into their basic repertoire of skills. 'Even when they are confronted with evidence that what they are doing doesn't work, people keep on doing it. Even when other procedures are shown to be demonstrably better, people keep on doing the same old things' (Ysseldyke 2001: 296).

On the other hand, practitioners often enthusiastically adopt methods with minimal or dubious research bases. Stoiber and Kratochwill (2000) conclude that the intuitive appeal of a procedure is more important than empirical 'evidence' to practitioners. This is not a new phenomenon, having been noted and commented on by Dewey who expressed his concern that teachers in his own day were 'far too susceptible to passing fads and lofty rhetoric' (cited in Shulman 1998: 514). For whatever reasons, numerous promising interventions and approaches fail to bridge the gap between the more rarefied, well-controlled laboratory settings and the somewhat 'messy' environments that are schools and classrooms.

Malouf and Schiller argue that this may be because the predominant thinking underlying the approach is that 'interventions should be "validated" by research, then translated, packaged, and disseminated to practitioners, who should then replicate them in the classroom, manipulating independent variables to achieve effects in important dependent variables' (1995: 414). In other words, classrooms should function as if they were research-replication sites. To improve better uptake of validated interventions, the focus has been on increased research and more effective dissemination systems. There is a consequent realization that more attention must be paid to the systemic factors related to the adoption, adaptation, and sustainability of interventions in school contexts (Graczyk *et al.* 2006; Hoagwood and Johnson 2003; Kratochwill and Hoagwood 2005; Kratochwill and Shernoff 2004; Schaughency and Ervin 2006; Sheridan 2000; Walker 2004).

However, there appears to be little empirically derived information available on transferability of evidence-based research (Graczyk *et al.* 2006; Hoagwood and Johnson 2003; Kratochwill and Hoagwood 2005; Kratochwill and Shernoff 2004; Walker 2004). There has been a failure to construct what Kratochwill and Hoagwood call 'an integrative science on implementation effectiveness' (2004: 504). Ways to cross the chasm between research and practice are poorly researched and what little research does exist in this area is still in its infancy. More information is needed, but funding agencies and researchers have, to date, shown little interest (Walker 2004). The emphasis (and also, it would appear, the research funding) is firmly on exploring and refining the technical adequacy of interventions. The practices with respect to implementation of interventions must begin to be examined with the same rigour (Adelman and Taylor 1998; Detrich 1999).

Despite quite widespread enthusiasm for evidence-based practice in some circles, a number of writers recognize that it is very much a work in progress. Gutkin (2002) notes that much controversy has emerged from efforts in recent times to develop a framework for evidence-based research; Waas (2002) predicts that vigorous discussion will likely continue on all aspects of evidence-based research in the future; and Kratochwill (2002) anticipates disagreement, controversy, and conceptual challenges will continue unabated for some time. Adelman and Taylor (1998) argue that the evidence is insufficient to support any policy that would restrict practitioners to the use of what are termed empirically supported interventions. In summing up the situation, Gutkin concludes: 'A very substantial number of questions remain unresolved and, as of this date, nobody can legitimately claim to provide a completed "road map" for evidence-based practice' (2002: 339).

In conclusion, while there is widespread agreement in the literature for the need to promote evidence-based practice in education and educational psychology, there is still much debate about exactly what this means and how to operationalize this. The discussion involves questions concerning appropriate methodology on at least two levels: first, there are questions about whether the methods used are sufficiently rigorous to demonstrate clearly a causal relationship between a specific strategy, intervention, or way of teaching and student outcomes; and second, there are questions about a way to practise education and educational psychology that is accountable and able to demonstrate the effectiveness of one's practices.

An additional and overarching line of argument is that the discussion should not be restricted to appropriate research methods but should ensure that meaningful and important questions are asked. One important question that has so far been largely neglected concerns the effective implementation or uptake of already proven effective practices. There is little point in investing sparse resources in identifying new strategies or interventions when we are incapable of changing teachers' practices towards the effective implementation of currently known best practice.

It can reasonably be argued that to think one approach, such as randomized group experimental design, is the only approach to produce valid evidence indicates a somewhat myopic view of the scope of educational research (Berliner 2002). One method of scientific enquiry should not be the sole driver of education policy and practice as it dangerously sets us on a path that leads to rigid definition of research quality and a narrow prescription of research methods (Feuer *et al.* 2002). To promote evidence-based practice in education so as to improve student outcomes will also require increased focus on crossing the research to practice gap. More research is required into how to engage teachers and principals in this process to promote effective practices in our classrooms. Answers to the research questions generated in this endeavour are likely to require diverse methodologies.

References

Adams, R.S. (1969) 'Location as a feature of instructional interaction', *Merrill Palmer Quarterly*, 15: 309–21.

Adelman, H.S. and Taylor, L. (1998) 'Mental health in schools: moving forward', *School Psychology Review*, 27: 83–90.

Alton-Lee, A. (2003) *Quality Teaching for Diverse Students in Schooling: Best Evidence Synthesis*, Wellington, NZ: Ministry of Education.

Berliner, D.C. (2002) 'Educational research: The hardest science of all', *Educational Researcher*, 31: 18–20.

Bruner, J. (1996) *The Culture of Education*, Cambridge, MA: Harvard University Press.

Brusling, C. (2005) 'Evidence-based practice in teaching and teacher education; What is it? What is the rationale? What is the criticism? Where to go now?', invited paper presented at the Conference of Professional Development of Teachers in a Lifelong Perspective Teacher Education, Knowledge Production and Institutional Reform, Centre for Higher Education Greater Copenhagen in collaboration with OECD, Copenhagen, November.

Carnine, D. (1995) 'Trustworthiness, usability, and accessibility of educational research', *Journal of Behavioural Education*, 5: 251–8.

Detrich, R. (1999) 'Increasing treatment fidelity by matching interventions to contextual variables within the educational setting', *School Psychology Review*, 28: 608–21.

Dirkx, J.M. (2006) 'Studying the complicated matter of what works: evidence-based research and the problem of practice', *Adult Education Quarterly*, 56: 273–90.

Dykman, B.M. and Reis, H.T. (1979) 'Personality correlates of classroom seating position', *Journal of Educational Psychology*, 71: 346–54.

Erickson, F. and Gutierrez, K. (2002) 'Culture, rigour and science in educational research', *Educational Researcher*, 31: 21–4.

Feuer, M.J., Towne, L. and Shavelson, R.J. (2002) 'Scientific culture and educational research', *Educational Researcher*, 31: 4–14.

Forness, S.R., Kavale, K.A., Blum, I.M. and Lloyd, J.W. (1997) 'Analysis of mega-analysis: what works in special education and related services?', *Teaching Exceptional Children*, 29: 4–9.

Fullan, M. (1991) *The New Meaning of Educational Change*, London: Cassell.

Gersten, R., Vaughn, S., Deshler, D. and Schiller, E. (1997) 'What we know about using research findings: implications for improving special education practice', *Journal of Learning Disabilities*, 30: 466–76.

Graczyk, P.A., Domitrovich, C.E., Small, M. and Zins, J.E. (2006) 'Serving all children: an implementation model framework', *School Psychology Review*, 35: 266–75.

Guba, E.G. and Lincoln, Y.S. (2005) 'Paradigmatic controversies, contradictions and emerging confluences', in N.K. Denzin and Y.S. Lincoln (eds) *The Sage Handbook of Qualitative Research* (pp. 191–215), Thousand Oaks, CA: Sage Publishing.

Gutkin, T.B. (2002) 'Evidence-based interventions in school psychology: state of the art and directions for the future', *School Psychology Quarterly*, 17: 339–40.

Herman, R. (2002) 'Comprehensive school reform: scientifically based research', paper presented at the seminar No Child Left Behind: Scientifically Based Research, Washington, DC, February.

Hoagwood, K.E. (2003–04) 'Evidence-based practice in child and adolescent mental health: its meaning, application and limitation', *Emotional and Behavioural Disorders in Youth*, 4: 7–8.

Hoagwood, K.E. and Johnson, J. (2003) 'School psychology: a public health framework: from evidence-based practices to evidence-based policies', *Journal of School Psychology*, 41: 3–21.

Horner, R.H., Carr, E.G., Halle, J., McGee, G., Odom, S., and Wolery, M. (2005) 'The use of single-subject research to identify evidence-based practice in special education', *Exceptional Children*, 71: 165–79.

Kagan, S. (1994) *Cooperative Learning*, San Juan Capistrano, CA: Kagan Cooperative Learning.

Kratochwill, T.R. (2002) 'Evidence-based interventions in school psychology: thoughts on thoughtful commentary', *School Psychology Quarterly*, 17: 518–33.

Kratochwill, T.R. and Hoagwood, K.E. (2005) 'Evidence-based parent and family interventions in school psychology: conceptual and methodological considerations in advancing best practice', *School Psychology Quarterly*, 20: 504–12.

Kratochwill, T.R. and Shernoff, E.S. (2004) 'Evidence-based practice: promoting evidence-based interventions in school psychology', *School Psychology Review*, 33: 34–48.

Malouf, D.B. and Schiller, E.P. (1995) 'Practice and research in special education', *Exceptional Children*, 61: 414–25.

Moore, D.W. and Glynn, T. (1984) 'Variation in question rate as a function of position in the classroom', *Educational Psychology*, 4: 233–48.

Nastasi, B.K. and Truscott, S.D. (2000) 'Acceptability research in school psychology: current trends and future directions', *School Psychology Quarterly*, 15: 117–23.

Odom, S.L., Brantlinger, E., Gersten, R. and Horner, R.H. (2005) 'Research in special education: scientific methods and evidence-based practices', *Exceptional Children*, 71: 137–49.

Pajares, F. (2007) 'Culturalizing educational psychology', in F. Salili and R. Hoosain (eds) *Culture, Motivation and Learning: A Multicultural Perspective* (pp. 19–42). Charlotte, NC: Information Age Publishing.

Pellegrino, J.W. and Goldman, S.R. (2002) 'Be careful what you wish for – you may get it: educational research in the spotlight', *Educational Researcher*, 31: 15–17.

Raudenbush, S.W. (2005) 'Learning from attempts to improve schooling: the contribution of methodological diversity', *Educational Researcher*, 34: 25–31.

Reid, D.K. and Robinson, S.J. (1995) 'Empiricism and beyond', *Remedial and Special Education*, 16: 131–41.

Reschly, D.J. (2004) 'Commentary: paradigm shift, outcomes criteria and behavioural interventions: foundations for the future of school psychology,' *School Psychology Review*, 33: 408–17.

Schaughency, E. and Ervin, R. (2006) 'Building capacity to implement and sustain effective practices to better serve children', *School Psychology Review*, 35: 155–67.

Shavelson, R.J. and Towne, L. (eds) (2002) *Scientific Research in Education*, Washington, DC: National Academy Press.

Sheridan, S.M. (2000) 'The science and theory of empirically supported treatments: a response to Hughes', *Journal of School Psychology*, 38: 377–82.

Shulman, L.S. (1998) 'Theory, practice and the education of professionals', *The Elementary School Journal*, 98: 511–26.

Slavin, P. (2002) 'Evidence-based educational policies: transforming educational practice and research', *Educational Researcher,* 31: 15–21.

Stanovich, P.J. and Stanovich, K.E. (1997) 'Research into practice in special education', *Journal of Learning Disabilities,* 30: 477–81.

St. Pierre, E.A. (2002) ' "Science" rejects postmodernism', *Educational Researcher,* 31: 25–7.

St. Pierre, E.A. (2006) 'Scientifically based research in education: epistemology and ethics', *Adult Education Quarterly,* 56: 239–66.

Stoiber, C.K. and Kratochwill, T.R. (2000) 'Empirically supported interventions and school psychology: rationale and methodological issues. Part I', *School Psychology Quarterly,* 15': 75–106.

Swanson, H.L. (2001) 'Searching for the best model for instructing students with learning disabilities', *Focus on Exceptional Children,* 34: 1–14.

Waas, G.A. (2002) 'Identifying evidence-based interventions in school psychology: building a bridge or jousting with windmills?', *School Psychology Quarterly,* 17: 508–17.

Walker, H.M. (2004) 'Commentary: use of evidence-based interventions in schools: where we've been, where we are, and where we need to go', *School Psychology Review,* 33: 398–408.

Ysseldyke, J. (2001) 'Reflections on a research career: generalizations from 25 years of research on assessment and instructional decision making', *Exceptional Children,* 67: 295–309.

Chapter 2

What is this lesson about?

Instructional processes and student understandings in writing lessons

Helen S. Timperley and Judy M. Parr

This chapter examines issues related to the quality of instructional goals in writing and how students come to understand them in classrooms settings in terms of deeper rather than surface or mechanical features. Our examination of instructional goals in writing is illustrated in a detailed study of 17 writing lessons. The theoretical framing of this examination used two different but converging perspectives: one with its origins and emphases on the development of self-regulatory learning processes both within and among individuals (e.g. Butler and Winne 1995; Zimmerman 2001), and the other with greater emphasis on the development of those learning processes through effective classroom teaching associated with formative assessment (e.g. Black and Wiliam 1998). Considered in combination, these perspectives have the potential to provide teachers with the necessary understanding of the links between the development of demanding learning goals and the instructional messages conveyed through various lesson activities.

Claims about the effectiveness of self-regulated learning are captured in Butler and Winne's extensive review which they begin with the statement 'Theoreticians seem unanimous – the most effective learners are self-regulating' (1995: 245). It is difficult to present a single definition of the concept of self-regulated learning because at least seven different theoretical perspectives have emerged (Zimmerman 2001). Butler and Winne capture many of the key elements when they describe self-regulated learners as those who 'judge performance relative to goals, generate internal feedback about amounts and rates of progress towards goals, and adjust further action based on that feedback' (1995: 258). It is, in their view, a deliberate, judgemental, adaptive process.

Much of the research on self-regulation, particularly that from a cognitive constructivist perspective, has examined how self-regulatory processes develop independently of any particular qualities in the learning environment (e.g. Son and Metcalfe 2000; Thiede and Dunlosky 1999). It is the more socially-oriented perspectives, however, that are of greater relevance to this chapter. Zimmerman proposes that to understand self-regulation is to understand how learners constantly adjust to the changing personal, behavioural, and environmental conditions in typical learning situations and proactively increase 'performance discrepancies by raising goals and seeking more challenging tasks' (2000: 14). This dynamic view of self-regulated learning is more reflective of constantly evolving classroom situations with their myriad of learning opportunities, and potentially has more to offer in identifying the kinds of teaching and learning environments that might lead to developing self-regulation (e.g. Butler and Cartier 2004).

A more deliberate teaching–learning relationship is evident in the Vygotskian perspective of self-regulation, which understands the learning process in essentially sociocultural terms. Through guided interactions with more skilled others, important concepts and skills in the external environment become internalized, and as learners are scaffolded into gaining greater control of the ideas, they are increasingly able to guide, plan and monitor their activities. Thus, 'for every individual at any point in time, there will be a mix of other regulation, self-regulation and other automatized processes' (Gallimore and Tharp 1990: 186). The points at which a teacher is likely to be most effective in developing self-regulation are those that focus on aspects of skills that are emerging but still require the assistance of others for their mastery.

These more socially-oriented perspectives on self-regulated learning are evident in the literature on formative assessment. Research in this area typically has a more direct focus on the role of classroom teaching activities and the effect of those activities on students. The parallels between the two research perspectives are obvious, however, when looking at the learning processes involved, as identified in the seminal review by Black and Wiliam (1998). They suggest the core of the activity of formative assessment lies in the sequence of two actions:

> The first is the perception by the learner of a gap between a desired goal and his or her present state (of knowledge, and/or understanding, and/or skill). The second is the action taken by the learner to close that gap in order to attain the desired goal.
>
> (ibid.: 20)

These authors calculated that those students whose teachers helped them understand what it was they were supposed to be learning, who fostered self-assessment, and gave appropriate feedback, by end of secondary school, showed an additional one to two years progress in achievement compared with their peers.

It appears from this review by Black and Wiliam that fostering effective self-regulation and realizing the benefits of formative assessment require teachers to help learners understand the learning goals and to provide opportunities for them to seek and receive feedback on progress towards those goals. Our study examined the extent to which teachers provided these conditions for their students and, further, whether the students were able to use them in ways that fostered self-regulated learning.

Goals and feedback

This section considers the literature on the qualities of goals and feedback likely to foster self-regulated learning. In its purest form, self-regulated learning involves learners formulating their own goals. However, we take the position that primary-aged students need guidance in doing this, and it is the role of teachers to make these goals clear to students so they know the purpose of classroom learning tasks and activities. Understanding what is to be learned is fundamental to successful task interpretation (Butler and Cartier 2004). Specific rather than general goals have been found to be more effective in focusing students' attention, developing greater commitment, and allowing more directed feedback (Bargh *et al.* 2001; Kluger and DeNisi 1996).

Learning goals need to be distinguished from performance goals because they are differentially effective in promoting self-regulated learning. Learning goals focus on understanding how to tackle new problems and learn new things, such as learning to formulate an argument, while performance goals focus on grades and have a strong focus on performance being associated with ability, such as doing better than one's peers. Newman and Schwager (1995) found that a focus on performance goals developed maladaptive questioning patterns and poorer problem-solving ability than those focused on learning goals.

Closely aligned to learning goals is the power of mastery learning, which involves the learner having an understanding of what success in that task might look like and receiving instruction and feedback directly related to it. Research reviews assessing the effect of mastery learning have found an average effect size of 0.82 (Guskey and Gates 1986) which is among the largest average effects reported for a teaching strategy (Kulik and Kulik 1989).

Although feedback features prominently in all the above accounts, it has highly variable effects. The right type of feedback, therefore, is important. Feedback about the learner's personal qualities invites a focus on social relationships rather than cognitive processes and can be detrimental to developing learning goals (Brophy 1981; Kluger and DeNisi 1996). Outcome feedback, sometimes called knowledge of results, gives binary information about whether or not a particular response is correct. This kind of feedback can also be problematic in developing learning goals. Typically, this type of feedback does not carry sufficient information to guide a learner about how to self-regulate. Feedback that is more cognitively oriented helps students identify cues indicative of progress towards particular goals, monitor task engagement, and assess the value of those cues in achieving task success (Butler and Winne 1995).

Feedback can also promote either minimal or deep learning. Feedback that promotes minimal learning is typically focused on the correctness of content in a domain and usually contains insufficient information to affect the development of knowledge construction. In contrast, feedback directed at deep learning, triggers other forms of cognitive processing, such as assembling ideas, searching for relationships, and developing knowledge with which to elaborate information

(Balzer *et al.* 1989). Thus, the most efficacious type of feedback is that which promotes self-monitoring, directing, and regulating activities associated with the learning goal at these deeper levels. It fosters autonomy, self-control, self-direction, and self-discipline (Zimmerman 2000).

Receiving information about progress towards a goal, however, is of little benefit unless a third condition is also met: that the feedback is linked to a corrective strategy (sometimes referred to as feed-forward). A key condition of self-regulated learning is that learners adjust future actions in response to feedback, so the quality of information contained in the feedback or feed-forward is fundamental to developing effective processes (Black and Wiliam 1998).

Learning goals, feedback, and feed-forward are closely interrelated. Locke and Latham (1990) identified that goals and feedback work both prospectively and retrospectively. Goals can inform learners about the quality of performance that needs to be attained so they can direct and evaluate their actions and efforts accordingly, while feedback allows learners to set reasonable goals and to track performance in relation to their goals.

How goals are defined also plays a role in determining feedback cues to which learners attend. Learners judge progress towards goals by selecting and monitoring cues perceived to be relevant to achieving a particular goal. If the writing purpose is to give an account of a ball game and the teacher has a specific learning goal, for example, learning about temporal markers, students will use the knowledge they have about order of events to select cues to monitor and generate internal feedback. They will then use this feedback to work out whether their writing efforts are meeting the learning goal. If the teacher's learning goals are unclear or inaccessible to students, the students are likely to construct alternative goals, for example, writing a whole page, and use these to assess their progress (Butler and Winne 1995). Alternatively, if teachers state one kind of learning goal but give feedback that is misaligned to those goals, the learners are likely to be confused about what it is they are to self-monitor and how best to make progress.

We examined these issues of goal quality, feedback, and self-regulation through an empirical study in which we analyzed a selection of writing lessons in elementary classrooms (year levels 4–8) and interviewed a sample of students to find out what sense they made of the information provided by their teachers on the learning goals, feedback and feed-forward.

Method

Our study analyzed the writing lessons of 15 teachers (one lesson per teacher). The 45-minute lessons were recorded and later transcribed. Two teachers whose students had the least understanding of the learning aims were re-observed four months after the initial observation and the changes the teachers made were analyzed to ascertain what would happen if they changed their practice.

Teachers were also asked to provide background information about the lesson, including the lesson aims, the extent to which the lesson was typical of others, and to complete a series of rating scales related to their confidence in teaching aspects of lessons central to developing self-regulated learning.

The lesson observation

The teachers' instructions and interactions with students were audio-taped for each writing lesson. We interviewed approximately six students per class who had been nominated by the teachers as representing the range of writing achievement within the class. The interview schedule consisted of four questions:

- What are you working on today? (Purpose – general introduction so students felt comfortable talking to researchers.)
- What are you learning about writing while you are doing this? (Purpose – to find out if students were aware of the writing learning aims for the lesson.)
- Can you tell me what a good [argument, recount] looks like? (Purpose – to find out if the students know the criteria for mastery.)
- What does your teacher tell you to work on in your writing? (Purpose – to find out students' understanding of any feedback or feed-forward received.)

The transcripts of the teachers' instructions and interactions during the lessons and the students' responses to the interviews were divided into three parts. The first two parts included the extent to which the lesson aims and mastery criteria were shared with, and understood by, the students. The third part related to the type of comments on students' work and students' understanding of those comments. To be included in the comments category, comments had to refer to some aspect of writing, rather than other behaviour. The comments were further divided into 'feedback' and 'feed-forward'. Feedback referred to an evaluative statement related to something the student had already written and feed-forward referred to something the student needed to do in relation to his or her writing in the future.

Questionnaires

For each of these parts of the lesson, teachers had previously indicated their confidence by rating the following items on a scale of 1 to 6:

- I know how to develop the important learning objectives for a writing lesson.
- I know how to make the criteria for successful learning in writing clear to my students.
- I know how to provide feedback about their writing to students in ways that support further learning.

Each scale point had a descriptor, with the extremes of 1 representing 'definitely not confident' to 6 representing 'highly confident'.

Achievement data

At the time of the initial observations of the two teachers who changed their practice, scripts of students' writing were scored independently by a member of the research team who had no other involvement in the project. We used scoring rubrics from the Assessment Tools for Teaching and Learning (asTTle) in writing, tools developed and normed in New Zealand (see Chapter 7). These criterion measures assess six dimensions of writing including both deep and surface features, for each of a range of writing purposes. Surface features concern the conventions of writing – the more mechanical aspects of spelling, grammar and punctuation. The deep features are those that require deeper level cognitive processing and take into account the audience and rhetorical situation; structure; content and use of language resources.

Results

The analysis of the 15 observed lessons is presented first. Throughout this analysis, we have provided more detail on contrasting transcripts from two teachers (teachers 4 and 15). We then present a detailed case of a third teacher (teacher 6) whose practice appeared to contain the conditions for self-regulated learning but whose students failed to understand the learning aims or feedback provided. Finally, we present an analysis of the changes made by two teachers (1 and 2) whose students initially had the least understanding of the learning aims, together with the different students' responses

Students' understanding of learning aims

Table 2.1 lists the learning aims and how well they were understood by the students. The teachers whose students had least understanding of what they were supposed to be learning are at the top of the table and those teachers whose students had most understanding are at the bottom. High confidence ratings (3 to 6 on the six-point scale) were given by teachers at all levels of the table but this was not related to how well students understood the learning aims of the lesson.

The learning aims, as stated by the teachers, were all focused on deeper rather than surface features of writing. The specificity of the aims, as written, was difficult to code reliably so verbatim aims are presented in Table 2.1. Several aims were expressed in terms of activities rather than what students were to learn but in all cases the learning aim could be inferred from the activity description. The aims as written were not indicative of whether students could understand what it was they were supposed to be learning. A better predictor of student understanding than the written learning aims was the clarity with which the aims were conveyed to the students during the lesson and linked to prior knowledge about writing. When clearly conveyed, they were typically not stated immediately on starting the lesson but rather as links made to prior knowledge through questioning the students.

Table 2.1 Teachers' lesson aims and students' understanding of them

Teacher	Year level	Aims as written	Aims shared with students	Students' response[a]
1	2–3	To help children to start their stories using an interesting beginning	No	1
2	4–5	Using English matrices from New Zealand curriculum exemplars 'Audience Purpose' (impact and voice) at Levels 1 iii, 2 and 3	No	1
3	5–6	Writing with the audience in mind as preparation for speeches later in term	No	1
4	5–8	To introduce to the students the concept of persuasive writing	No	1
5	3–4	Introducing a new form of poetry	Partly	1
6	3–4	Making a piece of writing better by adding or replacing certain words	Yes. Written	2
7	4–6	Introduction of new poetry style	Yes. Not written	2
8	7–8	Initial observation sheet had series of activities, not aims. As shared with students, 'We are learning to write a descriptive passage that creates a "picture" in the reader's mind, i.e. imagery'	Yes. Written	2
9	2–3	Children will write a poem entitled 'I like words like: . . .' using interesting sounding – lip-smacking words	Partly Not written	3
10	7–8	To identify and use alliteration in a poem	Yes Written	3
11	3–5	Language choice in poetry. Brainstorming adjectives related to a topic/theme and then finding more interesting synonyms to 'paint a picture with words'	Yes. Not written	3
12	7–8	Writing attention grabbing, descriptive informative orientations in the context of a recount	Yes. Written	3
13	4–5	To think about the reader (audience) and purpose when writing character descriptions	Yes. Oral	3
14	5–6	The opening sentence in a description to tell reader about the big picture of what describing	Yes. Oral	3

| 15 | 3–4 | Arguments. Persuasive writing – main components of an argument. Opening statement and opinion. Reasons and examples to support. Sequencing from strongest to weakest. | Yes. Written | 3 |

Notes

ᵃ= Coding for student understanding:

1 Surface features only e.g. length, punctuation and spelling (may include some undefined 'better writer' in the future, learning to write good stories).
2 Some mention of lesson aims (less than half responses).
3 Mostly focused on lesson aims (more than half responses).

Two contrasting examples from two different lessons on writing an argument are used to illustrate this. In the first example, teacher 15 began the lesson (the fourth in a series on writing an argument) as follows:

Teacher: What are the main parts of an argument? The main things we are working on? [Students' name]? One of them?
Student 1: Make sure your opinion is what you want to say.
Teacher: Say what you want to say, you write your opinion. [Student's name], what else?
Student 2: You give your reasons.
Teacher: What do we give reasons for?
Student 2: So they know why or why not to agree with us or agree with it.

The lesson continued with the introduction of the topic about which they were to write their argument; that is, whether Greedy Cat, a loved story character who was very overweight, should go on a diet. The students' opinions and reasons were then arranged in the order in which arguments are conventionally grouped, with the strongest reasons first and the weakest last. The students' interview responses indicated they were very clear that the notions of expressing an opinion and then organizing arguments in a hierarchy were what they were supposed to be learning.

Another lesson on writing arguments (teacher 4), one in which the students did not understand the learning aims so well, began in a different way.

Teacher: I want you to talk about this question in pairs, 'Should schools start at 10:00 and finish at 2:30?' You might want to modify it a wee bit. [Discussion about preferred starting and finishing times followed by paired discussion of opinions.]
Teacher: I want you to give me one positive about school starting at 10:00 and finishing up when you like it to and one negative. Who's going to give me one? [child's name]?
Student: I've got a negative. You wouldn't learn as much.

The lesson introduction continued to focus on identifying content – namely positive and negative reasons, and possible starting and finishing times – rather than making explicit how such content related to writing an argument. When interviewed, these students were unsure of what they were learning about writing during this lesson.

Students' understanding of mastery criteria

The extent to which students understood what counted as mastery criteria in relation to the lesson aims was closely related to how well they understood the learning aims themselves. Teachers who were more explicit about the learning aims were mostly explicit about what constituted mastery in that form of writing and so the sequence of lessons. Table 2.2 presents findings related to students' understanding of mastery criteria. It is in the same order as Table 2.1; that is, lessons for which students had a poor understanding of what counted as success in that particular writing function are at the top of the table. The exception was teacher 6 and this lesson is described in greater detail later. Again, teachers' confidence ratings in making the criteria clear to the students were unrelated to the extent to which students understood the criteria, so are not presented in Table 2.2. High ratings of 5 and 6 were given by teachers 3, 5, 6, 7, 13, 14 and 15. The lowest confidence rating of 3 was given by teacher 11.

Teacher 15, whose students were writing an argument about an overweight cat (described above), had worked during previous lessons to develop what he called criteria for success in writing an argument and these were displayed on the board. The criteria included:

- You need an opening statement that gives your opinion.
- Give reasons for your opinion and examples to support your reasons.
- Put your reasons in order from strongest to weakest.

Table 2.2 Teachers' explicitness when sharing mastery criteria and students' understanding of criteria

Teacher	Criteria explicit in task introduction	Criteria explicit through activities/individual assistance	Students' response[a]
1	No. General instruction to write first sentence	No. Mostly on mechanics and prompting content related to topic	1
2	No. Focus on generating content	No. Focus on generating content	1
3	No. Writing a story about topic – focus on generating content	No. Focused on topic of story and getting something written	1
4	Partly. Not written. In opening sentence should express an opinion	Minimal reference to learning aim. Unclear	3

5	Partly. Not written. Students told to note describing words to write poem from video	Yes. Most assistance focused on qualities of poem form	3
6	Partly – but non-specific 'to make the description more interesting'	Partly – but not specific enough to provide guidance for students	1
7	Yes. Not written. Gave rules for poem form	Partly. Focus on word quality within poem form	3
8	Yes. Written and re-stated but only partly aligned to the learning aim. Focused on using language features for fluency and effect	Yes, but links to learning aims and task unclear. Fluency equated with punctuation. Language features equated with creating a picture	4
9	Yes. Not written. Focused on generating appropriate vocabulary for poem	Yes. Focused on generating appropriate vocabulary for poem	4
10	No but very transparent in task introduction	Yes. Repeated activities reinforcing one another	4
11	Yes. Not written. Focused on generating appropriate vocabulary for poem	Yes. Focused on generating appropriate vocabulary	5
12	Yes for some aspects, rest to be made into explicit criteria next lesson	Mostly but indicated would make into explicit criteria in next lesson	5
13	Partly in that not written as mastery criteria but all oral activities, instructions and discussion explicitly focused on mastery criteria	Yes. Consistently referred to descriptive features	5
14	Partly in that not written as mastery criteria but all oral activities, instructions and discussion explicitly focused on mastery criteria	Yes. consistently referred to desirable features of opening sentences of a description	5
15	Yes. Written. Oral instructions focused on mastery criteria developed with students	Yes. All assistance focused on mastery criteria as written	5

Notes
[a]= Coding of students' understanding:
1 Focus on surface features.
2 Some mention of deeper features unrelated to lesson aims but most focus on surface features.
3 Some or all responses partially related to learning aim.
4 Fewer than half responses related to learning aim.
5 Half or more responses related to learning aim.

The lesson instruction was focused on the students' progress in relation to the criteria in terms of developing their arguments about Greedy Cat's diet. When interviewed, all students referred to these criteria when describing what effective persuasive writing looked like.

Students' understanding of feedback and feed-forward

Once again, the teachers' confidence ratings in providing feedback to students in ways that supported further learning were unrelated to how well the students understood this feedback in practice. High confidence ratings of 5 and 6 were given by teachers 3, 4, 6, 14 and 15. All other teachers gave ratings of 4.

An analysis of the oral feedback and feed-forward given to students during the lesson and the students' responses are presented in Table 2.3. The students' responses are paraphrased rather than coded because the variety of responses made coding difficult and failed to reflect the richness of their answers. The connectedness of the feedback and feed-forward to the learning aim followed a similar pattern to the relation of mastery criteria and learning aims. That is, with the exception of teacher 6, feedback and feed-forward relating to the learning aims were provided more frequently by those teachers who were explicit about the learning aim and mastery criteria. However, it is striking how little feed-forward

Table 2.3 Instances of teachers' oral feedback and feed-forward and students' understanding

Teacher	Feedback[a]	Feed-forward[a]	Students' responses[a]
1	Words x2 Content x3 Mechanics x3 General praise x1	Non-specific comment x2	Doesn't talk to us about improving work x2 Length x1 Non-specific praise x1
2	General praise x10 Mechanics x5 Words x1 Content x2 General comment x1	Mechanics x1 Words x1	Mechanics x4 Reference to content inclusion x4
3	Content x1		Mechanics x4 Make it interesting x1 Can't remember x1
4	General praise x10 Learning aim x6 Mechanics x3	General comment x1	Spelling x1 Working out hard words x3
5	General praise x4 Mechanics x1	Learning aim x3 Mechanics x1 Words x1	Make sure it makes sense x2 Punctuation x2 Good words x1
6	Learning aim x14 General praise x4 Content x1	Learning aim x5 Mechanics x1	Punctuation x1 Write good stories x1 Don't know x1

7	General praise x12 Words x1 Content x1 Mechanics x1	Content x1	Reference to prompting writing process x2 Work independently x1 Describing words x1 Reference to different genre x1 Reference to rules for a writing competition x1
8	No feedback given	No feed-forward given	Spelling x2 Handwriting x1 Form letters properly x1 Changing words to make them better x1
9	General praise x10 Learning aim x1 Mechanics x1	Content x1	Fix up words and spelling x3 Don't know x1 Have a go x1 Make more sense x1
10	No feedback given		Language features x2 (most unintelligible on tape)
11	Learning aim x7 General praise x6 Content x1 General comment x1	Deeper features x1	Procedures for spelling x9 Punctuation x2 Unspecified check x1 Make sense x1
12	No feedback given	Learning aim x1 Mechanics x1	Vocabulary, re-crafting, planning, audience related to learning aim x4 Tense in recounts x2; Punctuation x1
13	Learning aim x7 General praise x4	Mechanics x2 Learning aim x1	All referenced to mastery criteria of either character description or audience
14	General praise x5 Learning aim x3 Content x1	Learning aim x3	All apart from one related to mastery criteria
15	Learning aim x11 General praise x3 Mechanics x1	Mechanics x5 Learning aim x1	All referenced to mastery criteria

Notes
a = Descriptions of categories used in Table 2.3:
Learning aim: Related to learning aim or mastery criteria for lesson.
Deeper features: Refers to deeper essential features of writing but not specifically related to the learning aim or mastery criteria of lesson, e.g. sense, language use, structure.
Content: Refers to appropriateness of inclusion of particular content, e.g. 'You need to write about who else was there'.
Words: Refers to suggestions at the word level unrelated to learning aim or mastery criteria, e.g. addition, substitution, or deletion of words.
Mechanics: Mechanics and other surface features not related to writing aim, e.g. punctuation, capitals, date, spelling, miss a line etc.
General praise: Non-specific positive comment, e.g. 'Good work'.
General comment: A non-specific comment that does not give any particular direction for the student, e.g. 'There's lots to work on'.

was provided. Examples are from the contrasting lessons on persuasive writing. Teacher 4's only feed-forward was combined with non-specific feedback: 'You have done well and there's lots to work on.' In contrast, teacher 15, whose class was writing arguments about whether the overweight cat should go on a diet, commented on one child's efforts, 'Yes, the reasons support why he had to go on a diet.' An example of feed-forward was, 'You need to put these [the reasons] from strongest to weakest.'

The students of teacher 15 talked about the feedback their teacher gave them in terms of the deeper features of writing associated with particular lesson aims as did the students of teachers 12 and 13. In contrast, the students of teachers who gave non-specific feedback or who focused on surface or other features unrelated to the learning aim were more likely to refer to surface features when asked what their teachers told them to work on.

Instructional features and students' understanding

An analysis of teacher 6's lesson illustrates the importance of checking understanding with students, rather than assuming that, if particular instructional features are exhibited by the teacher, then the conditions for self-regulated learning will be present. Teacher 6 clearly specified the learning aims and wrote them on the board, yet less than half the students were able to articulate them. She was less clear in the mastery goals and the students responded to the interview questions by referring to surface features of writing. Nearly all her feedback and feed-forward related to the learning aim, yet her students referred to surface features when asked what their teacher told them they should work on.

Closer analysis of this lesson revealed the reasons for this pattern. The students were learning to re-craft their descriptions written the previous day, but the criteria for judging whether their re-crafting efforts were an improvement on their original attempts were unclear. At times it was 'to make the passage more interesting'; at other times it was 'to join sentences together to make them more complex' or to use 'more interesting words'. When students were given individual assistance, additional criteria mentioned more than once included changing or adding words (14 references), making longer sentences, or adding more information (3 references each). In no case were specific reasons given for these re-crafting actions or how they would improve on the students' original attempts.

When students were asked what they were learning, they mostly referred to actions, such as 'Describing a lot and breaking up sentences' (in direct contradiction to the teacher's emphasis on joining sentences), 'Put in describing words and make it make sense', and 'Fix the words.' One referred to more accurate spelling. When students were asked about mastery criteria and feedback, the only references to deeper features were general in nature, such as 'write good stories' and 'make our stories make sense', or the specifics of surface features such as neatness and punctuation.

Changes in practice and achievement

When teachers 1 and 2 were given feedback by the researchers from the observations about how students understood their lessons, they asked for assistance to change their practice. A consultant provided professional development and the researchers returned four months later and observed a new lesson, and once again interviewed the students.

In the initial observations, both lessons had begun with the topic of 'Getting Lost' with most of the lesson focused on motivating the students to recall a circumstance of becoming lost. This was done by reading the students a story about a child getting lost, recounting the teacher's personal experience and asking the students to share their experiences in pairs. Students were then told to write their story of what happened to them. While these strategies may be effective in motivating students, the criteria for an effective account were not divulged to the students during the introductory activities, which took up most of the lesson time.

In the initial lesson, teacher 1 also modelled a first sentence for the students, which was consistent with her aim 'to help children to start their stories using an interesting beginning', but all her references during the modelling were related to the mechanics of constructing words, not to the qualities of interesting beginnings (her lesson aim). Her only references to the qualities of interesting beginnings during the lesson occurred when the students began to write and she gave an instruction to write their first sentence and to 'think of an interesting beginning to your story'. Her assistance to individuals as they were writing included one suggestion to 'start off with a bang' and three specific wording suggestions for starting. She also suggested that two students use some speech in their first sentence and told two others that they should not start with 'once upon a time' because that beginning was for fairy tales.

In that initial lesson, she also gave many other suggestions as she stopped to help individuals during independent writing. These suggestions were not related to the beginning sentence but could be seen to constitute implicit references to information students could use to construct successful recounts. Most of the individual assistance was focused on helping the students with the mechanics of writing. Given all this information, it was not surprising that, when interviewed, the students explained that good writing of the type they were doing was neat, and had a title, capital letters, and full stops.

The feedback the teachers were given by the researchers about their students' understanding of their lessons surprised the teachers and provided a powerful catalyst for learning. They believed that what the students were to learn was transparent and that their instruction was goal-focused. During the change process, the teachers themselves became self-regulated learners with their self-identified goal being that their students understood the learning aims and mastery criteria for each writing lesson. They monitored their progress towards this goal by observing each other and checking students' understanding by asking them at regular intervals what it was they thought they were learning. Initially, despite their best efforts, their students failed to articulate what it was they were to learn, which, in turn, led the teachers to become more explicit. The teachers realized that part of their difficulty in being more explicit was their limited pedagogical content knowledge related to writing. They sought readings and instruction to develop this knowledge.

In the second observation four months later, teacher 1's lesson was, coincidentally, on recounting an experience with a focus on the deeper features of structure and order of events. The context was a birthday party. In this lesson she used the context to outline a structure for a written account, revising the qualities of beginning sentences, then instructing the students, 'so we're writing down everything that happened in the order that it happened . . . You can't have the thing that happened last at the top can you because it won't make sense.' After structuring some students' stories into beginning, middle and endings with the whole class, she then set the students the task of writing about a birthday party they had attended. All instructional assistance was aligned and coherent with the learning aims and mastery criteria. Feedback and feed-forward, however, were not consistently focused on the learning aim, with most comprising non-specific praise (14 instances) and surface features (four instances). Teacher 2 had changed her lesson in similar ways, with clear learning aims provided for the students and mastery criteria worked out with them, but her feedback also took the form of non-specific praise. It was notable that for both teachers, the majority of the first lesson was spent motivating students with several oral activities, whereas in the second lesson students concentrated on writing.

When interviewed during this second lesson, the students in both classes were able to articulate the learning aims and mastery criteria with a focus on the deeper features of writing. They spontaneously indicated how much they enjoyed writing, as did the teacher. Students were less clear in their responses to questions about feedback, however, with less than half mentioning deeper features of writing a clear account. It appeared that students' understanding of learning aims, mastery criteria or feedback and feed-forward was closely related to the specificity of each particular aspect of the lesson.

Achievement gains from the independently marked scripts showed an effect size of 1.04 over the four-month period. Notably, despite the second lesson focusing on deeper features, achievement gains were as great for surface as for deep features.

Conclusion

In this chapter, we examined attributes of classroom instruction identified in both the self-regulated learning and formative assessment literatures as likely to be most powerful in providing the conditions for students to focus on high quality learning goals and become successful writers. Our focus was on the interrelationship between teaching and student learning because, as Butler and Cartier (2004) argue, teachers influence students' task interpretation by virtue of how they structure learning environments. The aspects on which we focused included the clarity of learning goals throughout instruction, the explicitness of criteria for successful task mastery, and the extent to which feedback promoted further learning. All the participating teachers intended to convey learning goals focused on the deeper features of writing through the lesson activities, but they were differentially successful in doing so.

Students' understanding of learning goals and what it means to master them is fundamental to their success because without such an understanding they are unable to monitor their progress or to generate relevant internal feedback. In many of the observed lessons, despite the teachers having written substantive learning aims, these were not conveyed to the students and it was difficult for the observer, let alone the students, to deduce from activities during the lesson what was to be learned or what mastery of this learning might look like. As identified by both James and Pedder (2006) and Marshall and Drummond (2006) in the United Kingdom, assessment for learning practices make far greater demands on teachers' expertise than a more performance orientation towards instructional and assessment practices.

When the learning and mastery goals of the instruction were unclear, students in our study typically focused on surface features of the writing task or had some general learning aim such as becoming a better writer. It was as if students adopted these features as a default position when they were unclear about more sophisticated concepts of writing, giving weight to Butler and Cartier's contention that 'If task interpretation is absent or faulty, learning is derailed' (2004: 1735).

It could be argued that to become self-regulating, students should have the freedom to select their own goals, rather than meeting those pre-determined by their teachers. But from the lessons observed, it appears that until students have an in-depth understanding of what it means to be a writer for a particular purpose, learning is more likely if teachers assist students to understand the necessary learning goals and mastery criteria so that the students can monitor their learning progress.

Our study has clearly shown the link between students' understanding and instructional processes. It has also shown that rather than assume this understanding, it is vital that researchers check the students' perspectives. The problem with relying on an analysis of teaching practice in order to judge effectiveness was highlighted in the example of the teacher who appeared to present the learning aims and mastery criteria and provide learning-related feedback but her students failed to understand them. A more detailed analysis of this lesson revealed the mixed messages and unclear criteria evident during the instructional process. As Marshall and Drummond (2006) found when assisting teachers to understand assessment for learning principles and practices, the 'letter' rather than the 'spirit' of the relevant practices was frequently more evident in subsequent lessons.

Further, this study suggests that if teachers convey a learning goal that is understood by their students, they are also more likely to articulate mastery criteria and provide feedback related to these qualities. Indeed, integration and alignment were more important than just having a stated learning aim by itself. Such alignment is confirmed by a factor analysis of teachers' responses to questionnaire items in the United Kingdom where both attributes came together in a single factor of 'making learning explicit' (James and Pedder 2006). The ability to achieve either the separate parts or their integration, however, did not appear to be related to self-reported confidence or teaching experience. Rather, it would seem that considerable knowledge of both the writing process and how texts work for particular purposes is necessary.

If students have experienced low achievement and found the task of writing confusing, the results from this study indicate that those patterns of achievement can change if teachers reveal the secrets of how to be successful. Some students are able to ascertain from their teachers' implicit or confused messages what it is they are supposed to be learning and what mastery looks like and, consequently, have access to the conditions that will allow them to focus on mastery goals and to self-regulate their learning. But, for many, these features need to be made more explicit to help them understand what they are working towards and to realize that writing is more than getting the punctuation and spelling right in long and neatly presented pieces.

Acknowledgements

Copyright permission obtained from Routledge licence number 2205121252252 on June 09, 2009. Original article published in *The Curriculum Journal*, 20(1): 43–60.

References

Balzer, W.K., Doherty, M.E. and O'Connor, R. Jr. (1989) 'Effects of cognitive feedback on performance', *Psychological Bulletin*, 106: 410–33.

Bargh, J.A., Gollwitzer, P.M., Lee-Chai, A., Barndollar, K. and Troetschel, R. (2001) 'The automated will: nonconscious activation and pursuit of behavioural goals', *Journal of Personality and Social Psychology*, 81: 1014–27.

Black, P. and Wiliam, D. (1998) 'Assessment and classroom learning', *Assessment in Education: Principles, Policy and Practice*, 5: 7–74.

Brophy, J. (1981) 'Teacher praise: a functional analysis', *Review of Educational Research*, 51: 5–32.

Butler, D. and Cartier, S. (2004) 'Promoting effective task interpretation as an important work habit: a key to successful teaching and learning', *Teachers College Record*, 106: 1729–58.

Butler, D.L. and Winne, P.H. (1995) 'Feedback and self-regulated learning: a theoretical synthesis', *Review of Educational Research*, 65: 245–74.

Gallimore, R. and Tharp, R. (1990) 'Teaching mind in society: teaching, schooling, and literate discourse', in L.C. Moll (ed.) *Vygotsky and Education: Instructional Implications and Applications of Socio-historical Psychology* (pp. 175–205), New York: Cambridge University Press.

Guskey, T. and Gates, S. (1986) 'Synthesis of research on the effects of mastery learning in elementary and secondary classrooms', *Educational Leadership*, 33: 73–80.

James, M. and Pedder, D. (2006) 'Beyond method: assessment and learning practices and values', *The Curriculum Journal*, 17: 109–38.

Kluger, A.N. and DeNisi, A. (1996) 'The effects of feedback interventions on performance: a historical review, a meta-analysis, and a preliminary feedback intervention theory', *Psychological Bulletin*, 119: 254–84.

Kulik, J. and Kulik, C. (1989) 'Meta-analysis in education', *International Journal of Educational Research*, 13: 221–340.

Locke, E.A. and Latham, G.P. (1990) *A Theory of Goal Setting and Task Performance*, Englewood Cliffs, NJ: Prentice Hill.

Marshall, B. and Drummond, M. (2006) 'How teachers engage with assessment for learning: lessons from the classroom', *Research Papers in Education*, 21: 133–49.

Newman, R.S. and Schwager, M.T. (1995) 'Students' help seeking during problem solving: effects of grade, goal and prior achievement', *American Educational Research Journal*, 32: 352–76.

Son, L.K. and Metcalfe, J. (2000) 'Metacognitive and control strategies in study-time allocation', *Journal of Experimental Psychology: Learning, Memory and Cognition*, 26: 204–21.

Thiede, K. and Dunlosky, J. (1999) 'Toward a general model of self-regulated study: an analysis of selection of items for study and self-paced study time', *Journal of Experimental Psychology: Learning, Memory, and Cognition*, 25: 1024–37.

Zimmerman, B. (2000) 'Attaining self-regulation: a social cognitive perspective', in M. Boekaerts, P. Pintrich and M. Zeidner (eds) *Handbook of Self-regulation* (pp. 13–41), London: Academic Press.

Zimmerman, B. (2001) 'Theories of self-regulated learning and academic achievement: an overview and analysis', in E. Zimmerman and D. Schunk (eds) *Self-regulated Learning and Academic Achievement* (pp. 1–38), Mahwah, NJ: Lawrence Erlbaum.

Chapter 3

Reading

The great debate

Tom W. Nicholson and William E. Tunmer

It would be fair to say that the past 40 years have been turbulent times in regard to the psychology and teaching of reading. This is a good thing. Different theories have provoked disagreement and generated a lot of research and this has helped to make our understanding of reading a lot clearer. We are now a lot closer to understanding reading and how best to teach it, but we are not there yet. This chapter is in two parts. First, we give a brief overview of how two major theories of reading, top-down and bottom-up, have collided in the past four decades and how a lot of good has come from this. Second, we look at the implications of the theoretical debates for the teaching of reading.

The emergence of top-down theory

A major change in the psychology of reading in the 1960s was the emergence of psycholinguistics. Corballis called the period before psycholinguistics the 'dark ages' of behaviourism when psychology stopped being a study of the mind. The critical date for the cognitive revolution, according to Howard Gardner (1985), was September 11, 1956 at a conference at the Massachusetts Institute of Technology, when Chomsky made his famous challenge to behaviourism (Corballis 2006, see also Denett 1995). Chomsky's revolution was about language, but reading theorists at the time drew on Chomsky's idea of 'surface' and 'deep' structure in language processing. Chomsky suggested that the words we speak are the 'surface' structure of language and this can be different from the 'deep' meaning that we construct from those words.

Applied to reading, this idea suggested to some researchers that reading for meaning is an interaction of ideas already in our mind with words on the page, that the reader 'constructs' meaning, that reading is not an exact process but a meaning-getting process. Clay (1972), Smith (1971), K. Goodman (1965, 1967, 1970),and Y. Goodman (Goodman and Goodman 1981) drew on psycholinguistic theory to conceptualize reading as a meaning-getting process where it was not necessary to process every letter or even every word. This became the top-down theory of reading.

Top-down theory also drew on information processing research showing that we only process a small amount of information at any one time – about seven items (plus or minus two) (Miller 1956). This suggested that we could read a lot more effectively if we could reduce the amount of information to be processed. Our ability to comprehend information would depend on how quickly we took external information, made sense of it in short-term memory and then passed it on to long-term memory. In terms of top-down theory it seemed that good readers must minimize the amount of information that they process. One way to do this would be to make a calculated guess about information ahead of reading it. This was called prediction. A second way would be to process only a limited amount of printed information. To do this, top-down theorists looked at research on distinctive features theory which suggested substantial redundancy in letters and words and that the skilled reader only used a small subset of features to recognize them.

Does the skilled reader anticipate words by a process of calculated guesswork? This was the thinking of Goodman (1970), for example, who coined the phrase 'reading is a psycholinguistic guessing game'. His reasoning was that the skilled reader reduces the amount of information to be processed by sampling just enough visual detail to make sense of what is being read. We can do this because there is predictability that comes from sentence context and also from English spelling. Smith (1971) explained the predictability of spellings of words. He gave one example of the word 'stream' which could be guessed without having to process every letter. He also explained how to take advantage of predictability in sentences (e.g. 'ham and ____'). Predictability of letter sequences and of grammatical structure means that it is possible to reduce the amount of visual information we process in reading. Several studies at that time were able to confirm context effects with both adults (e.g. Tulving and Gold 1963) and children (e.g. Goodman 1965; Pearson and Studt 1975) showing that context clues helped in reading of words.

Clay argued along similar lines that 'although language skill does not ensure reading success', it can help in creating 'appropriate expectations which narrow the field of possible responses and make the final selection quicker and more accurate' (1972: 154), and quoted Goodman (1970) in support of this idea: 'It is in this respect that grammatical structure facilitates fluency in reading because it helps the child to anticipate what comes next' (Clay 1972: 154).

Top-down theories of reading led to a number of beliefs about reading that went against the idea that reading involved processing every letter in every word. One idea was that skilled readers do not read every word accurately, that they make approximations to the meaning of the word through effective use of context; for example, 'murky' instead of 'marshy'. A second idea was that skilled readers do not read every word, but that they read only 80 per cent of the words on the page. This idea may have come from Smith's writings: 'one word in five can be completely eliminated from most English texts . . . with scarcely any effect on its overall comprehensibility' (1971: 79). A third idea was that skilled readers look ahead and predict the meanings of upcoming words.

Goodman (1970) and Smith (1971) argued that context clues in reading were so powerful that the reader only needed to check the print to see if their expectations were correct. Gough parodied this idea by saying that the top-down reader would just check the print to see if they were thinking the right thoughts (Harrison and Gough 1996). At one level, young readers do seem to make use of context for word recognition. Picture clues, for example, enable the novice reader to read words that they might otherwise struggle with, for example, 'bear' if accompanied by a picture of a bear. Sentence context can help children predict words. If the context is rich, then predicting words is made easy; for example, 'The cat drank milk from the ____', where 'saucer' is at the end of the sentence and is the missing word (Hudson and Haworth 1983). For skilled readers, context speeds up word recognition time by about 10 per cent if the context is rich (Rayner and Pollatsek 1989).

A problem for top-down theory is that something else must do most of the work in word processing if context only speeds it up by 10 per cent. Another problem is that rich context is not typical. Gough *et al.* (1981) reported a study where they asked undergraduates to guess, one at a time, the first 100 words in 10 different reading selections from *Reader's Digest*; for example, 'The diary of Che Guevara'. They found that these intelligent, well-educated readers, given unlimited time, could only predict, on average, one word in four. Gough (1983) reported another study that found the probability of guessing function words was 40 per cent and of content words was 10 per cent. This suggests that context is a high-risk strategy to use once the child is beyond the beginning stages of reading, especially if your guess is correct on average only one time in four and if your guess is correct for content words only one time in ten.

Nicholson and Hill (1985) carried out context studies with 8-year-old children and reported similar findings that the good readers in the study could guess three out of four words when the first two letters of target words were shown in easy stories but that good readers could only guess one in four words when the stories were difficult. Prediction depended on whether words were at the beginning or end of the sentence. Words were harder to predict at the beginning of sentences than at the end. These results indicated that context clues are not consistently helpful. Context clues work better if words are at the end of the sentence and if text material is easy. Relying on context clues completely even for easy stories would only work 75 per cent of the time so it is not a complete strategy for reading words. Independent reading requires at least 95 per cent accuracy.

There is no doubt that context clues can make it easier to recognize words in text. The question is whether or not this is the best way to read words. Studies of good and poor readers show that good readers have developed good word recognition skills that can operate independently of guessing and do not have to rely on context, whereas beginner and poor readers rely on context clues to help in recognizing words (Stanovich 1980, 1984, 1986, 1994a, 1994b; Nicholson 1991, 1993; Nicholson *et al.* 1988; Nicholson *et al.* 1991; Wong and Underwood 1996). Gough (1996) summarized this weight of research, writing that good readers do not need the help of context because they are skilled at reading words in isolation.

Bottom-up theory

Bottom-up theory (Gough 1972) appealed to a lot of researchers when it first swept on the reading scene, but not to everyone. Gough's seminal paper, 'One second of reading', showed how words could be recognized through phonological recoding without any contextual help at all, basically rejecting top-down theory and arguing that the good reader reads word by word, letter by letter. It was a remarkable paper in that it was so different from the top-down view and yet came from the same psycholinguistic background.

Gough (1972) suggested that in one second of reading maybe five or six words are recognized. This is done very quickly. The letters in each word are mapped into phonological form (i.e. their sounds) and their meaning retrieved immediately from lexical memory, that is, from our mental dictionary. As words are looked up they are held briefly in working memory until they are parsed and interpreted. Parsing means working out the grammatical form, and interpretation refers to working out the meaning (Matthei and Roeper 1985).

Gough reasoned that skilled readers could in any one fixation (about a quarter of a second) process up to 12 letters – maybe one or two words. If this was the case, then the reader could easily process a normal word during a single fixation, and therefore several words a second, which was in line with the average speed of reading of adults, about 200 words a minute. In this way the model showed that a bottom-up process of reading could account for skilled reading without any prediction or guessing at all. The model did not say much about comprehension except that it was perfectly possible to read at 200 words a minute or more and still get meaning from each sentence as it was being read, in phrases and clauses. As the meanings of sentences were worked out, they were sent on to what Gough called 'the place where sentences go when they are understood', or TPWSGWTAU, which is a humorous way of describing long-term memory (see Rayner and Pollatsek 1989).

Bottom-up theory suggested that the skilled reader identified nearly every word and that the eye plodded along each line word by word. The eye of the skilled reader may not fixate on highly frequent and short words (usually function words like 'of', 'and', 'the') which means that they may or may not be processing these very high frequency words – but they do seem to process all other words.

Most skilled readers are oblivious as to what they do when they read words on the page. As Foss and Hakes (1978) pointed out, our intuitions about what our eyes do are not correct. Skilled readers often think that their eyes are on the move, skimming across each line of print. If you ask them to tell you what proportion of the time their eyes are moving, they will say that they are moving just about all the time. If you ask them to draw in the air with their finger what their eyes do when they read, they will probably make their finger move smoothly from left to right across an imaginary line of print in the air, then sweep back to beginning of the next imaginary line, and so on. But our eyes do not move smoothly across each line of print (see Rayner and Pollatsek 1989; Underwood and Batt 1996).

Instead of being on the move most of the time, our eyes are perfectly still for 95 per cent of the time. Obviously our eyes do move. They cover about 200 words or more per minute, but the process of moving from word to word, called saccadic movements, is extremely short, about 5 per cent of the time (Rayner and Pollatsek 1989). The typical pattern of eye movements has the eye fixating for about 250 milliseconds (a quarter of a second), then jerking to the next word in a saccadic motion that takes 20 milliseconds, just a very tiny fraction of a second. The eye jumps from one word to the next, jerking along each line of print and from one page to the next.

While eye movement studies suggest that the skilled reader processes just about every word on the page, there is still the question of whether this is done phonologically or visually. One theory is that there is an indirect, phonological route to the lexicon (our mental dictionary). There is evidence to support this idea. Proofreaders are more likely to pick up a spelling error if it does not sound right; for example, *wark* for *work* and miss it if it does sound right; for example, *werk* for *work* (Foss and Hakes 1978). We have more trouble deciding whether a word like 'rows' is or is not a flower which suggests that we process words by sound rather than by sight (Van Orden 1987). When we are asked to count the 'f's in words like 'off' and 'of', we are likely to miss 'of' words because the 'f' does not have its regular phoneme which again suggests that we convert letters into phonemes when we read words (Read 1983).

The other theory is called the direct, orthographic route. The research on this theory suggests that skilled readers process most words as 'sight' words. Words that are initially processed by phonemes are later, after a few exposures, stored as sight words and are processed visually (Ehri 1994, 1995; Thompson 1999). Or it could be that skilled readers use both a visual route to the mental lexicon and a phonological route. This is the dual route model (see Adams 1990; Rayner and Pollatsek 1989; Coltheart 2006). To summarize, the bottom-up model has stood up to scrutiny. There is debate about how we recognize words but there is agreement that the word reading process is a bottom-up one; that is, the skilled reader's eyes move along each line reading just about every word without having to rely on context clues.

Implications for learning to read

They say that there is nothing more practical than a good theory but this is probably not the case for reading. How we learn to read does not necessarily have anything to do with the theory that underpins the way we teach reading. The problem is that theory, on its own, will not settle the debate about how to teach reading. The question of how we read and how we learn to read is independent of how we teach reading (Gough and Tunmer 1986; Tunmer and Nicholson 2010). Even though children are taught to read a certain way, this may not be the way they finally read.

The two main approaches to teaching reading are phonics and whole language. Phonics seems closer to bottom-up theory and whole language to top-down theory, but this is not necessarily the case. The theoretical question is about how we learn to read. Good readers could use exactly the same processes yet learn to read with either phonics or whole language. The reading methods only provide the child with 'data'. The child has to take the data and use it to learn to read. The two reading methods can both work but only one theory of the process can be right – this is what researchers have to decide.

The fact that both methods succeed for a lot of children but still fail a lot of children prompted Gough's (1996) classic paper called 'A pox on both your houses' in which he explained why neither whole language nor phonics is sufficient to enable all children to work out the 'cipher' – the set of letter–sound correspondences needed to become a skilled reader. In his paper, Gough starts by praising the good things about whole language.

One good point about whole language is that teachers read children's literature to the class every day, they share interesting books with the class, and they guide groups of children as they read a story or article. Teachers provide the conditions that enable many children to learn to read, especially if children already have the basic building blocks of literacy; that is, knowledge of the alphabet and understanding of how spoken words can be decomposed into sounds, called phonemic awareness.

Imagine a group of children sitting on the mat while the teacher shares a book with them, such as *Greedy Cat*. Some children in the group, those with good knowledge of the alphabet and a good understanding that spoken words are made up of sounds (phonemic awareness) will look at a word like 'cat' and match up the letters with their existing knowledge of letters and sounds and begin to work out how to decipher 'cat' as the spoken word /kat/ and be in a good position to generalize this knowledge to similar words like 'mat' and 'hat'. In this way children learn to decode with whole language even if it does not explicitly encourage them to do this.

The whole-language view is that children will learn to read the way they learn to talk, that is, for reading, being exposed to lots of written language (as opposed to lots of spoken language for learning to talk). Whole-language proponents believe that we learn to read by reading just as we learn to talk by talking. They also believe that learning has to be authentic and this means that children should read authentic texts written by real children's authors not contrived texts that teach phonics such as 'the fat cat sat on the mat'.

This is a second good point about whole language. The research supports this view in that a good reader will only become good by doing lots of reading. Whole language tries to make this process of learning to read by reading as enjoyable as possible by only using interesting text material. This approach does not like drills and worksheets. Instead it provides lots of opportunities to read, with shared book reading and guided reading, and lots of writing as well. Children can learn phonics but they learn it in the context of reading and writing.

Whole language encourages children to use letter clues, especially the first couple of letters, to predict the meaning of words they read. Researchers believe that this is what good readers do, that they sample the print and then guess the meaning of the word. Whole language emphasizes the power of context clues to drive reading for meaning. Children will learn decoding skills but this will happen naturally, as a by-product of reading, and also as part of the process of phonologically encoding words when writing, given that an early emphasis on writing is also a major emphasis in whole-language teaching.

If all children learned to read this way, then whole language would have to be the preferred method of teaching reading. It is interesting, simple to implement, and makes reading enjoyable in that it exposes children to books from the very beginning stages. In contrast, phonics involves the child in learning a series of letter–sound correspondences that apply to Anglo-Saxon, Latin, and Greek words, some of which are intellectually sophisticated, like the final e marker rule, vowel teams, syllable-breaking strategies, and prefixes and suffixes (Moats 2000; Nicholson 2006). This is intellectually challenging for the pupil – and the teacher.

Whole language is very effective. Eighty per cent of children learn to read with this approach, but whole language also fails a significant minority of children, about 20 per cent. If you believe in whole-language teaching then the solution to this problem is to provide whole-language instruction in a more intensive way, with one-to-one instruction. This is what happens in Reading Recovery (Anand and Bennie 2004; Kerslake 2000, 2001; Lee 2008; Ng 2007).

Yet Reading Recovery has been criticized because the children who do not respond to this programme, and about 30 per cent do not, lack basic phonics skills and phonemic awareness skills (Nicholson 2008; Tunmer *et al*. 2008; White *et al*. 1999). Whole language is based on top-down theory so in its teaching of reading, it gives a very low profile to phonics. It argues that we read words using a multiple cueing system, that is, semantics, syntax, and grapho-phonics. Grapho-phonics is seen as the least important part of the multiple cueing system. Extreme whole-language enthusiasts would prefer a child to guess a word rather than sound it out as long as the meaning is about the same. This belief that sounding out words is a bad thing is the Achilles' heel of whole language. Whole language teaches some decoding, but not enough.

Whole language over-emphasizes the power of context in reading words. It believes that decoding ability, that is the ability to recode words phonologically, is unimportant even though numerous studies have shown that poor readers rely on context far more than do good readers (Gough 1996; Nicholson 1991; Stanovich 1986). Good readers are good decoders. When good readers are asked how they read words, they are much more likely to say they sound them out. Tunmer and Chapman (2002) reported that half of the children they interviewed in Year 1 of school in New Zealand, between the ages of 5 and 6 years, reported that they used 'sound it out' strategies and that these children were better readers than children who said they guessed from context even though both groups were taught in whole-language classrooms. The irony is that children who follow top-down theory in a whole-language classroom are more likely to be poor decoders because they try to guess words from context.

The good reader in a whole-language classroom benefits from the emphasis on context clues, only because they have better decoding skills. They are better able than poor readers to decode parts of an unfamiliar word so that when this is combined with the use of context clues, it is often sufficient to reveal the spoken form of the word (Groff 1983). For example, the good reader who decodes 'stomach' as 'stow-match' can better guess the word in a sentence like 'the football hit her in the stomach' than a poor reader who decodes 'stomach' as 'stotch' (Tunmer and Chapman 1999). This combination of partial decoding skill combined with use of context clues enables them to bootstrap themselves into skilled reading. The good reader rises to the top; the poor reader gets left behind.

Phonics can enable struggling readers to become better decoders by teaching the letter–sound correspondences that struggling readers have not yet learned and in this way bring them to a level of decoding skill where they can reap the same advantages from context as better readers. Knowledge of letter–sound rules empowers students to read 'in loco parentis' by giving them the ability to sound out words for themselves. Share and Stanovich (1995) argue that when a child decodes a word successfully, it is a self-teaching opportunity. Partial decoding of a word, when combined with context clues, can produce a correct decoding so that even partial decoding skill becomes a self-teaching tool. The strong correlations between word reading and the ability to read nonsense words, usually more than 0.70, supports this view that decoding skill helps children to teach themselves to read.

If all children learned to read with phonics, then it would be more popular than it is. Gough (1996) has argued that phonics, like whole language, is problematic in that it fails many children. He estimated about 10 per cent. Why does it fail? The problem is that phonics can only give the child a very basic sense of the cipher, that is, the letter-to-sound rules, of English. Phonics on its own cannot teach the cipher. The cipher is automatic, it is fast, and it is implicit. Phonics is slow, involves 'sounding out', and is approximate, unable to articulate the cipher exactly. Tunmer and Nicholson (2010) point out that the cipher is not phonics. The rules of phonics are explicit; the rules of the cipher are implicit. There are maybe 100 phonics rules that are taught but there are hundreds of cipher rules. Phonics rules are laborious to apply whereas cipher rules operate effortlessly. Cipher rules are acquired mostly by reading whereas phonics rules are usually taught by comparing patterns in isolated words. This is a big problem for phonics. There are so many spelling–sound correspondences to learn and many of them are subtle. We can teach some of them but the rest are complex, slightly irregular like 'steak' and 'pint' or very irregular like 'laugh' and 'shoe', and these words have to be acquired by doing lots and lots of reading, not by learning phonics. In summary, phonics has problems. It is often disconnected from reading of text, it teaches rules for sounding out words that are not 100 per cent reliable, it is slow, and this slowness interferes with getting the meaning of the text (Harrison and Gough 1996).

Gough (1996) criticized traditional phonics programmes for being overly teacher-centred and having a curriculum that is typically rigid, fixed, and lockstep, with the same lesson given to every child. The difficulty with phonics is that children differ in the amount of reading-related knowledge, skills, and experiences they bring to the classroom, in the explicitness and intensity of instruction they require to learn skills and strategies for identifying words, and in where they are located along the developmental progression from pre-reader to skilled reader.

Regarding the latter, learning to read is a process that takes place over time, involves qualitatively different (but perhaps overlapping) phases, and may break down at different points. Developmental theories of how children acquire automaticity in word recognition specify the critical cognitive skills and learning strategies (phonemic awareness, letter knowledge, understanding of the alphabetic principle, use of alphabetic coding skills, exposure to print, and so on) required to progress from one phase of word learning to the next, and provide frameworks for identifying the different learning needs of children according to the phase of reading development they have reached (Ehri and McCormick 1998).

Phonics and whole language each are not sufficient. As noted earlier, the research on how children learn to read indicates that comprehending text in an alphabetic orthography depends on the ability to recognize the words of text accurately and quickly. The development of automaticity in word recognition (i.e. sight word knowledge), in turn depends on the ability to make use of the cipher in identifying unknown words. The ability to use the cipher, that is, the ability to discover mappings between spelling patterns and sound patterns, in turn depends on the ability to detect phonemic sequences in spoken words (i.e. phonemic awareness).

Regarding the latter, Gough (1996) has suggested that we should start by teaching phonemic awareness in kindergarten. He has even developed his own programme called Turtletalk (Gough and Lee 2007) that gives children a 'sound' foundation for learning to read. Too many children start school lacking in phonemic awareness. It seems to be a universal problem in learning to read. Lundberg (1991), for example, studied 200 non-reading preschool children aged 6 to 7 years and only 10 had phoneme segmentation abilities. If phonemic awareness is a precursor to learning to read, which is what research is saying, then it makes sense to teach it early, before children start formal schooling (Nicholson 1998, 2005, 2006; Nicholson and Ng 2006). On the other hand, phonemic awareness on its own is not sufficient to learn the cipher. How does the child best learn the cipher? Which way is best to teach it? This takes us back to whole language and phonics.

As we have seen, phonics and whole language both have theoretical and practical weak points. This is why Gough (1996) called his paper 'A pox on both your houses', in that he felt there were too many weak points. Statistical comparisons, however, favour phonics over whole language. Hattie (2009) summarized 14 meta-analyses involving 12,000 students and found that phonics had a significant effect on learning to read (average effect size 0.6). Hattie concluded, 'Overall phonics instruction is powerful in the process of learning to read – both for reading skills and for reading comprehension' (ibid.: 134). In contrast, he summarized four meta-analyses of whole-language teaching involving 630 students and found that it had almost zero effect (average effect size 0.06). For whole language, he concluded:

> In summary, whole language programs have negligible effects on learning to read – be it on word recognition or on comprehension. Such methods might be of value to later reading but certainly not for the processes of learning to read; it appears that strategies of reading need to be deliberately taught, especially to students struggling to read.
>
> (2009: 138)

Other meta-analyses support this conclusion (Ehri *et al.* 2001; Torgerson *et al.* 2006).

Although the meta-analyses indicate that phonics is the better approach, the particular mix of phonics and whole-language activities depends on the particular learning needs of the child at the time, that is, in where they are located along the developmental progression from pre-reader to skilled reader (see above). In support of this suggestion are the results of a study by Juel and Minden-Cupp examining the effects of different instructional emphases on children possessing varying amounts of literacy-related skills at the beginning of school. They found that 'children who entered first grade with few literacy skills benefited from a heavy dose of phonics', whereas children who entered first grade with comparatively high levels of literacy and literacy-related skills 'did exceptionally well in a classroom that included a less structured phonics curriculum and more reading of trade books and writing of text' (2000: 484). Children with limited literacy skills on entry to school benefited more from explicit, code-emphasis approaches to beginning reading instruction than from whole-language/book experience approaches, whereas the opposite pattern occurred with children who had high levels of literacy-related abilities at the beginning of school. Perhaps most importantly, Juel and Minden-Cupp reported that 'the classroom . . . that had the very highest success both overall and with the low group had considerably different instruction across the groups' (ibid.: 482).

In support of child-by-instruction interactions, in which 'child' refers to high versus low reading-related skills and knowledge, and 'instruction' refers to code emphasis versus meaning emphasis, Connor *et al.* (2004) found that children who began first grade with below-average reading-related skills made greater reading gains in classrooms that provided more teacher-managed, code-focused instruction throughout the year than in classrooms that provided more child-managed, meaning-focused instruction. In contrast, for children with higher reading-related skills at school entry, better progress in reading was achieved in classrooms that provided less teacher-managed, code-focused instruction and more child-managed, meaning-focused instruction. On the basis of these and other similar findings,

Connor *et al.* (2007) concluded that instructional strategies that may be effective with some students may be ineffective when applied to other students with different skills. In support of this claim, Connor *et al.* reported that children in first-grade classrooms in which reading instruction was individualized by taking into account child-by-instruction interactions, made greater gains in reading achievement than children in control classrooms.

This research is saying that not only should the best bits of whole language and phonics be combined, but that the relative emphasis of each for any given child varies depending on individual learning needs. That is, the key to bringing phonics and whole language together in an optimal way is differential instruction based on a cognitive developmental model of how children learn to read. The model suggests that the relative effect of whole language and phonics will vary depending on the extent to which children have sufficient degrees of reading-related skills, in particular, high levels of phonological awareness and alphabet knowledge.

Conclusion

Overseas reports indicate that simply changing from one method to another is not an immediate solution. It may not even be the solution. In a media interview in 2008, the US Education Secretary commented that 'moving the needle on reading is a hard thing to do . . . I don't think anyone's going to assert that the cure will be less focus and fewer resources' (Toppo 2008). Literacy is obviously of immense importance to the individual and to society. The role of reading is to enable the child to grow as a person. The ability to read has an immense snowball effect. The best readers cover millions of words a year; poor readers only a small percentage of that. One of the messages of whole language is that children need to read but it does not provide poor readers with enough skills to catch up with good readers. Phonics can teach skills but these skills need to be combined with lots of text reading. The Achilles' heel of phonics is that it tends to be a licence to print worksheets rather than books (the internet is choked with phonics worksheets) and this is something that we need to be cautious of when teaching phonics.

The research suggested that we should differentiate our teaching in that children with low entry reading skills when they start school seem more likely to respond to a more code-oriented reading programme. If it is required that they start with whole language, then we need to have code-based instruction as an option for them very early on if they do not respond to whole-language teaching. Likewise, with children who have high-level entry reading skills when they start school, research suggests that they are likely to respond much better to a whole-language programme, but they also need the option of more code-based instruction if they do not respond to whole language as we thought they might.

Our theoretical understanding of reading says that the top-down model has to be discarded but this does not mean the teaching of whole language has to be discarded. Good readers are good decoders, not good guessers. At the same time, decoding is not all there is to reading. We do learn to read by reading. All the road signs point toward teaching whole language and phonics according to the needs of individual learners. Is this possible, given the politics of reading? We think it is.

References

Adams, M.J. (1990) *Beginning to Read: Thinking and Learning about Print*, Cambridge, MA: MIT Press.

Anand, V. and Bennie, N. (2004) *Annual Monitoring of Reading Recovery: The Data for 2002*, Wellington, NZ: Ministry of Education.

Clay, M.M. (1972) *Reading: The Patterning of Behaviour*, Auckland: Heinemann.

Coltheart, M. (2006) 'Dual route and connectionist models of reading: an overview', *London Review of Education*, 4: 5–17.

Connor, C.M., Morrison, F.J., Fishman, B.J., Schatschneider, C. and Underwood, P. (2007) 'Algorithm-guided individualized reading instruction', *Science*, 315: 464–5.

Connor, C.M., Morrison, F.J. and Katch, L.E. (2004) 'Beyond the reading wars: exploring the effect of child-instruction interactions on growth in early reading', *Scientific Studies of Reading*, 8: 305–36.

Corballis, M.C. (2006) 'The cognitive revolution', in G.M. Haberman and C.M. Fletcher-Flinn (eds) *Cognition and Language: Perspectives from New Zealand*, Bowen Hills, Queensland: Australian Academic Press.

Denett, D.C. (1995), *Darwin's dangerous idea: evolution and the meanings of life*. NY: Simon & Schuster.

Ehri, L.C. (1994) 'Development of the ability to read words: update', in R.B. Ruddell and M.R. Ruddell (eds) *Theoretical Models and Processes of Reading*, 4th edn (pp. 323–58), Newark, DE: International Reading Association.

Ehri, L.C. (1995) 'Phases of development in learning to read words by sight', *Journal of Research in Reading*, 18: 116–25.

Ehri, L.C. and McCormick, S. (1998) 'Phases of word learning: implications for instruction with delayed or disabled readers', *Reading and Writing Quarterly*, 14: 135–63.

Ehri, L.C., Nunes, S.R., Stahl, S.A. and Willows, D.M. (2001) 'Systematic phonics instruction helps students learn to read: evidence from the National Reading Panel's meta-analysis', *Review of Educational Research*, 71: 393–447.

Foss, D. and Hakes, D. (1978) *Psycholinguistics*, Englewood Cliffs, NJ: Prentice Hall.

Goodman, K.S. (1965) 'A linguistic study of cues and miscues in reading', *Elementary English*, 42: 639–43.

Goodman, K.S. (1967) 'Reading: a psycholinguistic guessing game', *Journal of the Reading Specialist*, 4: 126–35.

Goodman, K.S. (1970) 'Behind the eye: what happens in reading', in K.S. Goodman and O.S. Niles (eds) *Reading Process and Program* (pp. 3–38), Urbana, IL: National Council of Teachers of English.

Goodman, K. and Goodman, Y. (1981) 'Twenty questions about teaching language', *Educational Leadership*, 38: 437–42.

Gough, P.B. (1972) 'One second of reading', in J.F. Kavanagh and I.G. Mattingly (eds) *Language by Ear and by Eye* (pp. 331–58), Cambridge, MA: MIT Press.

Gough, P.B. (1983) 'Context, form and interaction', in K. Rayner (ed.) *Eye Movements in Reading: Perceptual and Language Processes* (pp. 203–11), San Diego, CA: Academic Press.

Gough, P.B. (1996) 'A pox on both your houses', paper presented to Symposium on Integrated Direct Instruction, sponsored by Language Arts Foundation of America and Oklahoma City Schools, Oklahoma City, February.

Gough, P.B., Alford, J.A. and Holley-Wilcox, P. (1981) 'Words and contexts', in O.L. Tzeng and H. Singer (eds) *Perception of Print: Reading Research in Experimental Psychology* (pp. 85–102), Hillsdale, NJ: Erlbaum.

Gough, P.B. and Lee, C.H. (2007) 'A step toward early phonemic awareness: the effects of Turtletalk training', *Psychologia*, 50: 54–66.

Gough. P.B. and Tunmer, W.E. (1986) 'Decoding, reading, and reading disability', *Remedial and Special Education*, 7: 6–10.

Groff, P. (1983) 'A test of the utility of phonics rules', *Reading Psychology*, 4: 217–25.

Harrison, C. and Gough, P.B. (1996) 'Compellingness in reading research', *Reading Research Quarterly*, 31: 334–41.

Hattie, J.A. (2009) *Visible Learning: A Synthesis of Over 800 Meta-Analyses Relating to Achievement*, London: Routledge.

Hudson, J. and Haworth, J. (1983) 'Dimensions of word recognition', *Reading*, 17: 87–94.

Juel, C. and Minden-Cupp, C. (2000) 'Learning to read words: linguistic units and instructional strategies', *Reading Research Quarterly*, 35: 458–92.

Kerslake, J. (2000) 'Annual monitoring of Reading Recovery: the data for 1999', *The Research Bulletin*, 11, Wellington, NZ: Ministry of Education.

Kerslake, J. (2001) 'Annual monitoring of Reading Recovery: the data for 2000', *The Research Bulletin*, 12, Wellington, NZ: Ministry of Education.

Lee, M. (2008) *Annual Monitoring for Reading Recovery: The Data for 2007*, Wellington, NZ: Ministry of Education.

Lundberg, I. (1991) 'Phonemic awareness can be developed without reading instruction', in S.A. Brady and D.P. Shankweiler (eds), *Phonological Processes in Literacy: A Tribute to Isabelle Y. Liberman* (pp. 47–53), Hillsdale, NJ: Erlbaum.

Matthei, E. and Roeper, T. (1985) *Understanding and Producing Speech*, New York: Universe Books.

Miller, G.A. (1956) 'The magical number 7, plus or minus two: some limits on our capacity for processing information', *Psychological Review*, 63: 81–97.

Moats, L.C. (2000) *Speech to Print: Language Essentials for Teachers*, Baltimore, MD: Paul H. Brookes.

Ng, L. (2007) *Annual Monitoring of Reading Recovery: The Data for 2006*, Wellington, NZ: Ministry of Education.

Nicholson, T. (1991) 'Do children read words better in context or in lists? A classic study revisited', *Journal of Educational Psychology*, 83: 444–50.

Nicholson, T. (1993) 'The case against context', in G.B. Thompson, W.E. Tunmer and T. Nicholson (eds) *Reading Acquisition Processes* (pp. 91–104), Clevedon: Multilingual Matters.

Nicholson, T. (1998) 'Phonological awareness and learning to read', in L. van Lier and D. Corson (eds) *Encyclopedia of Language and Education*, vol. 6, *Knowledge about Language* (pp. 53–61), Dordrecht: Kluwer.

Nicholson, T. (2005) *At the Cutting Edge: The Importance of Phonemic Awareness in Learning to Read*, 2nd edn, Wellington: New Zealand Council for Educational Research.

Nicholson, T. (2006) 'How to avoid reading failure: teach phonemic awareness', in A. McKeough, L.M. Phillips, V. Timmons and J.L. Lupart (eds) *Understanding Literacy Development: A Global View* (pp. 31–48), Mahwah, NJ: Lawrence Erlbaum.

Nicholson, T. (2008) 'Achieving equity for Māori children in reading by 2020', *New Zealand Annual Review of Education*, 18: 159–82.

Nicholson, T., Bailey, J. and McArthur, J. (1991) 'Context cues in reading: the gap between research and popular opinion', *Journal of Reading, Writing, and Learning Disabilities*, 7: 33–41.

Nicholson, T. and Hill, D. (1985) 'Good readers don't guess: taking another look at the issue of whether children read words better in context or in isolation', *Reading Psychology*, 6: 181–98.

Nicholson, T., Lillas, C. and Rzoska, A. (1988) 'Have we been misled by miscues?', *The Reading Teacher*, 42: 6–10.

Nicholson, T. and Ng, G.L. (2006) 'The case for teaching phonemic awareness and simple phonics to preschoolers', in R.M. Joshi and P.G. Aaron (eds) *Handbook of Orthography and Literacy* (pp. 637–48), Mahwah, NJ: Lawrence Erlbaum.

Pearson, D., Rouse, H., Doswell, S., Ainsworth, C., Dawson, O., Simms, K., Edwards, L. and Faulconbridge, J. (2001), 'Prevalence of imaginary companions in a normal child population', *Child Care, Health and Development*, 27: 13–22.

Pearson, P.D. and Studt, A. (1975) 'Effects of word frequency and contextual richness on children's word identification abilities', *Journal of Educational Psychology*, 67: 89–95.

Rayner, K. and Pollatsek, A. (1989) *Psychology of Reading*, Hillsdale, NJ: Erlbaum.

Read, J.D. (1983) 'Detection of Fs in a single statement: the role of phonetic recoding', *Memory and Cognition*, 11: 152–60.

Share, D. and Stanovich, K.E. (1995) 'Cognitive processes in early reading development: accommodating individual differences into a model of acquisition', *Issues in Education*, 1: 1–57.

Smith, F. (1971) *Understanding Reading*, New York: Holt, Rinehart and Winston.

Stanovich, K.E. (1980) 'Toward an interactive-compensatory model of individual differences in the development of reading fluency', *Reading Research Quarterly*, 16: 32–71.

Stanovich, K. (1984) 'The interactive-compensatory model of reading: a confluence of developmental, experimental and educational psychology', *Remedial and Special Education*, 5: 11–19.

Stanovich, K.E. (1986) 'Matthew effects in reading: some consequences of individual differences in the acquisition of literacy', *Reading Research Quarterly*, 21: 340–406.

Stanovich, K.E. (1994a) 'Constructivism in reading education', *The Journal of Special Education*, 28: 259–74.

Stanovich, K.E. (1994b) 'Romance and reality', *The Reading Teacher*, 47: 280–91.

Thompson, G.B. (1999) 'The process of learning to identify words', in G.B. Thompson and T. Nicholson (eds) *Learning to Read: Beyond Phonics and Whole Language* (pp. 25–55), New York: Teachers College Press.

Toppo, G. (2008) 'Study: Reading First has little impact on kids' scores', *USA Today*, May 2, p. 4A.

Torgerson, C.J., Brooks, G. and Hall, J. (2006) *A Systematic Review of the Research Literature on the Use of Phonics in the Teaching of Reading and Spelling*, Nottingham: Department for Education and Skills.

Tulving, E. and Gold, C. (1963) 'Stimulus information and contextual information as determinants of tachistoscopic recognition of words', *Journal of Experimental Psychology*, 66: 319–27.

Tunmer, W.E. and Chapman, J.W. (1999) 'Teaching strategies for word identification', in G.B. Thompson and T. Nicholson (eds) *Learning to Read: Beyond Phonics and Whole Language* (pp. 74–102) New York: Teachers College Press.

Tunmer, W.E. and Chapman, J.W. (2002) 'The relation of beginning readers' reported word identification strategies to reading achievement, reading related skills, and academic self-perceptions', *Reading and Writing*, 15: 341–58.

Tunmer, W.E. and Nicholson, T. (2010) 'The development and teaching of word recognition skill', in P.D. Pearson *et al.* (eds) *Handbook of Reading Research*, vol. 4, Mahwah, NJ: Lawrence Erlbaum.

Tunmer, W.E., Nicholson, T., Greaney, K., Prochnow, J.E., Chapman, J.W. and Arrow, A.W. (2008) 'PIRLS before swine: a critique of the National Literacy Strategy', *New Zealand Journal of Educational Studies*, 43: 105–19.

Underwood, G. and Batt, V. (1996) *Reading and Understanding*, Oxford: Blackwell.

Van Orden, G.C. (1987) 'A ROWS is a ROSE: spelling, sound and reading', *Memory and Cognition*, 15: 181–98.

White, C.Y., Fletcher-Flinn, C.M. and Nicholson, T. (1999) 'Does Reading Recovery improve phonological skills?', *Queensland Journal of Educational Research*, 14: 4–28.

Wong, M.Y and Underwood, G. (1996) 'Do bilingual children read words better in lists or in context?', *Journal of Research in Reading*, 19: 61–76.

Chapter 4

Writing in the curriculum

A complex act to teach and to evaluate

Judy M. Parr

As a theoretical construct, writing is complex. Writing is a social and cultural act; it is problematic to specify what 'develops' or progresses in writing; what it develops towards (Marshall 2004) and under which conditions. The complex and less than tangible nature of writing is an issue for both pedagogy and evaluation, where it affects the decision of what precisely is to be taught and what and how it is to be evaluated. In writing research, the links between theory, pedagogy and evaluation are not clearly articulated; the direction of influence seems to be from theory to pedagogy and, to a much lesser extent, to evaluation.

Evaluation of writing[1] is among the least studied areas, according to a recent overview of research in writing (Juzwik *et al.* 2006), and is under-theorized. Links between theory in writing and evaluation of writing are not well articulated (White *et al.* 1996). Equally, the links between evaluation and the teaching of writing are underdeveloped.

This chapter examines the current status of evaluating writing, particularly in relation to teaching. This is particularly apt, given that key ideas and principles from cognitive, constructivist and sociocultural theories have re-conceptualized assessment and its role in teaching and learning (Dwyer 1998; Gipps 1994). While the written form has long been used to examine knowledge, it is only relatively recently that evaluation of writing has been seen as a 'knowledge-making' endeavour that we can learn from (Yancey 1999), one that can inform teaching and learning. Assessment has come to be viewed as something embedded in, and integral to, teaching. Assessment with a formative intent and function has potential in terms of improving the quality of teaching and of learning (Black and Wiliam 1998; Black *et al.* 2003; Sadler 1989; Wiliam 1996).

Writing to examine knowledge

Writing is the means by which students in educational settings present and display what they know. As students move through schooling, competence in using writing for this purpose assumes greater importance. Writing is a cross-curricula endeavour. The widespread use of written tests to select, place, certify or hold to account has been a shaping influence on the field of composition studies (Traschel

1992). Some such tests examine the ability to write directly. Or, the ability to write may have an indirect effect when content is being tested in essay or similar form.

The emphasis in writing evaluation research has been on judgements whose purpose (and timing) suggest they are of a summative nature (Sadler 1989). Two camps, each with differing perspectives about knowledge and learning – psychological or educational measurement on the one hand and rhetoric or composition studies on the other – dominate contributions to this research literature. Theories underpinning psychological measurement assume educational achievements and aptitudes can be measured. Therefore, it follows that the nature of both writing ability and writing quality can be defined and measured with some consistency. This measurement emphasis led to the issues in the evaluation of writing being framed technically (Huot and Neal 2006). Indeed, scholars have often characterized the history of testing of writing as one of balancing the requirements of reliability and validity (Camp 1993; Yancey 1999), with a large body of literature discussing how to obtain, maintain and enhance agreement among markers (discussed in Williamson and Huot 1993). This includes efforts to make rating more reliable through specifying dimensions and related criteria. Most tests have used reliability estimates derived from classical test theory which account for only a single source of variance, rather than allowing the interactions of several independent sources of error variance – raters, occasions, prompts – to be estimated simultaneously (Schwartz et al. 1999). The question of consistency in a writer's performance and the extent of variability according to genre, topic or level of motivation have remained relatively unexplored, although seemingly such reliability is low even for take-home assignments (Hayes et al. 2000).

Critique regarding use of writing to make a judgement has centred on two major issues. The first concerns the fact that scholarship on testing of writing was based on outmoded notions of validity and seldom considered the implications of decisions including how testing might connect to and improve learning. The task of producing a piece of writing to be scored was seen as valid because it involved writing. Validity was assumed to be increased by using multiple samples over an extended period of time (White 2005). The notion of validity as 'an integrated, evaluative judgment to support the adequacy and appropriateness of inferences and actions based on test scores and modes of assessment' (Messick 1989: 5) was an idea that was slow to gain traction. This view of consequential validity involves questioning why some methods of evaluating writing are privileged and what the outcome of this is, particularly regarding the use to which assessment is put in terms of making the best educational decisions and taking cognisance of unintended consequences (Messick 1994; Moss 1996).

There has been limited research attention to the consequences of testing of writing. There have been attempts to explain how and why raters disagreed. The implications of differing interpretations of text in evaluating writing for decision-making about school or university placement are discussed by O'Neill (2003) who also enquires as to whether students receive the best placement as a result. Unintended consequences of testing have been the focus of some recent research.

Tests have an effect on curricula and instruction, a complex phenomenon referred to as 'washback' (Weigle 2002). Currently, widespread accountability testing has highlighted views regarding the negative effects of assessment on teaching (Lane and Stone 2002). Hillocks (2002) points out that assessments, not standards, influence what happens in classrooms in terms of rhetorical stance, instructional mode and writing process; they privilege curricula content that appears related to the assessment, like particular forms of writing. Assessments can downplay the interaction between writer and readers, defining writing as an act of formal display. Scoring rubrics can indicate what is regarded as important in writing (Mabry 1999). Tests promote unintended learning in schools including a narrow definition of writing by students (Luce-Kepler and Klinger 2005).

The second focus of critique centred on the idea that writing testing, unsupported by resources commonly used by writers, involving a single, often timed response to a prompt, was 'based upon theoretical and epistemological positions that do not reflect current knowledge of literacy and its teaching' (Huot 2002: 8). As writing theory advanced, the associated concepts no longer matched the construct implied in, and the information provided by, traditional formats for writing assessment (Camp 1993).

Moving beyond traditional assessment formats

The introduction of portfolios was, in part, a response to issues arising from use of tests involving writing to judge performance. Portfolios were introduced to gather writing for evaluation which seemed to encompass a view more aligned with theories of writing as social practice designed to accomplish communicative goals. Portfolios were launched when composition studies moved from a focus on form and products to the processes involved in writing. They were seen as an alternative, authentic, more equitable form of evaluating performance that might have a positive effect on instruction and student performance (Darling-Hammond *et al.* 1995; Wiggins 1993). The portfolio concept as it applied to writing has been discussed in a number of collections (e.g. Black *et al.* 1994; Calfee and Perfumo 1996; Hamp-Lyons and Condon 2000; Yancey and Weiser 1997) that incorporate diverse perspectives. Like the craft origin of the concept, portfolios essentially comprise multiple instances of writing which could be gathered over time to present richer, more complex information about a writer's efforts, progress or performance. This lends confidence to any generalization from the results (Weigle 2002). A portfolio created over time supported the notion of a process involving revision and crafting (Sommers 1982). Portfolios allowed writers to demonstrate writing for a range of purposes, for different audiences and in different contexts, although, arguably, social motives and functions of communication may still be absent (Reither and Hunt 1994). These potential features assumed significance as sociocultural theories entered the wider academic discourse.

Whether portfolios are or should be a form of evaluation has been questioned (Calfee 2000). Elbow (1994: 40) described a portfolio as 'nothing but a folder, a pouch – an emptiness: a collection device and not a form of assessment' and White (1994: 29) saw it as 'a pedagogically useful collection procedure that in some ways resembles an assessment procedure'. While not inaccurate, such observations suggest researchers had not yet conceptually linked to the notion that the purpose for the portfolio, together with the uses to which it is to be put, define the assessment.

Although originating in the classroom as part of a move to connect assessment to the process of learning, portfolios have 'hybridized' and, 'while designed for one set of uses, have been stretched and adapted to fit another set of assumptions' (Tierney *et al.* 1998: 475). They have been widely employed for large-scale assessment, for comparisons across classrooms at different levels from school to state (Kane and Mitchell 1996; Koretz 1998). These attempts to link classroom portfolio assessment to large-scale testing have been seen as problematic in terms of logistics, standardization, scoring and interference with instruction (e.g. Gearhart and Herman 1998; Koretz 1998). The limitations of portfolios – from pragmatic to questions of scoring to empirical validation – were widely addressed in scholarship of the 1990s (e.g. Applebee 1994; Belanoff 1994).

Ideally, portfolios would not be used to summarize performance but to link performance and ongoing assessment to guide the learning process; Gearhart and Herman (1998: 41) describe their potential as to 'capture a vision of assessment integrated with instruction'. Portfolios can have a formative purpose in assessment; in particular, they provide a site for writer reflection and self-assessment. They offer advantages to student writers, including developing a sense of control and ownership over their work and, in creating portfolios, students learn to exercise judgement about their own work (Murphy and Grant 1996). They also provide a potential site for collaborative enquiry (Tierney *et al.* 1998).

Assessment of writing for teaching and learning

Considering the student writer and his or her writing to obtain information about patterns of strengths and weaknesses and the use of this information to provide support and feedback to assist in the learning process, constitutes formative assessment (Shepard 2005; Torrance and Pryor 1998). While a major issue in testing writing has been aligning evaluation to theories of writing, the issue with formative assessment is related to working out how to move forward (Black and Wiliam 1998) along a progression (Harlen 1998) after noticing a 'gap' (Sadler 1989). Whether this is progression towards a defined goal or a broad horizon is a dilemma discussed by Marshall (2004). The goal model of progression is like a skills or knowledge model which assumes that what is necessary to be good at writing is 'known, quantifiable and reducible to a systematic teaching programme' (Marshall 2004: 102) while the horizon model suggests less specified outcomes and multiple pathways.

Little research addresses developmental progression in writing. There have been attempts such as that by Myhill (2009) to define progression in terms of, for example, linguistic features, notably grammar. Successful writers, however, adapt or subvert conventions and merge genre features, so progression is not linear. The systematic functional linguistics of the 'Sydney School' illustrates how genres are structured in specific ways and use particular language to achieve their purpose (Martin *et al.* 1987). These descriptions of structures and language use can function like criteria. When a complex phenomenon like writing is involved, fixed criteria are limiting (Sadler 1989). However, the strongest criticism of attempts to specify progression or criteria that mark development is that, in writing, the whole is greater than the sum of the parts so individual components underestimate the whole (Sadler 1987; Wiliam 1996).

To understand progression in writing, teachers may rely less on a knowledge model than on value judgements that are formed through the extensive process of making those judgements. Sadler wrote of the guild knowledge of teachers. The suggestion is that teachers make reliable judgements of written work through the process of construct referencing. Understanding of a construct is refined through experience and processes like moderation where collegial discussion is involved. The shared meaning that develops among those interpreting the evidence in the form of the writing is the guild knowledge.

In formative assessment, control of assessment approaches and the use of outcomes are in the hands of those responsible for teaching and learning in writing, teachers and their students. Underpinning formative assessment is the promotion of student autonomy and self-regulation (Marshall and Drummond 2006) with students initiated into the guild knowledge that guides teachers' judgements about student writing. Knowledge is built for students through classroom practices closely associated with formative assessment such as sharing goals and what counts as success with the learner, feedback, peer reviews, self-assessment and use of exemplars (Black *et al.* 2006; Marshall 2004).

The research community has barely begun to consider formative assessment in writing. Formative assessment can be seen to be of two kinds: planned and interactive (Cowie and Bell 1999). The purpose for planned formative assessment is to obtain information from the whole class about progress in learning through a specific activity. Conversely, interactive formative assessment is that which occurs during student–teacher interactions, arising out of a learning activity.

Potential for formative assessment: responding to developing writers

Writers need response in the form of feedback not only to monitor their own progress and move forward but also so they discover their readers' needs (Zellermayer 1989). Researchers struggle to delineate conditions for constructive feedback in writing (see Brannon and Knoblauch 1982; Sommers 1982). Teacher response is given in the context of an unequal power relationship; they have an ambiguous, often conflicting, role as facilitator, evaluator and audience (Hyland 2000; Muncie 2000) and the issues of text appropriation and ownership surface

(Reid 1994). Various vehicles for feedback on writing are possible including conferencing, written feedback from the teacher, and peer feedback. There is also feedback from self-assessment. While conferencing is more a feature of primary school writing classrooms, written feedback characterizes classrooms beyond this.

Conferencing as feedback on writing

Conferencing is viewed as fundamental to teaching and learning in process-oriented writing classrooms (Atwell 1987; Calkins 1994; Graves 1983). In conferences, developing writers learn to interact with, and craft meaning for, a reader. Effective conferences provide writers with opportunities to develop the metacognitive awareness related to the writing process and the self-regulatory strategies needed for reflecting on their texts, together with the personal responsibility needed to become a writer (Graves 2003).

Literature on conferencing is grounded in practice. Practice- and classroom-oriented writers (e.g. Anderson 2000; Calkins 1994; Graves 1983, 2003) clearly locate the role of the teacher as a follower of a developing writer's lead, rather than that of an instructor. Young writers are to take responsibility for managing and reflecting on their own learning. The role of the teacher is couched in terms of listening for cues about the kind of support writers need. Conferences contain opportunities for moment-by-moment decision-making by teachers that have the potential to move learners' development forward in meaningful ways.

However, detailed analyses of conferences in action show the reality of practice is different from the ideals of conferencing outlined above. For teachers, even the most skilled, conferencing is complex and challenging (Anderson 2000; Calkins 1994; Glasswell et al. 2003). Conferences have been shown to be predominantly teacher-controlled with the teacher adopting an overly authoritative role (Wong 1998). A narrow focus on low-level concerns has been noted (Freedman and Sperling 1985). Studies have described how similar patterns of organization and interaction can lead to both successful and less successful interactions for different writers (Lensmire 1994; McCarthey 1994). In particular, differences in the ways conferences have been conducted were found for low and high achieving writers (Freedman and Sperling 1985; Glasswell et al. 2003; Walker and Elias 1987) and for students from different cultural backgrounds (Pathey-Chavez and Ferris, 1997). However, the pedagogical effectiveness of any individual interaction is not in the formal properties of the interaction but in the way in which these properties are used to achieve targeted instructional purposes in a particular context (Haneda 2004). Research has, to date, provided few exemplifications of such use (but see Glasswell and Parr 2009).

Written comments as feedback on writing

Although feedback on writing has been considered a common form of writing instruction at secondary and tertiary levels, scholarship on response to student writing has not been a central theoretical concern (Phelps 2000). Written feedback is intended to improve student learning in writing, yet, ironically, most of the studies have been conducted outside of any context – pedagogical (Fife and O'Neill 2001) or, indeed, theoretical, or communicative (Huot 2002). The literature on response to writing is grounded in practice, focusing on ways teachers respond and the development of governing principles (for the latter, see Straub 2002). Research has treated texts that teacher-responders create as if they stand alone, ignoring the perspective that the meaning of text will be constructed differently depending on the 'discourses' brought to bear on the text by the reader (Murphy 2000). Also, research is largely divorced from explanations of why teachers respond in a particular way (Huot 2002).

Major early studies of written response show how college teacher comments focused on low-level technical concerns rather than on meaning making (e.g. Connors and Lunsford 1993; Sommers 1982). Similar undue consideration is given to surface features by teachers, particularly with regard to revision; they have also been portrayed as unable to articulate rhetorical concerns (Schwartz 1984). While several of these studies had methodological weaknesses (Ferris 1997), findings have been replicated (Stern and Solomon 2006). Written feedback has been considered possibly the least useful type of response students get to their writing. The traditional ways in which teachers make comments on students' drafts are seen, in general, as not effective in improving students' writing (Hyland 2000; Muncie 2000), perhaps because the work is not often viewed as one in progress and feedback is corrective rather than designed to foster development. In general, students do not find written feedback either helpful in itself or as a catalyst for discussion (Maclellan 2001). Studies examining student reaction to teacher comments illustrate how students often have difficulty in processing feedback (Zellermayer 1989); are often confused; misinterpret and misunderstand feedback; or cannot decipher comments (e.g. Nelson 1995; Richardson 2000).

There are two significant issues with respect to placing the literature on written response within a formative assessment frame where such response is intended to support and enhance learning. First, in acting as audience, corroborator, instructor or evaluator, the teacher as a reader does not respond to stable features in a text but rather interacts with a text, bringing to bear prior learning, expectations and experience. In particular, theoretical and cultural orientations affect interpretations (Ball 1997). Teachers respond to extra-textual features within the context of the classroom (Sperling 1994; Wyatt-Smith *et al.* 2003). In studying response, there is a need to go beyond considering the ways and nature of response and to recognize and understand the influence of the context (Huot 2002); of the writing classroom and student–teacher relationships (Prior 1991, 1995). There is partial recognition of this in the notion of a learning record system (Barr and Syverson 1999) which, for example, encourages teachers to record the context for the writing, the student's response to the writing, and what the piece shows about the student's development as a writer. In this way the teacher is likely to be conscious of the many factors that influence a consideration of student work.

This may also serve to focus the teacher on the developing writer rather than the writing *per se*.

Another stumbling block to instructive feedback is the non-dialogic nature of much of the reported practice. In commenting on drafts, teachers, in their role as expert and ultimate evaluator, have an effect on the decisions students make with respect to revision. Student writers, arguably, have a constrained level of choice about whether or not to use the feedback. Students are seldom co-negotiators, co-evaluators. The lack of critical involvement by the student lessens the likelihood of the feedback becoming internalized and having effect beyond the current piece (Muncie 2000). Huot argues that comments should be transformative; the comments 'open-ended, forcing students back into the text' (2002: 132).

Dialogic written feedback

Dialoguing is a means by which teachers help students think about their writing and writing processes and develop agency and control. Reflective and interactive logs are a way of realizing Huot's idea of forcing students back into their text. Logs have taken the form of a learning journal where the student records thoughts and goals and examines and explores these to better understand learning tasks (e.g. Kuhn 1999). Potentially, through the log, the student interacts with the teacher (or others) in an ongoing, formative and dialogic fashion which enhances their writing performance (Glenn 2009).

Self-assessment and peer assessment

Numerous teachers of writing (e.g. Bloom 1997; Elbow 1997; Yancey 1999) describe methods by which they incorporate student self-assessment into their classroom through reflective writing; through contracting criteria that describe the work required to reach a particular level or grade, and through written or oral dialogues in which student and teacher evaluate writing together. The benefits of reflection and self-assessment are readily claimed and there is a developed rationale for linking self-assessment to achievement (see Ross *et al.* 1999) but there is limited empirical support in terms of research into the forms and consequences of self-assessment. The literature suggests its use is not unproblematic. First, self-assessment is not necessarily employed formatively to inform and support learning. Second, the use of self-assessment without adequate support may differentially advantage some writers because effective writers have been characterized as capable self-evaluators (Perl 1979).

The dominant form of self-assessment in writing discussed in the literature involves selection of work for portfolios or reflection on the completed portfolio and recording of the evaluation often through a memo or covering letter. These acts are generally not for a formative purpose and are, arguably, too late to affect student learning. Inviting student input in an attempt to subvert the teacher–student dynamic of grading does not necessarily change the consequences or outcomes of the activity (Bloom 1997). The argument is made that the very nature of teaching makes it reasonable that, in self-assessing, students may simply reflect back teacher language and judgements (Yancey 1998); it is also noted that both selection and reflection are frequently teacher-guided (Hirvela and Pierson 2000). While self-assessment is touted as a means to democratize and to mitigate the negative effects of grading or testing writing and as a means to develop self-evaluation skills that may help students improve as writers, simultaneously it also contributes to the culture of testing whereby students participate in 'their own surveillance and domination' (Schendell and O'Neill 1999: 200).

There are a small number of studies examining specific ways to support self-assessment. Students can improve their ability to self-assess with certain sorts of instruction including involvement in rubric construction and receiving feedback on their applications of standards (Ross *et al.* 1999). In the formative assessment literature there has been an emphasis on explicit articulation of assessment criteria in order to promote understanding of what is needed. But, as Sadler (1987) pointed out, verbal descriptors of standards are always somewhat vague or fuzzy. They indicate relative, not absolute, placement and are context-dependent. Knowledge regarding standards is difficult to articulate and, therefore, to transmit directly through verbal descriptors. Sadler suggests it is best transferred in joint evaluative activity through using annotated exemplars, together with associated verbal descriptors. Developing students' understanding of assessment criteria and process through both tacit and explicit knowledge transfer improves learning (Rust *et al.* 2003).

In writing, such approaches to understanding assessment have used the principle of annotated samples, commonly used as a basis for training raters, and have modified the procedure for learners. In a small-scale study involving the provision of scripts annotated according to criteria specific to a writing task, each participant assessed their own writing and that of a peer. The samples, annotated according to criteria, helped students gain a sense of perspective regarding the quality of their written work and to both self- and peer assess appropriately (Brown 2005).

Peer response has been primarily employed to enable writers to receive feedback from an audience. It has been instantiated in practices in elementary school such as the author's chair. Peer feedback has the potential to broaden the act from assessment *of* learning to assessment *for* learning (O'Donovan *et al.* 2004). It is regarded as easier to evaluate and give feedback on a peer's work than on one's own (Sadler 1987). However, a recent study of methods teachers use in writing classrooms of 13- to 16-year-olds suggests peer evaluation and tasks that cede control to students are not a common occurrence (Hunter *et al.* 2006).

Supporting formative assessment practices in the classroom: planned assessment of writing

The message in many writing resource books for teachers presents a traditional view of classroom assessment as almost an afterthought phase in the planning cycle where what is taught is determined by curriculum objectives and writing process specifications (e.g. Tompkins 2004). A focus on instructional goals, however, does not help in decision-making about student learning needs. Planned formative assessment (Cowie and Bell 1999) can provide the teacher with insight into the particular learning needs of individual students and groups of students and form the basis for differentiated teaching.

A major issue with respect to enabling formative assessment in writing concerns the notion of guild knowledge. The capacity to make good teaching decisions in reading, for example, rests partly on a teacher's knowledge of the subtleties of word and text structure (Phelps and Schilling 2004). Teachers have been shown to lack knowledge of how language works (Moats 1994; Wong-Fillimore and Snow 2002).This knowledge is needed in order to notice and recognize what is significant in terms of language and then to respond. There is evidence that lack of explicit knowledge of how texts work limits the type and quality of feedback that can be given to students to assist their learning (Parr and Timperley 2005). Arguably, teachers of pre-tertiary students need considerable support in working out how to diagnose and teach to the needs of their developing writers (Parr *et al.* 2007). How to provide this support without an entirely prescriptive lockstep progression to a closely defined horizon was a problem addressed in the design of the writing assessment component within the Assessment Tools for Teaching and Learning (asTTle) package; what Cowie and Bell (1999) would term a planned formative assessment tool[2] to assist teachers gain in information from student writing in their classrooms (Glasswell *et al.* 2001).

The view of writing underpinning the tool is aligned with theory that writing is a social and cultural practice. The theoretical framing draws on the work of those who view writing broadly as serving social purposes (e.g. Chapman 1999; Knapp and Watkins 1994, 2005). Writing was conceptualized as serving six major purposes, a core set of generic processes that encapsulate what the text is doing (Knapp and Watkins 2005). An analytic rubric was developed for each major process or purpose of texts. The rubrics assess student performance using criterion statements relating to seven dimensions of writing. While all dimensions of analysis of the text are seen as interdependent in terms of judging the effectiveness of the piece of writing, for purposes of assessment, the dimensions are considered and scored separately. Within the same framework and dimensions, the criteria at each of the levels articulate a developmental progression. This helps teachers to work out what the next level of development would look like for any given writer. They map a writer's development, allowing diagnosis of strengths and difficulties in the context of the communicative purpose of the task.

The assessment tool is just one tool in the writing teacher's armory, albeit a powerful one. The classroom teacher who knows the students in a variety of contexts is able to view the results of a single assessment piece in the light of other sources of information and make informed decisions about the likely most efficacious instruction. This assessment tool allows consideration of the importance of context in relation to what judgments mean and in relation to decisions made on the basis of those judgments. The discussion about moderating writing samples builds teacher's knowledge (Parr *et al.* 2007). The use of this tool for formative purposes has been a major contributor to large effect-size gains (average 1.28 over two years) in student writing achievement in schools participating in a national literacy professional development project in New Zealand, one of the aims of which was to raise teacher knowledge in order to improve student achievement (Parr *et al.* 2006).

Conclusion

The scholarship on evaluation of writing has spent considerable time and effort on performance testing for summative purposes. It is an instance of a research literature which shows a surprising disconnection to practice. Although principles of sound written feedback or conferencing have been advocated, research has not established links between these and efficacious outcomes for developing writers. The field has been tardy in taking on board notions of validity that foreground the use and consequences of evaluation. There is a significant gap in the literature in terms of research that considers the assessment of writing for formative purposes, to inform teaching and support learning in a forward-looking manner.

Notes

1 The term 'evaluation' is used to refer to the process of making a judgement. If the use of the information is for an end-point type decision, a summative purpose, the word 'testing' is employed. If the purpose is to inform the teaching and learning of writing, then the term 'assessment' or 'formative assessment' is used.
2 A full description of Project asTTle is available at http://www.tki.org.nz/r/asttle.

References

Anderson, C. (2000) *How's It Going? A Practical Guide to Conferring with Student Writers*, Portsmouth, NH: Heinemann.

Applebee, A.N. (1994) 'English language arts assessment: lessons from the past', *English Journal*, 83: 40–6.

Atwell, N. (1987) *In the Middle: Writing, Reading, and Learning with Adolescents*, Portsmouth, NH: Boynton/Cook

Ball, A. (1997) 'Expanding the dialogue on culture as a critical component when assessing writing', *Assessing Writing*, 4: 169–202.

Barr, M.A., and Syverson, M.A. (1999) *Assessing Literacy with the Learning Record*, Portsmouth, NH: Heinemann.

Belanoff, P. (1994) 'Portfolios and literacy: why', in L. Black, D. Daiker, J. Sommers and G. Stygall (eds) *New Directions in Portfolio Assessment* (pp. 13–24), Portsmouth, NH: Boynton/Cook.

Black, L., Daiger, D., Sommers, J. and Stygall, G. (eds) (1994) *New Directions in Portfolio Assessment: Reflective Practice, Critical Theory, and Large-Scale Scoring*, Portsmouth, NH: Boynton.

Black, P., Harrison, C., Lee, C., Marshall, B. and Wiliam, D. (2003) *Assessment for Learning: Putting it into Practice*, Buckingham: Open University Press.

Black, P., McCormick, R., James, M. and Pedder, D. (2006) 'Learning how to learn and assessment for learning: a theoretical enquiry', *Research Papers in Education*, 21: 119–32.

Black, P. and Wiliam, D. (1998) 'Assessment and classroom learning', *Assessment in Education: Principles, Policy and Practice*, 5: 7–73.

Bloom, L.Z. (1997) 'Why I (used to) hate to give grades', *College Composition and Communication*, 48: 360–71.

Brannon, L. and Knoblauch, C.H. (1982) 'On students' rights to their own texts: a model of teacher response', *College Composition and Communication*, 33: 157–66.

Brown, A. (2005) 'Self-assessment of writing in independent language learning programs: the value of annotated samples', *Assessing Writing*, 10: 174–91.

Calfee, R.C. (2000) 'Writing portfolios: activity, assessment, authenticity', in R. Indrisano and J.R. Squires (eds) *Perspectives on Writing: Research, Theory and Practice* (pp. 278–304), Newark, NJ: International Reading Association.

Calfee, R.C. and Perfumo, P. (eds) (1996) *Writing Portfolios: Policy and Practice*, Hillsdale, NJ: Erlbaum.

Calkins, L. (1994) *The Art of Teaching Writing*, Portsmouth, NH: Heinemann.

Camp, R. (1993) 'Changing the model for the direct assessment of writing', in M.M. Williamson and B.A. Huot (eds) *Validating Holistic Scoring for Writing Assessment* (pp. 45–78), Cresskill, NJ: Hampton Press.

Chapman, M. (1999) 'Situated, social, active: rewriting genre in the elementary classroom', *Written Communication*, 16: 469–90.

Connors, R.J. and Lunsford, A.A. (1993) 'Teachers' rhetorical comments on student papers', *College Composition and Communication*, 44: 200–23.

Cowie, B. and Bell, B. (1999) 'A model of formative assessment in science education', *Assessment in Education*, 6: 101–16.

Darling-Hammond, L., Ancess, J. and Falk, B. (1995) *Authentic Assessment in Action*, New York: Teachers College Press.

Dywer, C.A. (1998) 'Assessment and classroom learning: theory and practice', *Assessment in Education: Principles, Policy and Practice*, 5: 131–7.

Elbow, P. (1994) 'Will the virtues of portfolio assessment blind us to their potential dangers?', in L. Black, D. Daiker, J. Sommers and G. Stygall (eds) *New Directions in Portfolio Assessment* (pp. 40–55), Portsmouth, NH: Boynton/Cook.

Elbow, P. (1997) 'Taking time out from grading and evaluating while working in a conventional system', *Assessing Writing*, 4: 5–28.

Ferris, D.R. (1997) 'The influence of teacher commentary on student revision', *TESOL Quarterly*, 31: 315–39.

Fife, J.M. and O'Neill, P. (2001) 'Moving beyond the written comment: narrowing the gap between response practice and research', *College Composition and Communication*, 53: 300–21.

Freedman, S. and Sperling, M. (1985) 'Written language acquisition: the role of response and the writing conference', in S.W. Freedman (ed.) *The Acquisition of Written Language* (pp. 106–30), Norwood, NJ: Ablex.

Gearhart, M. and Herman, J.L. (1998) 'Portfolio assessment: whose work is it?: Issues in the use of classroom assignments for accountability', *Educational Assessment*, 5: 41–56.

Gipps, C. (1994) *Beyond Testing: Towards a Theory of Educational Assessment*, London: Falmer.

Glasswell, K. and Parr, J.M. (2009) 'Teachable moments: linking assessment and teaching in talk around writing', *Language Arts*, 86: 352–61.

Glasswell, K., Parr, J.M. and Aikman, M. (2001) *Development of the asTTle Writing Assessment Rubrics for Scoring Extended Writing Tasks*, asTTle Technical Paper Report 26, Auckland: University of Auckland.

Glasswell, K., Parr, J.M. and McNaughton, S. (2003) 'Four ways to work against yourself when conferencing with struggling writers', *Language Arts*, 80: 291–8.

Glenn, J. (2009) 'Using a feedback log to improve academic writing in secondary classrooms', unpublished doctoral thesis, University of Auckland, New Zealand.

Graves, D. (1983) *Writing: Teachers and Children at Work*, Portsmouth, NH: Heinemann.

Graves, D. (2003) *Writing: Teachers and Children at Work*, 2nd edn, Portsmouth, NH: Heinemann.

Hamp-Lyons, L. and Condon, W. (2000) *Assessing the Portfolio: Principles for Practice, Theory and Research*, Cresskill, NJ: Hampton Press.

Haneda, M. (2004) 'The joint construction of meaning in writing conferences', *Applied Linguistics*, 25: 178–219.

Harlen, W. (1998) 'Classroom assessment: a dimension of purposes and procedures', paper presented at the Annual Conference of the New Zealand Association for Research in Education, Dunedin, December.

Hayes, J.R., Hatch, J.A. and Silk, C.M. (2000) 'Does holistic assessment predict writing performance? Estimating the consistency of student performance on holistically scored writing assessments', *Written Communication*, 17: 3–26.

Hillocks, G. (2002) *The Testing Trap: How State Writing Assessments Control Learning*, New York: Teachers College Press.

Hirvela, A. and Pierson, H. (2000) 'Portfolios: Vehicles for Self-assessment', in G. Ekbatani and H. Pierson (eds) *Learner Directed Assessment in ESL* (pp. 105–26), Mahwah, NJ: Lawrence Erlbaum.

Hunter, D., Mayenga, C. and Gambell, T. (2006) 'Classroom assessment tools and uses: Canadian English teachers' practices for writing', *Assessing Writing*, 11: 42–65.

Huot, B. (2002) *Re-articulating Writing*, Logan, UT: Utah State University Press.

Huot, B. and Neal, M. (2006) 'Writing assessment: a techno-history', in C.A. MacArthur, S. Graham and J. Fitzgerald (eds) *Handbook of Writing Research* (pp. 417–32), New York: Guilford.

Hyland, F. (2000) 'ESL writers and feedback: giving more autonomy to students', *Language Teaching Research*, 4: 33–54.

Juzwik, M., Curcic, S., Wolbers, K., Moxley, K., Dimling, L. and Shankland, R.K. (2006) 'Writing into the 21st century: an overview of research on writing 1999–2004', *Written Communication*, 23: 451–76.

Kane, M.S. and Mitchell, R. (eds) (1996) *Implementing Performance Assessment: Promises, Problems and Challenges*, Mahwah, NJ: Erlbaum.

Knapp, P. and Watkins, M. (1994) *Context-Text-Grammar: Teaching the Genres and Grammar of School Writing in Infant and Primary Classrooms*, Broadway, NSW: Text Productions.

Knapp, P. and Watkins, M. (2005) *Genre, Text, Grammar: Technologies for Teaching and Assessing Writing*, Sydney: University of New South Wales Press.

Koretz, D. (1998) 'Large-scale portfolio assessments in the US: evidence pertaining to the quality of measurement', in D. Koretz, A. Wolf, and P. Broadfoot (eds) *Records of Achievement*, Special issue of *Assessment in Education*, 5: 309–34.

Kuhn, C.G. (1999) 'Writing towards thoughtfulness through logs', in L. Reid and J. Golub (eds) *Reflective Activities: Helping Students Connect with Writing and Texts* (pp. 74–86), Urbana, IL: National Council of Teachers of English.

Lane, S. and Stone, C.A. (2002) 'Strategies for examining the consequences of assessment and accountability programs', *Educational Measurement: Issues and Practices*, 21: 23–30.

Lensmire, T. (1994) *When Children Write*, New York: Teacher College Press.

Luce-Kepler, R. and Klinger, D. (2005) 'Uneasy writing: the defining moments of high-stakes literacy testing', *Assessing Writing*, 10: 157–73.

Mabry, L. (1999) 'Writing to the rubric: lingering effects of traditional standardized testing on direct writing assessment', *Phi Delta Kappan*, 80: 673–86.

McCarthey, S. (1994) 'Authors, talk and text: the internalization of dialogue from social interaction during writing', *Reading Research Quarterly*, 29: 201–31.

Maclellan, E. (2001) 'Assessment for learning: the different perceptions of tutors and students', *Assessment and Evaluation in Higher Education*, 26: 307–18.

Marshall, B. (2004) 'Goals or horizons – the conundrum of progression in English: or a possible way of understanding formative assessment in English', *The Curriculum Journal*, 15: 101–13.

Marshall, B. and Drummond, M.J. (2006) 'How teachers engage with assessment for learning: lessons from the classroom', *Research Papers in Education*, 21: 133–49.

Martin, J.R, Christie, F, and Rothery, J. (1987) 'Social processes in education: a reply to Sawyer and Watson (and others)', in I. Reid (ed.) *The Place of Genre in Learning: Current Debates*, (pp. 55–8), Deakin University Press, Geelong, Australia.

Messick, S. (1989) 'Validity', in R.L. Linn (ed.) *Educational Measurement*, 3rd edn (pp. 13–103), New York: Macmillan.

Messick, S. (1994) 'The interplay of evidence and consequences in the validation of performance assessment', *Educational Researcher*, 23: 13–23.

Moats, L. (1994) 'The missing foundation in teacher education: knowledge of the structure of spoken and written language', *Annals of Dyslexia*, 44: 81–102.

Moss, P.A. (1996) 'Enlarging the dialogue in educational measurement: voices from interpretive traditions', *Educational Researcher*, 25: 20–8.

Muncie, J. (2000) 'Using written feedback in EFL composition classes', *ELT Journal*, 54: 47–53.

Murphy, S. (2000) 'A sociocultural perspective on teacher response: is there a student in the room?', *Assessing Writing*, 7: 79–90.

Murphy, S. and Grant, B. (1996) 'Portfolio approaches to assessment: breakthrough or more of the same?', in E.M. White, W.D. Lutz and S. Kamuskiri (eds) *Assessment of Writing: Politics, Policies, Practices* (pp. 284–301), New York: Modern Language Association.

Myhill, D. (2009) 'Becoming a designer: trajectories of linguistic development', in R. Beard, D. Myhill, J. Riley and M. Nystrand (eds) *Handbook of Writing Development*, London: Sage.

Nelson, J. (1995) 'Reading classrooms as text: exploring student writers' interpretive practices', *College Composition and Communication*, 46: 411–29.

O'Donovan, B., Price, M. and Rust, C. (2004) 'Know what I mean? Enhancing student understanding of assessment standards and criteria', *Teaching in Higher Education*, 3: 145–58.

O'Neill, P. (2003) 'Moving beyond holistic scoring through validity enquiry', *Journal of Writing Assessment*, 1: 47–65.

Parr, J.M., Glasswell, K. and Aikman, M. (2007) 'Supporting teacher learning and informed practice in writing through assessment tools for teaching and learning', *Asia-Pacific Journal of Teacher Education*, 35: 69–87.

Parr, J.M. and Timperley, H. (2005) 'Examining the role of teacher pedagogical content knowledge in literacy', paper presented to the Annual Meeting of the American Educational Research Association, San Francisco, March.

Parr, J.M., Timperley, H., Reddish, P, Jesson, R. and Adams, R. (2006) *Literacy Professional Development Project: Identifying Effective Teaching and Professional Development Practices for Enhanced Student Learning*, Wellington, New Zealand: Ministry of Education.

Pathey-Chavez, G. and Ferris, D. (1997) 'Writing conferences and the weaving of multi-voiced texts in college composition', *Research in the Teaching of English*, 31: 51–90.

Perl, S. (1979) 'The composing processes of unskilled college writers', *Research in the Teaching of English*, 13: 317–36.

Phelps, G. and Schilling, S. (2004) 'Developing measures of content knowledge for teaching reading', *Elementary School Journal*, 105: 31–49.

Phelps, L.W. (2000) 'Cyrano's nose: variations on the theme of response', *Assessing Writing*, 7: 91–110.

Prior, P. (1991) 'Contextualizing writing and response in a graduate seminar', *Written Communication*, 8: 267–310.

Prior, P. (1995) 'Tracing authoritative and internally persuasive discourses: a case study of response, revision and disciplinary enculturation', *Research in the Teaching of English*, 29: 288–325.

Reid, J. (1994) 'Responding to ESL students' texts: the myths of appropriation', *TESOL Quarterly*, 28: 273–94.

Reither, J.A. and Hunt, R.A. (1994) 'Beyond portfolios: scenes for dialogic reading and writing', in L. Black, D.A. Daiker, J. Sommers and G. Stygall (eds) *New Directions in Portfolio Assessment* (pp. 140–56), Portsmouth, NH: Boynton/Cook.

Richardson, S. (2000) 'Students' conditioned response to teachers' response: portfolio proponents, take note!', *Assessing Writing*, 10: 80–99.

Ross, J.A., Rolheiser, C. and Hogaboam-Gray, A. (1999) 'Effects of self-evaluation training on narrative writing', *Assessing Writing*, 6: 107–32.

Rust, C., Price, M. and Donovan, B. (2003) 'Improving students' learning by developing their understanding of assessment criteria and processes', *Assessment and Evaluation*, 28: 147–64.

Sadler, D.R. (1987) 'Specifying and promulgating achievement standards', *Oxford Review of Education*, 13: 191–209.

Sadler, R. (1989) 'Formative assessment and the design of instructional systems', *Instructional Science*, 18: 119–44.

Schendell, E. and O'Neill, P. (1999) 'Exploring the theories and consequences of self-assessment through ethical enquiry', *Assessing Writing*, 6: 199–227.

Schwartz, C.W., Hooper, S.R., Montgomery, J. and Wakely, M. (1999) 'Using generalizability theory to estimate the reliability of writing scores derived from holistic and analytic scoring methods', *Educational and Psychological Measurement*, 59: 492–506.

Schwartz, M. (1984) 'Response to writing: a college-wide perspective', *College English*, 46: 55–62.

Shepard, L.A. (2005) 'Linking formative assessment to scaffolding', *Educational Leadership*, 63: 66–70.

Sommers, N. (1982) 'Responding to student writing', *College Composition and Communication*, 33: 148–56.

Sperling, M (1994) 'Constructing the perspective of teacher as reader: a framework for studying response to student writing', *Research in the Teaching of English*, 28: 175–207.

Stern, L.A. and Solomon, A. (2006) 'Effective faculty feedback: the road less travelled', *Assessing Writing*, 11: 22–41.

Straub, R.E. (2002) 'Reading and responding to student writing: a heuristic for reflective practice', *Composition Studies*, 30: 15–60.

Tierney, R., Clark, C., Fenner, L., Herter, R.J., Simpson, C.S. and Wiser, B. (1998) 'Theory and research into practice: portfolios: assumptions, tensions, and possibilities', *Reading Research Quarterly*, 33: 474–86.

Tompkins, G. (2004) *Teaching Writing: Balancing Process and Product*, 4th edn, Columbus, OH: Merrill/Prentice Hall Inc.

Torrance, H. and Pryor, J. (1998) *Investigating Formative Assessment: Teaching, Learning and Assessment in the Classroom*, Buckingham: Open University Press.

Traschel, M. (1992) *Institutionalizing Literacy: The Historical Role of College Entrance Examinations in English*, Carbondale, IL: Southern Illinois University Press.

Walker, C.P. and Elias, D. (1987) 'Writing conference talk: factors associated with high and low rated conferences', *Research in the Teaching of English*, 21: 266–85.

Weigle, S.C. (2002) *Assessing Writing*, Cambridge: Cambridge University Press.

White, E.M. (1994) 'Portfolios as an assessment concept', in L. Black, D. Daiker, J. Sommers and G. Stygall (eds) *New Directions in Portfolio Assessment* (pp. 25–39), Portsmouth, NH: Boynton/Cook.

White, E.M. (2005) 'The scoring of writing portfolios: phase 2', *College Composition and Communication*, 56: 581–600.

White, E.M, Lutz, W.D and Kamuskiri, S. (eds) (1996) *Assessment of Writing: Politics, Policies, Practices*, New York: The Modern Language Association.

Wiggins, C. P. (1993) *Assessing Student Performance*, San Francisco: Jossey-Bass.

Wiliam, D. (1996) 'Standards in education: a matter of trust', *The Curriculum Journal*, 7: 293–306.

Williamson, M. and Huot, B. (1993) *Validating Holistic Scoring for Writing Assessment: Theoretical and Empirical Foundation*, Cresskill, NH: Hampton Press.

Wong, I. (1998) 'Teacher-student talk in technical writing conference', *Written Communication*, 5: 444–60.

Wong-Fillimore, L. and Snow, K. (2002) 'What teachers need to know about language', in C.T. Adger, C.E. Snow and D. Christian (eds) *What Teachers Need to Know About Language* (pp. 7–54), McHenry, IL: Delta Systems Co.

Wyatt-Smith, C., Castleton, G., Freebody, P. and Cooksey, R. (2003) 'Teachers' qualitative judgements: a matter of context and salience, Part 1', *Australian Journal of Language and Literacy*, 26: 11–32.

Yancey, K.B. (1998) *Reflection in the Writing Classroom*, Logan, UT: University of Utah Press.

Yancey, K.B. (1999) 'Historicizing writing assessment', *College Composition and Communication*, 50: 483–96.

Yancey, K.B. and Weiser, I. (eds) (1997) *Situating Portfolios: Four Perspectives*, Logan, UT: Utah State University Press.

Zellermayer, M. (1989) 'The study of teachers' written feedback to students' writing: changes in theoretical considerations and the expansion of research contexts', *Instructional Science*, 18: 145–65.

Chapter 5

The curriculum
Developing multiplicative thinking and reasoning in mathematics

Jennifer M. Young-Loveridge

Two main psychological theories have dominated the debates about how mathematics is learned – the *behavioural* and *cognitive* approaches (Young-Loveridge 1994), each reflecting different beliefs about the nature of knowledge, how it is acquired, and what it means to be knowledgeable.

Behavioural approaches (where learning occurs as a result of behaviour that is rewarded) are reflected in traditional approaches to teaching mathematics, emphasizing drill and practice, and the memorization of rote procedures and skills; for example, learning the associations between expressions such as '*8 times 5*' and '*40*' (Krause *et al.* 2007). This simple view of learning cannot easily account for the complexity of mental processes like mathematical thinking and reasoning. Bandura's social learning theory extends behavioural explanations to include the contribution of psychological factors to the learning process (Krause *et al.* 2007), seeing learning as more complex, involving observation (including vicarious learning), language (symbolic processes), and self-talk (self-regulation), and hence modelling and imitation.

Cognitive (or constructivist) approaches assume knowledge is structured and organized in meaningful ways that are actively constructed by the student (e.g. through reasoning). Learning results not just in the acquisition of further information, but in qualitative changes in patterns of thinking. For example, a student who knows that *four groups of 10 equal 40* might use this to work out *8 times 5*, reasoning that if the groups of 10 are halved (into 5s) there will be double the groups (8 not 4). Hence, *8 times 5* is equal to *4 times 10*, so both answers are *40*. Alternatively, the student might know that *two groups of 5* is *10*, and use a doubling strategy to reason that *4 times 5* is *20*, so *8 times 5* is *40*. The emphasis is not on training, but on learning about relationships and making connections between new ideas and existing concepts. Skemp (1971) contrasts this *relational* understanding where concepts are connected in meaningful ways, with the *instrumental* learning of rules and procedures. Evidence shows that students who are taught using an instrumental approach are reluctant later to make sense of what they have learned and build relational/conceptual understanding (Pesek and Kirshner 2000).

A major goal of today's mathematics instruction is to help students understand the structure of mathematics (Lambdin and Walcott 2007). For teachers working with 'middle years' students, an important challenge is helping them learn about the structure of multiplication and division to become multiplicative thinkers.

What is multiplicative thinking and reasoning?

According to Baek, 'understanding multiplication is central to knowing mathematics' (1998: 151). The importance of multiplicative thinking for understanding later mathematics is well established (Beckmann and Fuson 2008; Charles and Duckett 2008; National Council of Teachers of Mathematics [NCTM] n.d.). Multiplicative thinking is one of the crucial mathematics themes in the NCTM standards for the middle grades (NCTM 2000). It has been argued that students need to be multiplicative thinkers to engage with the formal algebra presented in secondary schools (Baek 2008; Brown and Quinn 2006; Lamon 2007).

The term *multiplicative thinking* refers to a particular type of thinking used to solve a range of problems, including multiplication, division, fraction, ratio, and other mathematical concepts involving multiplication and division (Mulligan and Vergnaud 2005; Vergnaud 1983). Importantly, proportional reasoning is inherently multiplicative (Sophian 2007) because the relative magnitude of the rational number (be it a fraction or a ratio) must be maintained.

Other useful definitions of multiplicative thinking include the 'capacity to work flexibly with the concepts, strategies, and representations of multiplication (and division) as they occur in a wide range of contexts' (Siemon 2005: 1); being able to 'think *simultaneously* about units of one and units of more than one [composite units]' (Clark and Kamii 1996: 43); being able to 'co-ordinate two composite units in such a way that one of the composite units is distributed across the elements of the other composite unit' (Steffe 1992: 264); and 'the construction and manipulation of factors (the numbers being multiplied) in response to a variety of contexts; [and] deriving unknown results from known facts using the properties of multiplication and division [e.g. commutative, associative, distributive, inverse]' (Ministry of Education 2008: 3).

The development of multiplicative thinking and reasoning

A key aspect of New Zealand's numeracy initiative, the Numeracy Development Project (discussed later), is a learning framework (the number framework), consisting of progressions, or stages, reflecting increasingly sophisticated strategies in several mathematical domains, including addition/subtraction, multiplication/ division, and proportion/ratios (Bobis *et al.* 2005; Ministry of Education 2007). Table 5.1 shows the progressions in thinking for students working with multiplication and division. The simplest strategies involve students counting all objects (stages two to three). A more sophisticated counting strategy is skip-counting in multiples (stage four). Combining known multiplication facts (e.g. x2, x5, x10 tables) with repeated addition or repeated subtraction helps in solving

Table 5.1 New Zealand's number framework for the domain of multiplication/division

Stage	Multiplication/Division
0	*Emergent* *Cannot* count or form a group of ten objects.
1	*One-to-One Counting* Can count a small collection up to 10, but *cannot* form groups of objects or use counting to solve multiplication or division problems.
2	*Counts from One on Materials* Solves multiplication or division problems by *counting*, but counts *all* the objects in the groups.
3	*Counts from One by Imaging* Solves multiplication or division problems by *counting all*, but counts mentally by imaging objects, and may stress multiples when counting.
4	*Skip Counting* Solves multiplication or division problems by *skip counting* groups, and may keep track of the counts using materials or imaging.
5	*Multiplication by Repeated Addition and Division by Repeated Subtraction* Understands that numbers can be partitioned and recombined (part–whole thinking). Solves simple multiplication problems by combination of known multiplication facts and *repeated addition*, and division problems by *repeated subtraction* or repeated addition.
6	*Derived Multiplication and Division* Uses a combination of known multiplication and division facts and mental strategies to *derive* answers to multiplication and division problems. Strategies may include place-value partitioning, doubling & halving, rounding & compensating, or reversibility.
7	*Advanced Multiplication and Division* Chooses appropriately from a broad range of different part–whole strategies to find answers to *multiplication and division problems* (with whole numbers). Partitioning may be additive or multiplicative.
8	*Multiplication and Division of Decimals and Fractions* Chooses appropriately from a broad range of different part–whole strategies to estimate answers and solve problems involving *multiplication and division of decimals and fractions*.

multiplication, division, or fraction problems (e.g. knowing that $5 + 5 = 10$, so $10 + 10 + 10 + 10 = 40$ so $8 \times 5 = 40$; stage five). Early multiplicative thinking is used in deriving the answers to simple multiplication and division problems using mental strategies such as place-value partitioning, doubling and halving, rounding and compensating, or reversibility (e.g. if $20 \times 3 = 60$ then $18 \times 3 = 60 - (2 \times 3) = 54$; stage six). Advanced multiplicative thinking involves the choice of an appropriate strategy from a broad range of mental strategies to solve multiplication and division problems with whole numbers, and fraction problems (e.g., $6 \times 24 = 6 \times 2 \times 12 = 12 \times 12 = 144$; stage seven). At stage eight, advanced proportional thinking, students can choose appropriately from a broad range of mental strategies to solve problems involving multiplication of fractions and decimals, or division with decimals. Strategies for fraction problems involve the use of common factors, re-unitizing of fractions, decimals, percentages, or finding relationships between and within ratios and simple rates.

Differences between multiplicative and additive thinking

To understand multiplicative thinking fully, it is useful to contrast it with additive thinking (Clark and Kamii 1996; Jacob and Willis 2001; Ministry of Education 2008). For example, multiplicative thinkers faced with the problem: 6×24, might use their knowledge that $4 \times 25 = 100$ to reason that $6 \times 25 = 150$, then make an adjustment: $6 \times 24 = (6 \times 25) - (6 \times 1) = 150 - 6 = 144$ (rounding and compensation). Alternatively, they might use the associative property to reason that doubling 6 and halving 24 becomes $12 \times 12 = 144$. Using the distributive property to partition the 24 into place-value units (two tens and four ones) leads to $(6 \times 20) + (6 \times 4) = 120 + 24 = 144$ (standard place-value partitioning). An additive thinker would be unable to manipulate factors in this way, and is more likely to use repeated addition to solve the problem (e.g. $24 + 24 = 48; 48 + 48 = 96; 96 + 24 = 120; 120 + 24 = 144$).

Another important feature of multiplication and division is their proportional structure, in contrast to the part–whole structure of addition and subtraction, this is a major difference between additive and multiplicative reasoning (Sophian 2007). Related to this is the fact that multiplicative partitioning always involves equal-sized parts or groups, whereas additive partitioning may involve breaking numbers up into unequal-sized parts. According to Sophian, the concept of a unit develops first in the context of additive reasoning, and 'an understanding of multiplicative relations depends on an understanding of the concept of a unit' (2007: 103). It is in considering units of quantification other than *one* that the need for multiplicative relations becomes clear – the unit may be a group (e.g. a pair, a trio, or any other composite unit) or it may be a fractional quantity (e.g. one-half, one-third). Young children often do not understand the importance of keeping units constant, and when equal sharing, tend to divide a continuous quantity into a particular number of pieces, ignoring the size of the pieces.

The two-dimensionality of multiplicative thinking (as groups of groups) is reinforced by teachers in Davis' group, who argued that 'the most flexible and robust interpretation of multiplication is based on a *rectangle*' (2008: 88, italics added). According to Davis, the word *multiplication* comes from the Latin *multi* (many) and *plicare* (to fold). Paper folding provides a powerful way of representing multiplication. For example, a rectangular sheet folded into three equal-sized pieces along one side, and four equal-sized pieces along the adjacent side results in twelve equal-sized regions altogether. The same paper-folding model for

$3 \times 4 = 12$ (3 groups of 4 equals 12) can be used to represent $\frac{1}{3} \times \frac{1}{4} = \frac{1}{12}$ ($\frac{1}{3}$ of $\frac{1}{4}$ equals $\frac{1}{12}$).

The two-dimensionality of multiplication can be modelled using arrays, with rows to represent the multiplier (the number of groups) and columns to represent the multiplicand (the number of items in the group), or vice versa (see Figure 5.1) (Young-Loveridge 2005a, 2005b; Young-Loveridge and Mills 2009). An area model provides a more abstract representation of the two dimensions (see Figure 5.2), and can be sketched by hand to show the partial products resulting from one or both factors being partitioned and the parts multiplied separately by the other factor (see Young-Loveridge 2005a, 2005b). Figure 5.2 shows the dividend being partitioned in various ways to enable the use of known multiplication/division facts to work out which parts comprise the quotient (the result of division).

In contrast to the rectangularity of multiplicative thinking, additive thinking is linear (one-dimensional). Number-line models show addition and subtraction as movement either forwards (addition) or backwards (subtraction) along the line

1. Solve the problem 23 × 37 =

Show on the dotty array how you would solve this problem. Explain your answer below.

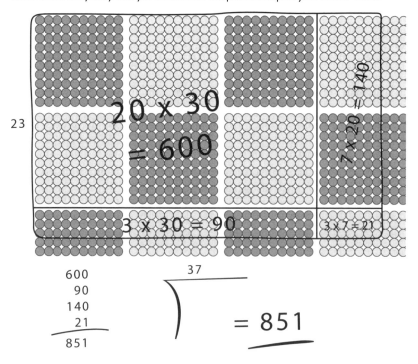

Figure 5.1 The solution to the multiplication problem: 23 × 37 using a dotty array by student B6.

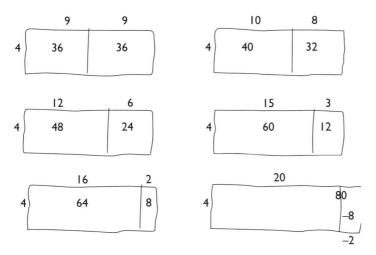

Figure 5.2 Multiple Solutions for 72 ÷ 4 using hand-drawn area models.

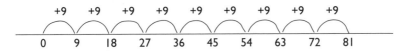

Figure 5.3 A number line model showing a repeated addition strategy for the multiplication problem: 9 × 9.

(see Beishuizen 1999). Figure 5.3 shows how repeated addition is less sophisticated than strategies involving partitioning, manipulating, and recombining quantities (as in Figure 5.2).

According to Sowder (2002), differences between additive and multiplicative thinking are reflected in absolute and relative difference. Most 10-year-olds, asked to compare an investment of $2 yielding $8, with one of $6 yielding $12, thought both deals were the same, not realizing one involved a four-fold increase, whereas the other was only double. Focusing on the absolute difference of $6 shows additive thinking, whereas comparing a relative difference of four times larger with double indicates the use of multiplicative thinking. When the advantage of thinking multiplicatively was even greater for the multiplicative scenario (a $1 investment yielding a $20 return) than the additive scenario (a $60 investment yielding a $79 return), one child recognized that investing more than $1 would soon yield much more than $79. Further examples of real-life distance comparisons are provided by Confrey and Harel (1994). One comparison makes sense as additive (e.g. a distance of 13 feet compared with a distance of 10 feet), while another example makes better sense as a multiplicative comparison (the distance to the moon [238,000 miles] compared with the distance to the sun [93 million miles]). Because of the magnitude of this second difference (the sun is nearly 400 times further away than the moon), a multiplicative comparison makes much more sense than an additive comparison.

The structure of multiplication and division

An important aspect of multiplication (grouping) and division (partitioning) is the way a problem is structured. In New Zealand, the convention is always to write the multiplier (number of groups) first, followed by the multiplicand (number in the group) (Anghileri 2006; Ministry of Education 2008). Hence *2 × 5* means two groups of five items. Although *5 × 2* gives the same answer as *2 × 5*, the structure of the problem is quite different. When the problem is written as *5 × 2*, it means five groups of two (five pairs), whereas *2 × 5* represents two groups of five (five doubled) (see Figure 5.4). In division, the dividend is the amount to be partitioned or divided, the divisor is what the dividend is being divided into, and the quotient is the result of the division process. There are two types of division – partitive and quotitive (see Ministry of Education 2008). Partitive division (sharing division) is so named because the divisor refers to the number of groups (or parts) into which the dividend is being partitioned or shared, while the unknown value (the quotient) refers to the number of items in each of the groups.

Quotitive division (measurement division) is so named because the divisor refers to the number of items in each group (the quota), while the quotient refers to the number of groups that can be formed from the dividend. Partitive division is the form of division most familiar to people. However, understanding quotitive division with whole numbers is important because it can be extended to fractions. Just as multiplication can be seen as repeated addition, division can be seen as repeated subtraction (e.g. *How many 2-metre skipping ropes can be cut from a length of rope 6 metres long?*). The examples below show how this applies:

$6 - 2 - 2 - 2 = ?$	How many groups of two in six? (three)
$6 \div 2 = ?$	How many groups of two in six? (three)
$6 \div 6 = ?$	How many groups of six in six? (one)
$2 \div \frac{1}{4} = ?$	How many groups of one quarter in two? (eight)
$0.5 \div 0.25 = ?$	How many groups of 0.25 $(\frac{1}{4})$ in 0.5 $(\frac{1}{2})$? (two)

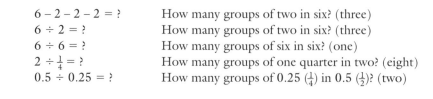

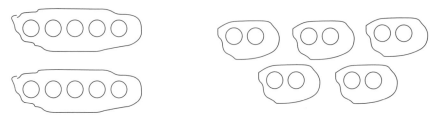

Figure 5.4 Representations showing the structure of 2 × 5 (left-hand side) and 5 × 2 (right-hand side).

Using quotitive division to explain the 'invert and multiply' rule

A hallmark of the current approach to mathematics education is the emphasis on understanding, rather than simply recall of rote procedures (see Skemp 1971). In the past, students were taught that when dividing by a fraction, they should 'invert the fraction and multiply'. Most people who learned this rule never understood why or how it works. Quotitive division helps to make sense of division by a fraction and can explain the 'invert and multiply' rule. In quotitive division, the divisor specifies the size of the group, while the quotient represents the number of groups that can be formed from the dividend (the amount being divided). Hence $2 \div \frac{1}{2}$ asks how many groups of $\frac{1}{2}$ can be found in 2. For every whole, there are 2 groups of $\frac{1}{2}$, so for 2 wholes, there are 2×2 groups of $\frac{1}{2}$ (4 groups). Inverting the fraction $\frac{1}{2}$ gives the number of groups of $\frac{1}{2}$ in each whole (two), then multiplying that by the dividend gives the number of groups of $\frac{1}{2}$ in the dividend altogether. Drawing a picture or using structured materials (e.g. fraction tiles) helps to make sense of this process.

Figure 5.5 shows how and why the 'invert and multiply' rule works. The value of pictures and diagrams for students' mathematics learning has been discussed (see Diezmann and English 2001; Presmeg 2006). NCTM *Curriculum Focal Points* suggest that students in Grade 3 (Year 4) should use representations such as arrays, area models, and equal-sized jumps on the number line to develop their understanding of multiplication and division further (Charles and Duckett 2008).

Working with fractions is confusing because computation often results in the opposite pattern to that found with whole numbers; for example, multiplication makes bigger (MMB) for whole numbers, but the reverse is true for fractions smaller than one. For example, $12 \times \frac{3}{4}$ represents 12 groups of three-quarters. An example is 12 lots of $\frac{3}{4}$ metre (for 12 tops), which would require 9 metres of fabric altogether (a product that is smaller than the multiplier). Likewise, division makes smaller (DMS) for whole numbers, but the reverse is true when the division involves fractions smaller than one. For example, $12 \div \frac{3}{4}$ means 12 divided into groups of three-quarters. An example is measuring 12 kilograms of sugar into bagfuls of $\frac{3}{4}$ kilogram. One solution is to get one bagful from each kilogram (12), leaving $\frac{1}{4}$ kilogram of sugar over from each of the 12 kilograms, and make four more bagfuls of $\frac{3}{4}$ kilogram (12 lots of $\frac{1}{4}$ grouped in threes), a total of 16 bagfuls (a quotient that is larger than the dividend). Alternatively, two

$2 \div \frac{1}{4}$ is the same as $2 \times \frac{4}{1}$

Figure 5.5 A drawing to show the solution to the problem: $2 \div \frac{1}{4}$ asking how many groups of one quarter are in two? (eight).

bags of $\frac{3}{4}$ kilogram could be made from $1\frac{1}{2}$ kilograms, so four bags could be made from 3 kilograms. As there is quadruple this amount, 16 (4 × 4) bags can be made from 12 kilograms of sugar. The answer '16' corresponds to the answer obtained by using the 'invert and multiply' rule.

Problem structures for multiplication and division

According to Vergnaud (1994: 47), 'multiplication and division are only the most visible part of an enormous conceptual iceberg' that is the multiplicative conceptual field. Different kinds of problems involving multiplication and division have been categorized in terms of problem structure (e.g. Carpenter *et al.* 1999; Ministry of Education 2008; Mulligan and Mitchelmore 1997). The six main types of problem structure involve the use of multiplication and division in slightly different ways, and include equal groups, rate (including price), multiplicative comparison (scale), part–whole ratio, Cartesian product (combinations), and area or array problems (see Table 5.2). For each type, there are multiplication problems and division problems. For four types, the division problems differ according to whether they are partitive (sharing) or quotitive (measuring/grouping) division problems. Cartesian product and area/array problems are symmetrical because the factors are equivalent (interchangeable), so the two versions of division problem for each type are identical in structure. Some writers have referred to this as the 'semantic structure' of the problem (e.g. Mulligan and Mitchelmore 1997). According to Carpenter *et al.*, problem structure is important for teachers to be aware of because 'it is important to provide opportunities for children to solve a variety of problems involving different kinds of quantities' (1999: 48–9). However, for Carpenter and

Table 5.2 Different problem structures for problems involving multiplication and division

Type	Multiplication	Partitive division	Quotitive division
1. Equal Groups	There are 5 tomato plants each with 4 tomatoes. How many tomatoes are there altogether?	Altogether there are 20 tomatoes on 5 tomato plants. If there is the same number of tomatoes on each plant, how many tomatoes are on each plant?	Altogether there are 20 tomatoes. If there are 4 tomatoes on each plant, how many tomato plants are there?
2. Rate	Sam walks for 5 hours at a speed of 3 kms per hour. How many kms does she walk?	Sam walks 15 kms, which took her 5 hours. If she walks at the same speed the whole way, how far does she walk in one hour?	Sam walks 15 kms. If she walks 3 kms each hour, how long will it take her to walk the whole way?

3. Price (a form of Rate)	John bought 7 pies costing $4 each. How much did he spend on pies altogether?	John spent a total of $28 on 7 pies. If each pie cost the same amount, how much did one pie cost?	How many pies can you buy for $28, if the pies cost $4 each?
4. Multiplicative Comparison (Scale)	The giraffe is 3 times as tall as the kangaroo, which is 2 metres tall. How tall is the giraffe?	The giraffe is 6 metres tall. She is 3 times as tall as the kangaroo. How tall is the kangaroo?	The giraffe is 6 metres tall. The kangaroo is 2 metres tall. The giraffe is how many times taller than the kangaroo?
5. Part–Whole Ratio	There are 20 girls in the class and the ratio of girls to boys is 4 to 3. How many children in the class altogether?	There are 20 girls in the class. For every 4 girls in the class, there are 3 boys. How many boys are in the class?	In a class of 35 students, 15 are boys. What is the ratio of boys to girls?
6. Area and Array	A farmer makes a garden that is 6 metres by 8 metres. How big is the garden altogether?	A farmer wants to plant a rectangular vegetable garden of 48 square metres. She has enough room to make the garden 6 metres along one side. How long does she have to make the adjacent side of the garden? *	
7. Combination Problems (Cartesian Product)	The ice cream shop has 4 different flavours and 3 different types of cones. How many different ice creams can be made?	The ice cream shop has different types of cones and different flavours of ice cream. They can make 12 different combinations using 4 different flavours. How many different cone types are there? *	

Note
* These problems are symmetrical because the sides of the garden (or the cones and flavours) can be interchanged.

his colleagues, the critical differences are between multiplication, measurement (quotitive) division, and partitive (sharing) division problems.

Number properties of multiplication

A number property unique to multiplication is the distributive property, referring to the way multiplication is distributed over addition (e.g. $4 \times 23 = (4 \times 20) + (4 \times 3) = 80 + 12 = 92$). The factors are partitioned (split) and the parts multiplied to form partial products that together form the overall total. Understanding the distributive property is indicative of being a multiplicative thinker. Understanding inverse relationships between operations is also important for multiplicative thinking. For example, division can be used to reverse the effect of multiplication (e.g. $7 \times 4 = 28$ so $28 \div 7 = 4$ and $28 \div 4 = 7$), as can multiplication by the reciprocal of one factor, (e.g. $7 \times 4 = 28$ so $\frac{1}{4}$ of $28 = 7$ and $\frac{1}{7}$ of $28 = 4$), which is equivalent to whole-number division ($28 \div 7 = 4$ so $\frac{1}{7}$ of $28 = 4$). Understanding the inverse relationship between multiplication of whole numbers and fractions (and the equivalence of whole-number division to multiplication by fractions) is considered another important aspect of multiplicative thinking (Thompson and Saldanha 2003). The following statements show the interrelationships:

$$8 + 8 + 8 = 24$$
$$3 \times 8 = 24$$
$$24 \div 3 = 8, \quad 24 \div 8 = 3$$
$$\tfrac{1}{3} \text{ of } 24 = 8, \quad \tfrac{1}{8} \text{ of } 24 = 3$$

How important is learning 'times tables'?

With the current emphasis firmly on building students' conceptual understanding, an obvious question arises about the importance of learning 'times tables'. New Zealand's number framework includes basic facts as one of the domains of knowledge needed for students to use with more sophisticated mental strategies. Although students are encouraged to use basic facts to work out answers to unfamiliar problems, it is important that learning of basic facts takes place in a meaningful way rather than just through 'rote learning'. For example, students can be shown how knowledge of all single-digit 'times tables' can be built up by using what is known about the '*two times*' (2x), '*times two*' (x2), and '*times ten*' (x10) tables. For example, the '*times four*' table can be derived from the '*times two*' table, by doubling the values, e.g. $7 \times 4 = 2 \times (7 \times 2) = 2 \times 14 = 28$. Likewise, the '*times eight*' table can be derived from the '*times four*' table, e.g. $7 \times 8 = 2 \times (7 \times 4) = 2 \times 28 = 56$. The '*times three*' table can be derived from the '*times two*' table, by adding one more item to each group, e.g. $7 \times 3 = (7 \times 2) + (7 \times 1) = 14 + 7 = 21$. The '*times five*' tables, can be derived from the '*times ten*' table by halving, e.g. $7 \times 5 = (7 \times 10) \div 2 = 70 \div 2 = 35$. The '*times six*' table, can be derived from the '*times five*' table by adding one more to each group, e.g. $7 \times 6 = (7 \times 5) + (7 \times 1) = 35 + 7 = 42$. Alternatively, the '*times six*' table can be derived by doubling the '*times three*' table, e.g. $7 \times 6 = 2 \times (7 \times 3) = 2 \times 21 = 42$. The '*times nine*' table can be derived from the '*times ten*' table by taking one from each group, e.g. $7 \times 9 = (7 \times 10) - (7 \times 1) = 70 - 7 = 63$. The '*times seven*' tables can be derived by adding the '*times two*' tables to the '*times five*' tables, e.g. $7 \times 7 = (7 \times 5) + (7 \times 2) = 35 + 14 = 49$. Once students understand how to generate new facts using what they already know, the number of different facts that need to be memorized is substantially reduced. The connectedness of mathematics concepts and relationships is exemplified in this process also.

Research on the effect of a numeracy initiative on children's multiplicative thinking

New Zealand's numeracy initiative, the Numeracy Development Project, has been under way for almost a decade. Almost all primary and intermediate schools have been involved in the initiative (more than 30,000 teachers of 800,000 Year 1–8 students in approximately 2500 schools), an example of an intervention 'going to scale' (Coburn 2003). Teachers at the early secondary level (Years 9 and 10) began the project in 2005, with more than 30,000 students participating so far. A major focus has been the improvement of teachers' capability through ongoing reflective professional development. Teachers have been helped to understand research information about the mathematical thinking of their students, reflect on it with colleagues, and adjust their planning for individual students and groups (Bobis *et al.* 2005). This process continued over months and in some cases years – in contrast to the 'one-shot' professional development programmes of earlier times. A key tool is the individual diagnostic interview for assessing students' understanding of mathematical strategies and knowledge against the number framework outlining the developmental progressions in number understanding. Professional development workshops spread throughout the school year, and in-class modelling by numeracy facilitators/consultants introduce new ways of supporting students' mathematics learning.

The Numeracy Project has had a substantial effect on children's mathematics achievement, including their multiplicative thinking (see Young-Loveridge 2006, 2007, 2008). Assessments of children at the beginning and end of the professional development programme show consistent improvements on the number framework (see Figure 5.6 and Table 5.3).

According to New Zealand's *Curriculum Expectations* (Ministry of Education n.d.), most students at curriculum level four (Year 8) should be at stage seven (advanced multiplicative/early proportional) or higher, yet only 42 per cent of students had reached stage seven by the end of Year 8 (Young-Loveridge 2008). Comparing end-of-first-year results with expectations showed, for example, that more than half (58 per cent) of the students were considered to be either 'cause for concern' or 'at risk'. There was little improvement at Year 9 on the multiplicative domain, with just 43 per cent of students being at stage seven or higher at end of year. When results were examined separately by socioeconomic status (using a school's decile ranking),[1] less than one quarter (23 per cent) of students at low-decile schools had reached stage seven on the multiplicative domain by end of Year 8 (see Table 5.3). Just over half (52 per cent) the students at high-decile schools had become multiplicative thinkers by the end of Year 8.

These results are consistent with international research showing it takes at least two years for educational change to affect students' learning (e.g. Lamon 2007). In a study of students' fraction understanding, Young-Loveridge and colleagues (Young-Loveridge *et al.* 2007) gave 238 Year 7 and 8 students a multiplicative task involving addition with fractions ($\frac{3}{4} + \frac{7}{8}$), presented in the context of a familiar

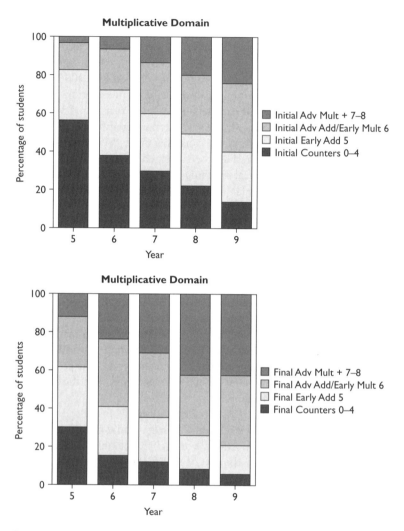

Figure 5.6 Percentage of students at stages on the number framework for the multiplicative domain (above: initial and below: final).

word problem about fractions of pizza. Only 32 students (13 per cent) found a correct answer for the problem, and some of those solved it using procedural knowledge rather than a deep conceptual understanding of fractions. Half the students gave an incorrect answer. The most common error (23 per cent) was to add the numerators and/or the denominators (the 'add across' error). More than a third of students did not attempt the problem. A potentially useful strategy shown by just a few students was the 'make a whole' strategy, analogous to the

Table 5.3 Percentages of students at stages on the number framework for the domain of multiplication/division as a function of timing (initial and final) and school decile

Stage	Year Level	5	6	7	8	9
	Approximate Age in years	9	10	11	12	13
	No. of students	*1415*	*1302*	*4049*	*3985*	*5900*
	Multiplicative Domain					
	Initial Overall					
0–4	Emergent to Skip Counting	56	38	30	22	13
5	Repeated Addition	27	34	30	28	27
6	Derived Multiplication/Division	14	22	26	30	36
7	Advanced Multiplication/Division	3	6	12	17	19
8	Multiplication/Division of Fractions/Decimals	0	1	2	3	5
	Total stages 7–8	***3***	***7***	***14***	***20***	***24***
	Final Overall					
0–4	Emergent to Skip Counting	30	15	12	8	6
5	Repeated Addition	32	26	23	17	16
6	Derived Multiplication/Division	26	35	34	32	35
7	Advanced Multiplication/Division	11	21	24	29	30
8	Multiplication/Division of Fractions/Decimals	1	3	7	13	13
	Total stages 7–8	***12***	***24***	***31***	***42***	***43***
	Final Low Decile (1–3)					
0–4	Emergent to Skip Counting	42	27	21	21	10
5	Repeated Addition	34	30	31	27	23
6	Derived Multiplication/Division	18	30	31	29	39
7	Advanced Multiplication/Division	5	13	16	19	21
8	Multiplication/Division of Fractions/Decimals	1	1	2	4	6
	Total stages 7–8	***6***	***14***	***18***	***23***	***27***
	Final High Decile (8–10)					
0–4	Emergent to Skip Counting	22	9	6	3	5
5	Repeated Addition	30	24	20	12	11
6	Derived Multiplication/Division	31	38	32	33	35
7	Advanced Multiplication/Division	16	24	31	34	35
8	Multiplication/Division of Fractions/Decimals	1	5	11	18	16
	Total stages 7–8	***17***	***29***	***42***	***52***	***51***

'make ten' strategy encouraged for whole-number addition. Most errors reflected the application of rote procedures involving symbol manipulation rather than a sense-making approach to the problem. The findings highlight the need for continued support for teachers as they grapple with a radically different way of approaching the teaching of mathematics. The findings are consistent with other research showing that many primary teachers do not have the deep understanding of fractions needed to teach their students effectively (Ward and Thomas 2007).

Multiplicative thinking in classrooms

Research on the effect of the Numeracy Project on students' mathematics achievement indicates that fewer than expected students become multiplicative thinkers by the end of primary school (e.g. Young-Loveridge 2006, 2007, 2008). Research on the classroom practices of seven teachers teaching a lesson on multi-digit multiplication using array-based materials shows the importance of teachers having a deep and connected understanding of the structure of multiplication/division (see Young-Loveridge and Mills 2009). For example, students in teacher E's class used a faulty algorithm to calculate the answers to multi-digit multiplication problems. For 11×99, students multiplied the tens ($10 \times 90 = 900$) then the ones ($1 \times 9 = 9$) and added just those products ($11 \times 99 = 900 + 9 = 909$). In teacher C's class, some students added the factors in 23×37, getting an answer of 60. Only two teachers (A and B) accurately judged which of their groups was ready to learn about multi-digit multiplication, and carefully scaffolded their students' learning using dotty arrays to represent the problem (see Figure 5.1). Teacher A emphasized the importance of putting a rectangular border around all the dots that represented the problem at the outset, and guided students in partitioning each of the factors into their place-value parts (23 into 20 and 3; 37 into 30 and 7), using this place-value partitioning to break up the array into four parts corresponding to each of the partial products ($20 \times 30 = 600, 20 \times 7 = 140, 30 \times 3 = 90, 3 \times 7 = 21; 600 + 140 + 90 + 21 = 851$). Later she helped them see how this array representation corresponded to the vertical written algorithm for multiplication ('long multiplication'). In the classes of teachers C, D and F, students first used a written algorithm to calculate their answers, and then created a series of unconnected arrays for each of the partial products. The teachers of these students appeared not to understand how an array could be used to represent the whole problem, and then solve it.

Ell's doctoral research explored the transition from additive to multiplicative thinking for a group of Year 5 and 6 students (Ell 2004). Ell found a hierarchy of increasing sophistication in the strategy use of the students she interviewed. The learning pathways of two case-study children, Le and Lo, were documented over eight mathematics lessons. The children differed in the range of strategies they used and in the paths they took towards understanding how multiplication works.

The challenge for teachers in supporting their students' multiplicative thinking raises questions about teacher education. A recent study on the effect of a university course for practising teachers on teachers' mathematics knowledge for teaching (their personal mathematics content knowledge and pedagogical content knowledge) focused on the mathematics of place-value, fractions, and decimals, and looked at how students construct mathematical knowledge, common misconceptions that students develop, and ways of presenting these concepts to students to ensure they develop robust ways of thinking (Ell *et al.* 2008). The percentage of teachers at stage seven (advanced multiplicative) rose from 15 per cent initially to 69 per cent by the end of the course. While this intervention showed substantial improvement, the fact that the final results were not closer to 100 per cent may reflect the difficulty and complexity of these ideas, and could help explain the relatively low percentages of Year 8 and 9 students reaching stage seven on the number framework (see Figure 5.6 and Table 5.3; Young-Loveridge 2008). These findings are consistent with other research showing the importance for teachers of having a deep and connected understanding of mathematics subject knowledge, as well as an appreciation of the ways that such knowledge can be introduced to their students (Ball *et al.* 2005; Hill *et al.* 2005).

Challenges for the future

Probably the greatest challenge is to use an understanding of psychology, particularly the work of constructivist and sociocultural theorists, to help teachers appreciate the complexity of multiplicative thinking and reasoning so they can make better instructional decisions about optimal ways of teaching students. This requires a deeper, more connected understanding of mathematics, and in particular, a better understanding of the structure of multiplication, division, fractions, ratios and proportions. There are some indications that strengthening teachers' knowledge and understanding of the multiplicative domain can enhance their confidence and attitude towards mathematics as well as helping them to become better teachers. However, more research is needed to find ways that teachers' understanding of multiplicative thinking and reasoning can be better supported to improve their students' learning.

Note

1 Each school has been assigned a decile ranking between 1 (low) and 10 (high) based on the latest Census information about the education and income levels of the adults living in the households of students who attend the school.

References

Anghileri, J. (2006) *Teaching Number Sense*, 2nd edn, London: Continuum.

Baek, J.M. (1998) 'Children's invented algorithms for multidigit multiplication problems', in L.J. Morrow (ed.), *The Teaching and Learning of Algorithms in School Mathematics: 1998 Yearbook* (pp. 151–60). Reston, VA: National Council of Teachers of Mathematics.

Baek, J.M. (2008) 'Developing algebraic thinking through explorations in multiplication', in C.E. Greenes and R. Rubenstein (eds) *Algebra and Algebraic Thinking in School Mathematics: Seventieth Yearbook* (pp. 141–54), Reston, VA: National Council of Teachers of Mathematics.

Ball, D.L., Hill, H.C. and Bass, H. (2005) 'Knowing mathematics for teaching: who knows mathematics well enough to teach third grade, and how can we decide?', *American Educator*, Fall, 14–22, 43–6.

Beckmann, S. and Fuson, K.C. (2008) 'Focal points – Grades 5 and 6', *Teaching Children Mathematics*, 14: 508–17.

Beishuizen, M. (1999) 'The empty number line as a new model', in I. Thompson (ed.) *Issues in Teaching Numeracy in Primary School*, Buckingham: Open University Press.

Bobis, J., Clarke, B., Clarke, D., Thomas, G., Wright, R., Young-Loveridge, J. and Gould, P. (2005) 'Supporting teachers in the development of young children's mathematical thinking: three large scale cases', *Mathematics Education Research Journal*, 16: 27–57.

Brown, G. and Quinn, R.J. (2006) 'Algebra students' difficulty with fractions: an error analysis', *Australian Mathematics Teacher*, 62: 28–40.

Carpenter, T.P., Fennema, E., Franke, M.L., Levi, L. and Empson, S.B. (1999) *Children's Mathematics: Cognitively Guided Instruction*, Portsmouth, NH: Heinemann.

Charles, R.I. and Duckett, P.B. (2008) 'Focal points – Grades 3 and 4', *Teaching Children Mathematics*, 14: 366–471.

Clark, F.B. and Kamii, C. (1996) 'Identification of multiplicative thinking in children in Grades 1–5', *Journal for Research in Mathematics Education*, 27: 41–51.

Coburn, C.E. (2003) 'Rethinking scale: moving beyond numbers to deep and lasting change', *Educational Researcher*, 32: 3–12.

Confrey, J. and Harel, G. (1994) 'Introduction', in G. Harel and J. Confrey (eds) *The Development of Multiplicative Reasoning in the Learning of Mathematics* (pp. vii–xxviii), Albany, NY: State University of New York.

Davis, B. (2008) 'Is 1 a prime number? Developing teacher knowledge through concept study', *Mathematics Teaching in the Middle School*, 14: 86–91.

Diezmann, C.M. and English, L.D. (2001) 'Promoting the use of diagrams as tools for thinking', in A.A. Cuoco and F.R. Curcio (eds) *The Role of Representation in School Mathematics: 2001 Yearbook* (pp. 77–89), Reston, VA: National Council of Teachers of Mathematics.

Ell, F. (2004) 'Learning about multiplication: an interpretation of a transition', unpublished doctoral thesis, University of Auckland.

Ell, F., Lomas, G., Cheeseman, L. and Nicholas, P. (2008) 'Improving knowledge of mathematics for teaching: investigating the effects of an in-service intervention', *Findings from the New Zealand Numeracy Development Projects 2007* (pp. 61–6), Wellington: Learning Media.

Hill, H., Rowan, B. and Ball, D. (2005) 'Effects of teachers' mathematical knowledge for teaching on student achievement', *American Educational Research Journal*, 42: 371–406.

Jacob, L. and Willis, S. (2001) 'Recognising the difference between additive and multiplicative thinking in young children', in J. Bobis, B. Perry and M. Mitchelmore (eds) *Numeracy and Beyond* (Proceedings of the 24th Annual Conference of the Mathematics Research Group of Australasia), Sydney (pp. 306–13).

Krause, K.L., Bochner, S. and Duchesne, S. (2007) *Educational Psychology for Learning and Teaching*, 2nd edn, South Melbourne, Vic: Thomson.

Lambdin, D.V. and Walcott, C. (2007) 'Changes through the years: connections between psychological learning theories and the school mathematics curriculum', in W.G. Martin, M.E. Struchens and P.C. Elliott (eds) *The Learning of Mathematics: Sixty-Ninth Yearbook* (pp. 3–25), Reston, VA: National Council of Teachers of Mathematics.

Lamon, S. (2007) 'Rational numbers and proportional reasoning: towards a theoretical framework for research', in F. Lester (ed.) *Second Handbook of Research on Mathematics Teaching and Learning* (pp. 629–67), Charlotte, NC: Information Age Publishing.

Ministry of Education (2007) *Book 1: The Number Framework: Revised Edition 2007*, Wellington, NZ: Author.

Ministry of Education (2008) *Book 6: Teaching Multiplication and Division: Revised Edition 2007*, Wellington, NZ: Author.

Ministry of Education (New Zealand) (n.d.) 'Curriculum expectations', retrieved on 30 November 2008 from: www.nzmaths.co.nz/numeracy/Principals/StudentData.aspx.

Mulligan, J.T. and Mitchelmore, M.C. (1997) 'Young children's intuitive models of multiplication and division', *Journal for Research in Mathematics Education*, 28: 309–30.

Mulligan, J. and Vergnaud, G. (2005) 'Research on children's early mathematical development: towards integrated perspectives', in A. Gutierrez and P. Boero (eds) *Handbook of Research on the Psychology of Mathematics Education: Past, Present and Future* (pp. 117–46), Rotterdam: Sense Publishers.

National Council of Teachers of Mathematics (NCTM) (2000) *Principles and Standards for School Mathematics: An Overview*, Reston, VA: Author.

National Council of Teachers of Mathematics (NCTM) (n.d.) *Curriculum Focal Points*, retrieved on 1 March 2007 from: www.nctm.org/standards/default.aspx?id=58.

Pesek, D. D. and Kirshner, D. (2000) 'Interference of instrumental instruction in subsequent relational learning', *Journal for Research in Mathematics Education*, 31: 524–40.

Presmeg, N. (2006) 'Research on visualization in learning and teaching mathematics', in A. Gutierrez and P. Boero (eds) *Handbook of Research on the Psychology of Mathematics Education: Past, Present and Future* (pp. 205–35), Rotterdam: Sense Publishers.

Siemon, D. (2005) 'Multiplicative thinking', retrieved on 19 May 2008 from www.eduweb.vic.gov.au/edulibrary/public/teachlearn/student/ppmultithinking.pdf.

Skemp, R.R. (1971) *The Psychology of Learning Mathematics*, Harmondsworth: Penguin.

Sophian, C. (2007) *The Origins of Mathematical Knowledge in Childhood*, New York: Erlbaum.

Sowder, J. (2002) 'Introduction', in B. Litwiller and G. Bright (eds) *Making Sense of Fractions, Ratios, and Proportions: 2002 Yearbook* (pp. 1–2), Reston, VA: NCTM.

Steffe, L. (1992) 'Schemes of action and operation involving composite units', *Learning and Individual Differences*, 4: 259–309.

Thompson, P.W. and Saldanha, L.A. (2003) 'Fractions and multiplicative reasoning', in J. Kilpatrick, W.G. Martin and D. Schifter (eds) *A Research Companion to Principles and Standards for School Mathematics* (pp. 95–113), Reston, VA: National Council of Teachers of Mathematics.

Vergnaud, G. (1983) 'Multiplicative structures', in R. Lesh and M. Landau (eds) *Acquisition of Mathematics Concepts and Processes* (pp. 127–74), Orlando, FL: Academic Press.

Vergnaud, G. (1994) 'Multiplicative conceptual field: what and why?', in G. Harel and J. Confrey (eds) *The Development of Multiplicative Reasoning in the Learning of Mathematics* (pp. 41–59), Albany, NY: State University of New York Press.

Ward, J. and Thomas, G. (2007) 'What do teachers know about fractions?', in *Findings from the New Zealand Numeracy Development Projects 2006* (pp. 128–38), Wellington, NZ: Ministry of Education.

Young-Loveridge, J. (1994) 'The psychology of learning mathematics', in J. Neyland (ed.) *Mathematics Education: A Handbook for Teachers* (vol. 1, pp. 307–18), Wellington: Wellington College of Education.

Young-Loveridge, J. (2005a) 'A developmental perspective on mathematics teaching and learning: the case of multiplicative thinking', *Teachers and Curriculum*, 8: 49–58.

Young-Loveridge, J. (2005b) 'Fostering multiplicative thinking using array-based materials', *Australian Mathematics Teacher*, 61: 34–40.

Young-Loveridge, J. (2006) 'Patterns of performance and progress on the Numeracy Development Project: looking back from 2005', *Findings from the New Zealand Numeracy Development Projects 2005* (pp. 6–21, 137–55), Wellington, NZ: Ministry of Education.

Young-Loveridge, J. (2007) 'Patterns of performance and progress on the Numeracy Development Projects: findings from 2006 for Years 5–9 students', *Findings from the New Zealand Numeracy Development Projects 2006* (pp. 16–32, 154–77), Wellington, NZ: Ministry of Education.

Young-Loveridge, J. (2008) 'Analysis of 2007 data from the Numeracy Development Projects: what does the picture show?', *Findings from the New Zealand Numeracy Development Projects 2007* (pp. 18–28, 191–211), Wellington, NZ: Ministry of Education.

Young-Loveridge, J. and Mills, J. (2009) 'Teaching multi-digit multiplication using array-based materials', in R. Hunter, B. Bicknell and T. Burgess (eds) *Crossing Divides*, proceedings of the annual conference of the Mathematics Education Research Group of Australasia (pp. 635–42), Wellington, NZ.

Young-Loveridge, J., Taylor, M., Hawera, N. and Sharma, S. (2007) 'Year 7–8 students' solution strategies for a task involving addition of unlike fractions', in B. Annan *et al.* *Findings from the New Zealand Numeracy Development Projects 2006* (pp. 67–86). Wellington, NZ: Ministry of Education.

Chapter 6

How research in educational psychology has contributed to instructional procedures

The case of cognitive load theory

Renae Low, Putai Jin and John Sweller

Educational psychology has thrown light on a variety of educational processes such as school administration, classroom management, and instructional design. In this chapter, we concentrate exclusively on instructional design. Specifically, we use cognitive load theory as an example of an instructional theory based on knowledge of psychological principles. We recognize, of course, that educational psychology extends beyond instruction and that, in turn, instructional psychology extends beyond cognitive load theory. Nevertheless, we believe it is useful to use cognitive load theory as an example of what educational psychology can contribute to more general issues of education. There are, of course, many alternative case studies that could be used.

When applied to cognitively generated instructional procedures, educational psychology can be considered as the nexus between instruction and learning in educational settings. It is concerned with the understanding of the interaction between instructional environments and learner characteristics that foster effective learning. In particular, this branch of educational psychology focuses on the scientific study of techniques for manipulating instructional processes and procedures and their interactions with learners' cognitive structures and processes.

Research in educational psychology has led to theories that form the foundation for understanding many critical issues faced by learners and educators. In the context of instruction and learning, the development of our knowledge of cognitive structures will have a significant effect on instructional issues. Knowing how students learn gives us information on how we should organize their learning environment. Similarly, discovering that some instructional procedures are better than others under certain conditions can provide insights into the cognitive structures and functions that constitute human cognitive architecture. Cognitive load theory, with its close links between human cognitive architecture and instructional design, provides an example of the advantages of linking the two areas.

Cognitive load theory

Cognitive load theory was born from studies on students learning to solve puzzle problems. Contrary to the widely held belief that students learn problem solving by having extensive practice in solving problems, extensive practice in solving puzzle problems did not result in learning (Sweller 1976). Subsequent work established that, as was the case for puzzle problems, minimal learning occurred when students solved school-based mathematics or science problems. For instance, students learned more and then performed better on subsequent problem-solving tests by studying worked examples rather than solving equivalent problems (e.g. Cooper and Sweller 1987). The two decades following this initial work saw cognitive load theory both develop and generate an increasing number of applications concerned with presenting information in ways to maximize learning. Many of these applications have been generated by our expanding knowledge of the cognitive processes involved in learning and understanding. The following section discusses elements of human cognitive architecture relevant to cognitive load theory.

Relevant aspects of human cognitive architecture

Cognitive load theory has recently been associated with an evolutionary view of human cognitive architecture to generate instructional design principles (Sweller 2003, 2004; Sweller and Sweller 2006). Before considering human cognitive architecture, we need to distinguish between two categories: biologically primary and biologically secondary knowledge, identified by Geary (2007). Biologically primary knowledge is knowledge we have evolved to acquire over many thousands of generations. Learning to listen and speak is an example. Because we have evolved to acquire these skills, we can do so simply by being immersed in a listening/speaking society. In contrast, biologically secondary knowledge is knowledge we can acquire, but which we have not explicitly evolved to acquire because it has only been part of human activity relatively recently. Learning to read and write is an example, as is all learning for which educational institutions have been devised. Biologically secondary knowledge needs to be explicitly taught and it is to this knowledge that cognitive load theory applies.

The cognitive architecture described next applies to biologically secondary knowledge. The five basic principles used to describe that architecture constitute a natural information processing system that also applies to the structures and functions of evolution by natural selection (Sweller and Sweller 2006).

Information store principle

Long-term memory contains a very large store of information governing most human cognitive activity. Evidence for the importance of information in long-term memory to problem solving came from the well-known work by De Groot ([1946] 1965), and Chase and Simon (1973), who found that the skill of chess masters derived from their extensive knowledge of chess board configurations.

Information stored in long-term memory is generally thought to be highly structured and organized. Schemas are often referred to as the building blocks of knowledge which provide the structure for long-term memory (Bartlett 1932; Gick and Holyoak 1983). They can operate under either automatic or conscious control. Novel tasks demand conscious effort, with the transition from controlled to automatic processing requiring considerable time and effort (Schneider and Shiffrin 1977). Consider the case of a child who has just begun to learn to read. Recognition of the letter *e* might occur only after considerable thought. However, after some time and practice, the child's recognition of the letter becomes automatic.

Borrowing and reorganizing principle

The bulk of information in long-term memory is obtained by borrowing information from other people, either directly or indirectly. We imitate what other people do (Bandura 1986), and listen to what they say and read what they write (Sweller 2003, 2004). Information obtained in this manner is combined with previously held information in long-term memory. Cognitive load theory is heavily based on the borrowing and reorganizing principle. It is concerned primarily with how information should be presented to learners and the activities they should engage in to maximize learning. In other words, the theory is concerned with the procedures that will assist in the acquisition and automation of schemas in long-term memory. Many of those procedures are discussed later in the section entitled 'Some instructional principles generated by cognitive load theory'.

Randomness as genesis principle

While most of the information in long-term memory is borrowed from others, at some point information has to be created. Creativity occurs while problem solving. When solving a novel problem, at various points, knowledge concerning the next, best move may not be available. Randomly generating a move and testing it for effectiveness may be the only procedure available. By necessity, when knowledge is unavailable, we must randomly choose a move. Furthermore, we cannot know the effect of that move until we have completed the particular move mentally or physically. Many moves so chosen, will, perhaps, lead to dead-ends. This can explain why we reach so many dead-ends when attempting to solve a novel, complex problem. Of course, almost all moves are a combination of knowledge and random generation and test. Therefore, when generating a problem-solving move, usually, a combination of knowledge held in long-term memory and a procedure of random generation and test is used.

Narrow limits of change principle

A large-scale random change could destroy the functionality of long-term memory, so change must be incremental. A working memory of limited duration and limited capacity ensures small, incremental changes to long-term memory. Working memory refers to the structure where information is processed for meaning.

Information enters working memory either via long-term memory as previously learned material (see the environmental organizing and linking principle discussed below) or via sensory memory as new information. The manner in which these two sources of information are processed by working memory is vastly different and has instructional consequences. Cognitive load theory was formulated to deal with these consequences.

Cognitive researchers have known for some time that, when new information enters working memory via sensory memory, no more than five to nine elements or chunks of information can be held in working memory at any given time and probably no more than two to three elements can be processed where processing involves comparing, combining, manipulating or working on elements in some fashion (Miller 1956; Newell and Simon 1972; Simon 1974). Not only is working memory limited in capacity, it is also limited in duration. Peterson and Peterson (1959) demonstrated the transitory nature of working memory when they found that if people are presented with sets of unfamiliar combinations of letters or digits to hold in memory, those stimuli can only be held for a few seconds without rehearsal. From an instructional perspective, the limited capacity and the transitory nature of working memory have important consequences. The limited capacity of working memory means that, when instruction requires learners to process more than a very few elements of new information at a time, that instruction is unlikely to be successful. Similarly, the transitory nature of working memory means that when learners are presented with new information, that information is lost within a few seconds unless the instruction is designed to take this characteristic of working memory into account.

Working memory was initially considered a unitary structure. More recent psychological research has indicated that working memory may consist of multiple processors rather than a single processor (Baddeley 1992; Schneider and Detweiler 1987). These processors are frequently associated with the independent processing of visual-spatial and language-based material. For example, Baddeley's model of working memory divides working memory into a visual-spatial sketch pad that processes visually based information such as diagrams and pictures and a phonological loop that processes auditory information (Baddeley 1986, 1992, 1999). A discussion of psychological research work supporting the notion that working memory can be subdivided into partially independent processors consisting of an auditory working memory system to deal with verbal material and a visual working memory system to deal with diagrammatical/pictorial information was presented by Low and Sweller (2005). From an instructional perspective, there are important consequences if two independent working memory systems co-exist. One obvious consequence is that the total amount of information that can be processed by working memory may be determined by the mode (visual or auditory) of presentation. Theoretically, it should be possible to increase effective working memory capacity by presenting information in a combined visual and auditory mode rather than a single mode.

Environmental linking and organizing principle

Limits on working memory apply only when dealing with novel information from the environment. Those limits disappear when dealing with organized information from long-term memory. Whereas the amount of information from sensory memory that can be processed by working memory is limited, there are no known limits to the amount of information from long-term memory that can be processed by working memory. Ericsson and Kintsch's (1995) work on long-term working memory provides evidence that there are no limits to working memory in terms of capacity or duration when dealing with information from long-term memory. Schemas are critical to this process.

Schemas are designed to store knowledge in long-term memory and, when brought into working memory, to bypass the limited capacity of working memory. They permit complex, generalized knowledge structures to be treated as single elements in memory. As a result, otherwise diverse entities can be treated as a single entity. For example, we can treat the infinite variety of forms that a handwritten letter *e* can take as being identical. Our schema for this letter not only allows us to ignore the variations and indeed all irrelevant details, but also enables us to treat all of the information encapsulated in the letter as a single element. In other words, schema acquisition allows us to bring a large amount of information into a very limited working memory and deal with what might otherwise be an impossibly large and complex collection of elements.

Conscious processing of information requires relatively more working memory resources than automatic processing. Thus, automatic processing is critical to learning as it reduces the load on working memory. This function of automatic processing is similar to schema acquisition. While schema acquisition seems to be an essential component in solving problems and exercises similar to those learned, automatic processing seems to be a key ingredient in transfer and in dealing with novel problems (Cooper and Sweller 1987; Kotovsky *et al.* 1985). Thus, schema acquisition and automatic processing are important factors in learning and understanding. Schemas that can be processed automatically are held in permanent long-term memory. They permit the processing of large amounts of information in working memory that would otherwise exceed the capacity of working memory, which is limited to processing no more than a few elements at a time. The large amount of information held in long-term memory permits us to link to and organize our complex environment.

This cognitive architecture as set out in the five principles discussed above is used by cognitive load theory to design instruction. From an instructional perspective, it is essential that we know the characteristics of the relevant cognitive structures because such knowledge can be used to generate principles for instructional design, which in turn can verify the existence of the relevant cognitive structures and their characteristics. The major function of instruction is to allow learners to make appropriate changes to information stored in long-term memory. This is because if there is no alteration to long-term memory, nothing has been learnt. Facilitating the acquisition of organized information in long-term memory is the major concern of cognitive load theory. Cognitive load theory suggests that instructional and training procedures should be designed to make optimal use of the limited processing capacity of working memory and to aid learning by accelerating the acquisition of schemas. Extensive research using cognitive load theory as a theoretical framework has demonstrated that many conventional and widely used instructional techniques and approaches to training ignore the fundamental components of the human cognitive architecture discussed above, especially the limitations of working memory.

Intrinsic, extraneous and germane cognitive load

The extent to which new material is learned and understood depends largely on the cognitive load imposed on working memory by the instruction. Cognitive load theory proposes three independent sources of cognitive load involved in learning any instructional material: intrinsic, extraneous and germane cognitive load.

Intrinsic cognitive load is generated by the intellectual demands of a task. It is influenced by the complexity of the information that must be processed and is determined by element interactivity, which is the number of elements contained in the learning material that have to be held simultaneously in working memory (Sweller 1994; Sweller and Chandler 1994). Some elements can be learned serially (i.e. element by element) and such material imposes a minimal intrinsic load on working memory. Consider the task of learning some vocabulary items of a foreign language. Learning the translation of a particular word can occur in isolation without reference to the translation of any other word. For example, one can learn the Chinese word for dog quite independently of learning the word for cat. The vocabulary task may be difficult because there are a lot of words to learn, but it does not impose a heavy intrinsic cognitive load because the elements (the vocabulary terms) do not interact and do not have to be processed simultaneously in working memory. In order to attain competence, a large number of words must be learned and so the task is difficult. However, because there is minimal interaction between the elements, intrinsic cognitive load remains low.

In contrast, some material can be understood and learned only by holding several elements simultaneously in working memory. Consider the task of learning the syntax of a language such as the required order of words in English. In order to learn word orders in a sentence, all the relevant words and their relations must be held in working memory simultaneously. Element interactivity and thus intrinsic cognitive load are likely to be relatively high.

It should be noted that what constitutes an element does not depend solely on the nature of the material; it also depends on the expertise level of the learner. For a beginning reader, each letter may constitute an element and because of limited working memory, reading may be a slow, laborious process. For an expert reader, entire words or even their synonyms and antonyms may have already been incorporated in schemas, with each schema acting as an element. While the number of elements processed in working memory may be identical for novices and experts, the amount of information dealt with can vary substantially because the size of those elements can differ. Experts can call on very complex, sophisticated schemas brought into working memory from long-term memory. In contrast, novices hold much simpler schemas in long-term memory. As a consequence, high element interactivity may not result in high cognitive load if sufficient expertise has been attained to incorporate interacting elements in a schema that acts as a single element. Accordingly, the intrinsic cognitive load of a task varies with level of expertise.

While intrinsic load is determined by the complexity of the learning material, extraneous load is determined by the format of the instructional material, which can take many forms (for example, written instructions, formal lectures, practical demonstrations), and by the activities required of learners. While intrinsic cognitive load is inalterable until schemas, preferably in automated form, have been acquired, it does have consequences for instructional design. Sweller and Chandler (1994), Chandler and Sweller (1996) and Tindall-Ford et al. (1997) found that instructional design was a significant factor for learning only when instructions involved an intrinsically high cognitive load because of high element interactivity. The explanation given for the finding was that when element interactivity was high and therefore intrinsic load was assumed to be high, then the extraneous load imposed by the instructional format became critical and the implementation of cognitively based instruction led to learning benefits. In areas where there was a low level of interaction between learning elements, intrinsic load was thought to be low and instructional design and associated extraneous load were assumed to be of little consequence. This interpretation of results was supported by comprehensive measures of both element interactivity and cognitive load.

A reduction in extraneous cognitive load cannot have instructional benefits if the working memory resources devoted to processing poorly designed instruction are not shifted to schema acquisition and automation once instruction is modified to reduce extraneous load. Germane cognitive load is the load imposed by acquiring schemas and automating them. A reduction in extraneous cognitive load allows an increase in germane cognitive load that leads to learning (Paas and Van Merrienboer 1994). Intrinsic, extraneous and germane cognitive load are additive and contribute to the total load on working memory (Sweller et al. 1998). While intrinsic cognitive load cannot be altered without altering understanding of the information, a reduction in extraneous cognitive load allows an increase in germane cognitive load leading to enhanced learning.

Some instructional principles generated by cognitive load theory

Cognitive load theory uses the cognitive architecture described above to generate instructional design principles, and many such principles have been generated. The vast bulk of that work has used relatively well-defined problems taken from areas such as mathematics, science and technology. Nevertheless, in recent times, many similar results have been obtained in the humanities, including in art and music-based areas, which suggests that the theory can be extended to wide areas of knowledge. The following sections summarize some of the instructional effects generated by cognitive load theory.

Goal-free effect

A conventional problem is one that specifies a desired variable (the goal). For example, a geometry problem that states 'Find the value of angle ABC' is a conventional (or goal-directed) problem, whereas the same problem stated as 'Find the values of as many angles as you can' has an unspecified goal. Solving conventional problems during learning imposes a heavy cognitive load. In order to solve a conventional problem, the problem solver must consider the current problem, the goal, and the differences between the two; find problem-solving operators that can reduce those differences; and maintain track of any subgoals that have been established. These cognitive activities can easily overload working memory. In contrast, goal-free or non-specific goal problems reduce the load on working memory by permitting the problem solver to simply find a set of givens that will allow something to be calculated, rather than requiring the problem solver to go through the complex procedure required by conventional goal-specific problems. When goal-free problems result in more learning than conventional problems, this is known as the goal-free effect. This effect has been demonstrated on many occasions with different learning materials (e.g. Sweller *et al.* 1983) but it should be noted that the effect is not likely to be obtained in areas in which, as a result of instructions to find as much as can possibly be found, there is a very large search space.

Worked example effect

The worked example effect occurs when learning is enhanced after studying worked examples that provide solutions to problems rather than solving equivalent problems. Searching for a solution places heavy demands on working memory and those demands interfere with schema construction. A worked example reduces extraneous cognitive load and thereby facilitates learning by eliminating problem-solving steps. Many experiments have demonstrated this basic worked example effect (e.g. Cooper and Sweller 1987).

Completion effect

Partially completed examples that provide some problem-solving steps and require learners to complete the missing steps are a variation of fully worked-out examples. This instructional format has been demonstrated to be as effective as using complete worked examples (e.g. Paas and Van Merrienboer 1994).

Split-attention effect

Studying worked examples can be ineffective under certain conditions. One such condition is where the worked example consists of two or more sources of information that require mental integration. The load on working memory imposed by the need to mentally integrate the disparate sources of information interferes with learning. Consider a conventionally structured geometry worked example consisting of a diagram and its associated solution statements. The diagram alone does not communicate the solution to the problem. The statements, in turn, are incomprehensible until they have been integrated with the diagram. Learners must mentally integrate the two sources of information (the diagram and the statements) in order to understand them. This process can be cognitively demanding, especially for a novice learner, thus imposing a cognitive load that is extraneous simply because of the particular format used. If the separate sources of related information are physically integrated, for example, by placing the verbal explanation at the appropriate places in the diagram, the need for learners to engage in mental integration would be obviated, thus freeing cognitive resources for learning. Learning conditions comparing split-attention and integrated formats that yield results demonstrating the superiority of the integrated format provide examples of the split-attention effect. The integrated format technique has been demonstrated to be effective in a range of instructional areas including English as a second language, mathematics, physics, electrical engineering, biology, basic computing, numerical control programming in both industrial and educational settings (see Ayres and Sweller 2005; Ginns 2006; Sweller *et al.* 1990; Yeung *et al.* 1997).

From an instructional perspective, the split-attention effect means that where the learning material includes multiple sources of information that must be integrated in order to make sense of the problem, those sources of information should be physically integrated in order to reduce extraneous cognitive load. This guideline is especially applicable in a multimedia context where there is always more than one source of information.

Redundancy effect

Physically integrated instructions may not always be beneficial. Integrated instructions are beneficial if sources of related information are unintelligible prior to mental integration. However, in some instructions, there may be two or more sources of related information with one information source being entirely self-explanatory. For example, a self-contained diagram with an associated text that merely re-describes the diagram adds no new information. Under such conditions, physical integration is unlikely to be beneficial, as processing unnecessary redundant information will impose an extraneous load on working memory. When a second source of information merely reiterates the information of the first source in a different form, it can be considered redundant. Cognitive load theory refers to the beneficial effect of removing the redundant information as the redundancy effect. The theory suggests that processing redundant information with essential information increases working memory load, which interferes with the transfer of information to long-term memory. Removing redundant information eliminates the requirement to process information that is not essential to learning. The redundancy effect has been demonstrated in a variety of contexts (see Chandler and Sweller 1991; Sweller 2005; Yeung *et al.* 1997). From an instructional perspective, while it is important to analyse the relation between multiple sources of information before the physical integration to avoid split attention, it is also vital to bear in mind that presentation of the same information in multiple formats has negative effects.

Modality effect

According to cognitive load theory, there are two ways in which extraneous cognitive load can be manipulated. First, instructional procedures can alleviate extraneous cognitive load by formatting instructional material in such a way that it minimizes the cognitive activities that are unnecessary to learning so that cognitive resources can be freed to concentrate on activities essential to learning. All of the effects discussed above fall into this category. The consequences of extraneous cognitive load can also be alleviated by increasing effective working memory capacity. As noted earlier, Baddeley's working memory model divides working memory into a visual-spatial sketch pad that processes visually based information such as diagrams and pictures, and a phonological loop that processes auditory information. It may be possible to increase the capacity of effective working memory by presenting information in a mixed visual and auditory mode rather than a single mode. If effective working memory can be increased by using dual-modality presentation techniques, theoretically this procedure may be just as effective in facilitating learning as physically integrating two sources of visually presented information.

The modality effect occurs when information presented in a mixed mode (partly visual and partly auditory) is more effective than when the same information is presented in a single mode (either visually or in auditory form alone). For example, consider a typical geometry problem consisting of a diagram and associated statements. Conventionally, the diagram and the associated statements are visually presented. However, although the diagram has to be presented visually, the associated statements can be presented either visually or orally. There is evidence to show that students learn better when the associated statements are narrated rather than presented visually (see Ginns 2005a; Low and Sweller 2005; Mousavi *et al.* 1995). From a cognitive load theory perspective, the modality effect can be explained by assuming the memory load due to a diagram (or picture) with text presentation induces a high load in the visual working memory system because both sources of information are processed in this system. In contrast, the diagram and narration version induces a lower load in visual working memory because auditory and visual information are each processed in their respective systems. Therefore, the total load induced by this version is spread between the visual and the auditory components in the working memory system. In other words, integration of the audio and visual information may not overload working memory if its capacity is effectively expanded by using a dual-mode presentation.

From an instructional perspective, the modality effect means that the cognitive load imposed on working memory by instruction that includes two visual sources of information (e.g. a diagram and text) that are unintelligible unless they are mentally integrated can be alleviated by spreading the load between the visual and the auditory components in the working memory system. In other words, integration of the audio and visual information may not overload working memory if its capacity is effectively expanded by using a dual-mode presentation.

Expertise reversal effect

All of the above effects can be demonstrated with novel instructional designs intended for novice students. It can be expected that as students' levels of knowledge increase, information presented to novices become less essential and may eventually become fully redundant. As mentioned previously, redundant information imposes an extraneous cognitive load compared to instruction that does not include the material, resulting in the expertise reversal effect (Kalyuga *et al.* 2003). An expertise reversal effect occurs when an instructional format that is beneficial for novices compared to other formats loses its advantage as the learners increase their expertise, and finally becomes disadvantageous for individuals with higher expertise. There are many demonstrations of this effect (e.g. Kalyuga *et al.* 1998; Yeung *et al.* 1997).

Guidance fading effect

The guidance effect is related to the expertise reversal effect, the completion effect, and the worked example effect. As the levels of expertise increase, the worked example effect associated with the full worked examples can be expected to decrease. It can be more advantageous at this stage of expertise to introduce partial worked examples for students to complete the problems. Once sufficient knowledge has been accumulated, full problems can replace the completion problems. The guidance fading effect occurs when this procedure is superior to one in which fading is not used (e.g. Renkl *et al.* 2002).

Isolated-integrated elements effect

If the element interactivity of new material is exceptionally high, it cannot be processed in working memory because there may be too many elements to process simultaneously. The solution is to present only some of the required elements in isolation for processing even if in doing so, understanding is compromised. The isolated elements can be processed in working memory and stored in isolated fashion in long-term memory. Full understanding subsequently can be facilitated by re-presenting the material including all elements in properly integrated fashion. Because the essential elements had previously been learned in isolation, they now can be integrated in working memory. Compared to learners who are presented with the full information twice, an isolated-integrated presentation facilitates learning (Pollock *et al.* 2002).

Imagination effect

Once students have learned a concept or procedure sufficiently to be able to run it through working memory, that is, to 'imagine' the concept or procedure, the act of imagining that concept or procedure should strengthen and further automate the schema held in working memory. It can be predicted that instructing learners to imagine a concept or procedure may be advantageous compared to merely having them engage in, for example, further study of worked examples. Several studies have demonstrated this imagination effect (see Cooper *et al.* 2001; Ginns 2005b). It needs to be noted that this effect is heavily influenced by the expertise reversal effect. If learners do not have sufficient levels of expertise to imagine the relevant concepts and procedures, instructions to imagine them have negative rather than positive consequences compared with 'studying' instructions (Leahy and Sweller 2005).

Element interactivity effect

None of the above effects is obtainable using low element interactivity information. If the information imposes a low intrinsic cognitive load, how it is presented may have little consequence because even with an increase in extraneous cognitive load, working memory resources may be sufficient to enable processing. Accordingly, no differences may be obtained between instructional procedures when using low element interactivity information (e.g. Sweller and Chandler 1994). Cognitive load effects can be obtained only when dealing with complex, high intrinsic cognitive load information.

Conclusion

The case of cognitive load theory provides one example of how research in educational psychology has contributed to instructional procedures. Developed from a combination of knowledge of human cognitive architecture and empirical problem-solving studies, cognitive load theory has generated a large range of effects, some of which have been surveyed in this chapter. In turn, instructional predictions that flow from these effects provide a theoretical base that leads to practical applications for instruction. It must be emphasized, of course, that there are many other examples of the importance of educational psychology to education.

Knowledge of human cognitive architecture is pivotal to the development of cognitive load theory. Without that knowledge, the effectiveness of instructional designs is likely to be random. Furthermore, all the cognitive load effects discussed above have been generated and replicated over many experiments and across a variety of domains. The instructional techniques associated with these cognitive load effects have been extensively tested experimentally for effectiveness. In this context, the importance of randomized, controlled experiments to those streams of educational psychology concerned with instructional procedures cannot be overlooked. Not only do randomized controlled experiments enhance theory development, but more importantly, they are critical when determining the effectiveness of instructional processes. For example, the isolation of optimal conditions for learning from goal-free problems, various forms of worked examples, and mixed mode presentations, and the conditions under which split-attention and redundancy can occur and therefore be avoided, would not have been possible without randomized controlled experimentation. Proper testing, using randomized, controlled experiments that takes into account learning processes, needs to be carried out before instructional procedures can be effectively introduced into education. The use of replicated, randomized, controlled experimental designs is a major strength of cognitive load theory and the instructional procedures that it has generated.

References

Ayres, P. and Sweller, J. (2005) 'The split-attention principle', in R.E. Mayer (ed.) *Cambridge Handbook of Multimedia Learning* (pp. 135–46), New York: Cambridge University Press.

Baddeley, A. (1986) *Working Memory*, Oxford: Oxford University Press.

Baddeley, A. (1992) 'Working memory', *Science*, 255: 556–9.

Baddeley, A. (1999) *Human Memory*, Boston: Allyn and Bacon.

Bandura, A. (1986) *Social Foundations of Thought and Action: A Social Cognitive Theory*, Englewoods Cliffs, NJ: Prentice Hall.

Bartlett, F.C. (1932) *Remembering: A Study in Experimental and Social Psychology*, Oxford: Macmillan.

Chandler, P. and Sweller, J. (1991) 'Cognitive load theory and the format of instruction', *Cognition and Instruction*, 8: 293–332.

Chandler, P. and Sweller, J. (1996) 'Cognitive load while learning to use a computer program', *Applied Cognitive Psychology*, 10: 151–70.

Chase, W.G. and Simon, H.A. (1973) 'Perception in chess', *Cognitive Psychology*, 4: 55–81.

Cooper, G. and Sweller, J. (1987) 'Effects of schema acquisition and rule automation on mathematical problem-solving transfer', *Journal of Educational Psychology*, 79: 347–62.

Cooper, G., Tindall-Ford, S., Chandler, P. and Sweller, J. (2001) 'Learning by imagining', *Journal of Experimental Psychology: Applied*, 7: 68–82.

De Groot, A. ([1946] 1965) *Thought and Choice in Chess*, The Hague: Mouton.

Ericsson, K.A. and Kintsch, W. (1995) 'Long-term working memory', *Psychological Review*, 102: 211–45.

Geary, D. (2007) 'Educating the evolved mind: conceptual foundations for an evolutionary educational psychology', in J.S. Carlson and J.R. Levin (eds) *Psychological Perspectives on Contemporary Educational Issues* (pp. 1–99), Greenwich, CT: Information Age Publishing.

Gick, M.L. and Holyoak, K.J. (1983) 'Schema induction and analogical transfer', *Cognitive Psychology*, 15: 1–38.

Ginns, P. (2005a) 'Meta-analysis of the modality effect', *Learning and Instruction*, 15: 313–31.

Ginns, P. (2005b) 'Imagining instructions: mental practice in highly cognitive domains', *Australian Journal of Education*, 49: 128–40.

Ginns, P. (2006) 'Integrating information: meta-analyses of the spatial contiguity and temporal contiguity effects', *Learning and Instruction*, 16: 511–25.

Kalyuga, S., Ayres, P., Chandler, P. and Sweller, J. (2003) 'The expertise reversal effect', *Educational Psychologist*, 38: 23–31.

Kalyuga, S., Chandler, P. and Sweller, J. (1998) 'Levels of expertise and instructional design', *Human Factors*, 40: 1–17.

Kotovsky, K., Hayes, J. and Simon, H. (1985) 'Why are some problems hard? Evidence from Tower of Hanoi', *Cognitive Psychology*, 17: 248–94.

Leahy, W. and Sweller, J. (2005) 'Interactions among the imagination, expertise reversal, and element interactivity effects', *Journal of Experimental Psychology: Applied*, 11: 266–76.

Low, R. and Sweller, J. (2005) 'The modality principle', in R.E. Mayer (ed.) *Cambridge Handbook of Multimedia Learning* (pp. 147–58), New York: Cambridge University Press.

Miller, G.A. (1956) 'The magical number seven, plus or minus two: some limits on our capacity for processing information', *Psychological Review*, 63: 81–97.

Mousavi, S.Y., Low, R. and Sweller, J. (1995) 'Reducing cognitive load by mixing auditory and visual presentation modes', *Journal of Educational Psychology*, 87: 319–34.

Newell, A. and Simon, H.A. (1972) *Human Problem Solving*, Englewood Cliffs, NJ: Prentice Hall.

Paas, F. and Van Merrienboer, J.J. (1994) 'Variability of worked examples and transfer of geometrical problem-solving skills: a cognitive-load approach', *Journal of Educational Psychology*, 86: 122–33.

Peterson, L. and Peterson, M.J. (1959) 'Short-term retention of individual verbal items', *Journal of Experimental Psychology*, 58: 193–8.

Pollock, E., Chandler, P. and Sweller, J. (2002) 'Assimilating complex information', *Learning and Instruction*, 12: 61–86.

Renkl, A., Atkinson, R.K., Maier, U.H. and Staley, R. (2002) 'From example study to problem solving: smooth transitions help learning', *Journal of Experimental Education*, 70: 293–315.

Schneider, W. and Detweiler, M. (1987) 'A connectionist/control architecture for working memory', in G. Bower (ed.) *The Psychology of Learning and Motivation* (vol. 21, pp. 53–119), New York: Academic Press.

Schneider, W. and Shiffrin, R.M. (1977) 'Controlled and automatic human information processing: I. Detection, search, and attention' *Psychological Review*, 84: 1–66.

Simon, H. (1974) 'How big is a chunk?', *Science*, 183: 482–8.

Sweller, J. (1976) 'The effect of task complexity and sequence on rule learning and problem solving', *British Journal of Psychology*, 67: 553–8.

Sweller, J. (1994) 'Cognitive load theory, learning difficulty, and instructional design', *Learning and Instruction*, 4: 295–312.

Sweller, J. (2003) 'Evolution of human cognitive architecture', in B. Ross (ed.) *The Psychology of Learning and Motivation* (vol. 43, pp. 215–66), San Diego: Academic Press.

Sweller, J. (2004) 'Instructional design consequences of an analogy between evolution by natural selection and human cognitive architecture', *Instructional Science*, 32: 9–31.

Sweller, J. (2005) 'The redundancy principle', in R.E. Mayer (ed.) *Cambridge Handbook of Multimedia Learning* (pp. 159–67), New York: Cambridge University Press.

Sweller, J. and Chandler, P. (1994) 'Why some material is difficult to learn', *Cognition and Instruction*, 12: 185–233.

Sweller, J., Chandler, P., Tierney, P. and Cooper, M. (1990) 'Cognitive load as a factor in the structuring of technical material', *Journal of Experimental Psychology: General*, 119: 176–92.

Sweller, J., Mawer, R.F. and Ward, M.R. (1983) 'Development of expertise in mathematical problem solving', *Journal of Experimental Psychology: General*, 112: 639–61.

Sweller, J. and Sweller, S. (2006) 'Natural information processing systems', *Evolutionary Psychology*, 4: 434–58.

Sweller, J., van Merrienboer, J.J. and Paas, F.G. (1998) 'Cognitive architecture and instructional design', *Educational Psychology Review*, 10: 251–96.

Tindall-Ford, S., Chandler, P. and Sweller, J. (1997) 'When two sensory modes are better than one', *Journal of Experimental Psychology: Applied*, 3: 257–87.

Yeung, A.S., Jin, P. and Sweller, J. (1997) 'Cognitive load and learner expertise: split-attention and redundancy effects in reading with explanatory notes', *Contemporary Educational Psychology*, 23: 1–21.

Chapter 7

Assessment and evaluation

John A. Hattie and Gavin T.L. Brown

The New Zealand education system values teacher and school professional judgements, but there is an ever-present pressure to have a layer of assessment to convince policy-makers and parents that 'all is well' in the system. In the past decade, a number of initiatives have been implemented to provide policy-makers with evidence of the success of the system. These include the development of the Assessment Tools for Teaching and Learning (asTTle) suite of assessments, with its emphasis on reporting to teachers, schools, students and the system; the remodelling of the long-standing Progressive Achievement Tests (PAT); the emergence of the National Certificate of Educational Achievement; a much more dependable University Scholarships examinations system; a re-examination of the School Entry Assessment Kit (which schools are encouraged to administer in the first weeks of schooling) and the Six Year Net (administered one year later); the use of value-added models (via the Centre for Evaluation and Monitoring); the development of exemplars to provide more consistency of standards; the regular use of a few standardized tests (e.g. Burt word reading, Schonell spelling, and so on); and the continuation of the National Education Monitoring Project (NEMP). (Details of each assessment can be found in Brown *et al* 2008a).

This chapter outlines two assessment-related issues – the measurement contributions that have accrued from the development of a national reporting engine for assessment (asTTle), and research on the conceptions of assessment held by teachers and how this affects their assessment decisions and interpretations.

The nature of assessment

Assessment relates to the identification of characteristics, and evaluation relates to the establishment of value and worth of a product, process, person, policy or programme. Assessment refers to 'What's so?' and evaluation to 'So what?' Both depend on high-quality measurement, and both focus on the qualities, degrees, and characteristics of student learning of the material deemed important by society and identified in the curriculum. The validity and reliability of such assessments and evaluations depend on our ability to specify what is to be learned and defensible measures of progress in each curriculum domain.

The process of assessing and evaluating learning involves designing and using appropriate methods of collecting information about learning, converting the collected data into metrics related to important stages of progression in learning, and interpreting those metrics in such a way that appropriate decisions and actions are taken (Messick 1989). Measurement of learning involves accepting that all assessment and evaluation processes are subject to error, mis-specification, and/or a degree of randomness (Lord and Novick 1968). A major point of measurement, then, is to identify confounding elements in the assessment of learning, allowing the identification of an accurate signal within the noisy web of information about student learning. Indeed, the educational measurement community has attempted to capture the relevant knowledge and expertise associated with measurement in four editions of a handbook (e.g. Brennan 2006), published jointly by the American Psychological Association (APA), the American Educational Research Association (AERA), and the National Council for Measurement in Education (NCME); and in *Standards for Educational and Psychological Testing*, published by the same three organizations (AERA, APA, and NCME 1999). Topics considered pertinent to high quality educational assessment include: validity, reliability and generalizability; item response theory; scaling and norming; linking and equating; test fairness and bias; standard setting; test development and construction; performance assessment; use of technology in testing; second language testing; testing for accountability in compulsory schooling; standardized assessment of individual achievement in schools; higher education admissions testing; monitoring educational progress; licensure and certification testing; and legal and ethical issues. Clearly, the range of concerns within educational measurement is large and test users (such as teachers) need some awareness of these fundamental issues. The consequences of inappropriately measuring student learning, regardless of the method used, and making the wrong decision are grave for test developers, test administrators, test-takers, and society in general.

Traditionally, educational assessment has used tests of curriculum knowledge, memory, understanding, analysis, or application. Shepard (2001, 2006) makes it clear that most educational assessment is carried out in classrooms by teachers and that significant improvements are needed in how testing might continue to play a part in that process. Kane (2006) has claimed that teachers are expected to make a series of qualitative interpretations about observed student performances, as well as interpretations of test scores. These interpretations occur as teachers interact with students in the classroom and are not simply recorded for later interpretation. In New Zealand, teachers are expected to observe, interact with, and respond to student learning activities within the context of in-the-moment instructional and learning programmes:

> The primary purpose of assessment is to improve students' learning and teachers' teaching as both student and teacher respond to the information that it provides. With this in mind, schools need to consider how they will

gather, analyze, and use assessment information so that it is effective in meeting this purpose.

(Ministry of Education 2007: 39)

Assessment for the purpose of improving student learning is best understood as an ongoing process that arises out of the interaction between teaching and learning. It involves the focused and timely gathering, analysis, interpretation, and use of information that can provide evidence of student progress. Much of this evidence is 'of the moment'. Analysis and interpretation often take place in the mind of the teachers, who then use the insights gained to shape their actions as they continue to work with their students.

It is assumed that the teacher, who has personal knowledge of the learner and the learning programme and who has sufficiently profound understanding of learning progressions and targets, will be able to assess and evaluate student learning accurately and validly without having to resort to formal measures (i.e. tests) of learning. Furthermore, given the persistent contact teachers have with learners and the multiple opportunities that provides for of-the-moment assessment, it must be assumed that any error, mis-specification or randomness in the decisions and actions taken by the teacher should have little or no negative effect on the learner. This type of educational assessment is often called assessment *for* learning (Black *et al.* 2003) or formative assessment (Sadler 1989).

This view dominates much of teacher education and teacher professional development; the interactive, on-the-fly judgement of the teacher who has intimate knowledge of students is considered the gold standard of assessment. Such a framework takes Sadler's (1989) position that formative assessment is a qualitatively different process from summative assessment, in contrast to Scriven's (1991) position that formative evaluations must be of equal quality to summative ones (and we would argue that if formative evaluation is deemed more important, maybe it needs to be of higher quality). Objectively-scored tests (e.g. asTTle, PAT) are often misleadingly perceived by many teachers as summative devices that add little or no formative value to the practice of classroom teaching (simply because they are 'objective'). Given these views, these assessments are often then treated as accountability tools by which schools can demonstrate effectiveness to inspectors, the Ministry of Education, and the public. This is clearly a misunderstanding of the notions of formative and summative.

Formative and summative debates

The terms formative and summative were introduced by Michael Scriven more than 30 years ago (Scriven 1967). As Scriven outlined, the distinction between formative and summative is more related to interpretations and time – as illustrated by Bob Stake's maxim (quoted in Scriven 1991): 'When the cook tastes the soup, it is formative, when the guests taste the soup, it is summative.' Thus, a key issue is timing, and it is possible that the same stimulus (e.g. tasting the soup) can be interpreted and used for both purposes of assessment. The key distinctions are the *timing* of the interpretation and the purpose to which the information is used.

It is not the test that is summative or formative, but the interpretations made from any test scores. Thus, it is possible to take what many (mistakenly) consider a 'summative test' (e.g. the PATs or asTTle) and use the feedback information from them to make decisions that enhance the programme (improve the soup) while it is still in progress, and/or to make statements about students when they have completed a programme of study. As Scriven (1991) has noted, it is a fallacy to assume that formative and summative represent two types of assessment. Instead, they refer to interpretations of information at two differing times – either to make interpretations that can then lead to changing a programme of learning or that can lead to a statement about the learning at the end of the programme.

In the same way that the goal of the cook is to make the best soup possible for the guests, it is imperative that teachers have excellent summative evaluation in place in their classes (and likewise principals for their schools) as such evaluation can be a powerful source of evidence that there is excellent formative evaluation in place. Poor soup for the guests is pretty powerful evidence of poor cooking. Similarly, if a school has poor summative assessment in place, then it is unlikely it will have the ability, purpose, or wherewithal to be concerned with high quality formative assessment. Serving poor soup to the guests is probably the best indicator that the cook was lousy at tasting it during the preparations. At the same time, too much reliance on tasting the soup may lead to inattention to key goals – such as serving tasty soup to the guests at the right temperature at the right time. The goals or learning intentions are critical aspects of this process, and can have major effects on the usefulness of the formative and/or summative evaluation. The soup tasting allows the chef to monitor whether the soup cooking is on track to reach the goals. Hence, assessment alone will not raise achievement, but without it teachers would lack insights as to what (different) instructional practices are effective and required.

There can be occasions when we do *not* know when administering an assessment whether only formative or summative interpretations will be made. For example, a teacher may consider evaluating the course of teaching by using an end-of-course test, but then find that remedial work is necessary, making the test interpretations more formative than originally intended. Similarly, formative interpretations can indicate to teachers that students have made adequate progress, suggesting that it is time to move on to other topics. Hence, formative intentions can be turned into summative interpretations and vice versa.

Without accurate in-course formative assessments, it is all too likely that teachers will send students in a wrong direction, possibly at wrong speed, and with less chance of reaching the goals. Too often we underestimate the importance of accuracy and dependability in formative assessment – diagnosis, feedback, and subsequent instruction need to be excellent. The major message is that teachers need to be constantly attending to the *quality* of the assessments they use for both summative and formative interpretations.

The stance we take here is in strong contrast to the currently popular view that assessment *for* learning or formative assessment is a completely different kind of process from measurement or testing (Sadler 1989). Two significant reviews of research on classroom or formative assessment practices have argued that greater achievement outcomes are found when non-summative assessment is used (Black and Wiliam 1998; Crooks 1988). (It is worth noting that evidence to the contrary is arising, see Dunn and Mulvenon 2009, suggesting that the virtuous claim of assessment for learning is still being tested.) Assessment *for* learning prioritizes the use of assessment as a means of discovering what children need to be taught next so as to engage and motivate them to monitor and regulate their own learning (e.g. Brookhart 2004; Harlen 2007; Weeden *et al.* 2002). Indeed, assessment *for* learning is seen by many as predominantly about engaging, motivating, and enabling students to improve their own learning (Black and Wiliam 1998; Brookhart 1997, 2009). Black and Wiliam (2006) have hinted that this approach is more than a theory of assessment, but is rather an incipient theory of pedagogy.

From this definition of formative assessment, some consensus has arisen as to strategies that make tangible the formative effects. Leahy *et al.* (2005: 20) identified

> five broad strategies to be equally powerful for teachers of all content areas and at all grade levels: clarifying and sharing learning intentions and criteria for success; engineering effective classroom discussions, questions, and learning tasks; providing feedback that moves learners forward; activating students as owners of their own learning; and activating students as instructional resources for one another.

There has been a great flurry of activity in educational circles to discover, test, and propagate these strategies (e.g. Black *et al.* 2003; Carless *et al.* 2006; Clarke 2005; Harlen 2007; Weeden *et al.* 2002). Shavelson provides an eloquent summary of the assessment for learning logic:

> Formative assessment should be carried out by teachers in the service of student learning because such assessment makes clear learning goals, indexes where students are with respect to those goals, and, consequently, reveals a gap between what is and what is not desired. Moreover, the logic goes, formative assessment would require teachers to use their knowledge of 'the gap' to provide timely feedback to students as to how they might close that gap . . . By embedding assessments that elicit students' explanations – formally within a unit, as part of a lesson plan, or as 'on-the-fly' teachable moments occur – teachers would take this opportunity to close the gap in student understanding. As a consequence students' learning would be expected to improve.
>
> (Shavelson 2008: 293)

It appears the major point of this approach to formative assessment is to reduce the emphasis on testing, which is seen as a mechanism of summative evaluation of students and/or schools, in order to emphasize a more student-centric approach to improved learning (Gipps 1994; Torrance and Pryor 1998). Harlen (2007: 121) stated baldly that assessment for learning 'is not a measurement; it does not lead to grades or levels'. Any assessment system that involves tests or regular activities that are interpreted in relation to performance criteria and which are reported are deemed summative assessment of learning; reliability of judgements against common criteria are key characteristics of this form of assessment (Harlen 2007). One might almost suspect that this strong antipathy towards testing and measurement among UK advocates of assessment for learning is based on a political rejection of the frequent high-stakes testing regime (i.e. Key Stage tests) practised in England for nearly the past two decades. It may well be that tests, in a low-stakes context such as New Zealand, are not automatically consigned to the rubbish bin of summative, accountability measures. For example, there is clear evidence that some New Zealand teachers are able to make use of standardized, curriculum-aligned tests for the improvement of their classroom teaching and students' learning (Archer 2009; Brown and Harris 2009; McDowall *et al.* 2007; Parr and Timperley 2008).

Strong arguments have been made that formative assessment is more powerful when students undertake these assessments relative to their own work (Absolum *et al.* 2009). For example, placing too much emphasis on the role of the teacher in formative assessment is believed to create a negative, over-dependence on the teacher (Weeden *et al.* 2002). Indeed, Brookhart (2009: 2) argued that formative assessment is a big deal because 'it puts feelings of power and control over learning in the hands of students'. While Brookhart (2009) grants a place for teachers in formative assessment, her priority is that, ultimately, it is students who are users of assessment information. At its extreme, this student-centric definition of formative assessment may seem to minimize the role for teachers. However, we contend there is an important role for teachers; students, as novices, must obtain high quality, accurate understanding and feedback from experts (i.e. the teachers) (Bloom *et al.* 1981). Indeed, the importance and relevance of teachers' role in formative assessment have been demonstrated in New Zealand by studies which show that student learning gains come when teachers develop simultaneously their knowledge of the content being taught and skills in interpreting assessment evidence (Parr and Timperley 2008).

Thus, assessment for learning, despite its laudable aims, has taken on a flavour which is antithetical to measurement, testing, and the legitimacy of those processes in the hands of teachers. Given the conflicts over how these terms are used, perhaps it is time to abandon them. Talking about formative and summative assessments, using informative assessment information for summative purposes, and so on are very misleading (consider also Newton 2007). We suggest that appropriate and defensible interpretation of assessment information is the primary aim of assessment, and more discussion about such interpretations (regardless of timing, purpose, tests used) may be a more fruitful debate. Providing evidence for appropriate and defensible interpretation of assessment information is at the heart of the concept of 'validity'. Tests are not valid, scores are not valid, but interpretations and actions can be valid – and sufficient evidence for these interpretations is the cornerstone of an excellent assessment system (Messick 1992).

The quality of teacher judgements

It would appear a measurement-free assessment community, practice, and mindset have grown up in New Zealand. The measurement-free community is represented by assessment advice delivered in some texts (e.g. Absolum 2006; Clarke *et al.* 2003), professional developers (e.g. those delivering the Assessment for Better Learning and Assess to Learn programmes), and subject experts or primary school specialists (e.g. Aitken 2000; Dixon and Williams 2002; Hill 2000; Knight 2003) who have developed an interest in assessment from their curriculum and pedagogy roles. This group views assessment primarily as professional teacher judgement about student learning.

Psychometric concerns (e.g. identifying and controlling for error and imprecision) are noticeably absent in this emphasis on teacher judgement. Apparently the position is that not only does every teacher make an accurate and valid evaluation, but no evidence is required to ascertain the degree of consistency within raters across times, persons, or tasks, the consistency between raters, or the consistency between raters and other measures. As well, the notion of measurement (i.e. location of performance on a scale of progression) appears to be given little but passing mention. While it is legitimate to emphasize a broader construction of classroom assessment than simply testing, it seems problematic in that the current emphasis appears to avoid measurement issues or concerns.

It is a given that any student may perform better or worse depending on the questions asked, the context of the questioning (particularly in front of peers), and the attitudinal and physical disposition of the student (he/she may be unwell), and different teachers may give different scores and interpretations for the same work. These issues are at the heart of the concept of reliability. It is surprising so little information is available on the degree of reliability of teacher assessments or even many public examinations (see Black and Wiliam 2006). For example, Wiliam (2001) concluded that the chances of a student's level in the Key Stage tests in England being wrong by one level were about 20 to 30 per cent! As Black and Wiliam concluded, that teachers 'may be unaware of the limited reliability of their own tests is thus a serious issue' (2006: 130). This lack of awareness can lead to students and teachers being seriously misled.

The use of modern measurement in New Zealand

To remedy this situation, there has been a move in New Zealand for teachers to introduce 'classroom' tests with known high levels of reliability to augment other teacher-made assessments and judgements. These assessments are based on internationally recognized high standards of measurement based on modern test methods. This measurement community is represented by some recent texts (e.g. Brown *et al* 2008a), test developers (e.g. asTTle, PAT, NEMP), and measurement experts who have sought to apply measurement theory and disciplines in the field of education. Related to this community are evidence-based professional developers and evaluators who argue for more dependable interpretations of assessment data (e.g. Parr and Timperley 2008; Robinson *et al.* 2002; Timperley 2003).

One such system is the asTTle application, and features of this system are used to illustrate the uses of modern measurement in the class. Teachers had access to the system via CD-ROM (Versions 1 to 4) and now e-asTTle (an internet-based version implemented over the past two years). They can use wizards to create tests with various 'constraints' such as the curriculum processes or objectives, the time of testing, the format of the test (paper, on-screen, computer sequential adaptive), the proportion of open to closed items in the test, and there are pre-specified constraints (e.g. ensuring that the test has at least 30 per cent surface and 30 per cent deep cognitive complexity). The 'objective function' that is maximized is the distribution of difficulty, which the teachers judge by estimating the proportion of students in their class at each of the New Zealand curriculum levels or years. A linear programming heuristic then searches a data base of 5,000 items in each of reading or mathematics to create the optimal test (Fletcher 2000; van der Linden 2005). Given this number of items, there are literally millions of tests possible using this method, all guaranteed to have high reliability and fidelity to the chosen specifications by the teachers. Such optimal tests have many desirable measurement properties (e.g. maximizing the information at each part of the difficulty distribution; fitting the curriculum objectives).

Each of the items was evaluated, initially by using a norm sample (about 90,000) and now by extracting data from trial items embedded in normed tests (school leaders can turn on permissions to allow these data to be extracted). Using a three-parameter item response model, items are checked for issues with guessing, then a two-parameter model is used to maximize discrimination, and finally a one-parameter model is used to estimate difficulty. Various standard setting methods (e.g. modified Angoff, bookmarking) have been used to set cut scores for the various curriculum levels, and normative and curriculum expectation data have been developed to be fed back to teachers via interpretative reports (all reports are published at www.asTTle.org.nz). A major study of the mode effects was conducted before moving from the paper to on-screen testing, and this identified the more important aspects, such as scrolling and reviewing, that needed closer vigilance to ensure both methods led to similar results (Leeson 2006).

The most critical development has been the processes for creating the various reports from the assessments. This process goes to the heart of the validity issues, so central to decades of debates about test theory. Over the various editions of the *Standards for Educational and Psychological Testing*, the essence of validity has moved from the characteristics of the test itself, through the interpretation of scores to the more recent emphasis on the adequacy and appropriateness of inferences and actions based on test scores. No longer do we worry about whether the 'test does the job it was employed to do' (Cureton 1951: 621), but we are now more concerned about a more prescriptive set of arguments about whether the decisions based on the test results are defensible (Kane 2006). The 1999 and latest set of *Standards* considered that validity referred to the 'degree to which evidence and theory support the interpretations of test scores entailed by proposed uses of tests' (AERA, APA and NCME 1999: 9). 'The process of validation involves accumulating evidence to provide a sound scientific basis for the proposed score interpretations. As noted earlier, it is the interpretations of test scores required by proposed uses that are evaluated, not the test itself' (ibid.: 9).

That there are many, and often unanticipated, readers of test reports means that any report must include sufficient information about the choice of the test, the context of administration of the test, and the psychometric evaluation for the defence of the test scores representing the student's proficiencies presented in the report. In a sense there is a four-part snooker operating – there are report validity arguments relating to: (1) the choice of the test; (2) the administration of the test (e.g. computer or pencil and paper); (3) the psychometric evaluation of the dependability of the scores; and (4) the accuracy and appropriateness with which the reader interprets this information. All are related, all are important, and all interact with each other.

The latest published version of the *Standards* has little to say about reports. There are admonitions that when 'test score information' is released to readers, 'those responsible for testing programmes should provide appropriate interpretations. The interpretations should describe in simple language what the test covers, what scores mean, the precision of the scores, common misinterpretations of test scores, and how scores will be used' (Standard 5.10). The *Standards* do stipulate that 'when computer prepared interpretations of test result protocols are reported, the sources, rationale, and empirical bias for these interpretations should be available, and their limitations described' (Standard 5.11). These statements are more cautions and they provide little guidance on the need for empirical evidence, and therefore there needs to be much more attention to the evidence to justify various interpretations *and ensuring that it is these interpretations that are appropriately made by the reader.*

We have argued that the validity of reports is a function of the reader's correct and appropriate inferences and/or actions about the test taker's performance based on the scores from the test. This claim places much reliance on the developer of reports to provide compelling evidence that readers make correct and appropriate inferences and actions based on the reports provided. To address this claim about validity, there is a minimum requirement to provide evidence that readers correctly answer two major questions: What do you see? What would you do next? These two questions focus on the two most critical aspects of validity: that appropriate interpretations and actions from reports are undertaken by readers and that how readers answer these questions is aligned with the intentions of the report developer. There can be many sources of validity evidence to ascertain whether a report can lead to valid interpretations of these two questions (Hattie 2009). From a series of formative evaluations, the asTTle development team has ascertained that accurate interpretation of the asTTle reports is obtained through appropriate professional development and through judicious adjustments to the report display (Hattie *et al.* 2006).

Conceptions of assessment

The emphasis on reports means we need to know much more about conceptions of assessment held by teachers, since these conceptions can potentially be influenced by providing teachers with knowledge about interpreting assessment information. Conceptions of assessment refer to the perceptions people have about assessment based on their experiences with and of assessment. Strong conceptions are more likely to predict behaviours (Ajzen 2002); hence, it matters to identify not only which conceptions are present, but also to know how those conceptions are structured and how they relate to other beliefs, behaviours, and outcomes. Using survey questionnaires and structural equation modelling, it has been possible to identify the structure of teachers' and secondary students' conceptions of assessment and relate those to conceptions of teaching, learning, curriculum, and efficacy; assessment practices; definitions of assessment; and student learning outcomes.

Teachers' conceptions of assessment

Teachers appear to have four major conceptions of assessment (Brown 2008). First, assessment can lead to improvement of both teaching and students' learning. A second perception is that assessment makes students accountable by scoring, grading, or certification; this conception is particularly evident among high school teachers (Brown 2007). A third conception is that assessment is used to hold schools and teachers accountable by showing the quality of education provided. Teachers in New Zealand and Queensland consistently give low mean scores to this conception (Brown and Lake 2006), but there is a moderate positive correlation between this and the improvement conception (average $r \approx .55$) suggesting that teachers understand high-quality schools cause improvements in learning and that this can be seen in assessment scores. The fourth perception, called 'irrelevance', is that assessment plays no meaningful purpose in education because it is bad for students, is ignored by teachers, and has error. This conception is inversely correlated with improvement – the more assessment is for improvement, the less it is viewed as irrelevant. Among teachers surveyed in New Zealand and Queensland (Brown 2007; Brown and Lake 2006), irrelevance is positively correlated with student accountability – grading students is seen as the negative aspect of assessment. In contrast, Hong Kong teachers surveyed with a Chinese language version of the inventory positively associated student accountability with improvement ($r = .91$) (Brown *et al.* 2009). These results indicate that cultural and policy factors can affect teachers' conceptions of assessment, suggesting that in societies with high-stakes student assessment, teachers will conceive and respond to assessment differently from teachers in low-stakes contexts.

New Zealand primary school teachers (in contrast to the overall findings reported above) appear to have four major integrated conceptions of teaching and assessment (Brown 2008). The first conception is a teacher-centred, content-focused orientation towards schooling in which students are taught to reproduce facts and details for assessments that are used for accountability for which teachers are confident they can prepare students. The second perception is a student-centred, learning-oriented, formative conception of teaching and assessing to improve. This conception suggests that teachers associate deep learning with nurturing, developmental, and apprenticeship teaching perspectives, and the use of assessment to improve the quality of teaching and learning. The third conception is a liberationist conception of teaching and curriculum as reform or reconstruction of society (Fenstermacher and Soltis 1998). This conception focuses on the role of instruction and curriculum to reform or reconstruct society through a deliberate focus on social issues and problems. The fourth conception, 'assessment against learning', is related to notions that assessment is bad, inaccurate, and ignored and that external obstacles interfere with teachers' sense of efficacy. This conception associates assessment with being bad for students or something to be ignored, with a sense of powerlessness within the teacher. However, among New Zealand primary teachers there is a low level of agreement with this negative conception of assessment. This may be attributable to the low-stakes assessment policies and practices in New Zealand primary schools. It is expected that this conception would be much more robust if stakes for students or teachers were raised within the assessment system. Maintaining low-stakes with government-authorized testing-systems (e.g. asTTle, Assessment Resource Bank, exemplars, etc.), as advocated by Hattie and Brown (2008), may be necessary to avoid teachers picking up a negative conception of assessment.

Teachers' assessment practices can be predicted by the teachers' conceptions of assessment. Based on responses of 239 New Zealand primary teachers, Brown (2009) identified four assessment practices: (1) test-like formats; (2) interactive-informal formats; (3) transformational cognitive processes; and (4) the reproduction of cognitive processes. Teachers claimed to use the interactive and transformational types of assessments significantly more than they used test-like or surface processing assessments. The links between these claimed practices and the teachers' conceptions of assessment were interesting. For example, the use of informal-interactive classroom assessments related to two negatively correlated conceptions of assessment (the conception of assessment as irrelevant, and the conception of assessment for improvement). Assessment of school quality was more likely measured by deeper processing (transformational cognitive processes), while student-accountability perceptions were associated with externally created assessments that measure surface knowledge. Much work is still needed to show teachers that this negative perception of tests could be misguided.

Students' conceptions of assessment

In similar vein, secondary students' conceptions of assessment have been investigated. In addition to developing a dependable inventory and measurement model for students' conceptions of assessment (Brown 2008), the research programme has linked students' conceptions to both their achievement in mathematics and reading and has linked conceptions to definitions of assessment. The proportion of variance explained in outcome measures by the pattern of students' conceptions of assessment has been substantial; some 24 per cent in reading (Brown and Hirschfeld 2008) and 20 per cent in mathematics (Brown *et al.* 2008b). In reading (Brown and Hirschfeld 2008), there were positive relations between students' conceptions that assessment is used to grade students and increased test performance, while conceptions that assessment is fun, is ignored, or is about school quality related to decreased achievement. In mathematics, students who perceived that assessment legitimately grades them, that they must actively use assessment to regulate their learning, and that teachers will use assessment to modify and improve instruction had higher academic performance (Brown *et al.* 2008b). At the same time, students who expected assessment to bring affective benefit to their class or themselves, believed assessment measured external factors such as intelligence, their future, or their school, and saw assessment as irrelevant received lower grades. Together these positive and negative predictions of academic outcomes are consistent with self-regulation practices founded on conceptions that assessment legitimately grades and can be used for improvement; while negative outcomes were associated with maladaptive motivations and external causal attributions founded on conceptions that assessment predicted external futures, was irrelevant, and was affectively beneficial.

It should be noted that while these structural models are robust, they have not proven consistently invariant among subpopulations. Hirschfeld and Brown (2009) reported that conceptions of assessment for Māori students were sub-stantially different from those of Pasifika, Pakeha, or Asian students; and concluded that the underlying model for Māori students was not appropriate. Walton (2009) has found that greater and lesser self-efficacy and interest in reading also create different structural relations between students' conceptions of assessment and academic performance.

Hence, it would appear that how students conceive assessment matters not only to outcomes, but also to relevant learning practices. The more assessment administrators and instructors are aware of the patterns and differences in how students conceive assessment events and processes, the better they will be able to help students achieve the best that they can. Conceptions of assessment seem to matter perhaps because assessment itself matters.

Discussion

The perceptions, beliefs, and intentions of teachers and students influence their learning behaviours and outcomes. Conceptions of assessment also detect real-world psychological responses to policy tensions (i.e. accountability and improvement) related to the use of assessment and contribute to our understanding of how various types of, and policies for, assessment might be evaluated by teachers and students. Given the psychometric community's current understanding of validation evidence, attention to conceptions of assessment is a relevant and powerful way to understand and predict the consequences of an assessment tool or policy.

Understanding teachers' and students' conceptions of assessment is critical if, as argued above, the appropriate and defensible interpretations and actions that follow from assessment are critical to the core concept of validity. There is a need not only to understand the optimal interpretations (and asTTle aims to provide such interpretations rather than provide scores and derivatives of scores, such as percentiles, stanines, and so on), but also to then understand how these provided interpretations intersect with the conceptions held by the major users – teachers and students. The development of a national reporting engine such as asTTle for the delivery of interpretative reports makes their understanding more accessible by teachers, school leaders and students. asTTle also provides a similar set of language terms (the lack of which often becomes a barrier to making valid interpretations), and curriculum-based functionalities linked to the most commonly used student and learning management systems.

There is a sound basis for the further development of measurement and assessment research in New Zealand. A major block is the lack of psychometricians and lack of training programmes, although the recently formed New Zealand Assessment Academy has this issue at the forefront of its agenda. As the developments in classroom assessment link more closely with the psychometric rigour of modern test theory, there is a strong basis for knowing 'Where are we going?' and 'How are we going?' and 'Where we should go next?' – in the classroom, in the school, and in the nation.

References

Absolum, M. (2006) *Clarity in the Classroom: Using Formative Assessment to Build Learning-Focused Relationships*, Auckland, NZ: Hachette Livre New Zealand.

Absolum, M., Flockton, L., Hattie, J.A.C., Hipkins, R. and Reid, I. (2009) *Directions for Assessment in New Zealand: Developing Students' Assessment Capabilities*, Wellington, NZ: Ministry of Education.

Aitken, R. (2000) 'Teacher perceptions of the use and value of formative assessment in secondary English programs', *Set: Research Information for Teachers*, 3: 15–20.

Ajzen, I. (2002) 'Residual effects of past on later behavior: habituation and reasoned action perspectives', *Personality and Social Psychology Review*, 6: 107–22.

American Educational Research Association (AERA), American Psychological Association (APA) and National Council for Measurement in Education (NCME) (1999)

Standards for Educational and Psychological Testing, Washington, DC: American Educational Research Association.

Archer, E. (2009) 'Beyond the rhetoric of formative assessment: seeking solutions for South Africa in New Zealand's Assessment Tools for Teaching and Learning', unpublished manuscript, University of Pretoria, South Africa.

Black, P., Harrison, C., Lee, C., Marshall, B. and Wiliam, D. (2003) *Assessment for Learning: Putting it into Practice*, Maidenhead: Open University Press.

Black, P. and Wiliam, D. (1998) 'Assessment and classroom learning', *Assessment in Education*, 5: 7–74.

Black, P. and Wiliam, D. (2006) 'Developing a theory of formative assessment', in J. Gardner (ed.) *Assessment and Learning* (pp. 81–100), London: Sage.

Bloom, B., Madaus, G.F. and Hastings, J.T. (1981) *Evaluation to Improve Learning*, New York: McGraw-Hill.

Brennan, R.L. (ed.) (2006) *Educational Measurement*, 4th edn, Westport, CT: Praeger.

Brookhart, S.M. (1997) 'A theoretical framework for the role of classroom assessment in motivating student effort and achievement', *Applied Measurement in Education*, 10: 161–80.

Brookhart, S.M. (2004) 'Classroom assessment: tensions and intersections in theory and practice', *Teachers College Record*, 106: 429–38.

Brookhart, S.M. (2009) 'Editorial', *Educational Measurement: Issues and Practice*, 28: 1–2.

Brown, G.T.L. (2007) 'Teachers' conceptions of assessment: comparing measurement models for primary and secondary teachers in New Zealand', paper presented at the New Zealand Association for Research in Education (NZARE) annual conference, Christchurch, NZ, December.

Brown, G.T.L. (2008) *Conceptions of Assessment: Understanding What Assessment Means to Teachers and Students*, New York: Nova Science Publishers.

Brown, G.T.L. (2009) 'Teachers' self-reported assessment practices and conceptions: using structural equation modelling to examine measurement and structural models', in T. Teo and M.S. Khine (eds) *Structural Equation Modeling in Educational Research: Concepts and Applications* (pp. 243–66), Rotterdam: Sense Publishers.

Brown, G.T.L. and Harris, L.R. (2009) 'Unintended consequences of using tests to improve learning: how improvement-oriented resources engender heightened conceptions of assessment as school accountability', *Journal of Multi-Disciplinary Evaluation*, 6: 68–91.

Brown, G.T.L. and Hirschfeld, G.H.F. (2008) 'Students' conceptions of assessment: links to outcomes', *Assessment in Education: Principles, Policy and Practice*, 15: 3–17.

Brown, G.T.L. Irving, S.E. and Keegan, P.J. (2008a) *An Introduction to Educational Assessment, Measurement, and Evaluation: Improving the Quality of Teacher-Based Assessment*, 2nd edn, Auckland, NZ: Pearson Education.

Brown, G.T.L., Irving, S.E. and Peterson, E.R. (2008b) 'Beliefs that make a difference: students' conceptions of assessment and academic performance,' paper presented at the Biannual Conference of the International Test Commission, Liverpool, July.

Brown, G.T.L., Kennedy, K.J., Fok, P.K., Chan, J.K.S. and Yu, W.M. (2009) 'Assessment for improvement: understanding Hong Kong teachers' conceptions and practices of assessment', *Assessment in Education: Policy, Principles and Practice*, 16: 347–63.

Brown, G.T.L. and Lake, R. (2006) 'Queensland teachers' conceptions of teaching, learning, curriculum and assessment: comparisons with New Zealand teachers', paper presented at the Annual Conference of the Australian Association for Research in Education (AARE), Adelaide, Australia, November.

Carless, D., Joughin, G., Liu, N.-F. and Associates (eds) (2006) *How Assessment Supports Learning: Learning-Oriented Assessment in Action*, Hong Kong: Hong Kong University Press.

Clarke, S. (2005) *Formative Assessment in the Secondary Classroom*, Abingdon: Hodder Murray.

Clarke, S., Timperley, H.S. and Hattie, J.A. (2003) *Unlocking Formative Assessment: Practical Strategies for Enhancing Students' Learning in the Primary and Intermediate Classroom*, New Zealand edn, Auckland, NZ: Hodder Moa Beckett.

Crooks, T. (1988) 'The impact of classroom evaluation practices on students', *Review of Educational Research*, 58: 438–81.

Cureton, E.E. (1951) 'Validity', in E.F. Lindquist (ed.) *Educational Measurement* (pp. 621–94), Washington, DC: American Council on Education.

Dixon, H. and Williams, R. (2002) 'Teachers' understanding and use of formative assessment in literacy learning', *New Zealand Annual Review of Education*, 12: 95–110.

Dunn, K.E. and Mulvenon, S.W. (2009) 'A critical review of research on formative assessments: the limited scientific evidence of the impact of formative assessments in education', *Practical Assessment Research and Evaluation*, 14, available at: http://pareonline.net/getvn.asp?v=14andn=17.

Fenstermacher, G.D. and Soltis, J.F. (1998) *Approaches to Teaching*, 3rd edn, New York: Teachers College Press.

Fletcher, R.B. (2000) *A Review of Linear Programming and its Application to the Assessment Tools for Teaching and Learning (asTTle) Projects* (Tech. Rep. No. 5), Auckland, NZ: University of Auckland, Project asTTle.

Gipps, C.V. (1994) *Beyond Testing: Towards a Theory of Educational Assessment*, London: Falmer Press.

Harlen, W. (2007) *Assessment of Learning*, Los Angeles: Sage.

Hattie, J.A. (2009) *Visible Learning: A Synthesis of Meta-Analyses in Education*, London: Routledge.

Hattie, J.A. and Brown, G.T.L. (2008) 'Technology for school-based assessment and assessment for learning: development principles from New Zealand', *Journal of Educational Technology Systems*, 36: 189–201.

Hattie, J.A., Brown, G.T.L., Ward, L., Irving, S.E. and Keegan, P.J. (2006) 'Formative evaluation of an educational assessment technology innovation: developers' insights into Assessment Tools for Teaching and Learning (asTTle)', *Journal of Multi-Disciplinary Evaluation*, 5, available at: http://survey.ate.wmich.edu/jmde/index.php/jmde_1/article/view/50/57.

Hill, M. (2000) 'Dot, slash, cross: how assessment can drive teachers to ticking instead of teaching', *Set: Research Information for Teachers*, pp. 21–5.

Hirschfeld, G.H.F. and Brown, G.T.L. (2009) 'Students' conceptions of assessment: factorial and structural invariance of the SCoA across sex, age, and ethnicity', *European Journal of Psychological Assessment*, 25: 30–8.

Kane, M.T. (2006) 'Validation', in R. L. Brennan (ed.) *Educational Measurement*, 4th edn (pp. 17–64), Westport, CT: Praeger.

Knight, N. (2003) 'Teacher feedback to students in numeracy lessons: are students getting good value?', *Set: Research Information for Teachers*, pp. 40–5.

Leahy, S., Lyon, C., Thompson, M. and Wiliam, D. (2005) 'Classroom assessment: minute by minute, day by day', *Educational Leadership*, 63: 18–24.

Leeson, H.V. (2006) 'The mode effect: a literature review of human and technological issues in computerized testing', *International Journal of Testing*, 6: 1–24.

Lord, F.M. and Novick, M.R. (1968) *Statistical Theories of Mental Test Scores*, Reading, MA: Addison-Wesley.

McDowall, S., Cameron, M., Dingle, R., Gilmore, A. and MacGibbon, L. (2007) *Evaluation of the Literacy Professional Development Project* (RMR No. 869), Wellington, NZ: Ministry of Education, Research Division.

Messick, S. (1989) 'Validity', in R. L. Linn (ed.) *Educational Measurement*, 3rd edn (pp. 13–103), Old Tappan, NJ: Macmillan.

Messick, S. (1992) 'The interplay of evidence and consequences in the validation of performance assessments', *Educational Researcher*, 23: 13–23.

Ministry of Education (2007) *The New Zealand Curriculum for English-Medium Teaching and Learning in Years 1–13*, Wellington, NZ: Learning Media.

Newton, P.E. (2007) 'Clarifying the purposes of educational assessment', *Assessment in Education: Principles, Policy and Practice*, 14: 149–70.

Parr, J.M. and Timperley, H. (2008) 'Teachers, schools and using evidence: considerations of preparedness', *Assessment in Education: Policy, Principles and Practice*, 15: 57–71.

Robinson, V., Phillips, G. and Timperley, H. (2002) 'Using achievement data for school-based curriculum review: a bridge too far?', *Leadership and Policy in Schools*, 1: 3–29.

Sadler, R. (1989) 'Formative assessment and the design of instructional systems', *Instructional Science*, 18: 119–44.

Scriven, M. (1967) 'The methodology of evaluation', in R.W. Tyler, R.M. Gagne and M. Scriven (eds) *Perspectives of Curriculum Evaluation* (vol. 1, pp. 39–83), Chicago: Rand McNally.

Scriven, M. (1991) 'Beyond formative and summative evaluation', in M.W. McLaughlin and D.C. Phillips (eds) *Evaluation and Education: At Quarter Century* (vol. 2, pp. 19–64), Chicago: NSSE.

Shavelson, R.J. (2008) 'Guest editor's introduction', *Applied Measurement in Education*, 21: 293–4.

Shepard, L.A. (2001) 'The role of classroom assessment in teaching and learning', in V. Richardson (ed.) *Handbook of Research on Teaching*, 4th edn (pp. 1066–101), Washington, DC: AERA.

Shepard, L.A. (2006) 'Classroom assessment', in R.L. Brennan (ed.) *Educational Measurement*, 4th edn (pp. 623–46), Westport, CT: Praeger.

Timperley, H. (2003) 'Evidence-based leadership: the use of running records', *New Zealand Journal of Educational Leadership*, 18: 65–76.

Torrance, H. and Pryor, J. (1998) *Investigating Formative Assessment: Teaching, Learning and Assessment in the Classroom*, Buckingham: Open University Press.

van der Linden, W.J. (2005) *Linear Models for Optimal Test Design*, New York: Springer.

Walton, F. (2009) 'Secondary students' conceptions of assessment mediated by self-motivational attitudes: effects on academic performance', unpublished master's thesis, University of Auckland, Auckland, NZ.

Weeden, P., Winter, J. and Broadfoot, P. (2002) *Assessment: What's in it for Schools?*, London: Routledge Falmer.

Wiliam, D. (2001) 'Reliability, validity, and all that jazz', *Education 3–13*, October: 17–21.

Chapter 8

Motivation, learning and instruction

Michael Townsend

In my recent experience, teacher requests for professional development on how to motivate students rank second only to requests about how to manage student behaviour. The irony is that solution of the second request would take care of the first. But, more importantly, the request implies that motivation is seen as something we 'do' or 'give' to students, rather than an internal state that students already have. A goal of this chapter is to encourage teachers to think less about how to motivate our students and more about how to instruct them in ways that encourage them to develop an internal motivational structure that is adaptive to learning.

Although the emphasis is on how our theoretical and scientific knowledge about motivation can be applied to instruction in educational contexts, much of what we need to know about motivation in classrooms can and should be found in our daily activities. Motivation is ever-present because all human behaviour is motivated. Further, our thinking about motivation has always been imbued with notions of practical utility. In education we are interested in motivation because we want children to enjoy learning, or be more likely to apply learning, or value school more highly. But the concepts of motivation that apply to stimulating a reluctant student to learn are the same as those involved in encouraging strangers to work together to keep a business profitable, or persuading nations to mutually address global threats.

Motivation in crisis

One of the difficulties in applying the concept of motivation is that it is not clear what motivation is. This inability to define motivation is seen as an 'identity crisis' by Martin Ford (1992). A similar view almost half a century ago, that the popularity of the concept of motivation was 'surprising' given that its meaning is 'scandalously vague' (Brown 1961: 24), is still reflected in most current writers who refer to the difficulties posed by the numerous, varied definitions that lead to disagreement about its precise nature (e.g. Pintrich and Schunk 2002). On the one hand, it can be defined so broadly that it embraces virtually everything we do; on the other, so narrowly that it explains only some behaviour some of the time.

In spite of this identity crisis, there are three elements at the heart of human motivation. First, what initiates people's behaviour or turns them on and off? In practical terms, what makes students want or not want to engage with school? Second, what determines the direction or choice of behaviour? For example, why do some students want to learn science yet others do not, or why do some students boast that they have *not* studied for an examination? Third, what determines the maintenance or regulation of our behaviour? For example, what makes one person persevere with a learning task, while another gives up?

These three elements are in a number of definitions of motivation. For example, Franken (1988) described motivation as concerned with the 'arousal, direction and, persistence of behaviour', while Bandura defines it as a multidimensional phenomenon that controls the 'selection, activation and sustained direction of behaviour' (1991: 158). In the context of achievement motivation, Stipek notes that theorists attempt to explain the 'initiation, direction and intensity of an individual's behaviour' (1988: 9).

Although there is some relative agreement that motivation refers to a force that impels us toward a chosen goal, it is easy to be overwhelmed by the variety of motivational theories. Some understanding of the range and variety of theoretical subconstructs that underlie motivation can be seen in Ford's (1992) summary of 32 different theories of motivation. Motivation has been studied from a number of major theoretical perspectives, including psychoanalytic theory, need or drive theories, operant learning theory, humanistic theory, social learning theory, cognitive theory and, more recently, sociocultural theory. Readers will also likely be familiar with expectancy value theory, field theory, cognitive dissonance theory, causal attribution theory, personal causation theory, learned helplessness theory, self-worth theory, self-determination theory, self-efficacy theory, goal-setting theory, and goal orientation theory. This list, while not exhaustive, provides a glimpse of the variety of mechanisms and processes that have been posited to underlie motivation. Motivation may be seen as a biological or physiological process, a hedonistic desire to seek pleasure and avoid pain, an unconscious or subconscious process, or as a conscious, goal-oriented, strategic process. Our commonsense beliefs about motivation and the ease with which we use the concept belie the complexity suggested here.

As a consequence of having many research programmes devoted to one theory or component of motivation, there has been relatively little integration of the field, such that the term itself has been described as a 'garbage pail' for a variety of poorly understood factors (Dewsbury 1978: 172).

This lack of an integrated view of motivation contributes to the confounding of motivation as internal psychological phenomena with aspects of the external environment. In education, many teachers feel a responsibility to 'give' motivation to their students, as though it exists independently of the students. Of course, it is important for teachers to create interesting lessons, to gather resources to support those lessons, to provide activities that meaningfully engage students and encourage self-belief, to model enthusiastic, mastery-oriented approaches to learning and to reinforce appropriate learning behaviours in their students. But these activities do not, in themselves, *create* motivation. As teachers we can influence the development of motivation but, ultimately, it remains an internal, self-developed, psychological state that cannot be given directly to someone. Nor can it be directly taken away!

The belief that motivation is a transportable entity influences our behaviour as teachers. For example, if we believe *task value* is an inherent quality of the task itself, we focus on which academic tasks to present to children, rather than on examining the existing values of the children we teach. Similarly, if we believe that *interest* is an inherent feature of a book, we focus on the selection of books rather than on understanding the existing interests of our students. Such conceptual confusion is not trivial since it may engender a simplified, mechanistic view of motivation that undermines attempts to influence motivational consequences. In the same way that punishment may lead to rebellion rather than the intended compliance, the teacher who attempts to encourage positive motivation in a child who has failed a task by saying 'Never mind, you did your best' may, in fact, encourage a negative self-belief that has negative consequences for motivation ('If the teacher thinks my best is still a failure, I must be dumb'). To reiterate, motivation is an *internal psychological* state that accounts for the initiation, direction and maintenance of behaviour.

Integration of motivation theories

Although research has become increasingly focused on components of motivation, made more diverse by different assumptions about human nature, there have been attempts to develop a meta-theory that organizes the major motivational constructs into a coherent model. One attempt to provide a comprehensive integration of motivational theory is Ford's (1992) motivational systems theory. Ford argued that public understanding of motivation is dominated by simplistic, mechanical conceptions of human motivation that view humans as at the mercy of internal or external forces beyond their control. In motivational systems theory, biological, environmental and behavioural influences on human behaviour are distinguished from motivational influences, the internal, psychological processes responsible for the initiation, direction and maintenance of behaviour. It is these processes we must understand for motivation to be a useful, unique and applicable concept. In Ford's synthesis of motivational theory there are three main components of motivation: goals, personal agency beliefs, and emotions. Goals refer to outcomes an individual hopes to achieve. Personal agency beliefs are similar to the constructs of self-efficacy (Bandura 1997) and control beliefs (e.g. deCharms 1968) where individuals develop expectancies of success at various tasks based on an understanding of their own skills, competencies and aptitudes. Emotions refer to the various forms of affect (e.g. pride, shame, guilt) that develop in learning contexts and serve to initiate and regulate learning behaviour. The remainder of this chapter focuses on these three components.

Goals

As people have different needs, so too do they have different goals that need to be satisfied. Different needs and goals may exist even among a group of students working on a common topic. While one child is trying to understand the instructional material, another wants to be accepted into the discussion group, while a third may feign interest to appear smart, and a fourth may wish to avoid doing any work. The attempt to satisfy these different needs and goals is what motivates different behaviours, thus goals are the cognitive representations of the force or energy that initiates arousal in motivation.

The variety of goals just mentioned has resulted in attempts to categorize types of goals. For example, Ford (1992) has described 24 human goals including three categories of within-person goals and three categories of person-environment goals. The *within-person* categories represent affective goals (e.g. be excited, happy, and healthy), cognitive goals (e.g. to explore, understand, and maintain self-worth), and personal organization goals (e.g. to feel in harmony with people and nature, and to experience heightened states of being). The *person-environment* categories represent self-assertive goals (e.g. to feel unique, able to make choices, validated, and 'a winner'), social relationship goals (e.g. feel we belong, meet social obligations, promote fairness and give support to others), and task goals (e.g. achieve mastery, be productive). All 24 goals are found in varying degrees in every child in every classroom in the country, and in every teacher.

Mastery and performance goals

Much research in education has focused on goal orientation, or the distinction between *mastery goals* and *performance goals* (Schunk *et al.* 2008). Mastery or learning goals focus on understanding, personal improvement and accomplishment; a student interested to know her family history is mastery goal-oriented. Performance goals focus on demonstrating superiority over others; a student wanting to be the highest scorer on a spelling test is performance goal-oriented.

Research has generally confirmed that, relative to performance-oriented students, those who adopt a mastery approach in classrooms show higher learning and motivation (ibid.) as a result of greater self-efficacy, greater persistence in the face of obstacles, greater appreciation of the value of their personal effort, greater willingness to accept academic challenges, and greater use of effective learning strategies, such as setting proximal goals and monitoring progress toward their goals. Students with a mastery orientation also maintain their interest and effort beyond their formal classroom lessons.

The effect of a performance approach to motivation is more complex. Our sporting heroes are often performance-oriented and aspire to be the best. But although they have achieved high levels of skill and maintain self-efficacious beliefs in their capacity to improve, such athletes may not give of their best in minor competitions, may avoid competition against comparable athletes if they are unsure of winning, and may even cheat (either by artificially enhancing their own performance or decreasing the chances of their competitors). In school, a performance-oriented student, even if trying to avoid being bottom of the class, may use low-level learning strategies such as memorization that discourage understanding, or make the minimal effort needed to reach the goal, or engage in self-handicapping behaviours (such as not studying) or cheating when they think the goal might be beyond them.

Another complexity to performance goals is that researchers have identified two kinds: performance-approach goals, where students want to look competent relative to others, and performance-avoidance goals, where students want to avoid looking incompetent relative to others. Motivation and achievement are most at risk when students adopt a performance-avoidance orientation (Midgley and Urdan 2001). In addition to their relatively low self-efficacy, low self-confidence, and relatively high anxiety about assessment (Midgley et al. 2001), such students are further disadvantaged by their self-handicapping behaviours of avoiding activities that would help further their learning. Performance-avoidance goals are maladaptive to learning.

Unfortunately, the longer students are at school, the more their performance orientation increases while their mastery orientation decreases (Elliot and McGregor 2000). This is likely because older students are more aware of individual differences between learners, that effort does not necessarily ensure success, and that assessment assumes greater importance at higher levels. This understanding of goal orientation has resulted in investigations of its applicability to classroom instruction (Schunk et al. 2008), particularly for students with a maladaptive learning orientation (Dowson and McInerney 2004). Some attention has been given to mathematics (Ryan et al. 2007), and to science education where student motivation contributes to international differences in science achievement (Jenkins and Nelson 2005; Martin et al. 2004). New Zealand, for example, has double the international average of students with a negative attitude toward science, and high school students are less confident about their ability to do science than students in countries such as Australia, Scotland and the United States (Jackman and Townsend 2009). These findings prompted an attempt to see whether a mastery and strategic approach to science learning would increase achievement in low-achieving Year 10 students in science classes in New Zealand (Jackman et al. 2008).

In that study, students were given an intervention for science achievement which specifically paralleled the mastery-oriented approach to sporting achievement used by two popular and charismatic social models who had achieved gold medal success for New Zealand at the 2004 Olympic Games in Athens: Hamish Carter in triathlon and Sarah Ulmer in cycling. The components of the intervention targeted three salient motivational beliefs: personal achievement goal orientation (where students identified personal mastery learning goals that would encourage adaptive engagement processes), academic self-efficacy (designed to establish a competence belief platform to energize engagement and persistence in science tasks), and academic task-value (where students identified their personal intrinsic and utility values for each science topic). The intervention also targeted two cognitive strategies: academic goal-setting, where students were taught to identify proximal and distal goals for each teaching unit so they could regulate their motivation and the strategies necessary to reach those goals; and self-generated annotated diagrams, to help students develop the understanding, analytical, explanatory and memory skills essential for learning and improved science grades.

Over one school term (10 weeks), intervention students were given class time to engage in the strategies just described and to keep weekly journal records of their mastery-oriented activities, together with their use and assessment of the intervention strategies. For students with a maladaptive motivation structure (i.e. a disproportionately high performance-avoidance orientation relative to a mastery orientation), those in the intervention group became significantly more mastery-oriented and also showed associated gains in self-efficacy and value for science than those in the non-intervention group. Students with an adaptive motivation structure maintained their motivational structure. The student diaries indicated considerable enthusiasm for the adaptive motivation strategies, a belief in their effectiveness, and a willingness to continue using them. Students also showed increased achievement on regular science tests and end-of-term examinations during the course of the intervention, but these gains only reached statistical significance for the adaptive motivational group over their non-intervention peers. That the improvement in achievement did not reach statistical significance for the maladaptive motivation group highlights the difficulty of linking achievement outcomes to changes in motivational structure in the short term.

Coordinating multiple goals

There are many types of goals that can motivate behaviour in classrooms, whether positively or negatively. Sometimes the goals overlap, for example, when a student is simultaneously motivated to understand something (a mastery goal) *and* to be the best in the class (a performance goal). Similarly, a single activity might meet several goals, such as when a group discussion might meet an affective goal (experiencing excitement), a cognitive goal (satisfying curiosity), a personal relationship goal (obtaining approval from others), a social relationship goal (a sense of belonging), and a task goal (gaining mastery). Thus, students may actively pursue multiple goals at the same time (Wentzel and Wigfield 1998).

However, sometimes student goals are in conflict with each other, in which case the goals must be coordinated or, in more difficult situations, one must yield. A common conflict in schools is between academic goals and social goals. If students discuss their plans for the weekend when grouped together to work on an assigned topic on parasitic bird nesting, a social goal has taken precedence over the academic goal. When a student elects to work on a homework assignment rather than join her friends going to a movie, the academic goal has taken precedence over the social goal. The presence or absence of goal conflict is dependent on each student's ability to coordinate or accommodate competing activities.

Five common strategies have been hypothesized to cope with multiple, competing goals (Dodge *et al.* 1989). Multiple goals may be combined into a single integrative strategy (where all goals are met), a multi-tasking strategy (where different goals are met concurrently, such as talking to friends on the phone while doing housework for parents), a deferred goal strategy (where one goal is deferred while others are pursued), a modified goal strategy (where the goal of an activity is modified so as to enable the satisfaction of other goals, such as reducing the personally satisfying level of work from 'A' to 'B' to meet other goals), and a 'generalized' strategy that involves meeting the higher order needs of competing goals; for example, a conflict between going to a movie with friends and baby-sitting a younger sibling might be solved by having the friends over to play board games while baby-sitting, thus meeting higher order goals of affiliation (maintaining friendships) and filial responsibility (obeying parents). Sometimes goal coordination is not possible, such as when a teacher puts her career on hold to travel overseas; this is a single goal pursuit strategy.

These hypothesized strategies were examined in an experimental study (Townsend and Lai 2007) in which New Zealand senior high school students responded to a conflict between completing an important homework assignment and going to a close friend's birthday party. Four versions of the scenario were developed which systematically varied the urgency of the academic goal (assignment due tomorrow, or in two days time) and the social goal (party is tonight, or can be postponed). Students rated the likelihood that they would adopt each of eight strategies based on the analysis by Dodge *et al.* (1989), where some strategies favoured the academic goal and others the social goal. For example, the single integrative strategy (which achieved both goals) was, '*I would go to the party with my friends. After the party I would work till late at night to finish the assignment. I would sacrifice my sleeping time to do both things fully.*' Students also rated the importance of the goals, and wrote their own comments about how they would handle the conflict. Some students were interviewed to explore goal coordination more broadly.

Although the most popular strategy was the single integrative strategy in which both goals were favoured without being modified in any way, students elected strategies that favoured the social goal. The strength of this preference was influenced by the urgency of the two goals. When the academic goal was not urgent, students overwhelmingly elected strategies that favoured the social goal. When the academic goal was urgent, students favoured strategies that met both the academic and social goals. However, at all times students perceived the social goal as more important. The social goal was rated much higher than the academic goal when the academic goal was not urgent, and still rated somewhat higher even when the academic goal was urgent. These results were similar for students at all achievement levels. Males valued the social goal more than females and were more likely to select strategies which favoured the social goal. The great majority of students interviewed were satisfied with this approach to conflicts between academic and social goals, though a small number admitted that this approach had limitations: '. . . *at least I have something [a grade] on the assignment . . . but not a good one . . . I could do heaps better*'.

There is still much to learn about the nature of goal coordination and its interaction with internal and external influences. It is encouraging that the multiple simultaneous strategy, '*I would do my assignment at the party*', was the least selected. However, teachers must temper their desire for academic excellence from their students with awareness that students are intent on pursuing both academic and social goals.

Beliefs

Motivation to learn is dramatically influenced by students' beliefs about themselves and their capabilities. These beliefs are self-evaluative thoughts about what they expect to happen if they pursue a goal based on their history of what has happened in their past pursuit of similar goals. It is not enough for teachers to believe students can reach their academic goals. Students must also believe they have the personal capabilities, the opportunity, and the support needed to achieve the goal. It is these beliefs that motivate students to create opportunities and acquire skills they do not yet possess (Bandura 1986). Thus, it is our perception of reality that determines our learning behaviour, rather than reality itself.

Beliefs can be adaptive or maladaptive to learning. It is adaptive for students to believe they can be successful on school tasks, especially for tasks that require skills they have not yet mastered. Students with high expectations of success elect more challenging tasks, persist longer when faced with difficulties, and generally have higher achievement than students with lower expectations of success (Eccles *et al.* 1998). Students with low achievement typically have low expectations of success which, when combined with their need to protect their sense of self-worth, frequently lead to maladaptive behaviour such as electing tasks that are easily mastered, giving up quickly, or avoiding the task. Students with maladaptive expectations are not beyond recovery; teachers can change expectations for success through carefully planned instruction in the students' zone of proximal development, scaffolded to encourage a view of ability that is not stable and can be increased with effort (Dweck 2000).

Capability beliefs

Beliefs about capability are critical to adaptive motivation. In particular, self-efficacy (Bandura 1986) strongly influences both motivation to learn and subsequent achievement. Self-efficacy is the conviction that one can successfully accomplish a specific task; that is, one has the prerequisite skills or can acquire them, has the necessary self-regulatory skills to evaluate progress, can modify goals when necessary, can persist when faced with difficulty, can find solutions to obstacles, and so on. Self-efficacy is domain specific so it is possible for students to feel highly self-efficacious in learning algebra but less so for learning geometry. Self-efficacy may change as students progress through school, especially as students become more realistic in their self-beliefs compared to peers (Eccles *et al.* 1998). However, it is important that the characteristics of students with high self-efficacy, such as attempting challenging tasks, expending greater effort to learn, persisting longer when success is not immediate, and making greater use of effective learning strategies, be encouraged by teachers. Brophy (1998) argues this is best accomplished by having students set specific and challenging, but attainable, goals and providing informative feedback about the causes of personal progress.

The role of self-efficacy in children's reading achievement has received some recent attention in New Zealand. For example, Townsend and Teo (2005) investigated Bandura's (1986) argument that self-efficacy beliefs have a primacy effect in influencing the self-regulatory skills of students, particularly the types of goals they pursue, their ability to stay task-oriented, and the quality of their analytical thinking. Thus, even if students are taught self-regulatory skills, they may not employ them if they do not have self-efficacy beliefs that would support their use. Both reading self-efficacy and reading self-regulation were found to have significant independent correlations with reading comprehension of children in Years 5 and 6. However, a different picture emerged when multiple regression analyses were used to examine achievement. Although the combined effect of self-regulation and self-efficacy accounted for a significant proportion of the variance in the reading comprehension scores of the children (24 per cent), this effect was due almost entirely to self-efficacy. Self-regulation was not a significant predictor of achievement. In a further analysis, 14 per cent of the variability in achievement was accounted for by gender, ethnicity and age entered as a first block. Self-efficacy and self-regulation measures were entered as a second block, explaining an additional 20 per cent of the variability in comprehension scores. Once again, only self-efficacy accounted for a significant component of the variability. The results highlight the importance of teacher attention to raising self-efficacy beliefs in their students.

In a methodologically similar study, Townsend and Choi (2004) examined whether parental self-efficacy (as assessed by the belief factors of *competence* to assist their child's reading and *attribution* of reading success to controllable causes) contributed to the reading success of Year 4 children independently of the children's own motivation to read as measured by reading self-concept and task value for reading. In an initial multiple regression analysis, parental self-efficacy was significantly related to children's reading scores, accounting for some 11 per cent of the variance in comprehension, although only the *attribution* factor made a significant contribution. In a second regression analysis, the two measures of children's motivation to read (*self-concept* and *task value* for reading) were entered as a first block, and the parental self-efficacy measures as a second block. The two blocks accounted for a significant proportion of the variance in children's comprehension (33 per cent) and although this was largely attributable to the children's motivation (26 per cent), parental self-efficacy still made a significant additional contribution to their children's reading (7 per cent), again largely due to the attribution factor.

This result supports the view that parental self-efficacy beliefs are positively related to children's academic achievement in reading, over and above the more immediate motivational factors of self-concept and task value held by the child. That is, parent and child effects are additive. Children whose parents believe more strongly that they can influence their children's reading development have children whose reading achievement is higher than those children whose parents do not hold such beliefs as strongly. This finding supports the theoretical benefits claimed for parental efficacy in children's achievement (Bandura *et al.* 1996) but, more importantly, indicates the interactive role between home and school in children's reading motivation.

Task value beliefs

The inclusion of *task value* in the study just described raises the importance of student beliefs about the value they ascribe to a learning activity since its perceived value is a strong determinant of whether a student would want to pursue it in the first place, and to stay engaged with it (Anderman and Wolters 2006; Townsend *et al.* 2001). Four types of values have been identified as influencing motivation for learning: *intrinsic value* is the enjoyment experienced in doing a task; *attainment value* is the importance the student attaches to doing well on the task; *utility value* is the belief the task is important for future goals; and *cost belief* refers to perceived negative aspects of engaging in the task, such as loss of time for other valued activities (Pintrich and Schunk 2002). If students enjoy an activity, want to do well at it, believe it is a useful activity, and perceive little or no cost in doing the activity, they will be more motivated to engage with the task.

Some research indicates that academic task values are influenced by classroom structure. Classrooms that use a cooperative learning structure (as opposed to individualistic or competitive structures) not only result in enhanced achievement (Abrami *et al.* 1995) but also enhanced social outcomes such as improved student relations and more positive attitudes to school (Jacques *et al.* 1998; Johnson and Johnson 1999). The relationship of classroom structure to task values was explored in Year 8 students in New Zealand taught in classrooms where teachers used cooperative learning structures or more traditional structures (Townsend and Hicks 1997). Task values for engagement in mathematics and language activities were higher and perceived costs lower, in classrooms using a cooperative learning structure. These effects were also associated with greater social satisfaction with their peers in cooperative learning classrooms, suggesting that cooperative structures allow students better opportunities to coordinate academic and social goals at school.

Attribution beliefs

Further beliefs that affect motivation are found in attribution theory (Weiner 2001). An attribution is a belief about the cause of an event. In the context of school, students make attributions about why they believe they were successful or not on learning tasks. Although there is an almost infinite variety of causes to 'explain' a single event, such as a low test mark, every cause is either internal or external to the learner, is stable or unstable over time, and is controllable or uncontrollable in its effects. For example, to believe that lack of success on a test was due to low effort the student is making an attribution that is internal (*I needed to try harder*), unstable (*I could have tried harder*), and controllable (*I can try harder*). In the context of school academic outcomes, the most common attributions are ability, effort, luck and difficulty of the task, but choice of study strategies, amount of assistance available, clarity of instruction, teacher practices (including perceived degree of favouritism), and level of interest and relevance for the topic are also fairly common (Weiner 2001).

Attributions relate to motivation in that they affect expectations for future success and effort. If someone fails at something through lack of effort, they open the possibility that they can be successful next time if they expend effort. But if the person fails because they perceive themselves as not smart enough, or 'no good' at it (a common attribution heard in statistics classes), then future motivation is decreased because these attributions are enduring. Reduced motivation will inevitably lead to lower achievement.

An interesting interplay between teacher and student attributions occurs in the context of excuses in classrooms. Excuses for lateness, failure to complete homework, poor performance, and so on are offered by students as part of classroom life. In essence, excuses are reasons or attributions given to 'explain' some aspect of negative or non-compliant behaviour, and are all reducible to the three components of locus, stability and controllability. Excuses are frequently a mechanism for preserving self-esteem; they are a way of saying, '*I have the ability to do the work but something prevented me.*' Self-esteem is further preserved if the excuse shifts responsibility away from the student, thus the attributions made in excuses often invoke an external locus ('*my computer crashed*').

In an interview study examining the locus of student excuses, teachers were asked to describe incidents in which male and female students offered an excuse for poor or non-compliant behaviour (Townsend 1997). The overwhelming locus of student excuses (80 per cent) was external. Teachers believed the excuses in approximately 50 per cent of the cases, especially if they contained an internal attribution ('*I forgot to take it home*'). There were no gender differences in the locus of student excuses, or in the likelihood that teachers would believe the excuse. Many teachers took no action against the student, even when the reason given was disbelieved, in order to preserve a positive ongoing relationship.

Student excuses are a unique aspect of social interchange in classrooms. By the age of 10 years, students recognize the role that excuses play in maintaining self-esteem and, perhaps, in deflecting disapproval from teachers. Many students have learned that a 'good' excuse can even encourage sympathy from a teacher by invoking external, uncontrollable attributions ('*I had to help my grandmother who broke her leg*'). There is a need for greater understanding of the role excuses play in image management, both for students and teachers, and the maintenance of self-esteem in classrooms.

Emotions

As just seen, attributions are linked to the emotions we have for events. Though much less studied, academic emotions are significantly related to students' motivation, learning strategies, cognitive resources, self-regulation, and academic achievement (Pekrun *et al.* 2002). Common classroom events cause pride, shame and guilt, but also hope, relief, anger, hopelessness, joy, sadness and boredom. These associations are often mediated through attributions (Weiner 2001). For example, pride can only be appropriately felt for an outcome for which one is responsible and has made an internal, controllable attribution. The feeling of pride contributes to increased motivation. In some instances, increased motivation may follow a negative emotion. For example, if failure is attributed to lack of effort, the subsequent guilt may trigger more effort; attributing the same failure to lack of ability may result in feelings of shame and lowered motivation.

Pekrun (1992) has noted that emotions affecting motivation may be categorized as occurring *before* the task (e.g. hope, anticipatory joy), *during* the task (e.g. enjoyment, boredom), and *after* the task (e.g. relief, disappointment). It is the latter, retrospective emotions that are likely to be most closely linked with the type and nature of attributions students make for performance on a task. However, positive prospective emotions such as hope or anticipated enjoyment associated with a task can encourage effort and persistence on the task, while negative prospective emotions such as anxiety, hopelessness, resignation or despair are more likely to reduce effort and persistence with the task. Similarly, effort, persistence, use of more effective strategies for learning, and likelihood of continued motivation in the future are likely if, during the task itself, the student experiences enjoyment rather than boredom.

Several pathways linking emotions, motivation and achievement have been proposed by Pekrun (1992). For example, differences in working memory may explain the effect of interest (a cognitive-emotional factor) in motivation and achievement (Pintrich and Schunk 2002; Townsend and Townsend 1990). Another pathway is through intrinsic and extrinsic motivation. In general, positive emotions create greater intrinsic motivation which increases the extent and quality of engagement with learning, whereas negative emotions (especially hopelessness, sadness, and despair) are likely to decrease intrinsic motivation. The deleterious effects of anxiety, particularly test anxiety, on learning and motivation in education have been extensively researched (Hill and Wigfield 1984; Ryan *et al.* 2007; Townsend and Mahoney 1981) and will not be discussed here other than to reinforce the point made earlier that cooperative learning structures can reduce the negative effects of anxiety (e.g. Townsend *et al.* 1998).

Perhaps the most detailed study of how emotions interact with cognitive and emotional processes in normal class discussion is the grounded theory study of Do and Schallert (2004). Student-teachers were observed and interviewed, using video playbacks, during discussions. Emotional reactions governed shifts between listening, talking and tuning-out. For example, positive emotions about the content of discussion prompted shifts to deep listening or to talking. Negative emotions, particularly about classmates who monopolized discussion, were likely to result in tuning-out. Even while waiting to contribute to discussion, attention was overlaid with emotions such as anger toward a speaker, anxiety about the likely popularity of the intended contribution, or aggravation at having to wait to participate. This research not only gives insights into our own experiences of the interplay between cognitive, affective and motivational processes in academic contexts such as staff meetings, it also challenges an uncritical acceptance of egalitarian, dialogic structures in which learning is constructed or co-constructed with peers (Parr and Townsend 2002). It is clear that much affect goes unnoticed in classrooms and there is much to understand about how affect can be used to support rather than inhibit learning and adaptive motivation.

Conclusion

The overwhelmingly complex array of loosely connected theories and concepts that fall under the umbrella of 'motivation' has rendered it a word in crisis. It survives largely because in classrooms and on the street everyone 'knows' what motivation is. In colloquial language we use it in a positive sense to describe the person who finds an interest in something, pursues it, and gains satisfaction in completing it. We use it in a negative sense to describe the person who appears directionless, listless and bored. When we use the term in a positive sense, we generally get it right; the students we call 'motivated' do seem to have an energy that initiates, directs and sustains effort in an activity. When we use it in a negative sense, we generally get it wrong; the students we call 'unmotivated' are not unmotivated, they are just not motivated by the activities of school. This cannot be solved by 'giving' motivation to students. The real skill in teaching is to structure learning experiences that encourage students to develop adaptive motivational structures for learning.

This chapter discussed three components that can be used by teachers to encourage students to adopt adaptive motivation structures: (a) helping students to identify personally meaningful and challenging, but achievable, goals; (b) encouraging stable personal beliefs in competency to achieve those goals; and (c) ensuring that students experience positive emotional affect at successful completion of those goals. For many of our students, this will take relatively little effort from teachers because the seeds of mastery, intrinsic interest, academic value, competency beliefs, adaptive attributions and the like are sown early. For other students, teachers will need to consciously model intrinsic interest and a mastery orientation, use feedback in more informative ways that indicate personal growth, use language in ways that imply an incremental view of ability, encourage self-efficacy and self-worth or promote adaptive attributions to success and failure, and ensure that students experience the emotional concomitants of success. For a small number of students, many of whom will have already adopted a maladaptive motivation structure, the task of encouraging a more adaptive framework is difficult but not impossible. Learned helplessness can be reversed. Inappropriate attributions for success (e.g. luck) and failure (lack of ability) can be retrained to attributions (particularly effort) that encourage motivation rather than undermine it. Self-worth can be raised and work-avoidance minimized by reducing or eliminating public comparisons of student performance. The use of classroom structures that encourage a positive, cooperative environment can meet students' academic needs without necessarily incurring costs to social or other needs.

Motivation is at the heart of school learning. The outcomes we want for our students extend beyond achievement to include attitudes, beliefs and values about what they are learning, and about themselves. It would not be inappropriate to make motivational instruction the heart of teacher training programmes.

References

Abrami, P.C., Chambers, B., Poulson, C., De Simone, C., D'Apollonia, S. and Howden, W. (1995) *Classroom Connections: Understanding and Using Cooperative Learning*, Toronto: Harcourt Brace.

Anderman, E.M. and Wolters, C.A. (2006) 'Goals, values and affect: influences on student motivation', in P. Alexander and P. Winne (eds) *Handbook of Educational Psychology* (pp. 369–89), Mahwah, NJ: Lawrence Erlbaum Associates.

Bandura, A. (1986) *Social Foundations of Thought and Action: A Social Cognitive Theory*, Upper Saddle River, NJ: Prentice Hall.

Bandura, A. (1991) 'Human agency: the rhetoric and the reality', *American Psychologist*, 46: 157–62.

Bandura, A. (1997) *Self-Efficacy: The Exercise of Control*, New York: W.H. Freeman.

Bandura, A., Barbaranelli, C., Caprara, G. and Pastorelli, C. (1996) 'Multifaceted impact of self-efficacy beliefs on academic functioning', *Child Development*, 67: 1206–22.

Brophy, J. (1998) *Motivating Students to Learn*, Boston: McGraw-Hill.

Brown, J.S. (1961) *The Motivation of Behaviour*, New York: McGraw-Hill.

deCharms, R. (1968) *Personal Causation*, New York: Academic Press.

Dewsbury, D.A. (1978) *Comparative Animal Behaviour*, New York: McGraw-Hill.

Do, S.L. and Schallert, D.L. (2004) 'Emotions and classroom talk: toward a model of the role of affect in students' experiences of classroom discussion', *Journal of Educational Psychology*, 96: 619–34.

Dodge, K.A., Asher, S.R. and Parkhurst, J.T. (1989) 'Social life as a goal coordination task', in C. Amers and R. Ames (eds) *Research on Motivation in Education*, vol. 3: *Goals and Cognitions* (pp. 107–35), San Diego, CA: Academic Press.

Dowson, M. and McInerny, D.M. (2004) 'The development and validation of the Goal Orientation and Learning Strategies Survey', *Educational and Psychological Measurement*, 64: 290–310.

Dweck, C. (2000) *Self Theories: Their Role in Motivation, Personality, and Development*, Philadelphia, PA: Psychology Press.

Eccles, J., Wigfield, A. and Schiefele, U. (1998) 'Motivation to succeed', in W. Damon (Series ed.) and N. Eisenberg (Vol. ed.) *Handbook of Child Psychology*: vol. 3, *Social, Emotional, and Personality Development*, 5th edn (pp. 1017–95), New York: Wiley.

Elliot, A. and McGregor, H. (2000, April) 'Approach and avoidance goals and autonomous-controlled regulation: empirical and conceptual relations', in A. Assor (Chair), *Self-determination Theory and Achievement Goal Theory: Convergences, Divergences and Educational Implications*, symposium conducted at the annual meeting of the American Educational Research Association, New Orleans.

Ford, M.E. (1992) *Motivating Humans*, Newbury Park, CA: Sage Publications.

Franken, R.E. (1988) *Human Motivation*, 2nd edn, Pacific Grove, CA: Brooks/Cole.

Hill, K.T. and Wigfield, A. (1984) 'Test anxiety: a major educational problem and what can be done about it', *Elementary School Journal*, 85: 105–26.

Jackman, W.C. and Townsend, M. (2009) 'Is a direct approach to student-level engagement factors the crucial missing link in science education? An international perspective with New Zealand as a case in point', *International Journal of Learning*, 16: 287–98.

Jackman, W.C., Townsend, M. and Hamilton (2008) 'Improving motivation and performance in secondary school science', in C. Rubie-Davies and C. Rawlinson (eds) *Challenging Thinking about Teaching and Learning* (pp. 41–51), New York: Nova Science Publishers.

Jacques, N., Wilton, K. and Townsend, M. (1998) 'Cooperative learning and social acceptance of children with mild intellectual disability', *Journal of Intellectual Disability Research*, 42: 29–36.

Jenkins, E.W. and Nelson, N.W. (2005) ' "Important but not for me": students' attitudes towards secondary school science in England', *Research in Science and Technological Education*, 23: 41–57.

Johnson, D.W. and Johnson, R.T. (1999) *Learning Together and Alone: Cooperation, Competition and Individualization*, 5th edn, Boston: Allyn and Bacon.

Martin, M.O., Mullis, I.V.S. and Chrostowski, S.J. (2004) *TIMMS 2003 Technical Report*, Chestnut Hill, MA: International Study Center, Boston College.

Midgley, C., Kaplan, A. and Middleton, M. (2001) 'Performance-approach goals: good for what, for whom, under what circumstances, and at what cost?', *Journal of Educational Psychology*, 93: 77–86.

Midgley, C. and Urdan, T. (2001) 'Academic self-handicapping and achievement goals: a further examination', *Educational Psychology*, 26: 61–75.

Parr, J. and Townsend, M. (2002) 'Environments, processes, and mechanisms in peer learning', *International Journal of Educational Research*, 37: 403–23.

Pekrun, R. (1992) 'The impact of emotions on learning and achievement: towards a theory of cognitive/motivational mediators', *Applied Psychology: An International Review*, 41: 359–76.

Pekrun, R., Goetz, T., Titz, W. and Perry, R. (2002) 'Academic emotions in students' self-regulated learning and achievement: a program of qualitative and quantitative research', *Educational Psychologist*, 37: 91–105.

Pintrich, P. and Schunk. D. (2002) *Motivation in Education*, Upper Saddle River, NJ: Merrill Prentice Hall.

Ryan, K.E., Ryan, A.M., Arbuthnot, K. and Samuels, M. (2007) 'Students' motivation for standardised math exams', *Educational Researcher*, 36: 5–13.

Schunk, D., Pintrich, P. and Meece, J. (2008) *Motivation in Education: Theory, Research, and Applications*, 3rd edn, Upper Saddle River, NJ: Merrill/Pearson.

Seligman, M.E.P. (1975) *Helplessness: On Depression, Development, and Death*, San Francisco, CA: Freeman.

Stipek, D. (1988) *Motivation to Learn*, Boston: Allyn and Bacon.

Townsend, M. (1997) 'Teachers' perceptions of students' excuses', paper presented at the annual conference of the New Zealand Association for Research in Education, Auckland, New Zealand, December.

Townsend, M. and Choi. S.F. (2004) 'Reading achievement in New Zealand: effects of parents' self-efficacy and children's motivation', paper presented at the annual conference of the British Educational Research Association, Manchester, United Kingdom, September.

Townsend, M. and Hicks, L. (1997) 'Classroom goal structures, social satisfaction, and the perceived value of academic tasks', *British Journal of Educational Psychology*, 67: 1–12.

Townsend, M. and Lai, M.K. (2007) 'Balancing social and academic goals at high school', paper presented at the European Association for Research on Learning and Instruction conference, Budapest, Hungary, August.

Townsend, M. and Mahoney, M. (1981) 'Humor and anxiety: effects on class test performance', *Psychology in the Schools*, 18: 228–34.

Townsend, M., Moore, D., Tuck, B. and Wilton, K. (1998) 'Self-concept and anxiety in university students studying social science statistics within a cooperative learning structure', *Educational Psychology*, 18: 41–54.

Townsend, M. and Teo, W.T. (2005) 'Self-efficacy and self-regulation in children's reading comprehension', paper presented at the European Association for Research on Learning and Instruction conference, Nikosia, Cyprus, August.

Townsend, M. and Townsend, J.E. (1990) 'Comprehension of high and low interest reading material among Māori, Pacific Island, and Pakeha children', *New Zealand Journal of Educational Studies*, 25: 141–53.

Townsend, M., Townsend, J.E. and Seo, J. (2001) 'Children's motivation to read following Reading Recovery', *National Reading Conference Yearbook*, 50: 584–96.

Weiner, B. (2001) 'Intrapersonal and interpersonal theories of motivation from an attribution perspective', in F. Salili, C. Chiu and Y. Hong (eds) *Student Motivation: The Culture and Context of Learning* (pp. 17–30), New York: Kluwer Academic/Plenum.

Wentzel, K. and Wigfield, A. (1998) 'Academic and social motivational influences on students' academic performance', *Educational Psychology Review*, 10: 155–75.

Chapter 9

Teacher expectations and beliefs

Influences on the socioemotional environment of the classroom

Christine M. Rubie-Davies and Elizabeth R. Peterson

It is generally accepted within education circles that teacher expectations have effects on student achievement. Much early research in this area concentrated on ways teachers interacted with students for whom they had correspondingly high or low expectations (Brophy 1982, 1983, 1985; Cooper and Good 1983). Several differentiating behaviours were identified. For example, teachers praised students for whom they held high expectations (high expectation students) more frequently than those for whom they had low expectations (low expectation students), and they criticized low expectation students far more often; allowed more wait time for high expectation students; and interacted with high expectation students in public and low expectation students in private (Brophy 1985; Cooper and Good 1983; Harris and Rosenthal 1985). It was argued that these differential behaviours provided students with messages about what was expected of them and that, over time, they began to perform in accordance with the teachers' expectations.

Opportunity to learn

The most important implication of teacher expectations, however, is the opportunity to learn that teachers provide as a result of their expectations. When teachers have high expectations for students, they introduce more concepts within each lesson, teach them at a faster pace, and include more challenging learning activities (Good and Brophy 2003; Page and Rosenthal 1990). The opposite occurs for low expectation students. Over time, these differential learning opportunities result in high expectation students learning more simply because they have been given more opportunity to do so. Zohar *et al.* (2001) found two-thirds of teachers believed higher-order questioning was not appropriate for low ability students and around one-third reported they never used such questions with low ability students. Another study found that some teachers believed that low ability students needed lots of repetitive exercises and concrete experiences rather than challenging learning opportunities (Rubie-Davies 2008). When students for whom teachers have low expectations are not provided with opportunities to extend and enhance their cognitive abilities, the probability they will improve is reduced. Arguably these students need more opportunity to learn rather than less if they are to progress and close the gap on their high achieving peers. Certainly they need at least equitable learning opportunities (Rubie-Davies 2009).

Increased and enhanced opportunities to learn are particularly relevant for students from disadvantaged backgrounds and those from minority groups because these students, in particular, are vulnerable to teachers' expectations and they are groups for whom teachers' expectations are often low (Bishop *et al.* 2009). In a recent study (McKown and Weinstein 2008), it was found that in classes of students where teachers did not discriminate in how they treated high and low expectation students (low differentiating teachers), teachers' expectations were similar for students from diverse ethnic backgrounds, and were based on achievement. However, in classes where teachers treated high and low expectation students differently (high differentiating teachers), teachers' expectations were between .75 and 1.00 standard deviations higher for Caucasian and Asian American students than they were for African American and Latino students with similar levels of achievement. In these classes, teacher expectations accounted for on average .29 of a standard deviation in the end-of-year achievement gap.

In situations where minority group students, or those from low socioeconomic backgrounds, have been given challenging learning opportunities, they have often performed above what might have been expected (Hacker *et al.* 1992; Rubie *et al.* 2004; Weinstein *et al.* 2004). For example, a study was conducted (Rubie *et al.* 2004) in which a group of Year 4 to 6 students were involved in an intensive Māori culture group training programme which resulted in them representing New Zealand at an international children's festival in Europe. The children were from a low socioeconomic area and their academic achievement was below average at the beginning of the study. As reported in interviews with the parents and teachers, being part of the culture group raised teacher, student, and parent expectations of the children's academic achievement. Not only were they involved in intensive practices and cultural performances but it was a condition of being a group member that all homework was completed and class behaviour was of a high standard. Hence more was expected of these children at school, not less, even though they had time away from school performing at various venues. Compared with a similar group in the same school and another in a local school, the children improved their academic abilities during the year of the study ($F(2,68) = 4.66$, $p < .05$, partial $\eta^2 = 0.120$); the other two groups either declined in relative performance or remained at similar levels. There was a corresponding picture for the social measures. The self-esteem and internal locus of control of the children in the Māori culture group improved significantly (self-esteem: $F(2,68) = 4.05$, $p < .05$, partial $\eta^2 = 0.107$; locus of control: $F(2,68) = 4.84$, $p < .01$, partial $\eta^2 = 0.125$) while the other two matched groups either showed a decline in scores or remained at similar levels. One limitation of this study, however, was that it was impossible to unravel the causal factors so it was not known whether the enhanced achievement and social factors were a result of involvement in the group, close contact with teachers, improvements in self-confidence and pride, or other factors.

There did, however, appear to be an association between the students being given an unusual and intense opportunity to learn, the high expectations placed on them, and their social and academic outcomes.

Teacher characteristics

The vast majority of the research on teacher expectations, however, has concentrated firmly on the instructional environment of the classroom in relation to teacher expectations and student outcomes. Studies have extensively investigated relationships between teacher expectations, teacher instructional behaviours, and student learning. Any differences in the socioemotional context of the classroom and implications for student learning when teacher expectations are considered have received little attention. Yet the classroom can be viewed as a community in which children not only learn but also interact with others, learn social rules, and develop self-esteem. They learn that the classroom, as a social grouping, does not have voluntary membership and has a pre-determined leader (the teacher) whose attitudes and beliefs frame the affective environment.

Nevertheless, the conception that individual teacher factors may contribute to differences in not only the classroom instructional environment but also the socioemotional environment has been little explored. While individual students may experience different instructional lives within one classroom, it is likely some teachers emphasize these differences more than others and therefore may have greater effects on student learning than others. One question frequently pursued in the research on teacher expectations is: What is it about students that means their teacher has high or low expectations for them? However, when expectations are viewed in relation to teacher rather than student characteristics, the question becomes: What is it about teachers that means they have high or low expectations for students? It has been suggested that overall expectations have a modest effect on student outcomes, making a difference of 5 to 10 per cent (Brophy 1985). However, research that has examined expectations over time (Blatchford *et al.* 1989) and expectations at class level (comparing teachers who have high expectations for all students with those whose expectations are consistently low) has found much greater differences for student outcomes (Rubie-Davies 2006, 2007, 2008). Brophy also concedes that even a 5 per cent difference could become very large if there is aggregation each year.

Brophy and Good (1974) proposed three types of teachers: proactive, reactive, or over-reactive. These categories related to how susceptible teachers were to creating expectation effects in students. Proactive teachers would design learning opportunities for students based on their expectations. This group would have clear goals for students and systematically move students towards those goals. So, proactive teachers would be likely to have positive expectation effects on students. Reactive teachers would not cling to their initial expectations and would adjust these as they received new information about students' progress. This group would be more likely to allow their goals to be based on student input and behaviour so may not perceive student potential. They would have minimal expectation effects on students as they would tend to maintain existing differences between high and low achieving students rather than having self-fulfilling prophecy effects on students. Over-reactive teachers would be those who treated students as stereotypes rather than as individuals and who developed rigid expectations. These were the teachers Brophy and Good described as potentially having negative expectation effects on students. However, whether or not these categories of teachers exist has not been empirically tested. This is despite the later suggestion by Brophy that 'Differential teacher treatment of intact groups and classes may well be a much more widespread and powerful mediator of self-fulfilling prophecy effects on student achievement than differential teacher treatment of individual students within the same group or class' (1985: 309).

This chapter will explore contextual differences across classrooms that result in very different experiences for students and that may ultimately have implications for student learning. While the discussion will highlight differences in the instructional environment between classes, the major focus will be on the socioe-motional environment of the classroom. It is argued that while the instructional environment influences opportunity to learn, the socioemotional environment in which learning is framed can also affect student outcomes. This is because a more positive, caring socioemotional environment has been shown to have effects on student motivation, self-esteem, and, ultimately, learning outcomes (Weinstein 2002; Wentzel 1999). Students learn more effectively within an environment where they feel valued, respected, and cared about (Weinstein 2002).

The socioemotional environment of the classroom

The investigation of the socioemotional environment of the classroom generally is a relatively new area of psychological research and very few researchers working in the area of teacher expectations have attempted to link their work to differences in the affective climate of classrooms (see Weinstein 2002 as an exception). Research that has been conducted suggests there is a link between the interpersonal relationships teachers enjoy with students and student motivation (Noddings 1992). Wentzel (1997) investigated this idea further in relation to students who had moved from elementary to middle school. Almost 400 students completed questionnaires which measured student perceptions of teacher caring, psychological distress, locus of control beliefs, pursuit of social goals, academic effort, irresponsible and pro-social behaviour, academic achievement, and characteristics of caring teachers. Controlling for prior motivation, achievement, locus of control beliefs and psychological distress, Wentzel reported strong evidence that students were more likely to engage in schoolwork if they felt valued and supported by teachers. Student perceptions that teachers cared about them were related to students' motivation, academic efforts, and their pursuit of pro-social and social responsibility goals. Ultimately, student sensitivity to teacher care affected academic outcomes.

High and low bias teachers and the socioemotional environment

Few researchers in the field of teacher expectations have explored the more subtle aspects or the affective features of the classroom environment which can provide students with messages about the social construction of their educational experience. In some earlier research, Babad and his colleagues (Babad *et al.* 1982) identified teachers they termed 'high bias' and 'low bias'. In an experimental study, the researchers provided teachers with information about students that indicated the students were either high or low ability. However, the data was randomly assigned to students. High bias teachers were those who were easily influenced by the information and interacted with students according to a manipulated expectation that children were high or low ability. These teachers allowed the evidence they had been given to override their own perceptions. Low bias teachers paid little regard to the information provided and interacted and planned student lessons according to their perceptions of current student achievement.

These findings led the researchers to conduct further investigations of the interactions of high bias teachers with their students. Babad and his colleagues conducted a series of studies in Israel and then a final study in New Zealand (Babad *et al.* 1989a, 1989b, 1991; Babad and Taylor 1992) in which teachers and 10-year-old students were shown very brief video clips (10 seconds per clip) of high bias teachers interacting with – or, in some cases, talking about – individual students. In some instances, the student was one for whom the teacher had high expectations and, in others, low expectations. All the clips showed the teacher only. The potential influence of verbal content was minimized by distorting the sound, or, in the New Zealand study, by the judges' inability to understand Hebrew. Hence the decisions about the type of students being spoken to or simply spoken about were based on teachers' non-verbal (rather than verbal) presentation. In all studies, both adults and 10-year-old students were readily able to determine what type of student the high bias teacher was interacting with or talking about. The non-verbal behaviour of the high bias teachers was described as revealing more negative affect towards low expectancy students. The attitudes of high bias teachers could be ascertained from facial expressions, voice tone and body language.

Debates about teacher expectations often centre on arguments about students' rights to equitable treatment in a classroom environment. All students should expect similar treatment from teachers. However, while teachers can control their verbal interactions, non-verbal behaviour is less easily controlled. Babad describes differences in the affective messages students receive from teachers via verbal and non-verbal communication channels as leakage (Babad *et al.* 1989a).

High and low differentiating teachers and the socioemotional environment

While Babad has carefully investigated teacher non-verbal behaviours in the communication of teacher expectations, Weinstein (2002) has investigated further class-level characteristics of teachers in relation to expectations for students. She has identified teachers she calls high and low differentiating (Weinstein *et al.* 1982). High differentiating teachers are those who strongly differentiate between high and low expectation students, while low differentiating teachers are those who do not strongly differentiate between the two sets of students. Weinstein found that high differentiating teachers made student ability differences salient (as will be described below) while low differentiating teachers did not. Following earlier studies involving interviews with students (Weinstein 1986, 1989, 1993) and careful observations in classrooms (Weinstein 2002), Weinstein (2002) has proposed five areas in which teachers' instructional decisions have implications for the socioemotional climate of the classroom: (1) grouping; (2) differentiation of curriculum; (3) beliefs about intelligence; (4) motivational strategies; and (5) beliefs about the teacher role. In her book she described the variable practices of one high and one low differentiating teacher who epitomized the beliefs and practices of these types of teachers.

In the classrooms of high differentiating teachers there were a number of distinctive features relating to grouping of students, the curriculum taught, motivation, and beliefs about intelligence.

In classrooms of high differentiating teachers, students were grouped and seated by ability. Student groupings were frequently referred to and students were made to feel valued or otherwise according to their group. Progress was considered the students' responsibility in that lack of progress was blamed on students rather than any need for the teacher to take ownership.

In terms of curriculum, the work high differentiating teachers assigned to the various groups often required convergent thinking. In other words, the work students produced was clearly either correct or incorrect. The learning tasks were sharply differentiated depending on the perceived ability of students. Students were often publicly reminded about the status of their performance.

Motivation was affected by the emphasis on grouping, which led to a strongly competitive atmosphere. As a result, there was a focus on performance and teachers actively used extrinsic rewards to foster motivation. High differentiating teachers also created a climate characterized by labelling (e.g. 'babies' and 'social misfits') and threats (e.g. students would be put in a lower a group if they did not perform; parents were used as threats). Many negative public exchanges were observed and students were frequently subjected to put-downs. Students who laughed at or made fun of others were not admonished by their teacher.

The high differentiating teachers had an 'entity' view of intelligence (a belief that intelligence is fixed at birth and little can be done to change it) and so did not believe they could have much influence on student achievement. In these classrooms, teachers generally maintained tight control of students and encouraged them to seek the teachers' help rather than peer support. Students were given little autonomy.

On the other hand, the low differentiating teachers described by Weinstein (2002) established a very different classroom community based on their beliefs about grouping, curriculum, motivation and intelligence.

Although low differentiating teachers did use ability grouping for instruction, students were seated in family groups which contained a mix of ability and social skills. Groups were changed frequently and students were expected to support each other. There were few references to student ability and the teacher took responsibility for student progress.

In terms of the curriculum provided for students, low differentiating teachers designed similar tasks for all students but the tasks required divergent processes. Hence there was a range of approaches students could use to complete tasks. This enabled similar tasks to be challenging for all students.

Low differentiating teachers provided students with a lot of positive feedback and students were encouraged to help each other when one of them was having difficulty. The teachers fostered intrinsic motivation, developing cooperation rather than competition. Hence students were viewed as resources for themselves as well as for each other. The classroom climate was characterized by trust, respect, dignity and humour.

Low differentiating teachers had 'incremental' notions of intelligence (a belief that all students can improve their intelligence and make progress given appropriate supports) and treated errors as informative for learning. Such teachers encouraged students to understand that success was more likely to be due to effort, and failure to task difficulty.

These differences in how high and low differentiating teachers create the socioemotional climate of the classroom and in how they view grouping, differentiation of curriculum, motivational strategies, intelligence, and the teacher role are important. Weinstein (Kuklinski and Weinstein 2001) has shown that in classes of low differentiating teachers only 1 to 5 per cent of the variance in student achievement can be explained by teacher expectations, whereas in high differentiating classrooms, this figure was 9 to 18 per cent.

In summary, Babad's work on the non-verbal interactions of high bias teachers and Weinstein's findings on the beliefs and practices of high and low differentiating teachers provide rich descriptions of particular types of teachers whose beliefs and attributes led to students becoming part of very different classroom communities. The messages the teachers delivered resulted in clear differences in the socioemotional climates of the classrooms in which students were located. Within these differing communities, students worked out levels of teacher support available, which was an indication of teacher interest in their learning; whether teachers cared about their emotional well-being; and how to negotiate the environment in ways which would maximize their self-esteem and dignity.

High and low expectation teachers and the socioemotional climate

The only other research on teacher expectations that has investigated the instructional and socioemotional environments created by different types of teachers is that of Rubie-Davies (Rubie-Davies 2006, 2007, 2008; Rubie-Davies *et al.* 2007). This research found similar results to those of Weinstein and Babad. Rubie-Davies (2006) proposed that some teachers would have high expectations for all students while others would have low. In a series of studies which identified teachers with high expectations for all their students (HiEx teachers) and those with low expectations for all their students (LoEx teachers), Rubie-Davies tracked student academic and social outcomes and also interviewed teachers about their beliefs and conducted observations in their classrooms.

In classes of HiEx teachers, students made considerable gains in reading across one year ($d > 1.0$) while in classes of LoEx teachers gains were much smaller ($d < .15$) (Rubie-Davies *et al.* 2007). The gains in HiEx teachers' classrooms are particularly powerful given that Hattie (2007) defines an effect size of .4 as having a meaningful and substantial affect on student achievement. Student self-perceptions were also examined (Rubie-Davies 2006). While student academic self-perceptions increased across one year in the classes of HiEx teachers, the most dramatic change was a large decrease in student academic self-concept for students with LoEx teachers. Moreover, students appeared to be aware of their teachers' expectations. When students were asked at the beginning and end of year to rate the statements: 'My teacher thinks I'm good at reading' and 'My teacher thinks I'm good at maths', those in classes with HiEx teachers increased their perceptions of how teachers rated their performance whereas those in the classes of LoEx teachers showed a large decline.

Differences between HiEx and LoEx teachers were also found in terms of their beliefs about instruction and self-reported practices (Rubie-Davies 2008). Differences in beliefs were related to grouping, student autonomy and goal setting, motivation of students, and peer support. The findings relating to classroom climate will be discussed below.

All teachers grouped students by ability for reading instruction. This was not a surprising finding given that Wilkinson and Townsend (2000) reported that New Zealand had the highest grouping rate of all OECD countries. However, while students were grouped for instruction, there were distinct differences in the types of activities students completed and with whom. In LoEx classes, students remained in instructional groups for learning experiences; the learning opportunities were quite separate for the groups. The teachers believed low ability students needed repetitive exercises while high ability students needed extended reading opportunities. Conversely, no HiEx teachers kept students in instructional groups for learning experiences. Some had similar activities that all students completed, some allowed students to choose their learning experiences, some encouraged peers of varying ability to work together on learning activities. There were no restrictions in terms of who could complete which activities. These teachers believed all students needed challenging learning opportunities if they were to progress.

Differences in teacher beliefs about grouping clearly contributed to the instructional environment of the classroom, but could arguably also be said to contribute to the socioemotional environment. In classes of LoEx teachers, it would seem that differences in ability would be made salient when students worked in quite separate groups, whereas these differences would be less obvious in classes of HiEx teachers. Moreover, there appeared to be far more movement of students between groups in HiEx classes than there was for those in LoEx classes.

The two groups of teachers also had quite different beliefs about student autonomy. As could be seen above, HiEx teachers gave students a lot of choice in the activities they completed, and with whom. Students made many decisions about their learning. Indeed, one teacher of Year 2 students consulted with them to gauge their views when she thought they should change groups. Coupled with this, all HiEx teachers reported using goal setting with their students. Each student negotiated academic goals with their teachers and worked towards them. Students and teachers monitored progress. Goal setting was individual and based on current needs, so students were well aware of 'where to next'. In contrast, in LoEx classes, teachers made the decisions about what activities students would complete, when they would complete them, how and with whom. Students were given very few choices about their learning and there was no goal setting.

In classes of HiEx teachers, students had ownership of their learning; they had choice, and they had clear learning goals. Teachers encouraged a mastery goal orientation by individualizing student goals, and students were able to monitor their individual progress. However, for LoEx teachers, by providing students with clearly differentiated activities over which they had little choice, and no individualized goals, it is likely the focus would have been on group comparison and hence a performance orientation rather than a mastery orientation. Research has shown students are always well aware of their grouping (Linchevski and Kutscher 1998) and this is likely to have implications for perceived ability and expectations. Moreover, it has been shown that the creation of a mastery goal orientation results in a more positive socioemotional climate for students, where the focus is on their own learning, they feel respected, and failure is viewed as part of the learning process. Hence in classrooms oriented to the mastery of goals, students tend to make greater progress than students within a classroom focused on performance goals (Midgley 2002).

HiEx teachers further reported during interviews that allowing students choices in learning experiences and setting clearly defined learning goals with them, encouraged intrinsic motivation and cognitive engagement. These teachers also believed that incorporating student interests into class activities fostered motivation and learning. For example, teachers would choose books for their classroom that reflected student interests; one teacher created mathematics activities that centred on cricket so that a group of boys who did not enjoy mathematics became enthusiastic. LoEx teachers, however, chose student activities based on perceived needs for students' learning rather than on student interest. They were concerned to provide appropriate activities for students at their instructional level regardless of student interests.

Midgley (2002) proposed that a mastery goal orientation among teachers aligns with a focus on intrinsic motivation and in the study reported above this was found for HiEx teachers. These teachers also appeared to recognize the value of fostering student motivation as other researchers have reported (Dweck *et al.* 2004). Indeed, one HiEx teacher in the study said:

> I just think that having mixed ability with the [high achievers] is really important so that they have all got a contribution to make and their skills, their particular skills are valued this way, because if you have a pecking order in the class, motivation can go out the window and you won't see star charts and stuff like that in my room. I am more interested in intrinsic motivation than extrinsic, so I don't have them.

These teachers appeared to recognize the role of student autonomy and interest in improving learning (Hidi *et al.* 2004; Reeve and Jang 2006) and could clearly articulate reasons for their teaching decisions. In contrast, LoEx teachers did not talk about how they motivated students other than speaking about students being told they could move upwards to another group if they worked hard.

Students in classes of both types of teachers were encouraged to work together. However, in the classes of LoEx teachers, because students remained in ability groups for instruction and learning activities, they worked only with their same ability peers. In contrast, children with HiEx teachers worked with a wide variety of peers. The opportunity to work with several peers of mixed ability can provide students with positive peer modelling (Stone 1998) and also serves to create a single classroom community rather than several autonomous groups within the class (Weinstein 2002). Again, it could be argued that these differential teacher practices would result in different affective classroom environments.

In addition to interviewing teachers and tracking students' academic progress, a further study (Rubie-Davies 2007) also observed the two types of teachers in their classrooms. One trained research assistant coded everything a teacher said during the observation while another audio-taped and completed a running record of each lesson. In all, three hours of observations were completed for each teacher. The researcher independently coded 25 per cent of the observations using the audio-tape recording, and inter-rater agreement for the sample of observations was 97 per cent. While the discussion below explores some differences in instructional practices, the emphasis is on those aspects of the behaviours of the two groups of teachers that could have implications for the socioemotional environment of the classroom.

While teachers whose expectations did not differ significantly from student achievement (teachers with average expectations) were included in the analyses, only differences between HiEx and LoEx teachers will be highlighted. HiEx teachers, significantly more often than LoEx teachers, spent time orienting students to the lesson (H $(1,2) = 7.87$, $p < .02$; Highs: Mean rank = 15.79, Lows: Mean rank = 5.92). They linked new ideas with prior learning (H $(1,2) = 8.76$, $p < .01$; Highs: Mean rank = 15.96, Lows: Mean rank = 5.67) and constantly monitored student understanding. For students, this meant their learning was being carefully scaffolded and may have led to them feeling more confident about completion of tasks related to their new learning. LoEx teachers provided only very brief introductions to new concepts and monitored student understanding significantly less frequently than did HiEx teachers. For students, this may have meant they were less certain about the new ideas and less confident in completing their tasks.

In line with HiEx teachers providing significantly more instructional talk, they also asked significantly more questions of students than did LoEx teachers. Moreover, while there was no statistical difference in numbers of closed questions asked by both groups of teachers, HiEx teachers asked students significantly more open questions (H (1,2) = 14.59, $p < .001$; Highs: Mean rank = 17.75, Lows: Mean rank = 5.00). Such questions required more divergent thinking from students of HiEx than LoEx teachers. Moreover, open questions were asked of all students, not just high ability students. Furthermore, when students were unable to answer a question independently, HiEx teachers commonly prompted and supported students until they could offer a response. LoEx teachers, however, simply answered the question themselves or asked another child. Again this difference was statistically significant. In the first scenario, students were made to feel they were able to respond to the question, to achieve success, whereas in the second instance they may have felt less competent and confident.

HiEx teachers provided students with significantly more feedback about their learning than did LoEx teachers (H (1,2) = 8.55, $p < .01$; Highs: Mean rank = 16.50, Lows: Mean rank = 6.92). Hattie (2007) has shown the importance of feedback for student learning. Student feedback related to students' individual learning goals. Hence the feedback helped to keep students focused on their goals and the ways they could achieve them. Students appeared to be given frequent clear directions for learning. Conversely, feedback was uncommon in the classes of LoEx teachers; praise was a more common practice with LoEx teachers although there was no statistical difference in the amount of praise used in the classes of the two groups of teachers.

Behaviour management also differed in the classes of the two groups of teachers. HiEx teachers used significantly more positive management statements than did LoEx teachers (H (1,2) = 16.57, $p < .001$; Highs: Mean rank = 18.33, Lows: Mean rank = 7.50), and significantly more positive than negative statements. Closer examination of these statements showed statistically significant differences between groups for positive preventive statements to students (H (1,2) = 16.03, $p < .001$; Highs: Mean rank = 18.04, Lows: Mean rank = 9.17) (e.g. *'What lovely quiet girls over there and these boys here as well'*) and for positive reactive statements (H (1,2) = 11.36, $p < .004$; Highs: Mean rank = 17.33, Lows: Mean rank = 7.25) (e.g. *'Ah, that red table, you're remembering your quiet voices* [said when other students were being noisy]'). On the other hand, LoEx teachers used similar numbers of negative behaviour management statements to those used by HiEx teachers but used significantly fewer positive statements. Hence LoEx teachers were significantly more likely to react negatively to unwanted behaviour while

HiEx teachers used significantly more positive statements aimed at preventing poor behaviour. Again, for students, a potential result of the differential types of behaviour management is that their experiences within a high expectation classroom are likely to be more positive and more comfortable than those of children in low expectation classrooms.

In a more recent study, Rubie-Davies and colleagues (Flint *et al.* 2009) explored relationships between teachers' expectations and personal teaching efficacy. In this study, teachers were identified as having high, low, and average expectations. Perhaps not surprisingly, a statistically significant difference was found between the teaching efficacy of HiEx and LoEx teachers. The mean for the HiEx teacher group was higher than that for the average-expectation group, which was higher than that for the LoEx teacher group. There was a statistically significant difference between the three teacher-expectation groups for efficacy in instructional strategies ($F(2,59) = 5.47$, $p < .007$), efficacy in influencing students, ($F(2,59) = 3.57$, $p < .04$) and efficacy in providing for individuals ($F(2,59) = 4.85$, $p = .01$). There was no statistically significant difference between the three groups for efficacy in classroom management ($F(2,59) = 1.64$, $p < .20$). Post hoc Hochberg's GT2 tests showed the statistically significant differences were between the HiEx and LoEx teachers for each factor. Overall, HiEx teachers had much greater personal teaching efficacy than did their counterparts. While this study did not examine further the affective and instructional environments of the classes of the particular groups of teachers, nevertheless it is one more study to reveal differences in individual teacher characteristics that may have implications for the classroom community in which students find themselves, and ultimately for their learning.

Different lives in classroom communities

While Weinstein, Babad, and Rubie-Davies are the only researchers who have explored ways in which particular types of teachers portray their expectations at a class level, it is interesting to note that all three have found important differences in the ways different types of teachers interact with students. All three researchers have also found important differences in outcomes for students. As Weinstein (2002) points out in her book, students live different lives in different classrooms. It is also interesting to find that both Weinstein and Rubie-Davies have found similarities in the differing instructional beliefs and practices of high and low differentiating teachers (those who treat high and low expectation students very differently) (Weinstein) and of high and low expectation teachers (those who have either very high or very low expectations for all their students) (Rubie-Davies). It may well be that when results are combined across a large group of teachers, the effects of individual teachers with differing beliefs and practices on their students are dissipated or muted. When results are more closely examined by teacher type, the differences become stark and effects on student outcomes much larger.

The reduction in teacher expectation effect when data are aggregated across large numbers of teachers ignores individual differences in teacher expectations. This is strongly illustrated in the recent study by McKown and Weinstein (2008) discussed above. Several earlier studies that aggregated data across teachers found small effects for ethnicity on teachers' expectations (e.g. Baron *et al.* 1985). However, when McKown and Weinstein separated teachers' expectations for African American and Caucasian students, the results were startling. The expectations of the high differentiating teachers, compared to those of the low differentiating teachers' expectations, were between .75 and 1.00 standard deviations higher for Caucasian students, despite similar levels of student achievement.

Considering the large differences in student outcomes found by teacher type by both Weinstein and Rubie-Davies, it seems pertinent that research on teacher expectations should switch from examining effects on individual students to investigating teacher expectations in terms of teacher moderators. It appears that at this level, the effect of teacher expectations has been largely unacknowledged, but that moderators may have substantial effects on student academic and social outcomes.

Contributions to the literature

The work of Weinstein, Babad and Rubie-Davies has served to re-energize the teacher expectation field. It has taken the focus away from the student and instead placed the teacher under the microscope. In this way, class-level expectations have been placed in the foreground, and a search for teacher characteristics that contribute to considerable differences in student outcomes should become the focus. The earlier studies of Rubie-Davies (see above) have shown large differences in the instructional environments of teachers based on whether they have high or low expectations for all students, while the current chapter has explored possible effects of some of these instructional practices on the socioemotional environment of the classroom. However, any differences in the affective environment have mostly been surmised from teacher behaviours, teacher beliefs, and changes in student self-perceptions.

Future research

It will therefore be important in future studies to more carefully and systematically examine how students feel when they attend different classrooms. Students could be interviewed to determine what the teacher practices and beliefs identified by researchers mean for students, what their perceptions are and how they observe this affects them. There is surprisingly little research of, or understanding about, the social psychology of the classroom. Research has shown how important teacher caring is in influencing student motivation and achievement (Wentzel 1999) and the socioemotional environment of the classroom, but there are other aspects of the socioemotional environment that could be explored in future research. For example, it might be interesting to explore more closely relationships between teachers' beliefs and how teachers design the affective environment of their classes.

It would also be interesting to determine whether teachers with a high expectation orientation (and those with low expectations) are located in particular schools. In other words, it may be that school climate has an effect on teachers' class level expectations.

While research in the teacher expectation area has been active for almost 50 years, there have been few studies conducted since the end of the 1980s. This decline is partly because there is a perception there is nothing new to find. However, the more recent focus on teachers rather than students in research on the role of expectation has produced some thought-provoking results and has once again highlighted teacher expectations as worthy of further research. Research on teacher expectations is important because it focuses on equality of educational opportunities for all students. Students have little choice about their teacher and the classroom environment into which they are placed. They are small voices not often heard and, while the vast majority of teachers want to do their best for students, the spotlight for enhancing teacher practice and student outcomes has remained firmly on the instructional environment. Focusing more closely on the social psychology of the classroom, ensuring that teacher education courses include research findings in this area, and providing professional development for teachers related to the affective climate and not just the instructional, could contribute substantially to moving towards the goal of equality for all students.

References

Babad, E., Bernieri, F. and Rosenthal, R. (1989a) 'Nonverbal communication and leakage in the behavior of biased and unbiased teachers', *Journal of Personality and Social Psychology*, 56: 89–94.

Babad, E., Bernieri, F. and Rosenthal, R. (1989b) 'When less information is more informative: diagnosing teacher expectations from brief samples of behaviour', *British Journal of Educational Psychology*, 59: 281–95.

Babad, E., Bernieri, F. and Rosenthal, R. (1991) 'Students as judges of teachers' verbal and nonverbal behavior', *American Educational Research Journal*, 28: 211–34.

Babad, E., Inbar, J. and Rosenthal, R. (1982) 'Pygmalion, Galatea and the Golem: investigations of biased and unbiased teachers', *Journal of Educational Psychology*, 74: 459–74.

Babad, E. and Taylor, P.B. (1992) 'Transparency of teacher expectancies across language, cultural boundaries', *Journal of Educational Research*, 86: 120–5.

Baron, R.M., Tom, D.Y.H. and Cooper, H.M. (1985) 'Social class, race and teacher expectations', in J.B. Dusek (ed.) *Teacher Expectancies* (pp. 251–69), Hillsdale, NJ: Lawrence Erlbaum Associates.

Bishop, R., Berryman, M., Cavanagh, T. and Teddy, L. (2009). 'Te Kotahitanga: addressing educational disparities facing Māori students in New Zealand', *Teaching and Teacher Education*, 22: 734–42.

Blatchford, P., Burke, J., Farquhar, C., Plewis, I. and Tizard, B. (1989) 'Teacher expectations in infant school: associations with attainment and progress, curriculum coverage and classroom interaction', *British Journal of Educational Psychology*, 59: 19–30.

Brophy, J.E. (1982) 'How teachers influence what is taught and learned in classrooms', *The Elementary School Journal*, 83: 1–13.

Brophy, J.E. (1983) 'Research on the self-fulfilling prophecy and teacher expectations', *Journal of Educational Psychology*, 75: 631–61.

Brophy, J.E. (1985) 'Teacher-student interaction', in J. B. Dusek (ed.) *Teacher Expectancies* (pp. 303–28), Hillsdale, NJ: Lawrence Erlbaum.

Brophy, J.E. and Good, T.L. (1974) *Teacher-Student Relationships: Causes and Consequences*, New York: Holt, Rinehart and Winston.

Cooper, H.M. and Good, T.L. (1983) *Pygmalion Grows Up: Studies in the Expectation Communication Process*, New York: Longman.

Dweck, C.S., Mangels, J.A. and Good, C. (2004) 'Motivational effects on attention, cognition, and performance', in D.Y. Dai and R.J. Sternberg (eds) *Motivation, Emotion, and Cognition: Integrative Perspectives on Intellectual Functioning and Development* (pp. 41–56), Mahwah, NJ: Lawrence Erlbaum.

Flint, A., Rubie-Davies, C.M. and McDonald, L. (2009) 'Exploring moderators in teacher expectancy effects', paper presented at the European Association for Research on Learning and Instruction Conference, Amsterdam, the Netherlands, August.

Good, T.L. and Brophy, J.E. (2003) *Looking in Classrooms*, 9th edn, Boston: Allyn and Bacon.

Hacker, R.G., Rowe, M.J. and Evans, R.D. (1992) 'The influences of ability groupings for secondary science lessons upon classroom processes: part 2', *School Science Review*, 73: 119–23.

Harris, M.J. and Rosenthal, R. (1985) 'Mediation of interpersonal expectancy effects: 31 meta-analyses', *Psychological Bulletin*, 97: 363–86.

Hattie, J. (2007) 'Developing potentials for learning: evidence, assessment, and progress', paper presented at the European Association for Research into Learning and Instruction, Keynote address, Budapest, Hungary, August.

Hidi, S., Renninger, K.A. and Krapp, A. (2004) 'Interest, a motivational variable that combines affective and cognitive functioning', in D.Y. Dai and R.J. Sternberg (eds) *Motivation, Emotion and Cognition: Integrative Perspectives on Intellectual Functioning and Development* (pp. 89–115), Mahwah, NJ: Lawrence Erlbaum.

Kuklinski, M.R. and Weinstein, R.S. (2001) 'Classroom and developmental differences in a path model of teacher expectancy effects', *Child Development*, 72: 1554–78.

Linchevski, L. and Kutscher, B. (1998) 'Tell me with whom you're learning, and I'll tell you how much you've learned: mixed ability versus same-ability grouping in mathematics', *Journal for Research in Mathematics Education*, 29: 533–54.

McKown, C. and Weinstein, R.S. (2008) 'Teacher expectations, classroom context and the achievement gap', *Journal of School Psychology*, 46: 235–61.

Midgley, C. (ed.) (2002) *Goals, Goal Structures, and Patterns of Adaptive Learning*, Mahwah, NJ: Lawrence Erlbaum.

Noddings, N. (1992) *The Challenge to Care in Schools: An Alternative Approach to Education*, New York: Teachers College Press.

Page, S. and Rosenthal, R. (1990) 'Sex and expectations of teachers and sex and race of students as determinants of teaching behavior and student performance', *Journal of School Psychology*, 28: 119–31.

Reeve, J. and Jang, H. (2006) 'What teachers say and do to support students' autonomy during a learning activity', *Journal of Educational Psychology*, 98: 209–18.

Rubie-Davies, C.M. (2006) 'Teacher expectations and student self-perceptions: exploring relationships', *Psychology in the Schools*, 43: 537–52.

Rubie-Davies, C.M. (2007) 'Classroom interactions: exploring the practices of high and low expectation teachers', *British Journal of Educational Psychology*, 77: 289–306.

Rubie-Davies, C.M. (2008) 'Teacher beliefs and expectations: relationships with student learning', in C.M. Rubie-Davies and C. Rawlinson (eds) *Challenging Thinking About Teaching and Learning* (pp. 25–39), Haupaugge, NY: Nova.

Rubie-Davies, C.M. (2009) 'Teacher expectations and labeling', in L.J. Saha and A.G. Dworkin (eds) *The New International Handbook of Teachers and Teaching* (pp. 695–707), Norwell, MA: Springer.

Rubie-Davies, C.M., Hattie, J., Townsend, M.A.R. and Hamilton, R.J. (2007) 'Aiming high: teachers and their students', in V.N. Galwye (ed.) *Progress in Educational Psychology Research* (pp. 65–91), Hauppauge, NY: Nova.

Rubie, C.M., Townsend, M.A.R. and Moore, D.W. (2004) 'Motivational and academic effects of cultural experiences for indigenous minority students in New Zealand', *Educational Psychology*, 24: 143–60.

Stone, S.J. (1998) 'Creating contexts for middle-age learning', *Childhood Education*, 74: 234–6.

Weinstein, R.S. (1986) 'The teaching of reading and children's awareness of teacher expectations', in T. Raphael (ed.) *The Contexts of School-Based Literacy* (pp. 233–52), New York: Random House.

Weinstein, R.S. (1989) 'Perceptions of classroom processes and student motivation: children's views of self-fulfilling prophecies', in R. Ames and C. Ames (eds) *Research on Motivation in Education* (vol. 3, pp. 187–221), New York: Academic Press.

Weinstein, R.S. (1993) 'Children's knowledge of differential treatment in school: implications for motivation', in T.M. Tomlinson (ed.) *Motivating Students to Learn: Overcoming Barriers to High Achievement* (pp. 197–224) Berkeley, CA: McCutchan.

Weinstein, R.S. (2002) *Reaching Higher: The Power of Expectations in Schooling*, Cambridge, MA: Harvard University Press.

Weinstein, R.S., Gregory, A. and Strambler, M.J. (2004) 'Intractable self-fulfilling prophecies fifty years after Brown v. Board of Education', *American Psychologist*, 59: 511–20.

Weinstein, R.S., Marshall, H.H., Brattesani, K.A. and Middlestadt, S.E. (1982) 'Student perceptions of differential teacher treatment in open and traditional classrooms', *Journal of Educational Psychology*, 74: 678–92.

Wentzel, K.R. (1997) 'Student motivation in middle school: the role of perceived pedagogical caring', *Journal of Educational Psychology*, 89: 411–19.

Wentzel, K.R. (1999) 'Social-motivational processes and interpersonal relationships: implications for understanding motivation at school', *Journal of Educational Psychology*, 91: 76–97.

Wilkinson, I.G. and Townsend, M.A.R. (2000) 'From Rata to Rimu: grouping for instruction in best practice New Zealand classrooms', *The Reading Teacher*, 53: 460–71.

Zohar, A., Degani, A. and Vaaknin, E. (2001) 'Teachers' beliefs about low-achieving students and higher order thinking', *Teaching and Teacher Education*, 17: 469–85.

Chapter 10

Managing classroom behaviour
Assertiveness and warmth

Jane E. Prochnow and Angus H. Macfarlane

This chapter examines evidence about the effect of quality classroom management on the learning and behaviour of students. We begin by identifying types of behaviours that challenge teachers and outlining the characteristics of teachers who create conditions for maximizing learning and minimizing unacceptable student behaviour. We build on international trends, in particular the changes brought about by adopting inclusive education philosophies, positive behaviour support, and examining student 'response to intervention' for challenging behaviours. These changes, notably those required to embrace the philosophy of inclusion, require teachers to accommodate a range of diverse student needs within the regular classroom and recommend best practices and interventions. We suggest that, despite the focus of interest on teacher characteristics and the associated effect of teaching quality in general, there is reason to focus on the principles of culturally responsive practice, particularly in the school and classroom environment.

Nature of the classroom

Classroom management is the careful orchestration of classroom life so that students are able to make the most of their opportunities to learn. Behaviour management is inherently enigmatic; comprehensive, and holistic on the one hand, while being a series of separate (yet interrelated) skills on the other. Creating conditions that are conducive to maximizing learning capability and promoting appropriate behaviour is not an easy task, yet it is essential as learning is impaired in classrooms with higher rates of unsafe and challenging behaviours (Prochnow 2004). The classroom is a unique space that is populated (generally) by a sole adult and many students engaged in a variety of different activities. The teacher is regularly required to implement multiple tasks simultaneously, with little time to pause or reflect. The classroom is also an unpredictable place where a combination of human personalities and attitudes (for example, non-compliance) and natural elements (for example, extreme weather conditions) can determine the mood that transpires within its walls. In addition and importantly, the classroom is a place to which each student and teacher brings their previous histories and experiences (Doyle 1986).

Teachers draw on a range of qualities required of their profession, namely attitudes, skills, knowledge, and experience. According to Jensen (1995), a further quality, acumen, describes the high professional standards that good teachers set for themselves. Acumen includes learning about the various cultures represented in the classroom; discovering what has been done by other teachers in the past; looking through school archives; and asking colleagues and community members about the local traditions, rituals, and legends of the community. Having acumen is similar to Blumberg's notion of 'developing a nose for things – having a sense of process' so that management of the classroom can be carried out efficiently (1989: 56).

Developing a 'nose' for potential trouble and maintaining a sense of process do not necessarily guarantee that everything will always go smoothly in a classroom. Acumen and process cannot provide an absolute assurance that disruptive behaviours will be totally eliminated from or never occur in the classroom. In a classic study, Wheldall and Merrett (1989) reported on disruptive behaviour in schools in the West Midlands of the United Kingdom. These researchers found that the types of behaviours teachers found most unacceptable disrupted quality learning time. Strong consensus was indicated among the respondents that 'talking out of turn' and 'hindering other children' were the most frequent and troublesome behaviours in primary classrooms. Teachers identified a range of student behaviours as particularly troublesome, including disobedience, idleness, and physical aggression. Notably, more than half of the teachers responded that they spent too much time managing behaviour (order and control) at the expense of valuable teaching time. Wheldall and Merrett argued that straightforward interventions by teachers can bring about dramatic results in improving classroom atmosphere and enhancing the quantity and quality of work achieved by students. Successfully implemented interventions can also yield a more satisfying and rewarding classroom experience for both teachers and students.

Further studies have elicited varying degrees of concerns that teachers and researchers have about classroom behaviour (Bishop and Berryman 2006; Church 2003; Macfarlane 2003; Prochnow 2006; Wearmouth *et al.* 2005). Frequently, the behaviours being managed are the more 'pesky' behaviours (Charles 2008) with regard to the types, severity, and prevalence of inappropriate behaviours. These behaviours, as listed by Charles (2008: 2), include:

1   Aggression: physical and verbal attacks on the teacher or other students.
2   Immorality: acts such as cheating, lying, and stealing.
3   Defiance of authority: refusal, sometimes hostile, to do as the teacher requests.
4   Class disruptions: talking loudly, calling out, walking about the room, clowning, tossing objects.
5   Goofing off: fooling around, out of seat, not doing assigned tasks, dawdling, daydreaming.

Teachers' judgements generally mirror those of social scientists regarding prevalence and severity of the five categories of behaviour advanced by Charles

(2008). While the first three are, understandably, the most dreaded, they occur less frequently. Consequently, the more inane behaviours of inattention and annoying talking are more of an imposition on teachers' instructional time and ultimately on students' learning.

Although it is difficult to be totally definitive about what constitutes inappropriate behaviours, it is possible to identify clusters of varying degrees of behaviours which have recognizable features. Conway (1998) contends that these clusters may be represented along a behaviour continuum. The location of the student on the continuum has significant implications for assessment, intervention strategy, and the type of support person likely to work with the student. The behaviour continuum in Table 10.1 differentiates between, yet links, mild, moderate, severe, and serious behaviours.

The first stage of the continuum describes mild to moderate behaviours which should be able to be addressed by the classroom teacher with class- and school-wide primary interventions. If the behaviours persist, then further school support needs to be enlisted (e.g. a school dean, senior teacher, or the school special needs teacher). At the moderate level of difficult behaviour, a specialist support teacher may undertake observations and gather data specific to the learning environment in order to offer more specific interventions. The data, in the main, would rely heavily on qualitative information.

Table 10.1 Macfarlane and Prochnow's bases for contexts of behaviour

1	2	3
Mild to Moderate	Moderate to Severe	Severe to Serious
Displays rather innocuous behaviours; seen as more to do with adjustment difficulties because of slowness to respond to the usual range of management strategies.	Displays more salient behaviours; consequently judged by more than one authoritative adult to be severely excessive, deficient or inappropriate within given social situations.	Displays more damaging behaviours; often seen as defiant or uncouth that consequently interfere seriously with either their own or other people's well-being, learning and teaching. Often continues at an unacceptable level, subsequent to intervention which has been implemented thoroughly and with integrity.
Affects quality instructional time in the classroom	Affects quality management time of school leaders	Affects quality time of teachers, school leaders, whanau, caregivers, and professional and voluntary services
Low-end need; inexpensive resourcing required per student or programme	Moderate need; medium resourcing required per student or programme	High-end need; costly resourcing required per student or programme

Source: Macfarlane and Prochnow (2008).

Behaviours located to the right of the continuum would attract other forms of intervention and support such as a counsellor, special education advisor, psychologist, psychiatrist, or community action group. The teacher is always included in the group of professionals who collaborate to make meaning of and respond to the student's behaviour, given their knowledge of the student. The data collected for the assessment of behaviour that is severe or serious would also include quantitative information regarding frequency, duration and intensity.

Theoretical background

For nearly 50 years educators have actively sought ways to promote acceptable student behaviour by preferring to employ positive strategies rather than intimidation and punishment with students. Nevertheless, in the past 30 years, discipline has remained at the top of the list of teacher concerns (Charles 2008). Pioneers in the field of student behaviour include Redl and Wattenberg, who focused on group behaviour and explored how individual behaviour within groups could more easily be understood and managed (cited in Charles 2008). Redl and Wattenberg's research greatly contributed to the understanding that group expectations strongly influence group and individual behaviour. In the 1960s Skinner's work with behaviour consequences employed the shaping of desired student behaviour through the principles of reinforcement (Skinner 1953). Skinner's research added immensely to our understanding of the environment and the contingencies that shape and control many human behaviours.

Notable research and publications continued, including Jacob Kounin's (1977) landmark studies on behaviour management through lesson control (that is, 'with-it' knowledge of the classroom), and Fredric Jones's (1987) *Positive Discipline*, which has been in use since 1979 but was published later. Table 10.2 lists selected researchers who have made significant contributions to our present understandings of and methods for supporting challenging behaviours, along with the fundamental propositions that underpin their respective works.

Greater emphasis on the use of behaviour support has emerged in response to the increasingly adverse reaction of public and parents to corporal punishment in schools. Several of the classroom management and disciplinary strategies that have emerged from early scholarship continue to be vehicles for establishing a positive classroom climate where students feel valued and motivated. For example, from previous research (Ginott 1971; Good and Brophy 1994), we are aware that effective communication is both fundamental to student motivation and based on positive and reciprocal teacher and student relationships, which are in turn integral to effective classroom management, because the particular strategies a teacher employs are more likely to be successful in a classroom climate of mutual respect (Macfarlane 2007). A climate of effective communication and mutual respect begins with positive behaviour support and culturally responsive classrooms.

Positive behaviour support is firmly rooted in the fundamental behavioural principles that behaviour is learned intentionally or unintentionally in interaction

Table 10.2 Guiding developments in classroom management

Researchers	Theoretical Perspectives
Fritz Redl and William Wattenburg	Emphasized understanding *group dynamics* as critical. Group expectations strongly influence behaviour, and vice versa. Recognition of causes precedes effective intervention.
Jacob Kounin	Championed the notion of *with-it-ness* in knowing what is going on in the classroom at all times. Key aspects include teacher organization, lesson presentation, classroom arrangement, and smooth transitions.
Haim Ginott	Promoted self-discipline in small steps over time based on the power of *congruent communication*.
Burrhis Frederick Skinner	Demonstrated that *consequences* as well as setting events (antecedents or environmental conditions) influenced behaviour and behaviour change. His influential work remains the basis of applied behaviour analysis.
Albert Bandura	Further examined the principles of environment and consequences to develop the *social cognitive theory* which explains how cognition, imitation and anticipation of consequences influence many behaviours and behaviour change.
Fredric Jones	Introduced positive classroom discipline that espouses *effective body language* and adroit incentive systems.
William Glasser	Advocated *quality education* in the curriculum, as well as teaching and learning from a 'lead' rather than 'boss' approach to meeting students' basic needs in a non-coercive way.
Herbert Grossman	Empowered teachers to select techniques that suit their own personalities, philosophies and values, while *accommodating diverse backgrounds*.
Lee Kern and Glen Dunlap	Demonstrated both *functional behaviour analysis and functional behaviour assessment*, based on the belief that behaviour generally serves a function for the person performing the behaviour, recommended examination of the purpose(s) the behaviour serves before attempting to change it.
George Sugai and Robert Horner	Redesigned a systems-oriented school environment that *supports positive behaviour* by being more preventive, predictable, and safe for all students.
Janice Wearmouth, Ted Glynn, and Mere Berryman	Focused on the underpinning concept of *belonging*. With appropriate support, students can adapt and respond positively within a learning environment where they are valued, respected and feel that they belong.
Luanna Meyer and Ian Evans	Argued for and demonstrated *positive-based interventions* to effect behavioural changes, particularly with developmentally delayed participants.
Angus Macfarlane and Jane Prochnow	Advocated *assertiveness and warmth*. In this paradigm the teacher holds firm priorities about academic and social skills, in a space that is both welcoming and engaging.

with the environment and can be changed through a behaviourally based systems approach with attention to past behaviours, student needs, effective interventions, positive consequences and careful planning (Sugai *et al.* 2000). Any plan based on positive behaviour support should be continually reviewed and realigned to the student's current behaviours and academic needs.

Application in New Zealand

Classroom management in New Zealand moved toward a school-based positive behaviour support programme when the Special Education 2000 policy oriented the delivery model to an inclusive structure for education. The Special Education 2000 model (Ministry of Education 1996) was based on primary prevention of mild behaviour problems with school- and classroom-wide interventions which are effective for approximately 90 per cent of students, followed by targeted secondary prevention offering individual interventions for approximately 7 to 9 per cent of students with moderate behaviour problems. The tertiary tier of prevention offers more intensive interventions to the 1 to 3 per cent of students with the most difficult and challenging behaviours (Kerr and Nelson 2006; Ministry of Education 1996).

In New Zealand, the inclusive education model requires teachers to be actively involved in accommodating the needs of children with diverse abilities. Teachers' direct responsibility for managing moderate behaviour challenges is supported in the second tier by Resource Teachers: Learning and Behaviour, while severely challenging behaviour is supported by behaviour support workers within the severe behaviour initiative of the Ministry of Education, Special Education. These specialists support the teacher in a consultative problem-solving process with specialist support oriented toward working with the teacher rather than working directly with the student. However, both specialists, notably the specialists working within the severe behaviour initiative, will also work directly with the children and their families.

Major assumptions inherent in this model are that teachers feel prepared and confident to manage secondary and tertiary prevention interventions, and further, that they can consistently discriminate moderate behaviours from severe behaviours; feel that they are responsible for managing more intensive interventions; and, perhaps more importantly, believe that learners requiring more intensive interventions belong in their classroom. These assumptions have not found widespread support among teachers (Prochnow 2006). Research examining classroom management and teacher attitudes conducted since the initiation of the Special Education 2000 policy continues to find resistance on the part of teachers for inclusion of students with severely challenging behaviours in their classrooms (Macfarlane 2003; Prochnow 2006; Wylie and Hogden 2007).

In response to the difficulties of full inclusion for students with severely challenging behaviours, principals have felt highly constrained with the limited response options of stand-downs and suspensions to remove a learner from the classroom and school (Macfarlane and Burke 1997; Prochnow 1998; Prochnow and Maw 2002). Not surprisingly, many schools have developed their own on- or off-campus alternative education placements to recognize and cater for the requirements of up to 10 per cent of the learner population with behavioural problems.

Students from diverse backgrounds

Behaviour problems are associated with ethnicity and gender. In a multicultural society the disproportionate representation of children from any cultural or ethnic background in problematic areas of education must be considered unacceptable (Achilles et al. 2007; Skiba 2002). In New Zealand, the relatively small population includes many nationalities in addition to indigenous Māori. We could reasonably expect that with such diversity of ethnic and cultural backgrounds, no one ethnic group would be over-represented in the most easily identifiable key indicators of challenging behaviours, for example, retention rates, stand-downs and suspensions. However, education statistics of New Zealand reveal a different picture.

The 2006 statistics on stand-downs (Ministry of Education 2007) reveal that 3.1 per cent of the student population were stood down in 2006. Māori students were stood down at the highest rate (5.8 per cent of Māori were stood down) followed by Pasifika students (4.3 per cent), European/Pākehā students (2.3 per cent), and the lowest rate was for Asian students at 0.8 per cent. Similar statistics were reported in previous years (Ministry of Education 2003, 2004, 2005, 2006). Over-representation of students by ethnic groups in the number of suspensions from 2002 to 2006 was very similar to the statistics for stand-downs. The most frequent reasons for suspensions and stand-downs were continual disobedience and physical assault on students or staff, and drug use in the case of suspensions (Ministry of Education 2003, 2004, 2005, 2006, 2007). Similar behaviours were highlighted in an earlier study by Prochnow (1998) with primary and intermediate school principals, who indicated that most students were suspended for defiant, violent, aggressive, destructive, and noncompliant behaviours.

Although the statistics based on teacher and principal reports are persuasive, it is important to be aware of the possibility that 'disproportionate representation is greater in the judgmental or "soft" disability categories' (Skiba et al. 2008: 269) which include emotional disturbance and learning disabilities. We suggest that the soft categories also include behavioural difficulties and disorders, which are very dependent on teacher expectations, attitudes, and culturally based behavioural expectations (Skiba et al. 2008). Behavioural data reported by teacher and principal rating scales frequently suggest that minority students' behaviours are more often considered to be unacceptable, inappropriate, and challenging to school staff. As rating scales have been questioned methodologically for their low level of reliability (Church 2003; Eddy et al. 1998), these data have to be considered 'soft' in their subjectivity, reliability, and validity.

Race and ethnic background remain predictors not only for judging behaviours as inappropriate and challenging but also for subsequent referral to the Ministry of Education, Special Education and to Resource Teachers: Learning and Behaviour. There are questions, particularly as children mature, of whether disproportionate referrals are based on students' more frequent and extreme behaviours or misinterpretation of the behaviours by teachers from culturally different backgrounds (Skiba *et al.* 2008; Townsend 2000). Teachers tend to see difficult classroom behaviours as an issue coming from outside the classroom, frequently the result of dysfunctional families or student attitudes which are exacerbated by ineffective and inappropriate interventions and lack of management support (Prochnow 2006). Teachers rarely see classroom processes and practices as contributing to troublesome student behaviour (Prochnow 2006).

Yet a recent panel meeting of the National Research Council in the United States, 'identified inadequate classroom management as a factor increasing the risk of overidentifying minority students' (Donovan and Cross 2002, cited in Skiba *et al.* 2008: 280). In support of this, Church (2003) has indicated that behaviour is highly interactive and a function of the teacher's expectations, abilities and background, school structure and attitudes, and student expectations and background struggling with unequal and changing levels of power and control. As most problems and complaints occur in the classroom, teachers are the first level of assessment and generally the person to refer students for behaviour support. This highlights the importance of teacher–student interaction. Their interactions are highly dependent on the students' behaviours and the teachers' ability to handle, channel, teach, and manage those behaviours, as well as on the teachers' behaviours and ability to build relationships with students, and the students' ability to understand and accept the teacher behaviours.

Application of culturally responsive instruction in New Zealand

Contemporary approaches to difficult behaviour indicate a clear movement away from the earlier spate of school-centred zero tolerance and lockstep assertive discipline programmes, which are being rejected internationally (Horner and Sugai 2000; Sugai *et al.* 2000) and in particular, in New Zealand, by teachers, schools, parents and students as inflexible and punitive. Current research focuses on restorative practices (Bateman and Berryman 2008; Hooper *et al.* 1999; Macfarlane 2005) and culturally responsive programmes, teachers, classrooms and instruction. Culturally responsive instruction is defined as instruction that allows children of diverse backgrounds to feel more comfortable with their own identities in school (Au 1998; Macfarlane *et al.* 2007; Macfarlane *et al.* 2008). This can be accomplished through making learning experiences more personally meaningful to students of diverse backgrounds by engaging them in activities that relate to their interests and experiences outside of school; using instructional materials that present minority cultures in an authentic manner, including presenting culturally relevant content in culturally familiar social contexts; and improving community involvement in learning by promoting stronger connections among schools, parents, and the community (Au 1998, 2000). Classrooms using more culturally responsive pedagogical approaches rely less (ideally, not at all) on punitive practices and methods of teacher control (Macfarlane 2007).

Culturally responsive teachers use differentiated instruction to tailor teaching to the different needs of the students (Foorman 2001; Tunmer *et al.* 2003) paying particular attention to the gaps early learners may have between their rate of learning and expected reasonable levels without fear of being accused of deficit thinking in addressing differences in academic growth (Trent *et al.* 2008; Tunmer and Prochnow 2009). Culturally responsive teachers will also be aware of and use effective teaching methods informed by updated assessment of student performance and progress (Cartledge and Kourea 2008). In addition to being pedagogically informed, the teacher concerned with culturally responsive teaching will develop personal cultural awareness and understanding of his or her own bias to develop that awareness and understanding in their learners to promote appropriate classroom behaviour.

In order to guide teachers to reflect on their own personal bias, Cartledge and Kourea (2008) suggest that teachers reflect on a series of introspective questions which may reveal their biases in practice. For this purpose, Cartledge and Kourea developed 11 questions to guide self-reflection. We present adaptations of the questions for use within the New Zealand education context below. The questions are open-ended to stimulate reflective analysis of teaching practices, attitudes, and critical awareness of how actions and intentions may be perceived by others:

1 Does the culture of the students in my class influence my perspectives/biases in terms of how I respond to and manage behaviour?
2 What is the correlation (negative/positive) between my behavioural inter-actions with students and their culture?
3 How are my responses being perceived by the students?
4 How are my responses being perceived by the students' peers?
5 Is the behaviour of my students improving? How do I know that? If not, why not?
6 How equitable and culturally-appropriate are my behaviour management responses? How do I know?
7 Do my behaviour management strategies facilitate long term change(s) or do they merely suppress behaviour?
8 How do I identify cultural influences on, and explanations for, various behaviour(s)?
9 How do I currently respond to/address positive and long-term behavioural change in my students? Do I influence and empower their pro-social skills?
10 What behaviour management skills do I need to develop? Do I effectively manage student behaviour?
11 How can I improve my management/instructional skills so that I am not resorting to punitive teaching ideology/processes?

Teachers must be aware of their own beliefs and practices through self-reflection in order to fully engage culturally responsive teaching (Howard 2003). These adapted questions could guide teachers through examining their own beliefs and biases, as well as the effect these beliefs have on their behaviour and the behaviour of the students in their classrooms.

Classroom management in culturally responsive classrooms is concerned with positive teaching and teaching opportunities for practice and interaction as opposed to punitive, reductive procedures (see reviews by Church 2003; Meyer and Evans 2006). Yet, culturally responsive classrooms are assertively disciplined (as opposed to being controlling or punishing), as well as academic, organized, warm, and careful to make use of teachable moments.

The positive sequence of culturally responsive learning should begin early before negative expectations develop, difficult behaviour becomes entrenched, academic losses occur, and mutual negative expectations and negative reinforcement cycles develop in the interactions of teachers, schools, students, and parents. There is also a sense of urgency, as learners who are one year behind in Year 2 may be four years behind in Year 10 and then may leave school with few or no qualifications. Further, time lost to truancy and disciplinary actions is not only precious time lost to academic attention but yet another signal that the student does not belong in the education community.

In summary, disproportional identification of students for special services, disciplinary action, and school completion rates are indicators that could alert communities that a school could benefit from a review of culturally responsive practices, teachers, attitudes, interventions, and goals. Teachers who are indifferent to culturally responsive practices pose difficulties in the school and potentially hinder students' learning progress (Cartledge and Kourea 2008). On the other hand, teachers who use the most effective teaching methods and research-based effective interventions are helping all students, but more importantly, those students at greatest risk of overcoming barriers and succeeding at school.

Nevertheless, we must bear in mind that the relationships of students, student home environment, teachers, school and classroom environments, learning and behaviour are so systemic and complex, it would be overly simplistic to credit or blame the attitudes of teachers for the differential responses of students to instruction, teachers to students, and parents to teachers (Nash and Prochnow 2004). It is far more important to recognize the delicate balance between teacher abilities, the support available to teachers, the barriers to achievement and inclusion of behaviour, attitudes, and ambivalence (Prochnow and Bourke 2001; Prochnow *et al*. 2000; Prochnow 2006).

Effective classroom practitioners

In a review of nine New Zealand studies, Macfarlane (2003) synthesized key factors of culturally responsive classroom management which were consistent with the research reported by Prochnow and her colleagues. It is clear that some schools, teachers, and approaches to teaching can make a significant difference in the quality of student learning outcomes for students from minority cultures, and indeed for all students. The findings emerging from the Hei Awhina Maatua programme of the Poutama Pounamu Research Centre (Glynn *et al.* 1997), the Te Kotahitanga project (Bishop and Berryman 2006; Bishop *et al.* 2002), and the Achievement in Multicultural High Schools (AIMHI) project coordinated by Hill and Hawk (2000) are particularly worth noting. These, not unlike others mentioned earlier, highlighted the importance of academic engagement, supportive environment, and recognition of cultural difference as key qualities that make teaching and learning more meaningful and responsive to the diverse composition of the conventional New Zealand classroom.

The following is an exploration of the case of a highly experienced female Māori teacher of a Year Two (8-year-old students) enrichment class (Macfarlane 2003, 2004). A range of classroom management strategies identified in the literature were effectively introduced in a classroom of 6-year-olds, with particular emphasis on communication processes between teacher and students. This enrichment class was part of a special project between local schools and their *iwi* (Māori tribe) where the emphasis was on improving the learning and behaviour of selected groups of students.

Research observations indicated that the case study classroom had a busy tone to it. The teacher was always well organized and each lesson was presented with precision and clarity. Room arrangement allowed for the teacher to 'work the crowd' and to attend to students, either individually or collectively. In line with some of Kounin's (1977) approaches to classroom management, her 'with-it-ness' enabled her to know what was going on in all parts of the classroom at all times. The classroom was bright, with rules of the class displayed, as were examples of students' work, awards, reminder notices, class timetables, and pictures promoting the cultural icons of the region. Māori translations of key concepts and words were evident on walls, tables, and charts. The room had a texture which incorporated real sight, sound, smell, and taste. Importantly, the students seemed to delight in being there, in the presence of a skilled practitioner who valued each of them for simply who they were.

Students reputed to have behaviour problems did not misbehave. Most were said to have learning difficulties, yet in this environment they were motivated to advance their achievement, and records of their progress attested to that. Withdrawn students became vocal contributors and those previously identified as impulsive seemed more in control of themselves. Her lessons had good momentum in the sense that she motivated students to apply themselves to assigned tasks; and she made sure activities had closure and a smooth transition to the next activity. Her demeanour had a powerful influence on her students' learning and behaviour. Her posture and body language displayed confidence and suggested leadership, enthusiasm and enjoyment, as well as appreciation of the content of the learning experiences and of the context in which this was taking place. The students respected and derived a sense of security from the assertive, no-nonsense approach that prevailed. Their engagement in learning and the delight they showed in being around her created opportunities for their teacher to attend to their respective needs, to challenge, and to signal approval (or disapproval) where appropriate.

Systems for gaining attention and clarifying expectations played an important part in this teacher's approach. Tactics included a repertoire of body language cues to encourage students to pay attention and stay on task. She was often observed using non-verbal behaviour management strategies, such as eye contact, proximity control, conversational pause, facial expressions, and gestures in classroom interactions with students (Jones 1987).

It is argued that a key characteristic of programmes that attend successfully to students' achievement – such as this enrichment class – is cultural responsiveness. This is not to stipulate that teachers must be of the same culture as their students in order to be effective. What matters is their ability to connect culturally and to promote a cultural presence in their respective learning environments, referred to by Macfarlane (2004) as 'educultural'.

The term 'educultural' is used when referring to five concepts that are likely to have an effect on students' learning and teachers' teaching; hence on classroom management. The New Zealand and Māori concepts are *whanaungatanga* (building relationships), *manaakitanga* (caring ethos), *rangatiratanga* (motivating strategies), *kotahitanga* (working together), and *pumanawatanga* (maintaining a classroom ambience). They do not stand alone; rather they vary together in patterned ways (Rogoff 2003). The presence of these concepts in the enrichment class was very real. Collectively they offer a framework that encourages teachers to adopt a position within their classrooms that is culturally relevant. The aim is to ensure that the concept meanings are evidenced in their practice, reciprocated by the students, and represented in the learning and the learning activities. These five concepts are considered to be at the core of a Māori world view; they drive Māori philosophies and functionalities. From an educational and cultural (educultural) perspective, these concepts are highly regarded because they are conducive to creating a collaborative classroom climate where individual dignity is valued, where teachers believe in students' ability to learn, and where classroom norms and routines are clearly explained.

Conclusion

We end by drawing attention to a Māori proverb which highlights the potential of sharing the different perspectives from which we have come:

Nau te rourou
Naku te rourou
Ka ora ai te iwi
With your food basket
And my food basket
There will be ample.

Our world views, shaped in part by quite different cultural and social forces, provide the imprint of what we believe to be a congruent consciousness. This involves a parallel respect for and acceptance of these forces so as to forge a paradigm premised on the *whakatauki* (proverb) that when each of us contributes, the imprint expands.

Culturally responsive teachers will recognize learners with diverse learning needs begin school with limited experiences and limited knowledge of the fundamental building blocks that facilitate further learning, and these teachers will respond with instruction that targets the skill gaps and allows the learners to progress with their peers (Cartledge and Kourea 2008). Our very different research examining the links between early literacy development, the New Zealand teaching response, and difficult behaviour highlights the importance of early intervention responsive to student needs (Macfarlane 2003; Tunmer *et al.* 2003, 2006).

Successful classroom management does not come into existence by waving a magic wand; success is incumbent on good teaching. Although the level of difference is disputed, Hattie (2003) asserts that teachers can make a difference in young people's lives such that teacher attitudes and skills should be constantly reviewed and reassessed on the basis of new policies, systems, and technologies. Critical questions relating to school culture and support should also be continually considered and evaluated (Fiedler *et al.* 2008). These include questions about seeing young people as 'our' students rather than 'my' students and 'your' students; forming teams of teachers and working collaboratively to support all students in the classroom; adopting a problem-solving approach that values assessment to drive instructional decisions; reaching out to parents and *whānau* members of students experiencing difficulties in school; and using culturally responsive behaviour management practices by considering the effect of culture on students' learning and teachers' teaching (ibid.).

What teachers do in their classrooms and how they infuse elements of sensitivity and sensibility into their practice are what make a difference for their students in terms of their attitudes and performance. Student engagement in learning is linked to such factors as relevant teaching, challenging work, receiving good feedback, and learning that takes place at the students' pace. Student engagement in school is also indicated by strong links to home support, supportive friendships, and having interests that extended the individuals outside the classroom walls.

In the face of the current outcry about student failure and school strife, research-based good practice may offer an alternative. Research on good teaching practices such as those discussed in this chapter serve to make real the claim that educators need to approach the practice of teaching as a moral craft – an approach that effectively brings into play the heart, the head, and the hand (Sergiovanni 1994). The heart is about having a philosophy and therefore incorporates beliefs, values, and vision. The head involves personal or cognitive theory. The hand is about practices – the skills, strategies and decisions that are both concrete and emphatic. Each without the other two results in vulnerability. Each, with the other two, signals authority. We believe that classroom management is about creating warmth in the classroom that accepts each member of the class making him or her (including the teacher) feel important as a member of the class while asserting the purpose of the classroom as a place to focus on using each individual's talents to be part of and benefit in the learning process. Finally, we believe that classroom management is about asserting the purpose of the classroom as a place to focus on using each individual's talents to be part of and benefit in the learning process.

References

Achilles, G.M., McLaughlin, M.J. and Croninger, R.G. (2007) 'Sociocultural correlates of disciplinary exclusion among students with emotional, behavioral, and learning disabilities in the SEELS national dataset', *Journal of Emotional and Behavioral Disorders*, 15: 33–45.

Au, K.H. (1998) 'Social constructivism and the school literacy learning of students of diverse backgrounds', *Journal of Literacy Research*, 20: 297–319.

Au, K.H. (2000) 'A multicultural perspective on policies for improving literacy achievement: equity and excellence', in M.L. Kamil, P.B. Mosenthal, P.D. Pearson and R. Barr (eds) *Handbook of Reading Research* (vol. 3, pp. 835–51), Mahwah, NJ: Lawrence Erlbaum Associates.

Bateman, S. and Berryman, M. (2008) 'He hui whakatika: culturally responsive, self determining interventions for restoring harmony', *Kairaranga*, 9: 6–12.

Bishop, R. and Berryman, M. (2006) *Culture Speaks: Cultural Relationships and Classroom Learning*, Wellington, NZ: Huia Publishers.

Bishop, R., Berryman, M., Tiakiwai, S. and Richardson, C. (2002) *Te Kōtahitanga: the Experiences of Year 9 and Year 10 Māori Students in Mainstream Classrooms*, a research report to the Ministry of Education, Hamilton, NZ: University of Waikato.

Blumberg, A. (1989) *School Administration as a Craft: Foundations of Practice*, Boston: Allyn and Bacon.

Cartledge, G. and Kourea, L. (2008) 'Culturally responsive classrooms for culturally diverse students with and at risk for disabilities', *Exceptional Children*, 74: 351–71.

Charles, C. (2008) *Building Classroom Discipline*, 9th edn, Boston: Pearson/Allyn and Bacon.

Church, J. (2003) *Church Report: The Definition, Diagnosis and Treatment of Children and Youth with Severe Behaviour Difficulties*, Wellington, NZ: Ministry of Education.

Conway, R. (1998) 'Meeting the needs of students with behavioural and emotional problems', in A. Ashman and J. Elkins (eds) *Educating Children with Special Needs*, 3rd edn (pp. 177–228), Sydney: Prentice Hall.

Doyle, W. (1986) 'Classroom organization and management', in M.C. Wittrock (ed.) *Handbook of Research on Teaching*, 3rd edn (pp. 341–92), New York: Macmillan.

Eddy, J.M., Dishion, T.J. and Stoolmiller, M. (1998) 'The analysis of intervention change in children and families: methodological and conceptual issues embedded in intervention studies', *Journal of Abnormal Child Psychology*, 26: 53–69.

Fiedler, C.R., Chiang, B., Van Haren, B., Jorgensen, J., Halberg, S. and Boreson, L. (2008) 'Culturally responsive practices in schools: a checklist to address disproportionality in Special Education', *Teaching Exceptional Children*, 40: 52–9.

Foorman, B.R. (2001) 'Critical elements of classroom and small-group instruction promote reading success in all children', *Learning Disabilities Research and Practice*, 16: 203–12.

Ginott, H. (1971) *Teacher and Child*, New York: Macmillan.

Glynn, T., Berryman, M., Atvars, K. and Harawira, W. (1997) *Hei Awhina Maatua: A Home and School Behavioural Programme*, final report to the Ministry of Education, Wellington, NZ: Ministry of Education.

Good, T. and Brophy, J. (1994) *Looking in Classrooms*, New York: HarperCollins.

Hattie, J. (2003) *New Zealand Education Snapshot: With Specific Reference to the Years 1–13*, presentation to Knowledge Wave 2003 – the Leadership Forum, Auckland, New Zealand: University of Auckland.

Hill, J. and Hawk, K. (2000) *Making a Difference in the Classroom: Effective Teaching Practice in Low Decile, Multicultural Schools*, a report prepared for the Ministry of Education and AIMHI Forum, Albany New Zealand: Institute for Professional Development and Educational Research, Massey University.

Hooper, S., Winslade, J., Drewery, W., Monk, G. and Macfarlane, A. (1999) 'School and Family Group Conferences: te hui whakatika (a time for making amends)', paper presented at the Keeping Young People in School Summit Conference, Auckland, July.

Horner, R.H. and Sugai, G. (2000) 'School-wide behaviour support: an emerging initiative', *Journal of Positive Behavior Interventions*, 2: 231–2.

Howard, T.C. (2003) 'Culturally relevant pedagogy: ingredients for critical teacher reflection', *Theory into Practice*, 42: 195–202.

Jensen, E. (1995) *Super Teaching*, San Diego, CA: The Brain Store.

Jones, F. (1987) *Positive Classroom Instruction*, New York: McGraw-Hill.

Kerr, M.M. and Nelson, C.M. (2006) *Strategies for Addressing Behavior Problems in the Classroom*, 5th edn, Upper Saddle River, NJ: Pearson Education Inc.

Kounin, J. (1977) *Discipline and Group Management in Classrooms*, revised edn, New York: Holt Rinehart Winston.

Macfarlane, A. (2003) 'Culturally inclusive pedagogy for Māori students experiencing learning and behaviour difficulties', unpublished doctoral dissertation, University of Waikato, Hamilton, New Zealand.

Macfarlane, A. (2004) *Kia Hiwa Rā! Listen to Culture: Māori Students' Plea to Educators*, Wellington: New Zealand Council for Educational Research Press.

Macfarlane, A. (2005) 'Inclusion and Māori ecologies: an educultural approach', in D. Fraser, R. Moltzen and K. Ryba (eds) *Learners with Special Needs in Aotearoa New Zealand* (pp. 99–116), Victoria, Australia: Thomson Dunmore Press.

Macfarlane, A. (2007) *Discipline, Democracy and Diversity: Working with Students with Behaviour Difficulties*, Wellington: New Zealand Council for Educational Research Press.

Macfarlane, A. and Burke, H. (1997) 'Experimenting with change, but taking no gambles at Melville experience unit', paper presented at the New Zealand Association for Research in Education, Auckland, New Zealand, December.

Macfarlane, A., Glynn, T., Cavanagh, T. and Bateman, S. (2007) 'Creating culturally safe schools for Māori students', *The Australian Journal of Indigenous Education*, 36: 65–76.

Macfarlane, A., Glynn, T., Grace, W., Penetito, W. and Bateman, S. (2008) 'Indigenous epistemology in a national curriculum framework?', *Ethnicities*, 8: 102–27.

Macfarlane, A. and Prochnow, J.E. (2008) 'Assertiveness and warmth in managing classroom behaviour', paper presented at the Educational Psychology Forum, Auckland, New Zealand, September.

Meyer, L.H. and Evans, I.M. (2006) *Literature Review on Intervention with Challenging Behaviour in Children and Youth with Developmental Disabilities. Final Report*, Wellington, NZ: Ministry of Education.

Ministry of Education (1996) *Special Education 2000*, Wellington, NZ: Author.

Ministry of Education (2003) *Education Statistics of New Zealand for 2002*, Wellington, NZ: Data Management and Analysis Division, Ministry of Education.

Ministry of Education (2004) *Education Statistics of New Zealand for 2003*, Wellington, NZ: Data Management and Analysis Division, Ministry of Education.

Ministry of Education (2005) *Education Statistics of New Zealand for 2004*, Wellington, NZ: Data Management and Analysis Division, Ministry of Education.

Ministry of Education (2006) *Education Statistics of New Zealand for 2005*, Wellington, NZ: Data Management and Analysis Division, Ministry of Education.

Ministry of Education (2007) *Education Statistics of New Zealand for 2006*, Wellington, NZ: Data Management and Analysis Division, Ministry of Education.

Nash, R. and Prochnow, J. (2004) 'Is it really the teachers? An analysis of the discourse of teacher effects on New Zealand educational policy', *New Zealand Journal of Educational Studies*, 39: 175–92.

Prochnow, J.E. (1998) 'Suspensions human cost: damned if you do, damned if you don't', *New Zealand Principal*, 13: 13–14.

Prochnow, J.E. (2004) 'The PIRLS 2001 study: what does it say about gender, learner literacy attitudes and behaviour in New Zealand?', *Delta*, 56: 97–108.

Prochnow, J.E. (2006) 'Barriers toward including students with difficult behaviour in regular classrooms', *New Zealand Journal of Educational Studies*, 41: 329–47.

Prochnow, J.E. and Bourke, R. (2001) 'What are we doing for difficult kids and is it helping?', *New Zealand Principal*, 16: 4–6.

Prochnow, J.E., Kearney, A.C. and Carroll-Lind, J. (2000) 'Successful inclusion: what do teachers say they need?', *New Zealand Journal of Educational Studies*, 35: 157–78.

Prochnow, J.E. and Maw, N. (2002) 'Principals dealing with severe student behaviour: what they have experienced and what they need', *New Zealand Principal*, 17: 8–13.

Rogoff, B. (2003) *The Cultural Nature of Human Development*, New York: Oxford University Press.

Sergiovanni, T. (1994) *Building Community in Schools*, San Francisco: Jossey-Bass.

Skiba, R.J. (2002) 'Special education and school discipline: a precarious balance', *Behavioral Disorders*, 27: 81–97.

Skiba, R.J., Simmons, A.B., Ritter, S., Gibb, A.S., Rausch, M.K., Cuadrado, J. and Chung, C-G. (2008) 'Achieving equity in special education: history, status, and current challenges', *Exceptional Children*, 74: 264–88.

Skinner, B.F. (1953) *Science and Human Behavior*, New York: Free Press.

Sugai, G., Horner, R.H., Dunlap, G., Hieneman, M., Lewis, T., Nelson, C.M., Scott, T., Liaupsin, C., Sailor, W., Turnbull, A.P., Turnbull III, H.R., Wickham, D., Wilcox, B. and Ruef, M. (2000) 'Applying positive behavior support and functional behavioral assessment in schools', *Journal of Positive Behavior Interventions*, 2: 131–43.

Townsend, B.L. (2000) 'The disproportionate discipline of African American learners: reducing school suspensions and expulsions' *Exceptional Children*, 66: 381–91.

Trent, S.C., Kea, C.D. and Oh, K. (2008) 'Preparing preservice educators for cultural diversity: how far have we come?', *Exceptional Children*, 74: 328–50.

Tunmer, W.E., Chapman, J.W. and Prochnow, J.E. (2003) 'Preventing negative Matthew effects in at-risk readers: a retrospective study', in B. Foorman (ed.) *Preventing and Remediating Reading Difficulties: Bringing Science to Scale* (pp. 121–62), Timonium, MD: York Press.

Tunmer, W.E., Chapman, J.W., and Prochnow, J.E. (2006) 'Literate cultural capital at school entry predicts later reading achievement: a seven year longitudinal study', *New Zealand Journal of Educational Studies*, 41: 183–204.

Tunmer, W.E. and Prochnow, J.E. (2009) 'Cultural relativism and literacy education: explicit teaching based on specific learning needs is not deficit theory', in R. Openshaw and E. Rata (eds) *The Politics Conformity in New Zealand* (pp. 154–90), Auckland: Pearson Education.

Wearmouth, J., Glynn, T. and Berryman, M. (2005) *Perspectives on Student Behaviour in Schools: Exploring Theory and Developing Practice*, London: Routledge.

Wheldall, K. and Merrett, F. (1989) 'Managing troublesome behaviour in primary and secondary classrooms', *The Best of Set: Discipline*, item 12, Wellington: New Zealand Council for Educational Research; Melbourne: Australian Council for Educational Research.

Wylie, C. and Hogden, E. (2007) *Hawke's Bay Primary and Intermediate Schools' Incidence of Severe Behaviour*, report prepared for Hawke's Bay Primary Principals Association.

Chapter 11

Applied behaviour analysis

Contributions to New Zealand educational psychology

Dennis Rose and John Church

This chapter provides an overview of applied behaviour analysis research in New Zealand educational settings. Applied behaviour analysis uses experimentally derived principles of behaviour to improve behaviour in natural settings. It contributes to a wide range of socially significant areas including gerontology, health and exercise, safety, parenting, sports, and regular and special education. In recent years, it has gained popularity through successful work with students with autism.

Baer *et al.* (1968) identified seven dimensions of applied behaviour analysis. Applied behaviour analysis research must be *applied* (focus on socially significant issues); *behavioural* (measure behaviours); *analytic* (demonstrate experimental control over behaviour); *technological* (provide sufficient detail for replication); *conceptually systematic* (use procedures and interpret results in terms of the principles from which they were derived); *effective* (behaviour should improve); and must have *generality* (change endures over time and occurs in different contexts).

The applied behaviour analysis research methodology differs from the methods commonly used in education. In particular, it reports the performance of each individual and does not average results; repeated measures over time and experimental designs permit visual inspection of graphs to identify relationships between independent and dependent variables; and generality of results is obtained through replication and variation.

Children's behaviour

Early studies in the Mangere Guidance Unit in South Auckland, New Zealand, involved children with behavioural and learning problems in intermediate schools and their teachers and parents (Glynn *et al.* 1978). The unit staff defined problems, gathered and analyzed baseline data and designed, implemented and evaluated interventions in collaboration with teachers, parents, and children. This was a departure from the usual practice which was to segregate the most disruptive children.

The 1970s was also the first decade when applied behaviour analysis was widely applied to classrooms internationally. The focus was on reinforcement; concepts such as functional analysis had yet to appear in the literature. However, the procedures of the Mangere Guidance Unit included consideration of variables such as how much success children experienced, and self-management procedures (Thomas 1976). Thomas *et al.* (1978) used Mangere Guidance Unit data to provide normative information regarding New Zealand teachers' use of approving and disapproving statements. This data confirmed that, like their contemporaries in the United States, New Zealand teachers at intermediate level (Years 7 and 8) provided very low rates of approval (once every five minutes) and about three times as many disapproving statements. Such data allows principals and trainers to evaluate whether the functioning of a particular classroom is typical.

Project Early (Church 1999c), a systematic approach to children's behaviour in classrooms and homes, provided interventions lasting about 20 school weeks. Parents and teachers were shown how to frame behavioural rules, teach social skills, use differential attention, use increased levels of praise for appropriate social behaviour, use behaviour charts to reinforce appropriate behaviour, and confront antisocial behaviour using timeout or response cost. In 80 per cent of cases, compliance levels at home and at school increased, and antisocial behaviour decreased to age-appropriate levels. Rose (2008) found similar results with Project Early in Auckland schools. These projects demonstrate that a well-designed but inexpensive intervention can interrupt the development of antisocial behaviour when children are young enough to re-engage with regular activities and communities of reinforcement and before their behaviour isolates and alienates them from the mainstream. Interventions become more expensive and experience less success as children become older (Church 2003).

Ellery *et al.* (1975) differentially reinforced other behaviours to reduce disruptive behaviour in a class for children classified as being emotionally disturbed or socially maladjusted. Dixon *et al.* (1989) found that delayed reinforcement of children in an intermediate school special class resulted in generalization of lower rates of disruption to another lesson.

Glynn *et al.* (1973) provided all children in a junior class with one minute of free time if there was no off-task behaviour when an audible signal occurred at variable intervals. A whole-class contingency increased on-task behaviour but further improvements were made when each child individually determined whether they had earned a point when they heard the signal. Glynn and Thomas (1974) adopted similar procedures but needed to display a poster specifying on-task behaviour and shorten the average interval length to achieve improvements in on-task behaviour. Rumsey and Ballard (1985) also used cueing, self-management and correspondence training (a 'say–do' match) in a writing task with children aged 9 to 11 years. Correspondence training produced greater increases in on-task behaviour and in the number of words written. Coleman and Blampied (1977) and Lewis and Blampied (1985) also reduced off-task behaviour of children in special classrooms using self-management procedures.

In 'token economies' children receive tokens (points, ticks, stars) for producing the correct behaviour and exchange tokens later for tangible reinforcers or access to an activity. Ringer (1973) used a 'token helper' who provided tokens to children aged 10 to 11 years when they were behaving appropriately. With practice, the teacher was eventually able to use the token economy as effectively when the token helper was no longer present. Lewis and Blampied (1985) taught children in a special class to self-administer tokens for being on-task. Both the self-managed and externally administered token procedures increased on-task behaviour.

Children's behaviour is subject to subtle influences. Clark (1982, cited in Glynn 1982) found that children seated alone were more likely to be on task than when seated at group tables or on the floor. Moore and Glynn (1984) studied two teachers, one of whom asked more questions of children in the back of the room while the other teacher directed more questions to children seated in the middle of the room. When the children were moved into 'high' or 'low' question areas of the classrooms, they received more or fewer questions as a function of where they were seated rather than because of their behaviour.

A more recent trend has been to identify the functions of behaviour. Moore *et al.* (2005) studied the off-task behaviour of a 6-year-old boy in a regular class. A curriculum-based assessment confirmed that he was capable of completing the academic tasks, and a functional assessment suggested much of the behaviour was escape-maintained. They continued baseline conditions some days and provided a legitimate escape (reduction of a long task into three or four short steps) on other days, decreasing escape-maintained off-task behaviour during independent work. This study demonstrates how applied behaviour analysis procedures have changed since the 1970s when this problem might have resulted in a programme to reinforce staying on task but without addressing the underlying function of the behaviour: to escape.

Self-management

Self-management strategies have also been used to promote academic behaviour. Ballard and Glynn (1975) taught 37 primary school children to record how many sentences they produced. This had no effect on the number of sentences, different verbs or different adjectives, nor on the quality of the stories. When they added self-determined and self-administered reinforcement, the children's output increased substantially, their stories received higher quality ratings, and on-task behaviour increased. Glynn *et al.* (1976) found that eight children in a special class who used similar procedures required more practice and more prompting to learn the procedures than did the children in the regular classroom. Six of the eight children improved their written language performance using self-management procedures and a subsequent phase of teacher-controlled reinforcement resulted in improved scores for all children. Moore *et al.* (2001) taught three 8-year-old boys to self-record and set goals to increase on-task behaviour (from about 50 per cent to 80–95 per cent) during language lessons. Glynn (1970) compared self-determined, experimenter-determined, and chance-determined token reinforcement on how well 128 female high school students learned history and geography.

Self-determined and experimenter-determined token reinforcement was superior to chance-determined token reinforcement and a no-token control condition.

Dixon *et al.* (1995) taught an 18-year-old woman with autism to monitor her own asking of questions; this reduced the number of questions and improved the quality of her questions. Lambert *et al.* (1999) taught four female gymnasts aged 12 to 13 years to set their own goals. Those gymnasts who had been assessed as having an internal locus of control exhibited higher levels of on-task behaviour when setting their own goals than when they practised coach-determined goals while those assessed as having an external locus of control were more on-task when pursuing coach-determined goals. This result suggests self-management procedures may not be beneficial to all learners, or at least not until they have also learned other skills.

Learning the curriculum

There have been numerous applied behaviour analysis evaluations of curriculum strategies. Teaching reading has received most attention, especially evaluations of the Pause, Prompt, Praise procedure (Glynn and McNaughton 1985; Glynn *et al.* 1979; McNaughton *et al.* 1981). The pause (a delay before prompting), prompt (to help the learner make a correct response), and praise (reinforcement for correct responding) are all well established in the applied behaviour analysis literature (e.g. Cooper *et al.* 2007). Further, applied behaviour analysis literature on peer tutoring (Limbrick *et al.* 1985) informed the design of tutoring arrangements, tutor training and monitoring, while applied behaviour analysis findings concerning self-management contributed to the self-monitoring and self-management procedures for tutors and tutees.

The Pause, Prompt, Praise procedure has been successfully used with parents of mildly retarded children (Love and Van Biervliet 1984), parents of low progress readers (Scott and Ballard 1983), workers in a residential facility (O'Connor *et al.* 1987) and teacher trainees who trained parents to work with their children (Henderson and Glynn 1986). There have been demonstrations of the value of cross-age peer tutoring (Limbrick *et al.* 1985) and same-age tutoring arrangements (Pickens and McNaughton 1988).

Reciprocal teaching comprises a group of children using problem-solving strategies (clarifying, predicting, questioning, summarizing) to collaboratively determine the meaning of a passage. Kelly *et al.* (1994) used reciprocal teaching procedures to improve children's comprehension of non-fiction material and these improvements were maintained at an eight-week follow-up. Reciprocal teaching has also been associated with the development of cognitive and metacognitive skills for both poor and adequate decoders (Le Fevre *et al.* 2003). Gilroy and Moore (1988) found that reciprocal teaching of Year 6 to 8 children resulted in significant improvements in comprehension which were maintained eight weeks later. Fung *et al.* (2003) assessed the effects of reciprocal teaching on the reading performance of students who were new migrants to New Zealand, who spoke Mandarin as their first language and read in Chinese at grade level but whose English reading was approximately four to six years behind their chronological ages. Reciprocal teaching procedures in Mandarin and English on alternating days resulted in the students making gains on tests of reading comprehension in both Mandarin and English.

Singh and Singh (1984) assessed the effects of having the teacher discuss the text with the children before they were required to read it. Oral reading errors decreased and self-corrections increased when the children previewed the target text, compared to previewing an unrelated text or not previewing any text. Knott and Moore (1988) provided prior context to a 7-year-old above-average reader who then read passages approximately one year in advance of his current reading level. He made few or no errors when he had prior context, while not having context resulted in an average of 5 per cent of words being read incorrectly. Tang and Moore (1992) improved the comprehension of three adult ESL (English as a second language) readers by using activities such as discussing the title and vocabulary of a passage before reading. They achieved better maintenance when they added a simple metacognitive procedure (self-questioning, predicting the likely content of the story and determining the meaning of five difficult words in the passage).

Nirbhay and Judy Singh and their colleagues studied responses teachers and tutors make to children's oral reading errors. Most of their research was in special schools with developmentally disabled children and many of their studies compared the effects of positive practice overcorrection with other types of teacher response. Positive practice overcorrection requires the student to make the correct response several times. In the Singh and Singh studies, this usually required the reader to point to the word and say it correctly five times before rereading the sentence. All of their studies showed that overcorrection was effective in decreasing oral reading errors. It was more effective than repeating flash cards until all words were read correctly (Singh and Singh 1986), and supplying the words when errors were made (Singh 1990). Overcorrection was less effective than the reader being required to attend to phonetic elements of the error and to sound out the word (Singh 1987; Singh and Singh 1988). Stewart and Singh (1986) also found overcorrection to be effective in improving spelling performance.

The Singhs and their colleagues found individual and group training formats for error correction procedures were equally effective (Singh 1987) and that immediate error correction and delayed error correction were both effective but that delayed error correction was more effective (Singh *et al.* 1985). In later investigations, they also discovered that having pictures and words presented simultaneously increased oral word reading errors. This was the case with readers in special education (Singh and Solman 1990) and with young readers in regular classes (Solman *et al.* 1992). These researchers concluded that a prior association between the picture and the naming response to the picture blocked the acquisition of a new association between the written word and the naming response to it.

Writing is a relatively solitary and silent activity requiring considerable self-management skills. Ballard and Glynn's (1975) and Glynn *et al.*'s (1976) self-management strategies increased the amount and quality of writing, although they were more successful with children in regular classes than those in special education.

Other approaches include having the teacher respond in writing to pupils' writing. Jerram *et al.* (1988) demonstrated a clear relationship between teacher's written feedback and the number of words children wrote and higher ratings for imaginative writing and writing in an interesting style. Hopman and Glynn (1989) studied four 13-year-old boys in a class for low-achieving students. The boys stated the number of words they would write that day and were socially reinforced if they reached that criterion (correspondence training). The boys and teacher negotiated a gradually increasing number of words to be written and this increased the number of words written, which was maintained once the procedures were no longer used. Scriven and Glynn (1983) publicly posted graphed feedback on rate and accuracy of the written work of nine low-achieving students aged 13 to 14 years. Feedback resulted in an increased rate of writing; on-task behaviour also improved and became more stable.

Studies of oral language acquisition in New Zealand applied behaviour analysis research have tended to focus on naturalistic teaching procedures as opposed to more direct teaching such as direct instruction and discrete trial training. Reducing teacher questions and increasing teacher pauses decreased child expansions of oral language in a junior class of 33 children, but reducing teacher questions and increasing teacher praise increased child expansions (Moore *et al.* 1989). While praise probably reinforced expansions, pauses may have extinguished it. Knott *et al.* (1992) found the more teachers reprimanded or issued instructions to children aged 5 to 7 years during morning news sessions, the less likely pupils were to speak. Orsborn *et al.* (1995) reduced teacher questions and replaced them with pauses or topic-related statements and this was associated with an increase in child discourse. Reducing teacher questions increased student discourse without adversely affecting classroom behaviour.

Baker *et al.* (1983) found that having an adult seated with preschool children and allowing them to serve their own food increased children's total language, especially self-initiated language. Charles *et al.* (1984) trained two childcare workers to use 'talking up' (remarking on or asking a question about a child's involvement in an activity) and 'incidental teaching' (responding to a child utterance and elaborating the child's language while reinforcing the child by meeting the request). Child-initiated language increased for both childcare workers when incidental teaching was introduced and for one of them when talking up was introduced.

Teacher education

Teacher education typically occurs away from applied settings and under constraints that do not correspond to conditions encountered once training has completed. Rose and Church (1998) could only find 49 international studies that directly recorded the effects of pre-service and in-service training in practical classroom teaching skills. They found stronger effects for training packages that included classroom practice with performance feedback and this was the main finding in Rose's (1993) investigation of teacher skill training.

Applied behaviour analysis studies of teacher training in New Zealand have all occurred in classrooms. In Rose's (1993) investigation, pre-service teacher trainees practised skills in classrooms and graphed data on their performance. This study identified practice and performance feedback on that practice as instrumental in acquisition and maintenance of teaching skills. Ringer's (1973) token helper demonstrated to the teacher procedures to dispense tokens and match them with praise. Once the teacher became proficient, the token helper left the classroom and the programme was maintained. Both these studies made important contributions to the literature on maintenance of teaching skills.

Charles *et al.* (1984) provided oral and written instructions, role play, modelling, and feedback to teachers following a lesson. Feedback identified successful use of positive feedback and also occasions when positive feedback could have been used but was not. In a later phase, teachers were asked to make specific plans to use positive feedback and were then provided with information about the match between the plans and their teaching. These procedures changed the teachers' behaviour. Glynn *et al.* (1984) used individual feedback and prompts to teach staff of a residential special school to implement incidental teaching of socially appropriate language, play, or motor skills, and Glynn and Vaigro (1984) analyzed staff use of timeouts and used this during staff development within a residential special school. More recently Evans-McLeod (2008) provided secondary classroom teachers with feedback on teaching performance and group-based instruction on essential behaviour management strategies. When post-training observation and feedback was added, teachers increased positive feedback statements and students increased their on-task behaviour.

Despite relatively few applied behaviour analysis studies of teacher education, these six studies all made direct observations of teaching behaviour in classrooms. Only Rose's (1993) study used pre-service teachers. This is possibly because pre-service teacher education does not typically focus on discrete teaching behaviours, even when trainees practise in classrooms.

Recent applied behaviour analysis research in education

Several recent studies have analyzed some assumptions underlying precision teaching. Clark (2001) examined the claim that a student who has mastered basic skills to a high level of fluency will acquire related but more complex skills more quickly. A 'high fluency' group of four students who could answer multiplication fact questions at a rate of 60 correct answers per minute learned to factorize algebraic equations of the form $x^2 + 7x + 12$ and achieved a fluency level of 20 correct responses per minute in four sessions or less. No members of a 'low fluency' group of seven students who all responded to multiplication fact questions at a rate of less than 30 correct answers per minute could achieve this. However, when the low fluency students practised their multiplication fact responses until they reached 60 corrects per minute, all acquired fluency in the factorizing skill in four sessions just as their high achieving classmates had done. Sometimes the problem to solve is not the problem which presents.

Darvell (2006) examined the claim that fluent responding leads to better maintenance and adaptation to new contexts. Darvell taught four adults with developmental disabilities to read self-selected words. The fastest these learners were able to read words was about 30 per minute, much slower than speeds reported in international literature. Clark (2007) used similar procedures to teach multiplication tables to 8-year-old school pupils and had the same difficulties in achieving fluent performances. In both studies, amount of practice and reinforcement was controlled to be the same in each condition. The learners maintained an initially higher accuracy and rate for the items learned in the fluency condition in both studies but, over time, the items in the accuracy condition became equally fluent and accurate and those gains were maintained for up to 12 weeks. McGregor (2006) also used precision teaching to teach multiplication facts using custom computer software that allowed either a fast or a controlled rate of responding. She had similar problems to Darvell and Clark in achieving high rates and achieved similar results.

In a series of studies, several postgraduate students have studied the effects (on progress in reading) of building decoding fluency in 8- and 9-year-old students with significant delays in learning to read (Church et al. 2005). These studies found that a lack of grapheme–phoneme decoding fluency is a critically important component skill in learning to read at this age (more so than a lack of phonemic awareness), that children who lack decoding fluency can build this skill to levels of 60 to 70 correct responses per minute in four to six weeks, and that improvements in decoding fluency generalize immediately to improvements in prose reading accuracy and fluency.

Other studies have used applied behaviour analysis procedures to examine commonly held beliefs about how to teach. For example, McLay (2003) used an alternating treatments design, controlling the number of practice opportunities to test the assumption which underlies incidental teaching; that is, children learn better when they initiate their learning interactions than when teachers initiate such interactions. McLay found 4-year-old children who were learning the names of model animals acquired the new names at the same rate when an adult 'teacher' initiated interactions as they did when the children initiated the learning inter-actions by asking for the name of an animal. These results supported the view that learning depends upon the number of learning interactions which the child experiences, not who initiates these interactions.

The current status of applied behaviour analysis in education

Applied behaviour analysis research constitutes less than 17 per cent of research in educational psychology (Church 1998). However, in less than 40 years, applied behaviour analysts have made considerable progress in understanding the variables on which human behaviour and human learning depend.

The principles of behaviour identified by applied behaviour analysis research over this period have a greater theoretical coherence and explanatory power than theories of most other branches of educational psychology (Baum 2005; Chiesa 1994; Cooper *et al.* 2007). This research is beginning to reframe our view of learning and relationships between teaching variables and learning (Church 1999b, 2006a).

Applied behaviour analysis theory is also proving to have a wider range of practical applications than most other educational and psychological theories. Lists of 'empirically supported' and 'well established' interventions are almost always headed by interventions which have been derived from applied behaviour analysis. This is true for effective treatments for childhood phobias and anxiety disorders (Ollendick and King 1998), for children and teenagers with depression (Kaslow and Thompson 1998), for children with disruptive and antisocial behaviour (Brestan and Eyberg 1998; Church 2003; Walker *et al.* 2004), for children who stutter (Gillon and Schwarz 1998), for children with intellectual disabilities (Snell 1997), and for children with autism (Rogers 1998). The conclusions of these reviews have been confirmed by later reviews; see, for example, Mash and Barkley (2006).

Applied behaviour analysis has made rapid progress in identifying many of the conditions necessary for motivation and persistence (Church 1999b; Cooper *et al.* 2007; Malott *et al.* 1993), for the management of misbehaviour and antisocial behaviour in the home and in the classroom (Church 2003; Martella *et al.* 2003; Meyer and Evans 2006), for the development of meaning (DeGrandpre 2000; Staats 1968), for the learning and remembering of different kinds of skills (Church 1999b; Engelmann and Carnine 1991), and for the development of reading, writing, and mathematical competencies (Church 2005, 2006b, 2007a). Applied behaviour analysis has identified prompting and scaffolding procedures (for teaching new skills, procedures, and metacognitive skills) which are much more effective than the ad hoc procedures currently used by classroom teachers (Church 1999a, 1999b; Wolery *et al.* 1988).

In New Zealand, and following on from the cognitively oriented classroom research of Graham Nuthall (e.g. Nuthall 1999), applied behaviour analysis researchers are working to identify the number of learning interactions during the acquisition of different types of academic skills (e.g. McLay 2003; McWilliams 2005). The work on response opportunity and the distribution of practice responses in time has profound implications for research on teaching because it means experimental analyses of teaching are only likely to generate interpretable results if the number of learning opportunities and their scheduling is controlled, or at least recorded, across all experimental conditions (McWilliams 2005).

By combining emerging scientific knowledge of the various learning processes in novel ways, applied behaviour analysis researchers have begun to develop instructional systems which are considerably more effective than anything previously reported in the educational research literature (e.g. Church 1999b; Gardner *et al.* 1994; Heward *et al.* 2005; Moran and Malott 2004). These emerging 'technologies of effective teaching' include direct instruction (Adams and Engelmann 1996), class-wide peer tutoring (Greenwood *et al.* 1984), precision teaching (Binder *et al.* 2002), generative instruction (Johnson and Layng 1992), decision rule systems (e.g. Liberty and Haring 1990), and mastery learning systems (e.g. Sherman *et al.* 1982). Each of these approaches has produced large, reproducible gains in rate of learning across individual learners, across teachers, and over time.

An exciting recent development is functional analysis and assessment procedures, especially in classrooms. These are diagnostic procedures that identify dysfunctional behaviours and contingencies (especially those preventing the emergence of desired skills) so that these can be replaced by more functional responses supported by more appropriate contingencies (Church 2007b).

The future of applied behaviour analysis research and teaching

The results of applied behaviour analysis research have yet to have any visible effect on classroom practice in New Zealand schools. This comes as no surprise given that teacher education programmes have been isolated in colleges of education for nearly 40 years and that this has prevented much contact between teacher educators and developments which have been occurring in applied behaviour analysis research and teaching (Church 1975, 2008). However, this observation does raise an important question. Will applied behaviour analysis research ever begin to influence teacher education or classroom practice?

Recent developments allow us to be cautiously optimistic. All New Zealand colleges of education have now merged with their local university and thus almost all initial teacher education programmes are now located within universities. In the majority of New Zealand universities, the staff of both the psychology department and the education faculty include at least one experienced behaviour analyst.

Professional training programmes of psychologists in education generally now include a strong behaviour analysis thread or orientation. Special education courses in most New Zealand universities include the opportunity for those who work with children with special teaching needs to study the implications and applications of behaviour analysis research. Most New Zealand universities include, within their Master of Education programmes, courses in applied behaviour analysis. Most of these courses are strongly research-oriented and are likely to generate a steady stream of research theses examining important teaching and learning questions using the experimental methods of applied behaviour analysis.

In addition, the principles of behaviour and their implications for teachers are beginning to appear in undergraduate education programmes and initial teacher education programmes (Church 1999a, 1999b). During the past 30 years, some 400 teachers have graduated from University of Canterbury masters-level courses in applied behaviour analysis and a similar pattern is occurring at other New Zealand universities. This is producing a steady infusion of teachers who are aware of applied behaviour analysis research and its results. The Ministry of Education is commissioning reports on what works with children with severe behaviour problems (Church 2003; Meyer and Evans 2006), and a review of applied behaviour analysis research into best practice with children with autism (Mudford *et al.* 2009). An applied behaviour analysis component has been included in the training of Resource Teachers: Learning and Behaviour (itinerant specialist teachers) and all Ministry of Education educational psychologists are now being trained in functional behavioural assessment and analysis using a training programme developed at Victoria University of Wellington. Behaviour analysts are being seconded to expert advisory groups such as the advisory group on the Youth Offending Strategy and the advisory group on the Interagency Plan for Children with Severe Antisocial Behaviour (Ministry of Social Development 2007). The training of special education teachers at the University of Auckland includes a core course in applied behaviour analysis and some of these teachers also take courses in behaviour change and instructional procedures based on applied behaviour analysis research.

All these developments have the effect of bringing the principles of behaviour and interventions derived from them to an increasingly wide audience of teachers, resource teachers, teacher educators and educational policy-makers. Hopefully this will eventually result in applied behaviour analysis becoming a core element in teacher preparation at both pre-service and in-service levels, leading to the widespread use of behavioural approaches to benefit all children and their teachers.

References

Adams, G.L. and Engelmann, S.E. (1996) *Research on Direct Instruction: 25 Years Beyond DISTAR*, Seattle, WA: Educational Achievement Systems.

Baer, D.M., Wolf, M.M. and Risley, T.R. (1968) 'Some current dimensions of applied behaviour analysis', *Journal of Applied Behavior Analysis*, 1: 91–7.

Baker, M., Foley, M.F., Glynn, T. and McNaughton, S. (1983) 'The effect of adult proximity and serving style and pre-schoolers' language and eating behaviour', *Educational Psychology*, 3: 137–48.

Ballard, K.D. and Glynn, T. (1975) 'Behavioural self-management in story writing with elementary school children', *Journal of Applied Behavior Analysis*, 8: 387–98.

Baum, W.M. (2005) *Understanding Behaviorism: Behavior, Culture, and Evolution*, 2nd edn, Malden, MA: Blackwell.

Binder, C.V., Haughton, E. and Bateman, B.D. (2002) 'Fluency: achieving true mastery in the learning process', *Professional Papers in Special Education*, available at: http://curry.edschool.virginia.edu/go/specialed/papers/ (accessed 9 November, 2007).

Brestan, E.V. and Eyberg, S.M. (1998) 'Effective psychosocial treatments of conduct-disordered children and adolescents: 29 years, 82 studies, and 5272 kids', *Journal of Clinical Child Psychology*, 27: 180–9.

Charles, H., Glynn, T. and McNaughton, S. (1984) 'Childcare workers' use of talking up and incidental teaching procedures under standard and self-management staff training packages', *Educational Psychology*, 4: 199–212.

Chiesa, M. (1994) *Radical Behaviorism: The Philosophy and the Science*, Boston: Authors Cooperative, Inc.

Church, R.J. (1975) 'Could teachers be doing worthwhile research?', *SET: Research Information for Teachers*, number 1, item 5.

Church, R.J. (1998) 'The relative utility of qualitative, social science, and behaviour analysis research into learning and teaching', paper presented at the Annual Conference of the New Zealand Association for Research in Education, Dunedin, New Zealand, December.

Church, R.J. (1999a) *Basic Learning Processes*, Christchurch, New Zealand: University of Canterbury, Education Department.

Church, R.J. (1999b) *Instructional Processes*, Christchurch, New Zealand: University of Canterbury, Education Department.

Church, R.J. (1999c) *Project EARLY: Second Evaluation Report*, Christchurch: Education Department, University of Canterbury.

Church, R.J. (2003) *The Definition, Diagnosis and Treatment of Children and Youth with Severe Behaviour Difficulties: A Review of Research*, available at: http://www.educationcounts.govt.nz/publications/special_education/15171 (accessed May 2003).

Church, R.J. (2005) 'The origins and treatment of delayed development in learning to read: a review of research', paper presented at the Annual Conference of the New Zealand Association for Research in Education, Dunedin, New Zealand, December.

Church, R.J. (2006a) 'Critical teaching variables which govern the rate of learning', in R.J. Church (ed.) *Course Reader: Introduction to Interventions*, Christchurch, New Zealand: University of Canterbury, School of Education.

Church, R.J. (2006b) 'The origins and treatment of delayed mathematical development', in R.J. Church (ed.) *Course Reader: Introduction to Interventions*, Christchurch, New Zealand: University of Canterbury, School of Education.

Church, R.J. (2007a) 'Accelerating the development of expressive writing skills in low achieving children: a review of research', paper presented at the Annual Conference of the New Zealand Association for Research in Education, Christchurch, New Zealand.

Church, R.J. (2007b) *Introduction to Interventions: Practical Work Manual*, Christchurch, New Zealand: University of Canterbury: School of Educational Studies and Human Development.

Church, R.J. (2008) *Transforming Initial Teacher Education Programmes at the University of Canterbury into Research Informed Teacher Education Programmes*, submission to the Panel Reviewing Initial Teacher Education Qualifications: University of Canterbury, School of Educational Studies and Human Development.

Church, R.J., Nixon, J., Williams, D. and Zintl, S. (2005) 'Building decoding fluency in 8- to 9-year old poor readers', paper presented at the Annual Conference of the New Zealand Association for Research in Education, Dunedin, New Zealand.

Clark, B. (2001) *Effects of Fluency Building in Multiplication Tables on the Rate of Learning to Factorise Quadratic Equations*, research project report, Christchurch, New Zealand: University of Canterbury, Education Department.

Clark, T. (2007) 'The relative effects of fluency and accuracy-based instruction on learning performance outcomes', unpublished Master of Education thesis, University of Auckland, Auckland.

Coleman, P. and Blampied, N.M. (1977) 'Effects of self-monitoring, token reinforcement and different back-up reinforcers on the classroom behavior of retardates', *The Exceptional Child*, 24: 95–107.

Cooper, J.O., Heron, T.E. and Heward, W.L. (2007) *Applied Behavior Analysis*, 2nd edn, Upper Saddle River, NJ: Prentice Hall.

Darvell, A. (2006) 'Fast and fluent or careful and correct: an empirical study of rate-building methods', unpublished Master of Science thesis, University of Auckland, Auckland.

DeGrandpre, R.J. (2000) 'A science of meaning: can behaviorism bring meaning to psychological science?', *American Psychologist*, 55: 721–39.

Dixon, R.S., Fitzharris, A. and Moore, D.W. (1989) 'Reinforcement delay and across-setting generalization in an intermediate school special class', *Behaviour Change*, 6: 29–34.

Dixon, R.S., Moore, D.W., Hartnett, N., Howard, R. and Petrie, K. (1995) 'Reducing inappropriate questioning behaviour in an autistic adolescent', *Behaviour Change*, 12: 163–6.

Ellery, M.D., Blampied, N.M. and Black, W.A. (1975) 'Reduction of disruptive behaviour in the classroom: group and individual reinforcement contingencies compared', *New Zealand Journal of Educational Studies*, 10: 59–65.

Engelmann, S.E. and Carnine, D.W. (1991) *Theory of Instruction: Principles and Applications*, revised edn, Eugene, OR: ADI Press.

Evans-McLeod, A. (2008) 'Positive teaching: challenges for success', unpublished Master of Applied Psychology (Applied Behaviour Analysis) thesis, Waikato, Hamilton.

Fung, I.Y.Y., Wilkinson, I.A.G. and Moore, D.W. (2003) 'L1-assisted reciprocal teaching to improve ESL students' comprehension of English expository text', *Learning and Instruction*, 13: 1–31.

Gardner, R. III, Sainato, D.M., Cooper, J.O., Heron, T.E., Heward, W.L., Eshleman, J.W. *et al.* (eds) (1994) *Behavior Analysis in Education: Focus on Measurably Superior Instruction*, Pacific Grove, CA: Brooks/Cole.

Gillon, G. and Schwarz, I. (1998) *An International Literature Review of Best Practices in Speech and Language Therapy*, Christchurch, New Zealand: University of Canterbury, Department of Speech and Language Therapy.

Gilroy, A. and Moore, D.W. (1988) 'Reciprocal teaching of comprehension-fostering and comprehension-monitoring activities with ten primary school girls', *Educational Psychology*, 8: 41–9.

Glynn, T. (1970) 'Classroom applications of self-determined reinforcement', *Journal of Applied Behavior Analysis*, 3: 123–32.

Glynn, T. (1982) 'Antecedent control of behaviour in educational contexts', *Educational Psychology*, 2: 215–29.

Glynn, T., Clark, B., Vaigro, W. and Lawless, S. (1984) 'A self-management strategy for increasing implementation of behavioural procedures by residential staff', *The Exceptional Child*, 31: 209–22.

Glynn, T. and McNaughton, S. (1985) 'The Mangere Home and school remedial reading procedures: continuing research on their effectiveness', *New Zealand Journal of Psychology*, 14: 66–77.

Glynn, T., McNaughton, S., Robinson, V.M.J. and Quinn, M. (1979) *Remedial Reading at Home: Helping You to Help Your Child*, Wellington: New Zealand Council for Educational Research.

Glynn, T. and Thomas, J.D. (1974) 'Effect of cueing on self-control of classroom behavior', *Journal of Applied Behavior Analysis*, 7: 299–306.

Glynn, T., Thomas, J.D. and Shee, S.M. (1973) 'Behavioral self-control of on-task behavior in an elementary classroom', *Journal of Applied Behavior Analysis*, 6: 105–13.

Glynn, T., Thomas, J.D. and Wotherspoon, A.T. (1978) 'Applied psychology in the Mangere Guidance Unit: implementing behavioural programmes in the school', *The Exceptional Child* 25: 115–26.

Glynn, T. and Vaigro, W. (1984) 'Accountability through systematic record keeping in a residential setting', *The Exceptional Child*, 31: 142–50.

Glynn, T. Wotherspoon, A.T. and Harbridge, R.J. (1976) 'Towards self-management of generative writing in the special class', *The Exceptional Child*, 23: 31–45.

Greenwood, C.R., Delquadri, J.C. and Hall, R.V. (1984) 'Opportunity to respond and student academic performance', in W.L. Heward, T.E. Heron, D.F. Hill and J. Trap-Porter (eds) *Focus on Behavior Analysis in Education* (pp. 58–88), Columbus, OH: Charles E. Merrill Publishing Co.

Henderson, W. and Glynn, T. (1986) 'A feedback procedure for teacher trainees working with parent tutors of reading', *Educational Psychology*, 6: 159–77.

Heward, W.L., Heron, T.E., Neef, N.A., Peterson, S.M., Sainato, D.M., Cartledge, G. *et al.* (eds) (2005) *Focus on Behavior Analysis in Education: Achievements, Challenges, and Opportunities*, Upper Saddle River, NJ: Pearson/Merrill/Prentice Hall.

Hopman, M. and Glynn, T. (1989) 'The effect of correspondence training on the rate and quality of written expression of four low achieving boys', *Educational Psychology*, 9: 197–213.

Jerram, H., Glynn, T. and Tuck, B. (1988) 'Responding to the message: providing a social context for children learning to write', *Educational Psychology*, 8: 31–40.

Johnson, K.R. and Layng, T.V.J. (1992) 'Breaking the structuralist barrier: literacy and numeracy with fluency', *American Psychologist*, 47: 1475–90.

Kaslow, N.J. and Thompson, M.P. (1998) 'Applying the criteria for empirically supported treatments to studies of psychosocial interventions for child and adolescent depression', *Journal of Clinical Child Psychology*, 27: 146–55.

Kelly, M., Moore, D.W. and Tuck, B. (1994) 'Reciprocal teaching in a regular primary school classroom', *Journal of Educational Research*, 88: 53–61.

Knott, T. and Moore, D.W. (1988) 'The effects of an introductory provision of context on the oral reading behaviour of an above average reader', *Educational Psychology*, 8: 123–6.

Knott, T., Moore, D.W., Dixon, R.S., Rowsell, H., Sheldon, L.L. and McNaughton, S. (1992) 'Whose morning news is it?', *New Zealand Journal of Educational Studies*, 27: 69–79.

Lambert, S., Moore, D.W. and Dixon, R.S. (1999) 'Gymnasts in training: the differential effects of self- and coach-set goals as a function of locus of control', *The Journal of Applied Sports Psychology*, 11: 72–82.

Le Fevre, D.M., Moore, D.W. and Wilkinson, I.A.G. (2003) 'Tape-assisted reciprocal teaching: cognitive bootstrapping for poor decoders', *British Journal of Educational Psychology*, 73: 37–58.

Lewis, R.O. and Blampied, N.M. (1985) 'Self-management in a special class', *Techniques*, 1: 346–54.

Liberty, K.A. and Haring, N.G. (1990) 'Introduction to decision rule systems', *Remedial and Special Education*, 11: 32–41.

Limbrick, E., McNaughton, S. and Glynn, T. (1985) 'Reading gains for underachieving tutors and tutees in a cross-age tutoring programme', *Journal of Child Psychology and Psychiatry*, 26: 939–53.

Love, J.M. and Van Biervliet, A. (1984) 'Training parents to be home reading tutors: generalization of children's reading skills from home to school', *The Exceptional Child*, 31: 114–27.

Malott, R.W., Whaley, D.L. and Malott, M.E. (1993) *Elementary Principles of Behavior*, 2nd edn, Englewood Cliffs, NJ: Prentice Hall.

Martella, R.C., Nelson, J.R. and Marchand-Martella, N.E. (2003) *Managing Disruptive Behaviors in the Schools*, Boston: Pearson Education.

Mash, E.J. and Barkley, R.A. (eds) (2006) *Treatment of Childhood Disorders*, New York: Guilford Press.

McGregor, S.J. (2006) 'Practice makes the difference: the effect of rate-building and rate-controlled practice on retention', unpublished Master of Social Sciences thesis, University of Waikato, Hamilton.

McLay, L.K. (2003) 'Acquisition, retention and generalisation of object names in 4 year old children during child initiated and adult initiated learning interactions', unpublished M.Ed. dissertation, University of Canterbury, School of Education, Christchurch, New Zealand.

McNaughton, S., Glynn, T. and Robinson, V.M.J. (1981) *Parents as Remedial Reading Tutors: Issues for Home and School*, Wellington: New Zealand Council for Education Research.

McWilliams, K. (2005) 'An analysis of variables affecting instructional efficiency', unpublished Ph.D. thesis, University of Canterbury, Christchurch, New Zealand.

Meyer, L.H. and Evans, I.M. (2006) *Literature Review on Intervention with Challenging Behaviour in Children and Youth with Developmental Disabilities*, Wellington, New Zealand: Victoria University of Wellington, College of Education.

Ministry of Social Development (2007) *Inter-agency Plan for Conduct Disorder/Severe Antisocial Behaviour 2007–2012*, Wellington, NZ: Ministry of Social Development.

Moore, D.W., Anderson, A. and Kumar, K. (2005) 'Instructional adaptation in the management of escape-maintained behavior in a classroom', *Journal of Positive Behavior Interventions*, 7: 216–23.

Moore, D.W. and Glynn, T. (1984) 'Variation in question rate as a function of position in the classroom', *Educational Psychology*, 4: 233–48.

Moore, D.W., Knott, T. and McNaughton, S. (1989) 'Pupil speech during morning news: the effects of reducing teacher questions and increasing pauses and praise', *Educational Psychology*, 9: 311–20.

Moore, D.W., Prebble, S., Robertson, J., Waetford, R. and Anderson, A. (2001) 'Self-recording with goal setting: a self-management programme for the classroom', *Educational Psychology*, 21: 254–65.

Moran, D.J. and Malott, R.W. (eds) (2004) *Evidence-Based Educational Methods*, San Diego, CA: Elsevier Academic Press.

Mudford, O.C., Blampied, N.M., Phillips, K.J., Harper, D., Foster, M., Church, R.J. *et al.* (2009) *Technical Review of Published Research on Applied Behaviour Analysis Interventions for People with Autism Spectrum Disorders: Auckland Uniservices Ltd*, Wellington, NZ: Ministry of Education.

Nuthall, G.A. (1999) 'The way students learn: acquiring knowledge from an integrated science and social studies unit', *Elementary School Journal*, 99: 303–41.

O'Connor, G., Glynn, T. and Tuck, B. (1987) 'Contexts for remedial reading: practice reading and pause, prompt and praise tutoring', *Educational Psychology*, 7: 207–23.

Ollendick, T.H. and King, N.J. (1998) 'Empirically supported treatments for children with phobic and anxiety disorders: current status', *Journal of Clinical Child Psychology*, 27: 156–67.

Orsborn, E., Patrick, H., Dixon, R.S. and Moore, D.W. (1995) 'The effects of reducing teacher questions and increasing pauses on child talk during Morning News', *Journal of Behavioral Education*, 5: 347–57.

Pickens, J. and McNaughton, S. (1988) 'Peer tutoring of comprehension strategies', *Educational Psychology*, 8: 67–80.

Ringer, V.M.J. (1973) 'The use of a "token helper" in the management of classroom behavior problems and in teacher training', *Journal of Applied Behavior Analysis*, 6: 671–7.

Rogers, S.J. (1998) 'Empirically supported comprehensive treatments for young children with autism', *Journal of Clinical Child Psychology*, 27: 168–79.

Rose, D.J. (1993) *From College to Classroom: The Acquisition and Maintenance of Teaching Skills*, Wellington, NZ: Ministry of Education (Document Number ER 35/269/5).

Rose, D.J. (2008) 'Project EARLY: an intervention for children aged 3–6 with behavioural difficulties', paper presented at the 2nd International Conference on Special Education, Marmaris, Turkey, June.

Rose, D.J. and Church, R.J. (1998) 'Learning to teach: the acquisition and maintenance of teaching skills', *Journal of Behavioral Education*, 8: 5–35.

Rumsey, I. and Ballard, K.D. (1985) 'Teaching self-management strategies for independent story writing to children with classroom behaviour difficulties', *Educational Psychology*, 5: 147–57.

Scott, J.M. and Ballard, K.D. (1983) 'Training parents and teachers in remedial reading procedures for children with learning difficulties', *Educational Psychology*, 3: 15–30.

Scriven, J. and Glynn, T. (1983) 'Performance feedback on written tasks for low-achieving secondary students', *New Zealand Journal of Educational Studies*, 18: 134–45.

Sherman, J.G., Ruskin, G. and Semb, G.B. (eds) (1982) *The Personalised System of Instruction: 48 Seminal Papers*, Lawrence, KS: TRI Publications.

Singh, N.N. (1987) 'Overcorrection of oral reading errors: a comparison of individual- and group-training formats', *Behavior Modification*, 11: 165–81.

Singh, N.N. (1990) 'Effects of two error-correction procedures on oral reading errors: word supply versus sentence repeat', *Behavior Modification*, 14: 188–99.

Singh, N.N. and Singh, J. (1984) 'Antecedent control of oral reading errors and self-corrections by mentally retarded children', *Journal of Applied Behavior Analysis*, 17: 111–19.

Singh, N.N. and Singh, J. (1986) 'A behavioural remediation program for oral reading: effects on errors and comprehension', *Educational Psychology*, 6: 105–14.

Singh, N.N. and Singh, J. (1988) 'Increasing oral reading proficiency through overcorrection and phonic analysis', *American Journal on Mental Retardation*, 93: 312–19.

Singh, N.N. and Solman, R.T. (1990) 'A stimulus control analysis of the picture-word problem in children who are mentally retarded: the blocking effect', *Journal of Applied Behavior Analysis*, 23: 525–32.

Singh, N.N., Winton, A.S.W. and Singh, J. (1985) 'Effects of delayed versus immediate attention to oral reading errors on the reading proficiency of mentally retarded children', *Applied Research in Mental Retardation*, 6: 283–93.

Snell, M.E. (1997) 'Teaching children and young adults with mental retardation in school programmes: current research', *Behaviour Change*, 14: 73–105.

Solman, R.T., Singh, N.N. and Kehoe, E.J. (1992) 'Pictures block the learning of sight words', *Educational Psychology*, 12: 143–53.

Staats, A.W. (1968) *Learning, Language, and Cognition*, New York: Holt, Rinehart and Winston.

Stewart, C.A. and Singh, N.N. (1986) 'Overcorrection of spelling deficits in moderately mentally retarded children', *Behavior Modification*, 10: 355–65.

Tang, H.N. and Moore, D.W. (1992) 'The effects of cognitive and metacognitive pre-reading activities on the reading comprehension of ESL learners', *Educational Psychology*, 12: 315–31.

Thomas, J.D. (1976) 'Accuracy of self-assessment of on-task behavior by elementary school children', *Journal of Applied Behavior Analysis*, 9: 209–10.

Thomas, J.D., Presland, I.E., Grant, M.D. and Glynn, T. (1978) 'Natural rates of teacher approval and disapproval in grade 7 classrooms', *Journal of Applied Behavior Analysis*, 11: 91–4.

Walker, H.M., Ramsey, E. and Gresham, F.M. (2004) *Antisocial Behavior in School: Evidence-based Practices*, 2nd edn, Belmont, CA: Thomson/Wadsworth.

Wolery, M., Bailey, D.B. Jr. and Sugai, G.M. (1988) *Effective Teaching: Principles and Procedures of Applied Behavior Analysis with Exceptional Students*, Boston: Allyn and Bacon.

Chapter 12

Reconceptualizing special education

Don Brown and Dennis Moore

This chapter reviews the history of special education and relates the New Zealand experience to trends in other developed countries. We consider the role educational psychology has played in the development of special education and comment on the facilitators and barriers to its further development. In particular, we trace the gradual movement toward inclusion and the possibility of bringing general and special education together to develop a more cohesive, equitable, and effective education system for all students.

From exclusion to an inclusive model

All countries in the Western world have struggled with the education and organization of students with special teaching needs. Working almost in parallel, developed countries have gradually opened the doors of education to successive groups of students previously considered either ineducable or without need of education. Whether through charitable, private, or state-supported systems, the expansion of eligibility followed similar patterns in most educational jurisdictions. The first groups of students to gain access to special education resources were those with sensory, physical, and intellectual needs – and readily identifiable medical diagnoses. Educational provision for those with less easily and sometimes poorly defined psycho-educational needs followed in more recent years (Heller *et al.* 1982). Medical diagnosis and the medical influence on special education played an important role in establishing 'treatment' practices. It was probably as late as the 1930s before special educators began to place a greater emphasis on pedagogy, thereby asserting their independence of the medical profession, and lessening its influence on children categorized as in need of additional support (Vislie 2006).

Special education developed into a significant force within most education systems over the past hundred or so years, generally operating with its own administrative infrastructure and budgetary allocation (Moore-Brown 2001). Present estimates indicate that somewhere between 8 and 12 per cent of the school-aged population present with 'special' educational needs because of an identified disability (Horn and Tynan 2001; Jordan 2001). Today, as well as hearing and vision impairment and developmental, physical and intellectual disabilities, identified disabilities typically include behavioural and emotional disorders and, in many jurisdictions, such diagnoses as specific learning disabilities, attention deficit disorder and attention deficit hyperactivity disorder (Dempsey *et al.* 2002). Importantly, the categorical systems are neither universal nor uncontested and may represent little more than an etiological myth.

As recently argued elsewhere (Sigafoos *et al.* 2010), there could be several reasons for the development of this dual system. One plausible reason, as Kauffman (1999) noted, is that historically special educational services have generally been reserved for students with identified disabilities. Because of their disabilities, these students were considered to have a clear and justifiable need for extra resources and specialized interventions over and above those provided to non-disabled students in the regular classroom (Pijl and Dyson 1998). These specialized services are often viewed as entitlements that should be reserved for students meeting predetermined eligibility requirements, with the funding for these entitlements directed only towards students identified as eligible and placed in special education (Reschly 1996).

It is also clear, however, that special education is more expensive than regular education. Estimates in the past decade are that special education costs at least twice as much as regular education (Jordan *et al.* 1997; Parrish 2000) with this differential escalating (Hartman 2001; Horn and Tynan 2001). This is perhaps not surprising if special education is seen as the provision of services and specialized interventions additional to those provided to typical students. However, the rising costs, together with growing unease regarding accountability of practice in special education and the possibility that funding formulae provide incentives for contraindicated practices, such as exclusion from mainstream and over-referral into special education (see Parrish 2000), have been cause for concern about how we currently support children in need of additional educational support.

That special education became so separate a system within education is understandable, given its beginning as an attempt to assist clearly identified children with special educational needs. It can be argued, however, that as special education evolved, an unwritten contract was formed between regular and special education in which those in special education took over the troublesome and troubling students from regular classes. In return, those in regular education supported special education to gain resources and staffing.

Internationally, educational psychologists have played a significant role in the development of special education systems, as well as serving as gatekeepers between regular and special education. In New Zealand, educational psychologists have been providing assistance to special education since the mid-1940s, initially as part of the Vocational Guidance Service and in university clinics in Wellington and Christchurch. Psychologists were formed into a separate service within the Department of Education in 1948, modelled in part on the child guidance system already established in the United Kingdom and the United States. Professor Ralph Winterbourne, who had established an informal training programme in

Christchurch University College (working closely with Professors Ernest Beaglehole, Colin Bailey, and Arthur Fieldhouse at Victoria University College), advocated strongly for an educational psychology service. Though the turf wars between education and health were less bitter in New Zealand than in Europe and the United States, these early pioneers drew a clear demarcation line between the fledgling child health clinics, psychiatry, and an educational psychology service. Winterbourne established the first formal training for educational psychologists in 1960 at the University of Auckland, with Dr David Barney as the principal lecturer organizing and delivering much of the programme in its early days.

Initially, the emphasis within the New Zealand Education Department Psychological Service was on selection for special classes, and practice was built on a psychometric 'test and tell' model to determine eligibility for special education. However, the service quickly extended into working more broadly within schools. Concerned that psychologists might be seen as a quick fix for schools, Winterbourne noted in his history of the guidance movements that 'casework alone will never solve the problems faced by schools in dealing with atypical children . . . the emphasis has always been on environmental and educational manipulation . . . the service has increasingly come to see its role, partly at least, as an advisory and consulting one' (1974: 126).

Thus there was a move away from testing toward a more curriculum-based assessment and a problem-solving, collaborative form of practice (Brown and Hallinan 1972; Gill 1986; Thomas and Glynn 1976). The development of innovative support strategies for children with additional educational needs, and for their teachers and schools, often involved a collaboration between the Department of Education special education leadership, Psychological Service field staff, and university academics engaged in the training of educational psychologists. The focus Winterbourne had noted on the identification and adaptation of environmental and educational influences continued to be evident in the work of the educational psychologists. In fact, in 1975, the acting Chief Psychologist rejected an opportunity to standardize the Wechsler Intelligence Scale for Children (WISC) in New Zealand on the grounds that it would be unproductive and inappropriate to cement in place the use of intelligence testing in the work of the Psychological Service. Ten years later, the Director Special Education issued a memorandum stating that intelligence test results were not necessary to obtain access to special education services (D. Brown, personal notes). Instead an emphasis was placed on development of curriculum-based assessment.

Since most recruits to the educational psychology training were already practising teachers with a good understanding of classrooms, the transition to supporting teaching colleagues was not difficult. As psychologists began to realize the real contribution they could make in school systems, they began to focus their work more closely on school development. In 1980, Professor Jack Bardon of the University of North Carolina, in an international comparison of the work of educational psychologists (Bardon 1980), offered a strong confirmation of this aspect of the role of the Psychological Service.

Until 1989, four universities participated in joint training initiatives with the Department of Education. The training ensured a supply of trainees for the service and, with joint selection procedures, a close relationship was possible. The consequent cooperation of the academic and practice teams allowed for a highly collaborative research and training process. In this period, educational psychologists made significant contributions as both researchers and advocates in a range of fields, most notably in applied behaviour analysis, bicultural studies, classroom management, intellectual disability, peer-assisted learning, and reading instruction (e.g. Ballard and Crooks 1984; Ballard and Glynn 1975; Clay 1977, 1982, 1991; Gilroy and Moore 1988; Glynn 1982, 1989; Glynn *et al.* 1992; McNaughton *et al.* 1981).

By the mid-1980s, mainstreaming (with some, but not sufficient, support) had become a dominant theme in special education service delivery. In a review of the special education services, the Department of Education (1987) opted for a mainstreaming approach but also suggested abandoning the parallel special/regular education system in favour of a combined general education system. The review pointed to a new direction for special education that would be universally available; integral with other education programmes; lifelong; unified across sectors, home and school; needs-based; and effective and accountable (ibid.: 2).

With the advent of government's Tomorrow's Schools policy and the establishment of the Ministry of Education in 1989 to replace the Department of Education, the Psychological Service was disbanded. Since then, the practice of psychology in education has gone through two phases. Initially a new Specialist Education Services (SES) was established. SES was set up on corporate lines, with psychologists employed alongside other specialists and teachers. Psychologists were deployed primarily under contract to the Ministry of Education but with service contracts with commercial organisations as well as schools. SES was relatively short-lived. In 2001, the Ministry of Education disbanded SES and brought the service into the ministry as Group Special Education (now called Ministry of Education-Special Education GSE), a multidisciplinary team established to support the Special Education 2000 (SE2000) policy (Ministry of Education 1996).

The new policy introduced a radical move to what the Ministry of Education's chief executive at the time, Howard Fancy, said would be a world class inclusive education system within a decade and that would 'find the best possible learning environment and learning strategies for each student' (Fancy 1999: 3). This new approach to special education involved a paradigmatic shift in thinking about the delivery of support for schools, a new administrative arrangement for staffing, and a new funding method. Somewhat ambiguously, the Ministry of Education now describes this approach as 'an inspirational target for its time' (2008: 4).

In the process of implementing SE2000, many of the tasks of psychologists have been taken up by a new cadre of educators – Resource Teachers: Learning and Behaviour (RTLB). The RTLB service replaced a range of itinerant and 'pull-out' staff in schools. These specialist teachers are trained at a postgraduate level in an ecological service model. Their role is to assist schools in providing an inclusive education system. They collaborate with teachers to develop problem-solving approaches to identified concerns with individual students, groups of students, or whole classes. They are also trained to assist schools in developing school-wide systems approaches to support students and their teachers (Thomson *et al.* 2000). RTLB represent a significant positive force supporting inclusive education within the New Zealand education system today. Educational psychologists working within GSE have been more generally focused on working with students with severe disabilities and on special projects.

Psychology has had a profound though conflicted effect on how we organize our children's education, and specifically on how the needs of students who struggle with the curriculum are addressed within an education system. In addition to the role of psychologists as gatekeepers to special education, three separate influences by psychology can be readily identified. The first is the development of the construct of intelligence and IQ assessment, which while less dominant now, has underpinned decision-making within special education since its inception. The second influence is the work of educators such as John Dewey (e.g. 1933; 1966), who led a school of humanistic psychology. Programmes such as cooperative learning (Johnson, Johnson and Holubec 1991, 1993; Johnson, Johnson and Smith 1991) have emerged from this background. The third influence is the field of behavioural psychology, dealt with extensively elsewhere in this book, which underpins much of what is currently established best practice in education.

Arguably, intelligence testing underpins the deficit model in education. Whether benign in origin or not (see Gould 1981, for an extensive review of the relationship of many prominent psychologists, in both the old world and the new, with the eugenics movement), the advent of intelligence testing rapidly became a gatekeeper to educational opportunity (Coles 1987). Importantly, it also allowed into education the notion of pathology, and a process of identifying students with deficits and placing them outside the general education system.

By positing a biological-neurological cause for learning difficulty, psychology has fostered a view of learning difficulties as a particular deficit. The intelligence quotient (IQ) has become the proxy for neurological functioning, without clear evidence that it represents anything other than its own scores. Westwood cites Bartolome as saying, 'The deficit model has the longest history of any model discussed in the educational literature' (1995: 7). Interestingly, Westwood's own research shows how pervasive is teacher attribution to causality within the child (or the family) and how seldom teachers will offer their own teaching approach or school environment as a cause of learning difficulty.

Stanovich (1991) makes the point that educators have never grappled seriously with why the benchmark should be an intelligence quotient. The notion of discrepancy between general functioning (IQ) and some disability, however, certainly allowed educators first to rank students, then to explain how some could not be expected to learn while others were unexpectedly not learning. The differential diagnosis model has developed from this notion of a biological-neurological causation for educational failure. Some diagnostic categories are thought to be organic in origin (e.g. intellectual disability, and possibly autism) while with others the etiology is less clear (e.g. specific learning disabilities). All are based upon soft, and often unreliable, diagnostic procedures (Coles 1987; Skellern *et al.* 2005; Ysseldyke 1984; Ysseldyke *et al.* 1988) but all involve psychologists in a search for pathology. All allow us to ignore or heavily discount the possibility of educational or environmental causation. In addition, the interpretation of 'conditions' clouds the possibility of (early) educational rather than clinical intervention; in other words, searching for ways to teach better rather than how to further analyze intrapersonal factors associated with failure to learn.

Intelligence testing, and psychometrics more generally, have contributed to the way we think of special education, in the process determining the ways in which children with additional teaching needs can be assisted. The deficit model has become a major impediment to an equitable education system.

Behavioural psychology has also had a major influence on special education. In contrast to the psychometric tradition, behavioural psychology is, in principle, ecological, taking as fundamental the relationship between the individual and the environment and maintaining a focus on the environment as influencing behaviour. The current emphasis upon functional assessment is a clear indication of the contribution of behavioural psychology to our understanding of the learning process. The function of behaviour is a critical element in any analysis of what is happening in a classroom, applying equally to the teacher and other students as it does to a student who is causing concern. Such an analysis is complex and in our experience of working with specialist teachers, takes some time and guidance to master, but it is fundamental to problem identification and to developing a transparent and testable hypothesis for the classroom or school.

Access to special education resources has been a motivator for parents and professionals to advocate special consideration be given to a growing range of conditions. The current enthusiasm for a return to diagnostic labelling is a sociopolitical phenomenon, not a psychological one, and the growing demand for recognition of ill-defined categories is a function of the relationship between such diagnosis and resource allocation. The re-emergence of this demand, together with the frustration parents express over funding and resources, is understandable but unhelpful.

Parents have been a driving force in obtaining special education for their children. Pioneers among parents of children with intellectual disability, who were deaf, or who had visual impairments fought for and won concessions from governments and administrators for additional resources. Many parents favoured a separate system for their children, although recent surveys of parents have shown that many would now prefer to have their children educated in the mainstream if only they could be assured the resources would be available for them. For example, in a recent review, it was reported that:

> Many parents wanted regular school options but said that for regular class placement to work well for more children and young people, attitudes and

funding needed to change. A large number of parents and educators support special schools and units because they feel they allow more access to resource teachers and specialist therapy staff.

(Ministry of Education 2005: 7)

There is a remarkable similarity in the views expressed by parents in New Zealand and the United Kingdom over their concerns about special education. For example, Mittler (2008) reports from the House of Commons Select Committee report of 2006 that parent concerns focus on access to resources, attitudes to minority groups and frustration over lack of support. Mittler (2008: 5) cites the Children's Commissioner for England stating in 2006 that the 'plight of disabled children and their families is "nothing short of a national scandal" '. Though the Ministry of Education in New Zealand offered a more benign commentary on parental viewpoints than the British one, the IHC Society (2008), representing parents, children and young adults with intellectual disability, were more robust in their commentary, noting that:

Schools are separate entities under the Crown Entities Act 2004, but government is responsible for funding schools to ensure statutory obligations are met. It is the omission of government to do so in a way that allows disabled students full access to the curriculum, after parents have exercised or attempted to exercise their choice of enrolment at a local school, which discriminates on the basis of disability.

(para. 52)

The society goes on to assert that 'Difficulties faced by disabled students accessing education at their local school have existed for too long, and demand immediate attention' (para. 55).

While many parents appear to favour regular school, given adequate resources, others do not; some believe their children are too delicate, too robust or need safety restrictions which simply may not be possible in general education. The number of special schools in New Zealand has reduced since the mid-1980s and now remains stable at 47 (including health camps with short-term care and hospital schools), which represents about 0.72 per cent of the population (Ministry of Education 2007). This compares with the United Kingdom where Norwich (2002) found that a similar trend existed with a national average of 1.39 per cent. New Zealand had proportionally little more than half the students in special schools than in England at the time of these publications. If the health camp schools are removed from this count, then New Zealand has clearly increased the level of inclusion compared with a comparable school population. In an interesting analysis of a New Zealand school catering for extreme special needs, Gasson (2008) outlines reasons some students may still require intensive resourcing. Whether this can be provided in a regular school remains unresolved, a matter raised by Simmonds and Bayliss (2007). But as Ainscow points out, if progress is to be made toward inclusion, it 'will require negotiations about values and principles and a much greater sharing of expertise and resources among schools' (2008: 252). Building capacity in schools for such a change is the next challenge.

However, it is not only those with intellectual disability, or those students who have readily identifiable needs, who require assistance. There is a diverse group of students who do not succeed at school, many of whom are Māori or Pasifika students, for whom there is a clear need for assistance. Commenting on the Programme for International Student Assessment (PISA) report of 2001, the Ministry of Education (2004) noted that critical factors in achievement include academic engagement in the tasks students attempt, the skilful use of learning strategies in solving problems and student self-concept or confidence in their capacity to achieve well. Students who are failing (i.e. deemed to be at risk) lack these fundamental skills and characteristics. Māori and Pasifika students were over-represented in the group who are failing, but Pākehā (New Zealand European) boys in particular are also present in the failing group.

The vexed question of funding is an issue which has bedevilled special education for close to a century and which remains unresolved. In a recent review of models for funding special education services (Sigafoos *et al.* 2010), we concluded that current funding models can be conceptualized as lying along two continua. One related to how the money is allocated (categorically-based models at one end and census-based – often with demographic and constitutional variables built in – at the other end). Orthogonal to this continuum might be another axis with anchors related to whether the funds go to the district, school, programme, or parents. Sadly the existing research leaves unaddressed the question of relative efficacy of the different models of delivery of services or, more importantly, outcomes for students. Currently, aspects of New Zealand special education are funded categorically (the Ongoing and Reviewable Resourcing Schemes, or ORRS) and others on a census basis (Special Education Grants, access to RTLB).

There appears to be no best way to fund a separate special education. If schools are left to their own devices, in a competitive and individualized system such as ours, then audit is essential. When schools are expected to identify students in need, careful definitions are required. Schools that act to meet the needs of students with significant disabilities soon attract the attention of parents and become magnet schools. Yet a central funding system still leaves a dissatisfied group at the margins and strong advocacy from special interest groups brings pressure at all levels.

The movement toward a more socially responsible and inclusive society is challenged by the current philosophy of individualism (see Ballard 2004). Schools are concerned about their ranking and many avoid enrolling students with special teaching needs lest they become a drain on resources which might otherwise be used for their high achieving students. According to Gasson (2008), this happens even with special schools. Without a systemic approach which includes all schools, we shall continue to have a divided system with continuing in-fighting over resources. Despite the successful introduction of SE2000, taking account of the flaws that are now apparent, it is our view that we remain in a traditional, divided model.

Special education has been built upon categorization of students. The issue of classification has resulted in polarized views over recent years: either that special education is necessary or that it impedes progress. Whether special education is seen as a separate or parallel service to schools, the demand for some kind of classification to determine eligibility for access to specialist resources will remain. While there remains a desire to categorize students (however well disguised) to obtain resources, there is a powerful motivation for its support. In education there is little evidence that differential diagnosis or categorization leads to differential interventions, and some 'treatments' (e.g. perceptual motor training) have scant support in the empirical literature (Hattie 2009).We argue that there is no justification for assuming that special education has a distinct pedagogy. There is no special formula for working with students with special teaching needs (Lewis and Norwich 2000). What works in special education works, too, in general education and in regular classrooms. The reverse is equally true.

The position we take is that the numbers of students in need of additional assistance is far greater than the 8 to 12 per cent of the school-aged population who are typically identified as having special educational needs because of an identified disability. Our position is that far more than these numbers require more intensive assistance in their education, and teachers need support in providing that assistance. It is also our view that for inclusion to be fully implemented, schools will have to recognize their responsibility to establish an environment into which students with additional needs will readily fit. When schools recognize their capacity to educate all students, there should be no need to provide special locations outside the general education system.

The recent review of initial teacher education (New Zealand Government Cabinet Paper, 28 May 2008) attends in part to the concerns expressed about the capacity of initially trained teachers (and by implication, all teachers) to manage children with additional teaching needs, particularly those with behavioural needs. The solution offered is to enhance the training of these teachers and to provide further support to them through the role of well-trained mentor teachers. In the words of the paper, 'All newly qualified teachers must be able to effectively personalize learning to meet the needs of all the children and young people for whom they have responsibility' (clause 38). This is seen not only as a matter of teacher effectiveness but also as one of human rights.

There is consistent evidence that teachers can make a difference when they apply effective strategies (Hattie 2009; Marzano 2000). Researchers, however, consistently express their concern that effective interventions are not being implemented by teachers (Carnine 1995; Gersten *et al.* 1997; Kauffman 1996; Vaughn *et al.* 2000; Wong 1997; Ysseldyke 2001), but there is only speculation as to why this should be the case. Researchers have so far failed to empirically identify the reasons (Walker 2004).

Part of this difficulty may be the issue of 'scaling up' innovative programmes which work well in trials and individual studies (McDonald *et al.* 2006). How this can be done successfully remains problematic (Pianta 2003).The concept of strong interventions, put forward by Lentz *et al.* (1996), may offer one solution. This ecological model is naturalistic in scope, contains elements from the research base that are predictive of success and has face validity for teachers. In this regard, the Ministry of Education has developed a wide-ranging effort to introduce a more sophisticated literacy and numeracy programme to schools, to develop authentic assessment systems for class teachers (Ministry of Education 1998; Ministry of Education and the University of Auckland 2003), and to establish uniform teacher in-service professional development programmes. Whether these programmes have a direct effect upon students who struggle with the curriculum remains to be seen. Should they do so, they may well contribute to establishing a more inclusive environment, particularly in secondary schools. Such an environment is essential if students with additional teaching needs are to gain success at school.

This kind of action is not enough, however, to unite teachers in a fully inclusive model. Schools themselves must find the solutions to catering for all their students within their own systemic organization. Hill (2008) has shown how a specialist educator was able to assist one New Zealand secondary school to move from a traditional retributive model of student management to a positive behaviour support model, and how such a programme can become systemic. Individual teachers can be supported to improve classroom strategies and students can achieve higher academic goals together with self-managing behaviour.

The same can be said for the development of an equitable education for Māori students. The over-representation of Māori students in special education and in statistics on educational failure has been noted, and innovative programmes initiated (Berryman and Glynn 2004; Berryman *et al.* 2001; Bishop 2003; Bishop and Glynn 2000; Glynn *et al.* 1997; Glynn *et al.* 1999). Like many other programmes, scaling up to ensure universal acceptance of such work is critical to meeting the needs of students struggling not only with the curriculum but also with cultural misunderstandings within schools. Bishop and colleagues' work (Bishop *et al.* 2007) combining culturally appropriate responses to young Māori with cooperative learning has proven to be of particular value in secondary education.

Until recently, improvements in special education internationally have been achieved by way of incremental advances (Deschler and Lenz 1989; Deschler and Schumaker 1994; Ellis and Worthington 1994; Lewis and Norwich 2000; McMaster and Fuchs 2002; Medcalf *et al.* 2004; Marzano 1998, 2000; Ysseldyke and Christenson 1993, 2003; Ysseldyke *et al.* 1988; Ysseldyke and Marston 1990). In New Zealand, the changes have been similarly incremental. The question now is, can this incremental kind of change continue under a decentralized system with autonomous schools? As Moore *et al.* (1999) note, we are in the midst of a paradigmatic change with the competing functional deficit paradigm continuing in place in our education system.

Conclusion

The future of educational psychology may lie in the choice between the paths of seeking to intervene in single case approaches (see Pajares 2007) or to seek explanations from enquiry into contextual, cultural, and systems analysis.

The future will not have to do with increased resources or the ratios of students to teachers. It will have to do with the application of well-established principles of teaching and learning. The ideological issues of matters such as inclusion are important and have a broader constituency than that of present special education. Those principles of which we speak must take up the energy and influence of psychologists as they make their unique contribution to the ongoing dialogue on how general education should work. The principles we speak about here are broad, inclusive ones taking in not just a narrow view of assessment or intervention strategies which are known to work. They must also include what we know about motivation, self-efficacy and the self. When we speak about systems and the management of learning, we go beyond the immediate problem-solving methods and strategies for intervention. Our hypotheses should have wider boundaries and address the ways in which students and their teachers face the challenges of their roles in education (see Marzano 1998). For an equitable education to be available to all, we must 'uncouple from the resolutely deficit-oriented history of exceptionality and mesh instead with contemporary currents of thinking on the ways in which children learn or fail to learn' (Thomas and Loxley 2007: 153).

In particular, psychologists in education should not allow themselves to become buried in assessment and 'placement' and 1:1 activities when the big picture of what is happening to students with a range of challenging needs, including just struggling with the curriculum, will not yield to a one-at-a-time solution. Challenges such as class and individual student management, usually brought to the attention of educational psychologists as a last station on the road to exclusion (and perhaps a criminal life), is no solution. Yet we keep doing it – or rather, we allow ourselves to have that done to us. We know about systems management, about early intervention, and about positive behaviour management. How much do we influence policy-makers and school principals to take up these well-documented approaches? We know about fads and snake oil solutions that are rife in our schools – even supported in some cases by the authorities – yet we allow them to persist, either by turning a blind eye, by passive support, or because we do not know any better. We know that inclusive education should be more than an inspirational goal.

As we noted earlier in this chapter, educational psychology has been closely tied to special education. Today we know that what is good in 'special' education is also good in general education. Educational psychology cannot afford to be bound only to working with a small percentage of the population of students and their teachers. Psychologists have a role to play in a new general education, to ensure a safe and effective learning environment for all students. The application of the principles of psychology and the theories that are the foundation of effective school management, teaching, and learning must be made available to all educators and learners. The world view of teachers will determine how schools respond to the notion of equity and success for all. There is fertile ground out there. Educational psychology should revive its early promise and re-energize itself to take a full part in a broad educational endeavour which is the challenge of educating all the nation's children.

References

Ainscow, M. (2008) 'Teaching for diversity: the next big challenge', in F.M. Connelly (ed.) *The Sage Handbook of Curriculum and Instruction* (pp. 240–59), Los Angeles: Sage Publications.

Ballard, K. (2004) 'Children and disability: special or included?', *Waikato Journal of Education*, 10: 315–26.

Ballard K.D. and Crooks T.J. (1984) 'Videotape modelling for preschool children with low levels of social interaction and low peer involvement in play', *Journal of Abnormal Child Psychology*, 12: 95–109.

Ballard, K.D. and Glynn, T. (1975) 'Behavioral self-management in story writing with elementary school children', *Journal of Applied Behavior Analysis*, 8: 387–98.

Bardon, J.I. (1980) *The New Zealand Educational Psychologist: A Comparative Analysis*, Wellington: NZCER.

Berryman, M., Atvars, K., Glynn, T. and Harawira, W. (2001) *Pause, Prompt, Praise: Resource Manual*, Tauranga: Specialist Education Services and Poutama Pounamu Education Research Centre.

Berryman, M. and Glynn, T. (2004) 'Culturally responsive school and community partnerships to avoid suspension', in J. Wearmouth, R.C. Richmond and T. Glynn (eds) *Addressing Pupils' Behaviour: Responses at District, School and Individual Levels* (pp. 30–41), London: David Fulton.

Bishop, R. (2003) 'Changing power relations in education: kaupapa Māori messages for "mainstream" education in Aotearoa/New Zealand [1]', *Comparative Education* 39: 221–38.

Bishop, R., Berryman, M., Powell, A. and Teddy, L. (2007) *Te Kotahitanga: Improving the Educational Achievement of Māori Students in Mainstream Education. Phase 2: Towards a Whole School Approach*, Wellington, NZ: Ministry of Education.

Bishop, R. and Glynn, T. (2000) 'Kaupapa Māori messages for the mainstream', *Set: Research Information for Teachers*, 1: 4–7, Wellington, NZ: NZCER.

Brown, D. and Hallinan, P. (1972) *An Experimental Approach to Psychological Service in Schools*, Wellington, NZ: Department of Education.

Carnine, D. (1995) 'Trustworthiness, usability, and accessibility of educational research', *Journal of Behavioral Education*, 5: 251–8.

Clay, M. (1977) *Reading: The Patterning of Complex Behaviour*, Auckland: Heinemann.

Clay, M. (1982) 'Looking and seeing in the classroom', *English Journal*, 71: 90–2.

Clay, M. (1991) *Becoming Literate: The Construction of Inner Control*, Auckland: Heinemann.

Coles, G. (1987) *The Learning Mystique: A Critical Look at 'Learning Disabilities'*, New York: Pantheon Books.

Dempsey, I., Foreman, P. and Jenkinson, J. (2002) 'Educational enrolment of students with a disability in New South Wales and Victoria', *International Journal of Disability, Development and Education*, 49: 31–46.

Deshler, D.D. and Lenz B.K. (1989) 'The strategies instructional approach', *International Journal of Disability, Development and Education*, 36: 203–24.

Deshler, D.D. and Schumaker, J.B. (1994) 'Grounding intervention research in the larger context of schooling: a response to Pressley and Harris', *Educational Psychology Review*, 6: 215–22.

Dewey, J. (1933) *How We Think*, Boston: D.C. Heath and Co.

Dewey, J. (1966) *Democracy and Education*, New York: Free Press.

Ellis, E.S. and Worthington, L.A. (1994) *Effective Teaching Principles and the Design of Quality Tools for Educators*, University of Oregon: Technical Report No. 5. National Center to Improve the Tools of Educators.

Fancy, H. (1999) Opening address, Special Education 2000 Research Conference, Auckland, New Zealand., February.

Gasson, N.R. (2008) 'High fences and locked gates: extreme special needs in the era of inclusion', New *Zealand Journal of Educational Studies*, 43: 107–26.

Gersten, R., Vaughn, S., Deshler, D. and Schiller, E. (1997) 'What we know about using research findings: implications for improving special education practice', *Journal of Learning Disabilities*, 30: 466–76.

Gill, D. (1986) *A Staff Sharing Scheme: A School-Based Management System for Working with Difficult Children*, Auckland: Department of Education.

Gilroy, A. and Moore, D.W. (1988) 'Reciprocal teaching of comprehension-fostering and comprehension-monitoring activities with ten primary school girls', *Educational Psychology*, 8: 41–9.

Glynn, T. (1982) 'Antecedent control of behaviour in educational contexts', *Educational Psychology*, 2: 215–29.

Glynn, T. (1989) 'Applied behavioural research and the learning of literacy skills', in D. Philips., G. Lealand and G. McDonald (eds.) *The Impact of American Ideas on New Zealand's Educational Policy, Practice and Thinking* (pp. 130–7). Wellington: NZ-US Educational Foundation/New Zealand Council for Educational Research.

Glynn. T., Atvars, K. and O'Brien, K. (1999) *Culturally Appropriate Strategies for Assisting Māori Students Experiencing Learning and Behavioural Difficulties*, Wellington, NZ: Ministry of Education.

Glynn. T., Berryman, M., Atvars, K. and Harawira, W. (1997) *Hei Awhina Matua: A Home and School Behavioural Programme*, Tauranga: Specialist Education Services and Poutama Pounamu Education Research Centre.

Glynn, T., Moore, D., Gold, M. and Sheldon, L. (1992) *Support Teams for Regular Education*, Wellington, NZ: Ministry of Education.

Gould, S.J. (1981) *The Mismeasure of Man*, New York: W.W. Norton.

Hartman, W.T. (2001) 'The impact of census-based special education funding in Pennsylvania', *Journal of Special Education Leadership*, 14: 13–20.

Hattie, J.A.C. (2009) *Visible Learning: A Synthesis of Over 800 Meta-Analyses Relating to Achievement*, London: Routledge.

Heller, K.A., Holtzman, W.H. and Messick, S. (eds) (1982) *Placing Children in Special Education: A Strategy for Equity*, Washington, DC: National Academy Press.

Hill, D. (2008) 'The development of a systemic approach to the positive management of behaviour in one secondary school', unpublished doctoral dissertation, Victoria University of Wellington, New Zealand.

Horn, W.F. and Tynan, D. (2001) 'Revamping special education', *Public Interest*, 144: 36–53.

IHC Society (2008) *Complaint to the Human Rights Commission under Part 1A of the Human Rights Act 1993*, Wellington, NZ: Author.

Johnson, D.W., Johnson, R.T. and Holubec, E.J. (1991) *Cooperation in the Classroom*, Edina, MN: Interaction Book Co.

Johnson, D.W., Johnson, R.T. and Holubec, E.J. (1993) *Circles of Learning: Cooperation in the Classroom*, 6th edn Edina, MN: Interaction Book Co.

Johnson, D.W., Johnson, R.T. and Smith, K.A. (1991) *Active Learning: Cooperation in the College Classroom*, Edina, MN: Interaction Book Co.

Jordan, A. (2001) 'Special education in Ontario, Canada: a case study of market-based reforms', *Cambridge Journal of Education*, 31: 349–71.

Jordan, T.S., Weiner, C.A. and Forbis Jordan, K. (1997) 'The interaction of shifting special education policies with state funding practices', *Journal of Educational Finance*, 23: 43–68.

Kauffman, J.M. (1996) 'Research to practice issues', *Behavior Disorders*, 22: 55–66.

Kauffman, J.M. (1999) 'Commentary: today's special education and its messages for tomorrow', *The Journal of Special Education*, 32: 244–54.

Lentz, F.E., Allen, S.J. and Ehrhardt, K.E. (1996) 'The conceptual elements of strong interventions in school settings', *School Psychology Quarterly*, 11: 118–36.

Lewis, A. and Norwich, B. (2000) *Mapping a Pedagogy for Learning Difficulties*, report submitted to the British Educational Research Association (BERA), February 2000, as part of the National Events Programme 1999.

Marzano, R.J. (1998) *A Theory Based Meta-analysis of Research on Instruction*, Aurora, Co: Mid Continent Research for Education and Learning.

Marzano, R.J. (2000) 'Twentieth century advances in instruction', *Education in a New Era: ASCD Yearbook 2000*, ed. R.S. Brandt. Alexandria, VA: ASCD.

McDonald, S-K., Keesler, V.A., Kauffman, N.J. and Schneider, B. (2006) 'Scaling-up exemplary interventions', *Educational Researcher*, 35: 15–24.

McMaster, K.N. and Fuchs, D. (2002) 'Effects of cooperative learning on the academic achievement of students with learning disabilities: an update of Tateyama-Sniezek's review', *Learning Disabilities Research and Practice*, 17: 107–17.

McNaughton, S.S., Glynn, T. and Robinson, V. (1981) *Parents as Remedial Tutors: Issues for Home and School*, Wellington, NZ: NZCER.

Medcalf, J., Glynn, T. and Moore, D. (2004) 'Peer tutoring in writing: a school systems approach', *Educational Psychology in Practice*, 20: 157–78.

Ministry of Education (1996) *Special Education 2000*, Wellington, NZ: Author.

Ministry of Education (1998) *Assessment for Success in Primary Schools*, Wellington, NZ: Author.

Ministry of Education (2004) *School Leavers (2002): Statistical Tables on School Leavers in 2002*, Wellington, NZ: Author.

Ministry of Education (2005) *Local Service Profiling: National Report*, Wellington, NZ: Author.

Ministry of Education (2007) *Special Schools*, retrieved 28 March 2008 from www.minedu.govt.nz.

Ministry of Education (2008) *Information on Special Education*, Wellington, NZ: Author, 4 June.

Ministry of Education and the University of Auckland (2003) *Assessment Tools for Teaching and Learning: he punaha aromatawi mo te whakaako me te ako, Version 2*, Wellington, NZ: Learning Media. (CD-ROM).

Mittler, P. (2008) 'Planning for the 2040s: everybody's "business" ' [Electronic version], *British Journal of Special Education*, 35: 3–10.

Moore, D.W., Anderson, A., Timperley, H., Glynn, T., Macfarlane, A., Brown, D. and Thomson, C. (1999) *Caught Between Stories: Special Education in New Zealand*, Literature Review Monograph Series, Wellington, NZ: New Zealand Council for Educational Research.

Moore-Brown, B. (2001) 'Case in point: the administrative predicament of special education funding', *Journal of Special Education Leadership*, 14: 42–3.

New Zealand Department of Education (1987) *Draft Review of Special Education*, Wellington, NZ: Author.

New Zealand Government (2008) 'Cabinet Paper SDC', (08) 56, 28 May.

Norwich, B. (2002) 'LEA inclusion trends in England, 1997–2001: statistics on special school placements and pupils with statements in special schools', [electronic version], Bristol: Centre for Studies on Inclusive Education.

Pajares, F. (2007) 'Culturalizing educational psychology', in F. Salili and R. Hoosain (eds) *Culture, Motivation and Learning: A Multicultural Perspective* (pp. 19–42), Charlotte, NC: Information Age Publishing, Inc.

Parrish, T.B. (2000) 'Restructuring special education funding in New York to promote the objective of high learning standards for all students', *Economics of Education Review*, 19: 431–45.

Pianta, R. (2003) 'Commentary: implementation, sustainability, and scaling up in school contexts: can school psychology make the shift?', *School Psychology Review*, 32: 331–6.

Pijl, S.J. and Dyson, A. (1998) 'Funding special education: a three-country study of demand-oriented models', *Comparative Education*, 34: 261–79.

Reschly, D.J. (1996) 'Identification and assessment of students with disabilities: the future of children', *Special Education for Students with Disabilities*, 6: 40–53.

Sigafoos, J., Moore, D.W., Brown, D., Green, V.A., O'Reilly, M.F. and Lancioni, G.E. (2010) 'Special education funding reform: a review of impact studies', *Australasian Journal of Special Education*, 34: 17–35.

Simmonds, B. and Bayliss, P. (2007) 'Profound and multiple learning difficulties: is segregation always best?', *British Journal of Special Education*, 34: 19–24.

Skellern, C., Schluter, P. and McDowell, M. (2005) 'From complexity to category: responding to diagnostic uncertainties of autistic spectrum disorders', *Journal of Paediatrics and Child Health*, 41: 407–12.

Stanovich, K.E. (1991) 'Discrepancy definitions of reading disability: has intelligence led us astray?', *Reading Research Quarterly*, 26: 7–29.

Thomas, G. and Loxley, A. (2007) *Deconstructing Special Education and Constructing Inclusion*, 2nd edn, Maidenhead: Open University Press.

Thomas, J.D. and Glynn, E.L. (1976) *Mangere Guidance Unit: An Examination of Behavioural Programmes*, research report, University of Auckland, Auckland.

Thomson, C., Brown, D., Jones, E. and Manins, E. (2000) 'The development of resource teachers in New Zealand: a quarter century of paradigm change', in I. Livingstone (ed.)

The New Zealand Review of Education, Wellington, NZ: Victoria University of Wellington.

Vaughn, S., Klinger, J. and Hughes, M. (2000) 'Sustainability of research-based practices', *Exceptional Children*, 66: 163–72.

Vislie, L. (2006) 'Special education under modernity: from restricted liberty to organized modernity, to extend liberty and a plurality of practice', [electronic version], *European Journal of Special Needs Education*, 21: 395–414.

Walker, H.M. (2004) 'Commentary: use of evidence-based interventions in schools: where we've been, where we are, and where we need to go', *School Psychology Review*, 33: 398–408.

Westwood, P. (1995) *Behaviour Management: Learning Disabilities*, Adelaide: Institute for the Study of Learning Difficulties.

Winterbourne, R. (1974) *Guidance Services in New Zealand Education*, Wellington, NZ: NZCER.

Wong, B.Y.L. (1997) 'Clearing hurdles in teacher adoption and sustained use of research-based instruction', *Journal of Learning Disabilities*, 30: 482–5.

Ysseldyke, J. (1984) 'Lookin' for LD in all the wrong places', paper presented to the Penn State conference on school psychology.

Ysseldyke, J. (2001) 'Reflections on a research career: generalizations from 25 years of research on assessment and instructional decision making', *Exceptional Children*, 67: 295–309.

Ysseldyke, J.E. and Christenson, S.L. (1993) *TIES II The Instructional Environment System – II: A System to Identify a Student's Instructional Needs*, Longmont, CO: Sopris West.

Ysseldyke, J.E. and Christenson, S.L. (2003) *Functional Assessment of Academic Behavior*, Longmont, CO: Sopris West.

Ysseldyke, J.E., Christenson, S.L. and Thurlow, M.L. (1988) *Instructional Factors that Influence Student Achievement: An Integrative Review*, Instructional alternatives project, Monograph No 7, University of Minnesota.

Ysseldyke, J.E. and Marston, D. (1990) 'The use of assessment information to plan instructional interventions: a review of the research (26)', in T.B. Gutkin and C.R. Reynolds (eds) *The Handbook of School Psychology*, 2nd edn (pp. 661–81), New York: John Wiley and Sons.

Chapter 13

Children's friendships: real and imaginary

Tom W. Nicholson and Michael Townsend

Children need friends. Friends will spend time with them and will help them with their social and emotional development. Siblings can be friends but children are also drawn to other children about the same age outside the family, in the neighbourhood, at school, and at other places where children are likely to meet. By 4 years of age nearly 80 per cent of children have a real friend. Even lonely, neglected, or rejected children can have at least one friend. On the other hand, 10 per cent of preschool and primary school children have no friends and 20 per cent have only one friend. In this chapter we discuss why this is so. Young children also can invent imaginary friends. It was once thought that a child with an imaginary friend might have psychological issues but more recent research shows that this is not the case, and that up to 60 per cent of children report having had an imaginary friend. In this chapter, we also discuss the value of imaginary friends.

Children's real friends

Is it a good thing for children to have friends? Parents are often not sure about that. They worry about the possibility of their child making friends with the 'wrong crowd'. Even at the early childhood level, they worry. If they have friends visiting and their child yells out an expression that shocks everyone, parents will say defensively, 'Oh, sorry. She must have picked that word up from the kids next door.' Then there are stories of teenagers making the 'wrong' kinds of friends, getting into trouble, and maybe even getting stood down from school. This can upset parents to the extent that they wonder what they did for this to happen. There is a Chinese proverb, 'If you mix with dark you will be dark; if you mix with light you will be light.' It is a proverb that fits the mind of many a worried parent.

But the peer group is not all bad news for parents. In fact, the bad side of friendships is far outweighed by the good side. Friends are important. Children learn social skills by hanging out with friends. Children need friends. They need their parents as well. Teenagers often do not realize that their parents are actually their best friends. Parents can help their children to make friends and teach them how to keep their friends. If their children still end up with the wrong crowd, parents cannot take the blame for their children's choice of friends. Children each have their own unique personality and will choose friends that they want. Friendship is complex. Even lonely, neglected, or rejected children may have at least one friend. In contrast, some children may be popular yet not have a good friend.

When do children start making friends?

Children make friends early on. Even before preschool toddlers can miss the company of friends who move away. At preschool age young children tend to have friends who live nearby, or who have fun things like a trampoline, a red tricycle, or a Lego set, so they do not have far to go to play games together. Friends at that age help each other and are nice to each other. Those who are not nice are avoided. Once children go to school, they will have school friends that may not live nearby, but they will see each other at school, so proximity is not a problem. Once children have bicycles, this seems to help as well. At this age children frequently pick their friends because of qualities we value in our society, like being good at school, or good at sport, or being open and friendly. When in high school the basis of friendship changes again. Now children want friends they can trust, who can keep secrets, who they can talk to about things they will not tell their parents, and so on. These are the kinds of friends children might cycle a long distance to visit.

The influence of parents

Parents often try consciously or unconsciously to influence children's friendships. By living in a certain suburb, they are determining to some extent the pool of likely friends, especially through the influence of the local school. Parents also introduce their children to other children that they think will be nice friends. When people reflect on how they met their friends from primary school days, they mostly say they met at school, or lived nearby. But occasionally someone will say they met their best friend at church, or through friends of their parents, or even at a birthday party. These are friendships that have been partly influenced by parents. Parents may also coach their children in how to be a friend. It turns out that popular children often have parents who give them good advice in how to make friends.

Characteristics of friendships

An essential characteristic of friendship is that there is giving as well as taking, helping each other. Another characteristic is commitment, while a sense of equality, of each friend seeing the other as no more or less in status, is also important. A friend is like a security blanket, a support system. A friend can help a child to face new adventures that are slightly scary.

What are the job specifications for being a friend? This depends on your age level. The features of friendships vary as children get older. For children aged 3 to 7 years, the main features of friends is that they will play games with you, help you, and be nice to you. We once asked a group of 7-year-olds some questions about friends. One question was: 'What does a friend look like?' They immediately started describing each other: 'Short brown hair, undercut, purple tracksuit with blonde hair', and so on. Another question was: 'How do you make friends?' They said things like: 'bump into them', 'walk up to them and talk to them', 'ask them to play with you', 'ask them if you can be their friend', 'go to their house'. Another question was: 'What do friends do?' Replies included 'they help you', 'they are kind to you', 'they are funny', 'they cheer you up', 'they play with you', and 'they care for you'. As children reach preadolescence, they want a friend to be someone they can trust, who will not tease or gossip about them.

During the teenage years children want a friend who understands them, who will talk them through a problem, who they can rely on, who they can share thoughts with about their family, their future and taboo topics. This trust, caring, understanding and mutual acceptance form the basis of intimate friendships. Teenagers become friends with peers who share their attitudes and activities (Brown and Klute 2003).

Some researchers say the skills needed to make friends are more complex and subtle as one grows older and as friendships become more sophisticated – this suggests it is harder to make friends as one ages (Parker and Seal 1996). However, it is possible that adults simply become more careful in making new friendships as a result of disappointments or difficulties associated with earlier friendships. During the 50th anniversary of the end of World War II, one of the authors interviewed older adults about their friendships during the war. Although some servicemen reported that battle drew them closer to their comrades in arms, others consciously avoided making friends to protect themselves from the potential agony of losing a friend in battle. Interestingly, women who stayed at 'home' during the war often reported that their best friendships were formed in factories and activities associated with the war effort. Such women often said that they were bridesmaids at each other's wedding and had remained friends in the intervening fifty or more years. Some even said that their wartime friend was still their best friend, even though she had been dead for some years.

The incidence of children's friendships

Nicholson *et al.* (2002) reported on initial data collected from 100 respondents as an assignment carried out by students in an introductory course on developmental psychology. Students gave an anonymous questionnaire on friendships to another person, either someone in the class or not in the class. The full analysis of data involved 551 respondents (Nicholson 2008). Eighteen per cent of respondents were from the developmental psychology course itself. There were 150 males (27 per cent) and 401 females (72 per cent). The ethnicities were: 72 per cent European, 7 per cent Māori, 8 per cent Pasifika, 5 per cent Asian, and 8 per cent a mix of nationalities. Most respondents (83 per cent) were under 30 years of age. The survey results showed that nearly all (97 per cent) remembered having friends in primary school. Their friends were typically of the same age (93 per cent), same gender (85 per cent) or a mix (12 per cent), and followed the same dress code (82 per cent). The main thing they did together was play – 90 per cent mentioned this. When asked why they became friends, 91 per cent said in order to play games and other activities. When asked where they met their friends of those who responded 69 per cent said at school (23 per cent in the same class), 18 per cent said they lived in the same area, 5 per cent said they had similar hobbies, and 4 per cent said sports.

At secondary school, 98 per cent reported they had friends (22 per cent mentioned that their friends were in the same class as them and 54 per cent said their friends were in other classes). When asked about activities they did together, none mentioned play as such though 17 per cent mentioned they met through sports teams. Shared activities included watching movies, eating meals, parties, talking, shopping. They tended to follow the same dress code (84 per cent) and their friends tended to be the same gender (82 per cent). Most said that their friendships changed after they left high school. The most common reasons were that their personalities had changed (48 per cent) or that they had gone different ways such as got married, moved to other places, and so on (22 per cent). Since that study, however, much has changed in terms of the technology for keeping contact with friends, with the advent of mobile phones, the internet, and Facebook, and it may be that school friends in the future will keep much more in contact than in the past.

The above findings are remarkably positive, yet they are based on a university survey of students who are likely to be advantaged in making friends because they are more competent and socially skilled than average. It is also not known whether the friends they reported were actual friends or not. Lloyd *et al.* (2000) found that some children believe they are popular and socially accepted when in fact they are not. Most research on childhood friendships is not as positive as suggested in the university student survey described above. Based on overseas research, and on his personal studies of friendships in New Zealand, Townsend (1993) estimates that 10 per cent of preschool and primary school children have no friends and that 20 per cent have only one friend. This suggests that the average classroom of 30 pupils is likely to have two or three children without friends and another five who may have just one friend. The costs of not having friends may be high in that not having a friend in school is associated with low achievement, learning difficulties, dropping out of school, social problems, and, in adulthood, of not having a job, as well as emotional and psychological health problems (Townsend 1993).

The recognition of these costs has resulted in a number of postgraduate research studies at the University of Auckland examining the effects of friends and social acceptance in at-risk groups such as those with ADHD (Attention Deficit

Hyperactivity Disorder) (Lavery 1998), hearing loss (Wilzek 1999), intellectual disability (Townsend *et al.* 1997), and visual impairment (Inyega 2000). Concern about media coverage of several teenage suicides in New Zealand prompted an investigation of school teachers' beliefs about their role in promoting friendships in school in an effort to reduce suicide ideation in students (Craig 2003).

Also in the context of schools, other related studies have examined the extent to which different types of teaching strategies promote positive social relationships in classrooms (Parr and Townsend 2002), in particular, the use of cooperative learning strategies in increasing social acceptance (Jacques *et al.* 1998). Some of these studies have examined the nature of friendships in adolescents with serious social behaviour difficulties (e.g. Townsend and Hansen 1986), and how interpersonal relationships can be improved with intensive school-based intervention in how to take another person's perspective into account in social situations (Chalmers and Townsend 1990). Although we generally think of schools as places of academic learning, they are also places where friendships are formed and nourished. Recent research has shown that senior secondary school students place a high value on friendship activities and when academic goals conflict with social goals, such as when completion of a major assignment for credit conflicts with going to a party with friends, students adopt strategies (e.g. going to the party then working through the night to complete the assignment) that give precedence to the friendship goal (Townsend and Lai 2007).

Friends, popularity and peer acceptance

Friendship is a relationship of care, trust and respect that is reciprocated between two people and stable over time. Most people have a 'best friend' or 'intimate friend' as distinct from 'work-friend', 'bridge friend', and so on. Best or intimate friends can be recognized by whether they share common activities, trust each other with secrets, help each other in times of need, and so on. In describing a best friend it is not uncommon for a person to imply an ethereal quality to the friendship, 'When I'm feeling really down, the phone will ring and it will be her [my best friend]. She just seems to know.' Popularity is the extent to which you are claimed as a friend by your peer group. If 25 children in a classroom were asked to name their three best friends in the room, the child receiving the most nominations would be the most popular. However, even the most popular child in the room may still not have a best or intimate friend as described above. Finally, peer or social acceptance refers to how much a person is liked, ignored, or disliked by their peer group (Ladd *et al.* 2004). In a classroom we might ask every child to rate how close they feel to (or how much they like) every other child in the room. A mean social acceptance 'score' can thus be obtained for every child in the room and used by the teacher to identify problematic relationships, or as a way of seeing whether an intervention to increase the acceptance of a child (e.g. a child with a disability) has been effective.

Is it better to be popular or to have a best (or 'intimate') friend? In an initial investigation of this question Townsend *et al.* (1988) asked secondary school adolescents to nominate their three best friends at school (from which the popularity of each child was determined) and complete a checklist of activities that indicate close friendship (e.g. sharing secrets, talking about their future, and so on). 'Intimate' friendships were defined as those in which students nominated each other, the nominations were still present at a later date, and where both students engaged in a high number of activities. Four groups of students were identified: those who were popular and had an intimate friend, those who were popular but did not have an intimate friend, those who were not popular but did have an intimate friend, and those who were neither popular nor had a best friend. All children completed a self-esteem scale, a measure of psychological well-being. Overall, self-esteem was similar regardless of whether students were popular or not. However, self-esteem was much higher for students with an intimate friend than those without an intimate friend. As might be expected, self-esteem was highest for children in the popular/intimate friend group. Although it was expected that self-esteem would be least positive in the not-popular/no intimate friend group, the lowest self-esteem was found in children who were popular but did not have an intimate friend. Subsequent similar studies looking at other aspects of mental health (e.g. degree of loneliness, personal identity formation) have replicated the finding that positive well-being is associated with having a close friend but not with being popular (Laurie 1997; Laverick 1999; McIntyre 1998).

In contrast, Harris (1998, 2006) argues that not having the liking of your peer group is more costly than not having a best friend on other aspects of development. For example, while a close friendship is important in personal and social development, it may be less critical to life outcomes than popularity among the peer group (Hartup and Abecassis 2004). Some children are liked by the peer group but are not good at personal relationships. Likewise, some children are not good socially but can still have a friend (Harris 2006).

An evolutionary perspective on friends and peers is that although you can be a nice person and have one or more friends, what you eventually think of yourself as a person will depend on the judgement of your peers. Parents may be really positive toward their children or really negative but 'what matters in determining status in the group and desirability in the mating market is not how you see yourself but how others see you – how they rate you in comparison with others in your age group' (ibid.: 221).

Using friendship nominations or peer acceptance ratings (described earlier), researchers find out how others see you. Children are doing this all the time in their minds – finding out what others think of them. Children at school are constantly assessing the meanings of feedback from the group in terms of what others say to them or about them, by the looks they get from others, and by the extent to which others want to spend time with them. In turn, these beliefs ('they think I'm dumb', 'they think I'm pretty') can affect both a child's sense of self as well as the child's interactions with the peer group.

Friendship skills

Researchers have been able to teach children how to make friends. These children can be shown how to ask positive questions, offer useful suggestions, to be supportive, to be persistent if ignored or rejected, and to try different strategies if the first strategy fails. Activities such as cooperative learning can also build social skills (Townsend 1993).

More importantly, if you want to be liked by your peer group and you want to have friends, it is better to be good at something that other children value, like doing well at school or sport (Male 2007). While this is generally the case, it may not be the case in terms of doing well in any one subject area. For example, one of our students looked at this issue in a small study of 11-year-old good and poor readers and did not find any difference in the number of friends in each group. What she did find was that good readers' friends also tended to be good readers whereas poor readers were less likely to have good reader friends (Liu 2000).

It also helps if you have an ordinary or popular name, are good-looking, and able to mix well socially. This is because the peer group does not like children who look different, who wear different clothes, have an accent, or have funny names. One of our students said she was ridiculed at school because her name was 'Carmella'. Another student, whose name was Giselle, was called Gee-Gee for short, and then re-named 'Horse'. To help children to be more accepted, parents must do all they can to avoid peer stigma such as by giving them ordinary names and making their children look as normal as possible and as attractive as possible – which means trips to the dermatologist for children with bad skin and trips to the orthodontist for children with crooked teeth (Harris 1998). Not being liked by your childhood peers can have long-lasting effects on self-esteem and life status.

This, of course, is not a good prognosis for children who cannot help being different, such as children with disabilities. Children with developmental disabilities are not completely rejected, but they are excluded. They may not fall into the rejected category, but they will be less liked and more disliked (Townsend 1993). Programmes to improve social acceptance for these children to date have not shown sustained gain effects or generalization to new settings (Shonkoff and Phillips 2003). Children with a chronic illness such as cystic fibrosis or cancer also have similar issues. They are rejected by the peer group. In one study, chronically ill adolescents mentioned in interviews that they felt rejected, socially isolated, and misunderstood by their peers and friends (Smith 1994).

As adults, we know how critical the peer group can be. They will reject and/or make fun of those who wear unusual clothes or who have a different point of view from that of the group. Parents often despair at their children's insistence on wearing the same clothes as the peer group, doing the same things, having the same consumer items, such as Ipods, cell-phones, and spending so much time with friends on the internet. One way to look at this set of behaviours is to think of them as survival strategies so that they are liked by their peers. In one recent study, online communication among adolescents was associated with positive effects in that adolescents who did this were accepted by their peer group, had strong friendships and were more connected to school (Lee 2008).

It seems that if you want to be different from your peer group but feel okay about yourself, then you need to keep your opinions to yourself or be different in ways that are not noticed. Another way to be different but to be accepted is for boys to be bigger and tougher; for girls to be prettier and nicer. If you cannot be these things, to be different and be accepted by the group you will need to stand out in terms of an amazing personality, imagination, cleverness, athletic skill, and sense of humour. The peer group does seem to respect those who stand out in this way – but in reality these qualities are hard tasks for the average child to achieve (Harris 1998).

We learn early on that to be liked, we will need to fit in with the group. Popular children will have ordinary names, will be good-looking, and will be sociable. They will be nice to be with. The least likely person to have friends is someone who is aggressive, disruptive, and/or uncooperative. The peer group prefers someone who is nice and cooperative and agrees with them. When there is a fraction too much friction, the peer group will squeeze out the difficult one. Adults use expressions like 'team player', 'mucks in', 'offers to help', 'joins in', 'friendly', 'sociable'. These are qualities the peer group admires.

One can be neglected or ignored by one's peers. Children who are shy, withdrawn, and less talkative are not necessarily disliked, but they are ignored by the peer group. Garrison Keillor has made fun of our insistence that shy people join in with the rest of us. On one of his radio programmes he talks about an exclusive club that he is a member of. It is made up of people from Minnesota, in the Mid-West of the United States. He says, 'I belong to this club. It is limited to people from Minnesota. You can tell if someone is from Minnesota by standing silently next to them. If it bothers them, they're not from Minnesota.' It seems that shy children are in an exclusive club. They are 'neglected' by their peers. It is much better to be neglected than to be rejected. The research shows rejected children have a poorer prognosis for later success.

The dark side of friendships

Friendship is not always positive. Friendships can have their dark side in that they can hold a person back from realizing their true potential and they can also get one into trouble if the friends are aggressive and anti-social. Much of early research on children's social development has emphasized the major role of parents and the peer group, but there is also debate about the extent to which heredity is going to play a considerable part in one's ability to make or lose friends (Harris 1998). A child's temperament is going to play a large part in the making of friends. Insecurely attached infants are likely to have a difficult temperament which in turn is likely to produce negative behaviours such as aggressiveness and seeing the actions of others as hostile. On the other hand, environmental influences, such as parents and peers, seem to play a moderating role – and friendships can help social adaptation (Hartup and Stevens 1997; Newcomb and Bagwell 1995). One important contribution of the environment is that it brings children together; for example, when families move to an area where there are many other families with children of similar ages, when children meet other children at the same schools, churches, and so on. Initial contacts of friends are based on common interests, but friendships are not stable in the initial stages. Hartup and Abecassis write that 'on many occasions, children simply drift apart (and sometimes regret it) but cannot explain exactly why' (2004: 288). Sometimes, when this happens, friendships can seem perilous.

The friendships of some children are not good omens for social adjustment especially when the association is with other children who are anti-social friends. This kind of friendship is likely to increase anti-social behaviour partly because none of these friends is socially skilled. It is much better to have a friend who is well adjusted (Dishion 1990). Parents cannot compete against their child's friends if the group is anti-social but they can try other tactics such as changing to another local school or moving out of the area altogether. This may or may not be successful in that no school is free of anti-social children – but it is worth a try.

Children's imaginary friends

Many children create their own friends and peers by inventing imaginary companions. Research on this topic has changed dramatically over the past 100 years (Klausen and Passman 2007). In the past, children who had imaginary friends were seen as atypical or disturbed children. In recent years, Taylor (1999) turned much of this thinking on its head, arguing that earlier findings were often based on case studies or had selection bias in that children chosen for the studies were from institutions. Taylor's research showed that normal children were just as likely to have imaginary friends.

Svendsen defined an imaginary companion as 'an invisible, name-bearing person who presents for the constructor a psychic reality over an extended period of time and whom he can refer to in his everyday life communication.' (1934: 985). More recent definitions, however, have extended the definition to include stuffed animals (Taylor et al. 1993). For example, the cartoon strip Calvin and Hobbes is about a boy who has a stuffed tiger called Hobbes. In Calvin's mind, Hobbes is a real tiger, much bigger than him and he treats Hobbes like a real person. The definition also can be extended to include objects (Brookes and Knowles 1982). Another extension of definition is that the child invents the imaginary companion. This is different to belief in imaginary figures invented by adults such as elves, goblins, patupaiahere (Māori wood fairies), Santa Claus, the Easter Rabbit, or the Tooth Fairy (Prentice et al. 1978; Trinkaus 2007).

Researchers who have used experimental–control group research designs have found that children with imaginary companions are sometimes more shy than children who do not have imaginary companions. On the other hand, they are better able to focus attention on tasks, such as pretending to sit quietly in a space capsule, like an astronaut (Taylor 1999). But not all studies have found these differences. Some researchers have found that children with imaginary friends tend to be more intelligent and more creative, although not all studies have come to the same conclusions. Children with imaginary companions are also sometimes (but not always) found to be the first-born child. Children also sometimes invent imaginary friends after the birth of a sibling, perhaps to compensate for the lesser amount of parent attention they then receive.

Imaginary friends appear across cultures. Bouldin and Pratt (1999) surveyed 900 Australia parents and found only 17 per cent with imaginary friends. The authors reasoned that the role of imaginary friends is to alleviate loneliness and promote emotional and cognitive development. Pearson *et al.* (2001) surveyed 1800 children from 5 to 12 years of age and found that 46 per cent had imaginary friends including some 12-year-olds who still had imaginary friends. In Italy, Gallino (1991) found that 147 out of 357 Italian children (41 per cent) in the 4- to 10-year age groups reported having an imaginary friend. Inuzuka *et al.* (1991) surveyed Japanese college students. Their conclusions were that imaginary friends had a positive role in children's development. In the United States estimates are as high as 65 per cent of children with imaginary friends (Taylor *et al.* 1993).

Are imaginary friends scary or nice? They tend to be nice, someone the child can talk to, who will be a companion and a playmate. Children with imaginary friends tend to be sociable, creative, forthcoming, and have lots of real friends (Taylor *et al.* 1993). Creativity extends to being able to think about the same thing in two ways at once; for example, a pencil can become a toothbrush; a broom can become a pony. Taylor and Carlson (1997) found that children with imaginary friends were also better at 'theory of mind' tasks where the child understands that two people can have different understandings of the same thing.

There are gender differences in imaginary friends. Carlson and Taylor (2005) interviewed 152 children aged 3 and 4 years, and their parents. They found that girls were more likely to have imaginary friends than boys and that boys were more likely to impersonate characters, for example, Power Rangers, when they created imaginary friends.

How do parents feel about imaginary friends? Brookes and Knowles (1982) interviewed 100 parents who had children who were aged between 3 and 5 years. They gave parents various 'scenarios' to comment on. An innocuous scenario was where the child talks to an imaginary friend on an imaginary telephone. Only 5 per cent of parents said they would discourage this. A more testing scenario was where the child uses the imaginary friend to get her own way; for example, the child insists that the imaginary friend be seated at the dinner table even though the seating was already crowded, or the child carries around a teddy bear with her and will only do something if the teddy bear agrees. In the case of the testing scenario, 62 per cent of parents said they would discourage this behaviour.

In general, though, parents seem to be accepting of imaginary friends. Some parents set an extra place at table for the friend, dry them at bath-time, leave the television on while the family is away so that the friend does not get bored, and take them on outings. The period of having imaginary friends is about three years. There may be benefits to having imaginary friends in that they can help children role play everyday concerns they might have, such as the thought that there is a monster under the bed, or being scared of the dark.

In the Nicholson *et al.* (2002) New Zealand survey, 51 per cent of adult respondents remembered having some kind of imaginary friend as a child. The friend was a person (50 per cent) who was real or who was a soft toy (34 per cent). The friend was often the same gender (50 per cent) and the same age (64 per cent). The main reason given for having a friend was to have a companion (91 per cent). Names for imaginary friends included Beep-beep, Yoo-jia (Chinese name), Director, Max, Sooky, Cabbo, Baby Raha and Gay-Gay, Wiri and Gag, Mimi, Polly, Flopsy, Mopsy, and Cottontail, and Herman. One person mentioned that she had several pretend friends. They used to come to her house every morning. Her mother hung their coats up at the door. She played tea parties and 'house' with her imaginary friends. Another person said she had an imaginary friend called 'Selena'. Selena would come to visit and do the dishes. She used to tell her Dad, 'Dad, Selena's washing up,' And her Dad would say, 'I wish Selena would come over more often.' One in four (26 per cent) said that their parents did not know about their imaginary friend. This seems to be supported in the literature as well (Taylor *et al.* 1993). Also, parents seem to know more about children's invisible friends than personified objects; for example, a pillow that becomes an imaginary friend (Gleason 2004).

The only negative finding about imaginary friends in the literature is that children with imaginary friends may be less secure than other children. Researchers have found that girls invent imaginary friends that are less capable than them so that they can be more competent than them. Boys tended to invent imaginary friends who are larger than life so that the friend can protect them.

In all, imaginary friends seem to be just as useful as real friends in terms of having companionship and someone to share ideas with. They are more common than we used to think. For example, some well-known television and movie stars have had imaginary friends. Matthew Perry, who played Chandler in the television sit-com *Friends* said, 'I had an imaginary friend who my parents actually preferred' ('Just good friends' 1996). Robin Williams, the well known actor in *Good Morning Vietnam* and other movies, was an only child and came from a well-to-do professional family. It was reported in the media that he invented imaginary friends and had a 2000-strong army of toy soldiers (Barlow 1999).

Conclusion

A short summary of what we know about children's friendships is as follows (Hartup and Abecassis 2004). By 4 years of age, 75 per cent of young children have mutual friends (between one and two friends) and by middle childhood this rises to 85 per cent with between three and five friends. Time spent with friends increases during childhood to nearly 30 per cent in adolescence. This seems to be an important factor, spending time with each other. Opposite sex friends are infrequent in childhood. Children do like other children who are similar to themselves. Opposites do not attract. Children also will generally not make friends with threatening, uncooperative or aggressive peers. Social skills are likely to win a child more friends. Well-adapted children with no emotional difficulties are more likely to have friends. It is better to have more than one friend – and attributes such as leadership, having a sense of humour, and not being teased are associated with multiple friendships. Having friends in middle childhood is linked with positive self-esteem in adulthood and having successful romantic relationships in adolescence (Bagwell *et al.* 1998; Neeman *et al.* 1995). Preschool children with imaginary friends also tend very much to have real friends as well. If one has a good friend, one is likely to have higher self-esteem, more success in romance and to have good relationships with others. In the bigger scheme of things, though, it is worth keeping in mind the evolutionary idea that, to survive, one needs the approval of the peer group. This is more important than friends. It seems that parents need to do everything they can to ensure that their children are liked by their peers.

References

Bagwell, C.L., Newcomb, A.F. and Bukowski, W.M. (1998) 'Preadolescent friendship and peer rejection as predictors of adult adjustment', *Child Development*, 69: 140–53.

Barlow, H. (1999) 'Dad still knows best', *Courier Mail* (Brisbane), November 6.

Bouldin, P. and Pratt, C. (1999) 'Characteristics of pre-school and school-age children with imaginary companions', *The Journal of Genetic Psychology*, 160: 397–410.

Brookes, M. and Knowles, D. (1982) 'Parents' views of children's imaginary companions', *Child Welfare*, 61: 25–33.

Brown, B.B. and Klute, C. (2003) 'Friendships, cliques, and crowds', in G.R. Adams and M.D. Berzonsky (eds) *Blackwell Handbook of Adolescence* (pp. 330–48) Oxford: Blackwell.

Carlson, S.M. and Taylor, M. (2005) 'Imaginary companions and impersonated characters: sex differences in children's fantasy play', *Merrill-Palmer Quarterly*, 51: 93–118.

Chalmers, J.B. and Townsend, M. (1990) 'The effects of training in social perspective taking on socially maladjusted girls', *Child Development*, 61: 178–90.

Craig, A.L. (2003) 'Promoting peer friendships as a means of suicide prevention in New Zealand schools', unpublished Master's thesis, the University of Auckland, New Zealand.

Dishion, T.J. (1990) 'The peer context of troublesome child and adolescent behavior', in P. Leone (ed.) *Understanding Troubled and Troublesome Youth* (pp. 128–53), Newbury Park, CA: Sage.

Gallino, T.G. (1991) 'Children with and without an imaginary friend: their creative and social abilities', *Eta evolutiva*, 39: 33–44.

Gleason, T.R. (2004) 'Imaginary companions: an evaluation of parents as reporters', *Infant and Child Development*, 13: 199–215.

Harris, J.R. (1998) *The Nurture Assumption: Why Children Turn Out the Way They Do. Parents Matter Less Than You Think and Peers Matter More*, New York: Free Press.

Harris, J.R. (2000) 'Socialization, personality development, and the child's environment: comment on Vandell (2000)', *Developmental Psychology*, 36: 711–23.

Harris, J.R. (2006) *No Two Alike: Human Nature and Human Personality*, New York: W.H. Norton.

Hartup, W.W. and Abecassis, M. (2004) 'Friends and enemies', in P.K. Smith and C.H. Hart (eds) *Blackwell Handbook of Childhood Social Development* (pp. 285–306), London: Blackwell.

Hartup, W.W. and Stevens, N. (1997) 'Friendships and adaptation in the life course', *Psychological Bulletin*, 121: 335–70.

Inuzuka, M., Satoh, Y. and Wada, K. (1991) 'The imaginary companion: a questionnaire study', *Japanese Journal of Child and Adolescent Psychiatry*, 32: 32–48.

Inyega, H. (2000) 'Friendships and sense of well-being of visually impaired and sighted adolescents', unpublished Master's thesis, the University of Auckland, New Zealand.

Jacques, N., Wilton, K.M. and Townsend, M. (1998) 'Cooperative learning and social acceptance of children with mild intellectual disability', *Journal of Intellectual Disability Research*, 42: 29–36.

'Just good friends' (1996) *Sunday Mail*, October 20.

Klausen, E. and Passman, R.H. (2007) 'Pretend companions (imaginary playmates): the emergence of a field', *The Journal of Genetic Psychology*, 167: 349–64.

Ladd, G.W., Buhs, E.S. and Troop, W. (2004) 'Children's interpersonal skills and relationships in school settings: adaptive significance and implications for school-based prevention and intervention programs', in P.K. Smith and C.H. Hart (eds) *Blackwell Handbook of Childhood Social Development* (pp. 394–415), London: Blackwell.

Laurie, C. (1997) 'The functions of intimacy and popularity within same-sex adolescent friendships', unpublished Master's thesis, the University of Auckland, New Zealand.

Laverick, J. (1999) 'Adolescent friendships and social relations: intimacy as a predictor of social competence and loneliness', unpublished Master's thesis, the University of Auckland, New Zealand.

Lavery, L. (1998) 'Peer relations of children with attention deficit hyperactivity disorder: a comparison of liked and disliked groups', unpublished Master's thesis, the University of Auckland, New Zealand.

Lee, S.J. (2008) 'Online communication and adolescent social ties: who benefits more from internet use?', *Journal of Computer-Mediated Communication*, 14: 509–31.

Liu, S. (2000) 'Friendships, attitudes toward reading, and reading achievement', unpublished Master's thesis, University of Auckland, New Zealand.

Lloyd, C., Wilton, K.M. and Townsend, M. (2000) 'Children at high risk for mild intellectual disability in regular classrooms: six New Zealand case studies', *Education and Training in Mental Retardation and Developmental Disabilities*, 35: 44–54.

Male, D.B. (2007) 'The friendships and peer relationships of children and young people who experience difficulties in learning', in L. Florian (ed.) *Sage Handbook of Special Education*, London: Sage.

McIntyre, A.M. (1998) 'Peer relations and psychological adjustment during adolescence', unpublished Master's thesis, the University of Auckland, New Zealand.

Neeman, J., Hubbard, J. and Masten, A. (1995) 'The changing importance of romantic relationship involvement to competence from late childhood to late adolescence', *Development and Psychopathology*, 7: 727–50.

Newcomb, A.F. and Bagwell, C.L. (1995) 'Children's friendship relations: a meta-analytic review', *Psychological Bulletin*, 117: 306–47.

Nicholson, T. (2008) 'Children's friendships', paper presented to the First Educational Psychology Forum, Faculty of Education, The University of Auckland, New Zealand, September.

Nicholson, T., Adair, V., Boyd, A. and McArthur, B. (2002) 'Some preliminary results of a survey of childhood friendships including their imaginary friends', paper presented to New Zealand Association for Research in Education, Hamilton, New Zealand, December.

Parker, J.G. and Seal, J. (1996) 'Forming, losing, renewing, and replacing friendships: applying temporal parameters to the assessment of children's friendship experiences', *Child Development*, 67: 2248–68.

Parr, J.M. and Townsend, M. (2002) 'Environments, processes and mechanisms in peer learning', *International Journal of Education Research*, 37: 403–23.

Pearson, D., Rouse, H., Doswell, S., Ainsworth, C., Dawson, O., Simms, K., Edwards, L. and Faulconbridge, J. (2001), 'Prevalence of imaginary companions in a normal child population', *Child Care, Health and Development*, 27: 13–22.

Prentice, N.M., Manosevitch, M. and Hubbs, L. (1978) *American Journal of Orthopsychiatry*, 48: 618–28.

Shonkoff, J.P. and Phillips, D.A. (2003) *From Neurons to Neighborhoods: The Science of Early Childhood Development*, Washington, DC: National Academy Press.

Smith, D. (1994) 'The social networks and friendships of chronically ill adolescents', unpublished Master's thesis, the University of Auckland, New Zealand.

Svendsen, M. (1934) 'Children's imaginary companions', *Archives of Neurology and Psychiatry*, 32: 985–99.

Taylor, M. (1999) *Imaginary Companions and the Children Who Create Them*, New York: Oxford University Press.

Taylor, M. and Carlson, S.M. (1997) 'The relation between individual differences in fantasy and theory of mind', *Child Development*, 68: 436–55.

Taylor, M., Cartwright, B.S. and Carlson, S.M. (1993) 'A developmental investigation of children's imaginary companions', *Developmental Psychology*, 29: 276–85.

Townsend, M. (1993) *Children's Friendships and Social Development*, Palmerston North, New Zealand: Dunmore Press.

Townsend, M. and Hansen, J.B. (1986) 'The nature of friendships, leadership and social support among adolescent girls in a social welfare home', *New Zealand Journal of Educational Studies*, 21: 158–67.

Townsend, M. and Lai, M.K. (2007) 'Balancing social and academic goals at school', paper presented at the European Association for Research in Learning and Instruction, Budapest, Hungary, August.

Townsend, M., Lashley, M.L. and Wilton, K.M. (1997) 'Effects of friendship on social cognition', paper presented at the national conference of the New Zealand Special Education Association, Auckland, New Zealand, April.

Townsend, M., McCracken, H.E. and Wilton, K.M. (1988) 'Popularity and intimacy as determinants of psychological well-being in adolescent friendships', *Journal of Early Adolescence*, 8: 421–36.

Trinkaus, J. (2007) 'Visiting Santa: an additional look', *Psychological Reports*, 101: 779–83.

Vandell, D.L. (2000) 'Parents, peer groups, and other socializing influences', *Developmental Psychology*, 28: 700–13.

Wilzek, J. (1999) 'Friendships and social activities of adolescents who are deaf and hearing impaired', unpublished Master's thesis, the University of Auckland, New Zealand.

Chapter 14

Atypical behaviour development

Preschool hyperactivity and parent–child relationships

Louise J. Keown

Hyperactivity refers to an enduring set of behaviours characterized by developmentally inappropriate levels of restlessness, inattention, and impulsiveness (Barkley 1996; Danckaerts and Taylor 1995), while attention deficit hyperactivity disorder (ADHD) represents an extreme expression of hyperactivity (Sonuga-Barke *et al.* 2005). Children who show these patterns of hyperactive behaviour frequently experience a range of associated problems including disrupted family interactions, difficulties with peers, learning disabilities, academic underachievement, and conduct disordered behaviours such as aggression, lying and stealing (Henker and Whalen 1999; Hinshaw 1994; Taylor 1994). Furthermore, hyperactive behaviour problems and ADHD place children at risk for poor long-term outcomes including impaired social adjustment, the development of later psychiatric and substance use disorders, violence, antisocial behaviours, driving difficulties, and educational failure (Barkley *et al.* 1990; Fergusson *et al.* 1997; Mannuzza and Klein 1999; Taylor *et al.* 1996; Weiss and Hechtman 1993; Woodward *et al.* 2000). Thus, it is important to identify factors that contribute to the amelioration, as well as the continuation, of hyperactive behaviour problems.

There is general agreement that a mixture of biological–genetic and psychosocial factors lead to the development and maintenance of hyperactive behaviours, with family environment variables playing a primary role in some cases (Johnston and Mash 2001; Samudra and Cantwell 1999; Sonuga-Barke *et al.* 2005). While there have been advances in knowledge about the biological and cognitive nature of hyperactivity, research into families of children with hyperactivity has received relatively less attention (Johnston and Mash 2001). It has been argued that family context effects must be better understood in order to fully account for the developmental trajectory of hyperactive behaviour problems (Whalen and Henker 1999). In particular, more research needs to be undertaken with preschool samples.

Preschool hyperactivity

Studies of the family relationships of hyperactive children have been confined mainly to school-age samples. This is despite recognition of the early origins of hyperactive behaviour problems and their relative stability from preschool to school (Lavigne *et al.* 1998; Sonuga-Barke *et al.* 1997) especially in high risk samples (Lavigne *et al.* 1998; Marakovitz and Campbell 1998). For example, in a 12-year follow-up study of a sample of 1037 children, McGee *et al.* (1991) found that preschool children with hyperactive behaviour problems showed significantly more pervasive inattentive–hyperactive and general problem behaviours during their early school years than comparison group children. By adolescence, the rate of disorders (as defined in the *Diagnostic and Statistical Manual of Mental Disorders*, Third Edition (DSM-III)) for the hyperactive group was more than twice that of the comparison groups.

Internationally, there has been a rapid increase in the recognition of preschool ADHD and its treatment with psycho-stimulant medication, despite our fragmented understanding of the nature of preschool ADHD and the best way to treat it (Dopfner *et al.* 2004). Furthermore, it is questionable whether current ADHD diagnostic criteria are developmentally appropriate for preschool children. For example, many young children exhibit behaviours that contribute to a diagnosis of ADHD, such as difficulty with staying seated, playing quietly, and waiting their turn. However, criteria which define age-appropriate levels of activity and shifts in attention are not specified in the DSM-III, making it difficult to distinguish between normative behaviour and symptoms of disorder (Campbell 2002). Nevertheless, there are some similarities in the characteristics of preschool and school-age hyperactivity with regard to symptom structure, associated impairment and developmental risk, and neuropsychological deficits (Sonuga-Barke *et al.* 2005). There is general agreement that clinically significant preschool hyperactivity includes a cluster of behaviours that are frequent, pervasive (i.e. occur across settings), persistent (i.e. present for more than six months) and severe enough to interfere with developmental progress (Campbell 2002).

Possible therapies for clinically significant hyperactivity in young children include pharmacological and psychosocial approaches. Well-developed evidence is lacking about the efficacy and short- and long-term side effects of treating preschool hyperactivity with psycho-stimulant medication (Dopfner *et al.* 2004). There is, however, some suggestion that extreme and impairing expressions of preschool hyperactivity may be more amenable to treatment with parent training in child management techniques than ADHD behaviours during the school years, which tend to be compounded by school failure and deterioration of adult–child interactions (Dopfner *et al.* 2004). For example, in a randomized control trial of parent training for preschool ADHD with a specific focus on improving attention and self-regulation, there was a reduction in ADHD symptoms at the 15-week follow-up (Sonuga-Barke *et al.* 2001).

The potential importance of parent training for preschool hyperactivity is also supported by early observational research that negative parent–child interactions of hyperactive children tend to be at their worst during the preschool years (Mash and Johnston 1982), at a time when children may be particularly vulnerable to the effects of adverse parenting given their dependence on parents for emotional support and guidance (Campbell *et al.* 1996). In summary, from both a developmental and early intervention perspective, the preschool period represents a key time for examining family processes that may be related to the development of hyperactive behaviour problems.

Against this backdrop, the aim of this chapter is to review some recent work on the parenting correlates of hyperactivity during the preschool years and in particular, to discuss the possible role of father–child relationships in the development of children with hyperactivity, and identify areas for further research. It is acknowledged that studies of the family correlates of hyperactivity do not directly address the causes of either child hyperactive behaviour or parenting behaviour. In accordance with the transactional model, it is likely that both hyperactive child characteristics and parenting behaviour shape each other over time and that child behavioural outcomes arise from the continual interplay of parent and child (Johnston and Mash 2001; Shaw and Bell 1993). Nonetheless, understanding of family correlates is a key type of data necessary to clarify the processes by which child hyperactive behaviour develops and is maintained over time (Jester *et al.* 2005).

Associations between parent–child relationships and preschool hyperactivity

While many studies indicate that preschool children are likely to be rated as inattentive and overactive by their parents (for a review, see Campbell 1995), preschool children with extreme and durable patterns of these behaviours may be particularly difficult to socialize (Barkley 1998). Evidence for this possibility is provided by findings from a small number of cross-sectional studies of high-risk and clinical preschool samples. For example, in a clinical study of 94 ADHD and control children between 3 and 5 years of age, DuPaul *et al.* (2001) found that parents of ADHD children reported higher levels of parenting stress and displayed more negative behaviour towards their children than control parents during free play and structured situations. Similarly, in a study of 40 preschool children classified into two groups on the basis of teacher ratings of impulsivity, inattention and hyperactivity, Winsler *et al.* (1999) found that mothers of behaviourally at-risk children showed more negative control, less praise, and less contingent withdrawal of support during a teaching task compared to mothers of comparison children. Additionally, in research using self-report measures, mothers of preschool children with hyperactive-impulsive-inattentive behaviour rated themselves as employing less effective child management practices than comparison group mothers (Shelton *et al.* 1998). Results from a community study extend this body of work. Specifically, in a sample of 33 pervasively hyperactive and 34 comparison preschool boys, Keown and Woodward (2002) found that mothers of boys with hyperactivity reported using more lax and over-reactive disciplinary practices, less efficient maternal coping with child behaviour problems, lower rates of mother–child communication and showed less synchronous parent–child interactions in a free play setting than comparison mothers. In this last study, maternal coping and synchrony tapped the importance of the parent being in tune with the child. For example, coping referred to the parent's sensitivity in anticipating and responding to child behaviour and modifying parental actions according to events and to the individual child. Synchrony was defined as the reciprocity and responsiveness of parent–child interactions.

Prospective research findings suggest that for some children experiential factors may play a role in the development of hyperactivity (Carlson *et al*. 1995; Jacobitz and Sroufe 1987; Silverman and Ragusa 1992). For example, maternal intrusive care and over-stimulation assessed at 6 months and 42 months respectively, have been found to predict hyperactivity at 5 or 6 years (Jacobitz and Sroufe 1987) and middle childhood (Carlson *et al*. 1995) as measured by clinically validated teacher ratings. Similarly, Silverman and Ragusa (1992) found that maternal negativity and child rearing attitudes reflecting warmth and aggravation at 2 years of age predicted dimensional ratings of inattention, hyperactivity and impulsivity at 4 years. These predictions continued to hold after the child's behaviour at age 2, as an elicitor of maternal behaviour, was controlled.

Other longitudinal research findings suggest that parental behaviours may play an important role in the maintenance of early problem behaviours of hyperactive children (Carlson *et al*. 1995; Whalen and Henker 1999). For example, in two cohorts of children, initially identified at age 3 with hyperactive and conduct behaviour problems, where mothers were observed as showing negative affective behaviour and intrusive control of their children aged 4 years, this was predictive of these children having externalizing (attention deficit/hyperactivity, conduct and oppositional symptoms), problems at 9 years (Campbell and Ewing 1990; Campbell *et al*. 1996). As well as finding marked stability in child problems, the latter study found there were strong concurrent associations between child problems and maternal discipline at both ages (Campbell *et al*. 1996). While the stability in maternal control was accounted for by the stability in child behaviour problems, intrusive maternal control of the children at age 4 still predicted externalizing behaviour at age 9 even with all other variables controlled. These findings highlight the importance of early mother–child interactions for children's functioning in middle childhood (Campbell *et al*. 1996) and, more generally, reinforce the need to further examine the parenting practices of parents of preschoolers with hyperactivity. Additionally, research needs to expand from a primary focus on mothers to include both parents (Whalen and Henker 1999; Johnston and Mash 2001). In general, we know relatively little about the role of fathers in the development of children with hyperactivity.

Fathers and preschool behaviour problems

Where research has examined associations between parenting and broad patterns of disruptive behaviours, there is some indication that fathers of preschool children with externalizing behaviours use more authoritarian and less authoritative child rearing practices (Baker and Heller 1996), and that fathers of clinic-referred boys interact more negatively (Stormshak *et al.* 1997) and show less positive involvement with their sons (DeKlyen *et al.* 1998). More recently, Burbach *et al.* (2004) found that greater use of corporal and verbal punishment by fathers was associated with higher rates of challenging behaviours in young children. Conversely, longitudinal findings suggest that greater paternal involvement in the care of 'difficult to raise' preschool boys is linked with a lower likelihood that these children will develop more behaviour problems at school age (Aldous and Mulligan 2002). Likewise Denham *et al.* (2000) found that positive paternal behaviours were related to improved outcomes in middle childhood, among preschool children at high risk of developing of disruptive behaviour problems. These paternal behaviours included observed proactive parenting (supportive presence, clear instruction, and limit setting) and lack of reported hostility and anger.

In relation to early onset hyperactivity, findings from one of the few studies that include fathers indicate that preschoolers with hyperactivity plus aggression have more restrictive fathers than hyperactive preschoolers who are not aggressive (Stormont-Spurgin and Zentall 1995). There is also some evidence, based on maternal reports, that less efficient paternal coping with child behaviour and lower rates of father–child communication are associated with preschool hyperactivity (Keown and Woodward 2002). Similarly, only a small number of studies of hyperactivity in school-age children have examined fathers' parenting. In these studies, fathers of hyperactive children were more directive (Buhrmester *et al.* 1992; Tallmadge and Barkley 1983), over-reactive and lax (Harvey *et al.* 2001), and endorsed more indulgent or permissive child-rearing beliefs (Stormont-Spurgin and Zentall 1996) than fathers of comparison children. Given this small body of findings, there is a need to further investigate the father–child relationships of children with hyperactivity, especially in preschool samples.

Unique contribution of paternal parenting to children's behavioural development

There are a number of reasons we might expect fathers to play a significant role in the development of children with hyperactivity. First, fathers are particularly likely to be involved with sons (Pleck 1997), who are at higher risk than daughters of developing hyperactivity. Second, although there is growing evidence from studies of typically developing children that mothers and fathers influence their children in similar ways, evidence is also emerging that fathers make a unique contribution to their children's behavioural and social development (Parke 2002; Phares 1996).

For example, Isley *et al.* (1996) found that fathers' level of affect and control predicted children's social adaptation with peers after maternal effects were controlled for. While in a study of 994 families from the United States National

Survey of Families and Households, Amato and Rivera (1999) found that fathers' positive involvement, as reflected in shared activities (meals, play, homework) and supportive behaviour (praise, physical affection), was associated with fewer behaviour problems in children, independently of mothers' parenting. Other findings indicate that paternal sensitivity contributes uniquely to young children's behavioural and social competence outside the family (NICHD Early Child Care Research Network, 2004).

While an increasing number of studies are finding links between fathers' parenting and children's development, the majority of this research has not examined whether fathers' and mothers' parenting make similar or separate contributions to children's development. Maternal and paternal behaviours are highly correlated in many studies, yet past research has often not controlled for the quality of the mother–child relationship when estimating the effect of the father–child relationship (Amato and Rivera 1999; Marsiglio et al. 2000). High correlations may reflect the fact that effective mothers encourage fathers to be highly involved with their children. Thus to determine if fathers have a unique influence on children's development, it is necessary to include the quality of the mother–son relationship in these types of analyses.

Measurement and sampling issues

Parenting constructs

There are several additional measurement and sampling issues that should be addressed when examining how fathers' parenting might relate to the development and maintenance of preschool children's hyperactive behaviour problems. First, there is a need to target the type of parent–child interactions that are likely to be particularly important in the development of children's attentional and self-organizing skills. Much of the early socialization research undertaken with hyperactive children focused mainly on issues of parental control and child compliance. However, more recently researchers have identified other influential parenting qualities related to the development of young children's self-regulation that are highly relevant for understanding the parent–child relationships of hyperactive children (Whalen and Henker 1999; Winsler 1998). These include mutual responsiveness, emotional warmth, scaffolding, and authoritative parenting (Campbell 1995; Jester et al. 2005; Winsler 1998). For example, sensitive, responsive parenting behaviours, and synchronous interactions between parent and child during the preschool years are likely to foster the development of attention and impulse control in children (Olson et al. 1990; Keown and Woodward 2006). As these are skills that often prove difficult for hyperactive children to develop, this suggests that further attention should be given to the role of positive, reciprocal, and mutually focused maternal and paternal parent–child interactions in the development of children with hyperactive behaviour problems.

Comorbidity with conduct problems

Second, while the importance of considering hyperactivity separately from other disruptive behaviour problems is recognized (Johnston and Mash 2001), less is known about how family processes exert their influence on child hyperactive behaviour problems in comparison with conduct problems and other externalizing behaviours. This is partly because early research on the family relationships of hyperactive children often did not use the type of sampling and statistical procedures that enabled the contributions of hyperactivity and conduct problems to be independently examined. Some progress has been made in addressing this issue, with several studies showing that parent–child interactions tend to be more difficult among children with mixed hyperactive and conduct problems than among children with hyperactive behaviour problems alone (Barkley *et al.* 1991; Cunningham and Boyle 2002; Gomez and Sanson 1994). However, the extent to which different parenting variables are influential for conduct problems and hyperactivity among preschoolers has received very little research attention.

An exception is a recent study by Gardner *et al.* (1999), which found that the use of reactive parenting strategies was predictive of the continuation of conduct problems, but not of hyperactivity. Reactive strategies refer to tactics that are introduced after the child has misbehaved to gain compliance, in contrast to proactive parenting that involves interventions that anticipate and prevent misbehaviour occurring. Mothers and children for this research were recruited from an epidemiological study of parent-reported child behaviour problems. The study consisted of observations of strategies that parents used to prevent parent–child conflict with preschool children with behaviour problems. Results showed that mothers of children in the group with behaviour problems were more likely to use reactive strategies in a toy tidy-up situation than mothers of comparison children. Gardner *et al.* (1999) showed that mothers' use of reactive strategies with their 3-year-old children were predictive of child conduct problems at age 5, even after controlling for initial levels of child problem behaviours. However, this longitudinal association did not hold between mothers' use of reactive strategies and child hyperactive problems.

In contrast, in community samples where a dimensional approach to attentional and conduct problems is taken, some consistent results have recently emerged about associations between hyperactivity and parenting practices (Keown and Woodward 2002; Stormshak *et al.* 2000; Woodward *et al.* 1998). For example, Keown and Woodward (2002) examined the quality of parent–child relationships in a sample of preschool boys with pervasive hyperactivity and comparison children and used statistical methods to control for the effects of conduct problems. Results of the study showed that higher rates of lax disciplinary practices, less efficient maternal coping with child behaviour problems, and less synchronous parent–child interactions were associated with hyperactivity following statistical adjustment for the effects of conduct problems. These results suggest that the problematic behaviours of hyperactive children, such as poor sustained attention, over-activity, and distractibility, may present additional challenges for parents that influence their ability to parent effectively, and may contribute to the persistence of hyperactive behaviour problems.

This possibility is supported by Jester *et al.* (2005), who examined the influence of the early childhood home environment on trajectories of inattention/hyperactivity and aggression in a sample of 335 children from school entry throughout adolescence. Membership in the high inattention/hyperactivity groups was predicted by lower levels of intellectual stimulation and emotional support in early childhood, when the trajectory of aggression was held constant. Jester *et al.* acknowledged that in family studies measures of parenting are likely to be mediated by genetic influences via parental personality. Also, that inattention/hyperactivity problems may have been present in the children from a very young age before the measurement of preschool family environment. Therefore, the ability of the parents to provide intellectual stimulation may have been made more difficult because of the behaviour of the child. However, Jester *et al.* also noted that 'this does not change the importance of understanding the mediating mechanisms in the home environment by which such effects may be actualized' (ibid.: 121).

Future directions

The research reviewed in the previous sections indicates some consistent findings about the maternal parenting correlates of preschool hyperactivity. In particular, mothers of preschool children with hyperactivity tend to report using less effective parenting practices and show more negative, less synchronous parent–child interactions than mothers of comparison children. Furthermore, findings from a few longitudinal studies offer some support for the role of maternal parenting behaviours in the origin and developmental course of preschool hyperactive behaviour, especially in the context of family stress. There are compelling reasons for undertaking further research with preschool samples. These include the high rates of diagnosis of preschool ADHD and treatment with medication despite lack of consensus about the validity of this diagnostic category in preschool children and the best interventions for young children with clinically significant levels of hyperactivity. There is also a need to have a better understanding of the role of family context in determining outcomes for preschool children at risk of early onset hyperactivity. Emerging evidence of fathers' unique contribution to children's behavioural development underscores the need to include both parents in future studies. Specific areas that need further research attention include the assessment of a broader range of parenting behaviours, especially positive parental involvement and practices which might mitigate the effects of hyperactivity. Also of importance is that research on the socialization of children with hyperactivity should be designed to allow the independent contributions of hyperactivity and conduct problems to be examined.

Current models that seek to predict how ADHD characteristics develop over time propose a number of possible pathways depending on the relative influence of various child and environmental risk and protective factors (Johnston and Mash 2001; Sonuga-Barke *et al.* 2005). In one pathway, family dysfunction and severe preschool hyperactivity in combination with an explosive temperament may interact and lead to early severe ADHD and oppositional behaviours that are exacerbated by coercive family interactions. An alternative pathway is where family factors interrupt trajectories to disorder in the presence of significant preschool hyperactivity (Sonuga-Barke *et al.* 2005). For example, extremely sensitive, responsive parenting might act as a protective factor that facilitates self-regulation development and attenuates ADHD symptoms in children who are biologically at risk for the disorder (Johnston and Mash 2001). Of particular interest in relation to the research discussed in this chapter, is whether fathers' sensitive, responsive parenting might make a unique contribution, independently of maternal parenting, to the behavioural development of boys in this 'at-risk' category.

In order to address some of the gaps in the research addressed by this review, the author and colleagues are currently carrying out a study to identify paternal and maternal parenting factors that are associated with patterns of preschool activity, attention, and impulse control by comparing a community sample of 50 hyperactive 4-year-old boys with a comparison sample of 50 boys (Keown 2005). In addition to this general aim, there are some more specific questions that we are currently researching.

First, there is the question of whether fathers' and mothers' parenting make similar or separate contributions to the development and functioning of children with hyperactivity. There is a specific focus on parent–child relationship qualities important for the development of children's self-regulation including observed sensitivity, intrusiveness, positive regard, and supportive presence. Few, if any, previous studies of preschool hyperactivity have included observations of both fathers and mothers interacting with their children. The inclusion of observational data allows for an examination of actual, rather than self-reported, parenting behaviour in these dyads. The study is also comparing self-reports of paternal and maternal lax and over-reactive disciplinary practices, authoritative parenting style, parenting childcare involvement, parenting satisfaction, and child-rearing difficulties.

Second, there is the question of whether other child behaviours that commonly occur with hyperactivity, such as non-compliance, explain any links that may be found between parenting and hyperactivity. Our study extends previous research by assessing whether *both* fathers' and mothers' parenting are related to hyperactivity, once conduct problems are controlled for. Additionally, the study design allows a more precise estimate to be made of the relationship between parental behaviour and child outcomes by including multiple sources of information on child behaviour, such as teacher and interviewer ratings. Researchers frequently use parents as the sole source of information about their parenting and their children's behaviour, resulting in a likely inflation of the true association between these variables (Marsiglio *et al.* 2000).

Preliminary analyses of data for 46 boys and their fathers (23 per group), suggest that observed paternal sensitivity and fathers' self-reports' of over-reactive disciplinary strategies may be associated with preschool hyperactivity, especially where fathers report child-rearing difficulties and less satisfaction with their parenting role (Keown 2006). We are currently analysing observational data of maternal and child behaviours which will allow the following question to be addressed: What is the relationship between paternal parenting and child hyperactive behaviour once maternal effects and child conduct problems are controlled for? In order to clarify the possible direction of effects between paternal and maternal parenting and child hyperactive behaviour, the next step will be a longitudinal study that examines parent–child interactions and child development over time.

References

Aldous, J. and Mulligan, G.M. (2002) 'Fathers' child care and children's behavior problems', *Journal of Family Issues*, 23: 624–47.

Amato, P.R. and Rivera, F. (1999) 'Paternal involvement and children's behavior problems', *Journal of Marriage and the Family*, 61: 375–84.

Baker, B.L. and Heller, T.L. (1996) 'Preschool children with externalizing behaviors: experience of fathers and mothers', *Journal of Abnormal Child Psychology*, 24: 513–32.

Barkley, R.A. (1996) 'Attention-deficit/hyperactivity disorder', in E.J. Mash and R.A. Barkley (eds) *Child Psychopathology* (pp. 63–112), New York: Guilford Press.

Barkley, R.A. (1998) *Attention-deficit Hyperactivity Disorder: A Handbook for Diagnosis and Treatment*, 2nd edn, New York: Guilford Press.

Barkley, R.A., Fisher, M., Edelbrock, C.S. and Smallish, L. (1990) 'The adolescent outcome of hyperactive children diagnosed by research criteria: an 8-year prospective follow-up study', *Journal of the American Academy of Child and Adolescent Psychiatry*, 29: 546–57.

Barkley, R.A., Fisher, M., Edelbrock, C. and Smallish, L. (1991) 'The adolescent outcome of hyperactive children diagnosed by research criteria-III: mother–child interactions, family conflicts and maternal psychopathology', *Journal of Child Psychology and Psychiatry*, 32: 233–55.

Buhrmester, D., Camparo, L., Christensen, A., Gonzalez, L.S. and Hinshaw, S.P. (1992) 'Mothers and fathers interacting in dyads and triads with normal and hyperactive sons', *Developmental Psychology*, 28: 500–9.

Burbach, A.D., Fox, R.A. and Nicholson, B.C. (2004) 'Challenging behaviors in young children: the father's role', *Journal of Genetic Psychology*, 165: 169–83.

Campbell, S.B. (1995) 'Behavior problems in preschool children: a review of recent research', *Journal of Child Psychology and Psychiatry and Allied Disciplines*, 36: 113–49.

Campbell, S.B. (2002) *Behavior Problems in Preschool Children: Clinical and Developmental Issues*, 2nd edn, New York: Guilford Press.

Campbell, S.B. and Ewing, L.J. (1990) 'Hard-to-manage preschoolers: adjustment at age nine and predictors of continuing symptoms', *Journal of Child Psychology and Psychiatry*, 31: 473–88.

Campbell, S.B., Pierce, E.W., Moore, G., Marakovitz, S. and Newby, K. (1996) 'Boys' externalizing problems at elementary school age: pathways from early behavior problems, maternal control, and family stress', *Development and Psychopathology*, 8: 701–19.

Carlson, E.A., Jacobvitz, D. and Sroufe, L.A. (1995) 'A developmental investigation of inattentiveness and hyperactivity', *Child Development*, 66: 37–54.

Cunningham, C.E. and Boyle, M.H. (2002) 'Preschoolers at risk for attention-deficit hyperactivity disorder and oppositional defiant disorder: family, parenting, and behavioral correlates', *Journal of Abnormal Child Psychology*, 30: 555–69.

Danckaerts, M. and Taylor, E.A. (1995) 'The epidemiology of childhood hyperactivity', in F.C. Verhulst and H.M. Koot (eds) *The Epidemiology of Child and Adolescent Psychopathology* (pp. 178–209), London: Oxford University Press.

DeKlyen, M., Biernbaum, M.A., Speltz, M.L. and Greenberg, M.T. (1998) 'Fathers and preschool behavior problems', *Developmental Psychology*, 34: 264–75.

Denham, S.A., Workman, E., Cole, P.M., Weissbrod, C., Kendziora, K.T. and Zahn-Waxler, C. (2000) 'Prediction of externalizing behavior problems from early to middle childhood: the role of parental socialization and emotion expression', *Development and Psychopathology*, 12: 23–45.

Dopfner, M., Rothenberger, A. and Sonuga-Barke, E. (2004) 'Areas for future investment in the field of ADHD: preschoolers and clinical networks', *European Child and Adolescent Psychiatry*, 13: 130–5.

DuPaul, G.J., McGoey, K.E., Eckert, T.L. and VanBrakle, J. (2001) 'Preschool children with attention-deficit/hyperactivity disorder: impairments in behavioral, social, and school functioning', *Journal of the American Academy of Child and Adolescent Psychiatry*, 40: 508–15.

Fergusson, D.M., Lynskey, M.T. and Horwood, L. (1997) 'Attentional difficulties in middle childhood and psychosocial outcomes in young adulthood', *Journal of Child Psychology and Psychiatry and Allied Disciplines*, 38: 633–44.

Gardner, F.E.M., Sonuga-Barke, E.J.S. and Sayal, K. (1999) 'Parents anticipating misbehavior: an observational study of strategies parents use to prevent conflict with behavior problem children', *Journal of Child Psychology and Psychiatry*, 8: 1185–96.

Gomez, R. and Sanson, A.V. (1994) 'Mother–child interactions and noncompliance in hyperactive boys with and without conduct problems', *Journal of Child Psychology and Psychiatry*, 35: 477–90.

Harvey, E., Danforth, J.S., Ulaszek, W.R. and Eberhardt, T.L. (2001) 'Validity of the parenting scale for parents of children with attention-deficit/hyperactivity disorder', *Behavior Research and Therapy*, 39: 731–43.

Henker, B. and Whalen, C.K. (1999) 'The child with Attention-Deficit/Hyperactivity Disorder in school and peer settings', in H.C. Quay and A.E. Hogan (eds) *Handbook of Disruptive Behavior Disorders* (pp. 157–78), New York: Kluwer Academic.

Hinshaw, S.P. (1994) *Attention Deficits and Hyperactivity in Children*, Thousand Oaks, CA: Sage.

Isley, S., O'Neil, R. and Parke, R.D. (1996) 'The relation of parental affect and control behaviors to children's classroom acceptance: a concurrent and predictive analysis', *Early Education and Development*, 7: 7–23.

Jacobitz, D. and Sroufe, A. (1987) 'The early caregiver-child relationship and attention-deficit disorder with hyperactivity in kindergarten: a prospective study', *Child Development*, 58: 1488–95.

Jester, J.M., Nigg, J.T., Adams. K., Fitzgerald, H.E., Puttler, L.I., Wong, M.M. and Zucker, R.A. (2005) 'Inattention/hyperactivity and aggression from early childhood to adolescence: heterogeneity of trajectories and differential influence of family environment characteristics', *Development and Psychopathology*, 17: 99–125.

Johnston, C. and Mash, E.J. (2001) 'Families of children with Attention-Deficit/Hyperactivity Disorder: review and recommendations for future research', *Clinical Child and Family Psychology Review*, 4: 183–207.

Keown, L.J. (2005) 'Fathering, mothering, and preschool hyperactivity: preliminary findings', paper presented at the 14th biennial conference of the Australasian Human Development Association, Perth, July.

Keown, L.J. (2006) 'Fathering and hyperactive behaviour in 4-year-old boys', poster presented at the 19th biennial meeting of the International Society for the Study of Behavioral Development, Melbourne, July.

Keown, L.J. and Woodward, L.J. (2002) 'Early parent–child relations and family functioning of preschool boys with pervasive hyperactivity', *Journal of Abnormal Child Psychology*, 30: 541–53.

Keown, L.J. and Woodward, L.J. (2006) 'Early peer functioning and parent–child relationships of preschool boys with pervasive hyperactivity', *Social Development*, 15: 23–45.

Lavigne, J.V., Arend, R., Rosenbaum, D., Binns, H.J., Christoffel, K.K. and Gibbons, R.D. (1998) 'Psychiatric disorders with onset in the preschool years: I. Stability of diagnoses', *Journal of the American Academy of Child and Adolescent Psychiatry*, 37: 1246–54.

Mannuzza, S. and Klein, R.G. (1999) 'Adolescent and adult outcomes in attention-deficit/hyperactivity disorder', in H.C. Quay and A.E. Hogan (eds) *Handbook of Disruptive Behavior Disorders* (pp. 279–94), Dordrecht: Kluwer Academic Publishers.

Marakovitz, S.E. and Campbell, S.B. (1998) 'Inattention, impulsivity, and hyperactivity from preschool to school age: performance of hard-to-manage boys on laboratory measures', *Journal of Child Psychology and Psychiatry and Allied Disciplines*, 39: 841–51.

Marsiglio, W., Amato, P., Day, R.D. and Lamb, M.E. (2000) 'Scholarship on fatherhood in the 1990s and beyond', *Journal of Marriage and the Family*, 62: 1173–91.

Mash, E.J. and Johnston, C. (1982) 'A comparison of the mother–child interactions of younger and older hyperactive and normal children', *Child Development*, 53: 1371–81.

McGee, R., Partridge, F., Williams, S. and Silva, P.A. (1991) 'A twelve-year follow-up of preschool hyperactive children', *Journal of the American Academy of Child and Adolescent Psychiatry*, 30: 224–32.

NICHD Early Child Care Research Network (2004) 'Fathers' and mothers' parenting behavior and beliefs as predictors of children's social adjustment in the transition to school', *Journal of Family Psychology*, 18: 628–38.

Olson, S.L., Bates, J.E. and Bayles, K. (1990) 'Early antecedents of childhood impulsivity: the role of parent–child interaction, cognitive competence, and temperament', *Journal of Abnormal Child Psychology*, 18: 317–34.

Parke, R.D. (2002) 'Fathers and families', in M.H. Bornstein (ed.) *Handbook of Parenting:* vol. 3: *Being and Becoming a Parent*, 2nd edn (pp. 27–73), Mahwah, NJ: Lawrence Erlbaum.

Phares, V. (1996) *Fathers and Developmental Psychopathology*, Oxford: Wiley.

Pleck, J.H. (1997) 'Paternal involvement: levels, sources, and consequences', in M.E. Lamb (ed.) *The Role of the Father in Child Development*, 3rd edn (pp. 66–103), New York: Wiley.

Samudra, K. and Cantwell, D.P. (1999) 'Risk factors for attention-deficit/hyperactivity disorder', in H.C. Quay and A.E. Hogan (eds) *Handbook of Disruptive Behavior Disorders* (pp.199–220) New York: Kluwer Academic/Plenum Publishers.

Shaw, D.S. and Bell, R.Q. (1993) 'Developmental theories of parental contributors to antisocial behavior', *Journal of Abnormal Child Psychology*, 21: 493–518.

Shelton, T.L., Barkley, R.A., Crosswaite, C., Moorehouse, M., Fletcher, K., Barrett, S., Jenkins, L. and Metevia, L. (1998) 'Psychiatric and psychological morbidity as a function of adaptive disability in preschool children with aggressive and hyperactive-impulse-inattentive behavior', *Journal of Abnormal Child Psychology*, 26: 475–94.

Silverman, I.W. and Ragusa, D.M. (1992) 'A short-term longitudinal study of the early development of self-regulation', *Journal of Abnormal Child Psychology*, 20: 415–35.

Sonuga-Barke, E.J.S., Auerbach, J., Campbell, S.B., Daley, D. and Thompson, M. (2005) 'Varieties of preschool hyperactivity: multiple pathways from risk to disorder', *Developmental Science*, 8: 141–50.

Sonuga-Barke, E.J.S., Daley, D., Thompson, M., Laver-Bradbury, C. and Weeks, A. (2001) 'Parent-based therapies for preschool attention-deficit/hyperactivity disorder: a randomized, control trial with a community sample', *Journal of the American Academy of Child and Adolescent Psychiatry*, 40: 402–8.

Sonuga-Barke, E.J.S, Thompson, M., Stevenson, J. and Viney, D. (1997) 'Patterns of behavior problems among pre-school children.', *Psychological Medicine*, 27: 909–18.

Stormont-Spurgin, M. and Zentall, S.S. (1995) 'Contributing factors in the manifestation of aggression in preschoolers with hyperactivity', *Journal of Child Psychology and Psychiatry and Allied Disciplines*, 36: 491–509.

Stormont-Spurgin, M. and Zentall, S. (1996) 'Child-rearing practices associated with aggression in youth with and without ADHD: an exploratory study', *International Journal of Disability, Development and Education*, 43: 135–46.

Stormshak, E.A., Bierman, K.L., McMahon, R.J. and Lengua, L.J. (2000) 'Parenting practices and child disruptive behavior problems in early elementary school', *Journal of Clinical Child Psychology*, 29: 17–29.

Stormshak, E.A., Speltz, M.L., DeKlyen, M. and Greenberg, M.T. (1997) 'Observed family interaction during clinical interviews: a comparison of families containing preschool boys with and without disruptive behavior', *Journal of Abnormal Child Psychology*, 25: 345–57.

Tallmadge, J. and Barkley, R.A. (1983) 'The interactions of hyperactive and normal boys with their fathers and mothers', *Journal of Abnormal Child Psychology*, 11: 565–79.

Taylor, E. (1994) 'Syndromes of attention deficit and overactivity', in M. Rutter, E. Taylor and L. Hersov (eds) *Child and Adolescent Psychiatry: Modern Approaches*, 3rd edn (pp. 285–307), Oxford: Blackwell Scientific Publications.

Taylor, E., Chadwick, O., Heptinstall, E. and Danckaerts, M. (1996) 'Hyperactivity and conduct problems as risk factors for adolescent development', *Journal of the American Academy of Child and Adolescent Psychiatry*, 35: 1213–26.

Weiss, G. and Hechtman, L.T. (1993) *Hyperactive Children Grown Up: ADHD in Children, Adolescents, and Adults*, 2nd edn, New York: Guilford Press.

Whalen, C.K. and Henker, B. (1999) 'The child with attention-deficit/hyperactivity disorder in family contexts', in H.C. Quay and A.E. Hogan (eds) *Handbook of Disruptive Behavior Disorders* (pp. 139–55), Dordrecht: Kluwer Academic/Plenum Publishers.

Winsler, A. (1998) 'Parent–child interaction and private speech in boys with ADHD', *Applied Developmental Science*, 2: 17–39.

Winsler, A., Diaz, R.M., McCarthy, E.M., Atencio, D.J. and Chabay, L.A. (1999) 'Mother–child interaction, private speech, and task performance in preschool children with behavior problems', *Journal of Child Psychology and Psychiatry and Allied Disciplines*, 40: 891–904.

Woodward, L.J., Fergusson, D.M. and Horwood, L. (2000) 'Driving outcomes of young people with attentional difficulties in adolescence', *Journal of the American Academy of Child and Adolescent Psychiatry*, 39: 627–34.

Woodward, L., Taylor, E. and Dowdney, L. (1998) 'The parenting and family functioning of children with hyperactivity', *Journal of Child Psychology and Child Psychiatry*, 39: 161–9.

Chapter 15

Family literacy practices and the promise of optimization

A Vietnamese study

Thanh-Binh Tran, Stuart McNaughton and Judy M. Parr

There is a long history of optimism about how psychology in general and educational and developmental psychology in particular might contribute to child rearing and education. The flavour of the early enthusiasm by educators with a developmental or psychological perspective is captured by John Dewey's lectures in 1899 to an audience of parents interested in the University of Chicago's own experimental elementary school:

> The school is a laboratory of applied psychology. That is, it has a place for the study of mind as manifested and developed in the child and for the search after materials and agencies that seem most likely to fulfill and further the condition of normal growth.

A similar enthusiasm was present in England at the same time with William McDougall, writing about child psychology and education: 'Here then is an immense field for research, the extent and importance of which we are now beginning fully to realize. And it is a field for the psychologist' ([1912] 1952: 139).

Developmentalists in the 1970s saw a natural progression in developmental research. A prescription for developmental psychology was to engage in description, move on to explanation and thence to 'optimization' (Baltes *et al.* 1980). This grand vision has some notable success stories. One is Marie Clay's design of the highly successful Reading Recovery programme (Clay 1972, 2005). Clay first studied demonstrably effective teachers to determine the features of their expertise. She then designed and experimentally tested the intervention. From then, she moved to optimization nationally in New Zealand, working to develop a policy context and an ongoing training regime that would mean the intervention was bedded in, across the unique features of both urban and rural schools.

Despite the Reading Recovery example, the initial optimism of developmental psychology generally has not been widely fulfilled, especially in relationship to substantial educational change, and especially in the context of cultural and linguistic diversity (Consortium for Longitudinal Studies 1983; Zigler and Styfco 1994). In subsequent reevaluations and redevelopment of projects, the scientific community has realized that the optimism needs to be tempered; we need to guard against overselling benefits and we need to be realistic about what can be accomplished (Zigler and Styfco 1994). This has led to rethinking basic concepts about development (Ramey and Ramey 1998). Recent formulations now describe an 'applied developmental science' (Lerner *et al.* 2000), which would recognize the grounded and contextualized nature of children's development, and, with interdisciplinary help and better designed research strategies, would be able to study how historical and contemporary forces of economy, politics and social, physical and policy contexts create conditions for development. And then, having studied these, it would contribute to the design of new systems.

In this chapter, we focus on one of area of optimization, family literacy practices and, in particular, reading books to children as a vehicle for promoting particular types of language and literacy skills. We first outline the descriptive base to the research as well as the experimental analyses from such research. We then propose a theoretical model for looking at the nature of storybook reading as a contextualized activity and describe a test of the model and its outcomes with an intervention designed to optimize the use of the activity. A central argument is that for this programme of research to be influential, it needs to be contextualized so that what is described, explained and optimized is done so in relationship to known sociocultural contexts. It is the grounding of our research in everyday contexts and knowing the properties of those contexts that are key determinants of effectiveness.

Reading storybooks and child language development

Reading storybooks to children is part of family literacy practices, those activities and practices around print that occur within daily family life (Morrow 1995; Taylor 1995). By watching and participating in daily literacy events within their families and communities, children learn what it means to read and write before they know how to read and write (Heath 1983; McNaughton 1995; Spielberger and Halpern 2002; Taylor 1995). From the perspective of family literacy, styles of interactions in family literacy activities such as reading storybooks reflect general cultural practices, but there are also differences from one family to another family, from one community to another community. This means that the nature of cultural practices is collective and dynamic. Differences in family literacy practices mostly reflect cultural identity, socioeconomic status, and place of residence (Heath 1983; McNaughton 1995; Schieffelin and Cochran-Smith 1984; Taylor 1995; Tran 2003). According to Teale, reading stories not only promotes literacy development, but also serves 'to familiarize the child with the literacy heritage of the culture' (1984: 118). Through reading stories of a culture, the child is socialized into a particular pattern of attitudes and values (Wan 2000).

Reading storybooks to, with, and by children in the home setting has come to be regarded as an especially significant family literacy activity (McNaughton 1995).

It is claimed that shared storybook reading activity affects parent/child relationships, and also provides a vehicle for aspects of emergent literacy such as alphabet knowledge, print awareness, and narrative schema (Bus *et al.* 1995; Justice and Ezell 2000). Importantly, storybook reading is also considered an effective means to enhance oral language (Bus *et al.* 1995).

Descriptive, correlational, and analytic studies have examined these features of the activity and its association with children's language acquisition. Early research established that early readers came from families where they were read to frequently (Durkin 1966; McNaughton 1995). Frequency, however, was not the only dimension associated with developmental features. Many studies have found that qualitative differences in how parents read storybooks to their children are likely to be reflected in their children's development of different literacy skills (Haden *et al.* 1996; Hayden and Fagan 1987; Heath 1982, 1983). The variations in reading styles, reading environments or contexts, attitudes, and interactive behaviours likely influenced the potential of storybook reading for promoting literacy development (Meyer *et al.* 1994). Hence, we need to understand fully how the core dimensions interact to influence development (Teale 1984).

Family literacy intervention programmes

A number of experimental programmes have provided precise tests of the predicted relationship. The studies of Feitelson and her colleagues (Feitelson, Rosenhouse, Charadon and Givon-Oz 1991, cited in Meyer *et al.* 1999) show the effects of storybook reading on language skills such as the literacy register, the vocabulary, syntax, and tone used in school. Their experimental storybook reading programme also appears to have long-term effects in terms of children's transition to school and school achievement.

Another intervention programme is 'dialogic reading', an approach based on adults' use of questions during shared book reading to promote young children's vocabulary development. The programme is based on three general principles: (1) encourage the child to participate; (2) provide feedback to the child; and (3) adapt the adult's scaffold to the child's growing linguistic ability. Using 'what' and other types of open-ended questions and praise during reading enabled more expressive vocabulary gains for young children than for those whose parents used a regular reading style (Whitehurst *et al.* 1988, 1994, 1999).

Justice (2002) examined a different dimension, parental labelling, in a small-scale study with children from 3 to 5 years old. Justice pointed out that adults' labelling of new words, in contrast to questioning, resulted in significantly greater gains in preschool children's receptive word learning. However, this differential effect was not observed for children's expressive word learning: labelling and questioning resulted in similar new word learning gains. Methodological differences may be one source for the discrepancy in findings, but the differences across these studies suggest that the differential effects of various types of child–adult interactional styles have not yet been fully determined.

Another intervention programme, Early Access to Success in Education (Project EASE), designed by Jordan *et al.* (2000), aimed to provide European American low-income parents with both a theoretical understanding of how to help their preschool children and scaffolded interactive practices to facilitate their children's early literacy development through book-centred activities. Specifically, parents received information about ways to strengthen vocabulary, extend narrative understanding, develop letter recognition and sound awareness, produce narrative retellings, and understand exposition. Findings have shown that children whose families engaged in the at-school and at-home activities made significantly greater gains in language scores as measured on subtests of vocabulary, story comprehension, and sequencing in storytelling, than comparison children. The greatest gains were found in those low-achieving students who started out with low language skills at pretest and who had strong home literacy support. This study demonstrates the potential for schools to engage parents in meaningful ways in supporting their preschool children's literacy development.

Thus, in Western countries, there is evidence of positive effects of family storybook reading on children's vocabulary and comprehension development, though the effects of various sorts of adult input on preschool children's learning of receptive and expressive words still need to be examined (Justice 2002). The following study attempted to extend findings to the context of an emerging economy, Vietnam, seeking to optimize conditions for language development through family storybook reading using a theoretical model of shared activity as a basis for the design and implementation of an intervention programme.

A theoretical model of family shared reading activity

The descriptive and experimental research base provides evidence for a shared reading activity in the home setting. This activity consists of multiple dimensions. The dimensions have complex relationships with each other and with language development. There is a need for an encompassing explanatory framework, which would provide a more comprehensive model from which programmes could be developed for optimization in new contexts such as Vietnam. The following model, briefly outlined here, provided an explanatory base for developing an effective intervention in Vietnam. The model integrates dimensions such as interactional styles, parental ideas and beliefs, and dynamic changes for participants. We have used a combination of Soviet psychological concepts (Gal'perin 1969; Leont'ev 1981; Vygotsky 1962, 1978) and Western psychological concepts (Bronfenbrenner 1979; Bruner 1977; McNaughton 1995; Rogoff 2003) to model the structure of this activity. Then, based on this theoretical framework, an intervention on shared storybook reading in Vietnamese families was conducted to examine the efficacy of the theoretical model, to design more optimal conditions for language development.

Leont'ev described an activity as a system with its own structure which is created by its basic components and interrelationships among these components and the environment in which the activity exists (1978, 1981). This suggests that when investigating the activity of shared storybook reading, the activity's components and the interrelations among those components need to be understood. In the present study, the shared storybook reading in a home setting is seen as a collaborative activity between a parent or a family member (subject 1) and a preschool child (subject 2). This joint activity has 16 components, with reciprocal relationships between and among the components, as illustrated by the double-headed arrows in Figure 15.1.

Although each subject has his or her own needs, both often aim at the child's development. When they find a shared object that can satisfy their different needs, a common motive appears and they engage in this joint activity. Each subject carries out his or her individual activity with different actions and operations, while sharing the same object, motive, goal, and condition. To achieve a joint outcome, which meets their shared object, their individual activities become well-matched at all levels, including actions and operations. Therefore, the process of the subjects' execution requires being not only self-regulated, but also joint-regulated. Moreover, as in the general structure of activity, the components of each individual activity exist in interdependent relationships. They determine and reflect each other, and are even transformed (see Figure 15.1).

Shared storybook reading also needs to be identified within a social context or a system of social relations. In this research, the immediate setting is a home environment in which the joint reading activity is embedded. Following Bronfenbrenner's ecological systems theory (1979), the home setting is seen as affected by relations between it and other immediate settings such as kindergarten, school, and neighbourhood. In addition, the immediate settings are also influenced by relations between them and the larger contexts by which they are surrounded. Accordingly, in the following study, the shared reading activity was examined in the context of a national community of Vietnam, a local community, a neighbourhood, a kindergarten, a primary school and a family.

In summary, the shared reading activity consists of two individual activities, specifically the parent's reading activity and the child's listening activity which requires the child's active participation. Although the individual activities are performed by different people, they come to share the same object, motivation, goal, and condition, which need to be well-matched to one another. This activity occurs in a specific home setting, with its own social relations and with its own physical and material conditions. The home setting is not isolated but it is affected by its relations with other contexts, such as school and community.

Applying the model to a new context: Vietnam

The context

Vietnam is a multiethnic and multilingual nation with 54 ethnic groups and approximately 100 languages spoken by the more than 83 million inhabitants.

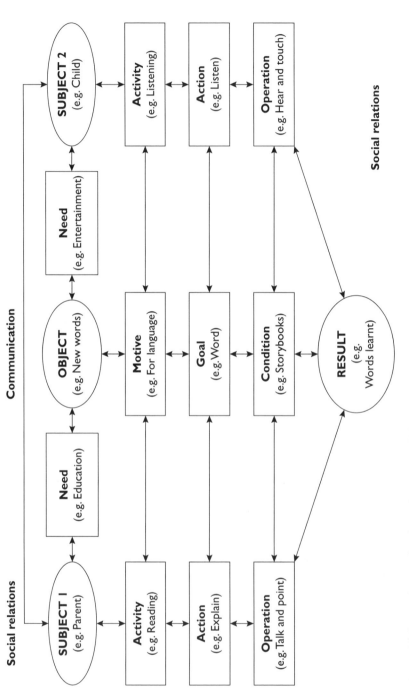

Figure 15.1 Family storybook reading as a collaborative activity.

The national language is Vietnamese. It is used as the first language (or one of the first languages of bilingual people) by about 90 percent of the population (Kosonen 2004) and three million Vietnamese people living overseas.

People living in specific areas of Vietnam have developed their own dialects and accents. Those who are born and living in Thua Thien Hue province, where this project was conducted, often use Hue dialect and accent which differ from Quốc Ngữ' or school language. This causes difficulties for young children in Thua Thien Hue in adapting to the school environment and school activities when making the transition to formal education. They often make language errors that are influenced by the Hue dialect and accent, especially when speaking, reading aloud, and writing (Hoang Thao Nguyen 2000; Tran 2003). The current early literacy intervention was concerned with the maintenance of Hue dialect as a vital part of Hue culture, and the development of Vietnamese standard language (or Quốc Ngữ') for young children. At the time of this study, no language intervention programme through family storybook sharing existed for less well-educated parents to use with their preschool children. Key aims of the current research were to enhance the quality of the community–school–family partnership, and also to provide a supportive learning environment for young children from disadvantaged Vietnamese families.

The research was carried out with six preschoolers (two girls and four boys), aged from 5 to 6 years, without special needs for health care, from an urban preschool and a rural preschool in Thua Thien Hue province, Vietnam, in 2006. The children came from low-income families. Their parents' education ranged from Year 5 to Year 12.[1] All the parents worked but their employment was unstable. Half of the families read storybooks to their children occasionally, but descriptions and interviews showed they found it difficult to provide their children with suggestions that helped them to understand stories. Parents in the other three families never shared storybooks with their children at home, because they did not think it was necessary to read stories to their children before the children knew how to read. In some families, the parents were very busy earning their living. They could just afford to buy food, clothes, textbooks, notebooks, pens, and pay school fees for their children. Buying storybooks for their children was considered a low priority, while public libraries and school libraries were not easily accessible or convenient for them to borrow books for home reading. The preschools and the government did not have any family literacy programme to support them.

However, all the parents wanted their children to be good students who studied well and also behaved well. As a daily routine, all the parents, including the parents who never read stories to their children, often encouraged and guided their children to learn how to read and write the Vietnamese alphabet and numbers at home. They often socialized their children with moral values and behaviours through telling legends and stories that they remembered or invented, using their own dialect and accent. In each Vietnamese family, telling stories is still a very popular activity. It is the main way which adult family members entertain and educate young children.

Procedure

The literature provided a descriptive and experimental base for developing the explanatory model. The project drew four components from the model. The components were introduced through a combination of workshop, modelling, coaching, and feedback, followed by individual coaching sessions in the home setting. Specifically, the educational programme focused on development of parental ideas, parents' practices, their skills for designing the activity, and their selection of storybooks for children.

Development of parental ideas

The intervention started with a workshop on family storybook reading, organized at Thua Thien Hue College of Education. The parents workshopped with other parents and professionals involved in the programme, including preschool principals and teachers, primary school teachers, and language teaching experts.

Examples of books to be read were introduced. The books all used Vietnamese standard language. The purposes of reading each book, ways of reading to achieve the purposes, and the conditions and tools (e.g. storybooks, reading places, children's existing experiences, and home language) were discussed.

The idea of a joint activity comprising the parent's reading, the child's listening and their interactions was explained. The role of parent's questions, explanations and suggestions was explained in terms of suitability to the child's ability and interest, and also as encouragement for the child to participate actively. It was suggested that parents use Hue dialect as a language learning support vehicle to explain and discuss points with their children. This would help their children understand the meaning of new words in Vietnamese standard language better. Also, this would help their children distinguish and use correctly home language and school language.

Ten picture storybook reading techniques were introduced, which were similar to those of 'dialogic reading' (Zevenbergen and Whitehurst 2003). They were also similar to effective reading techniques of highly educated Vietnamese parents identified in a previous study (Tran 2003). These shared reading techniques, which mainly focused on developing children's attention, reading interest, vocabulary and comprehension, are summarized in Table 15.1.

The parents taking part in the research were shown a video of shared reading that featured mother–child dyads who were experienced in the techniques of shared storybook reading. The parents were also coached to develop their shared reading skills.

Development of parents' practices

At the workshop, the parents practised their shared storybook reading with their own child, with coaching by the first author and a preschool teacher. Then each

Table 15.1 Ten picture storybook reading techniques

Reading techniques	Applying each technique
1. Warming-up	Activate the child's prior knowledge, interest and attention by questions, gestures or statements relating to the story that will be read
2. Identifying and labelling	Discuss with the child the way to hold, to read the books, and objects, settings, characters pictured, or some letters printed in the books
3. Explaining	Provide the children with suggestions or explanations to help them make meaning of a new word or of an incomprehensible sentence, when necessary
4. Recalling	Ask the child to remember main information presented explicitly in the story
5. Inferring	Discuss with the child how to make inference about information presented implicitly in the story by what, where and why questions or by suggestions, comments and models
6. Relating	Require the child to relate the content of the story to the real world around him/her or his/her experiences
7. Commenting	Ask or suggest the child to state his/her own thinking and feelings about the content or/and the form of the story
8. Elaborating	Provide an appropriate, accurate response when the child's statement is inadequate
9. Praising and encouraging	Give the child praise and encouragement by both gestures and statements whenever he or she makes a good response
10. Having fun	Create a comfortable and enjoyable atmosphere for shared reading by choosing a suitable place; giving the child a smiling face and gentle gestures; using an expressive reading voice and, sometimes, taking a game-like approach to discussing the story with the child

family was provided, at different times during the project, with a total of 22 commercially available picture storybooks in Vietnamese (including target books), chosen because of their high standard of content, form, and language style. Furthermore, they were suitable to the children's ability and interest, but unfamiliar to them. The storybooks were also consistent with Vietnamese moral and cultural values that Hue parents often emphasized when educating their children (Le Nguyen Luu 2006; Tran 2003).

The families were also provided with a DVD copy of the family shared reading samples, a family shared storybook reading brochure, and a Vietnamese dictionary, and given guidance on how to use them. The primary researcher (Tran) visited each family once a week, for 10 weeks, to encourage and support the parents in sharing storybooks with their own child. During this time, they were guided to read three target books which had target words and comprehension outcomes (identified by the primary researcher) for the children's learning. Each target book was introduced separately, with three sessions of coaching and feedback, over three weeks. On an overlapping basis, after three coaching sessions had been completed for reading book one, coaching was provided for book two reading, then for book three. When the intervention for each individual target book finished, the families could continue their shared reading of these books (without coaching and feedback). They also could read other storybooks for their own purposes.

During the project, language tests in Vietnamese were used to measure the children's vocabulary and comprehension development through shared reading. Expressive and receptive vocabulary was measured through 14 testing sessions, including at least three times for baseline (no treatment condition, see below). To prevent reactive responses of repeated measurements for narrative comprehension, baseline data of narrative comprehension were collected only once before starting the intervention for each target storybook.

Development of parents' skills for designing the activity

The intervention with the three target storybooks took 10 weeks. The 10-week summer holiday followed and the families continued to receive storybooks for children (as part of the total of 22 books). The parents were guided to design shared reading goals that were suitable to their own child's ability and interest, suitable to the content and form of each story, and also suitable to educational values that the parents held. Every three weeks, the researcher visited the families and worked with the parents and the children to evaluate if they achieved their proposed reading goals. The parents were also guided to identify and solve any difficulties that appeared and to make plans for improving their shared reading practices.

Book selection

When the children went to primary schools, the families did not receive any more books. They were funded a small amount of money, and suggestions were made about how to use the money to buy books that were appropriately matched for their children. Other suggestions were made about how to assess storybooks from their neighbourhood resources, such as from libraries in their communities. Following their own child's developmental changes, the parents were encouraged to give their child opportunities to practise identifying letters; decoding words and sentences; reading stories with his or her parents and siblings, and then reading stories by him or herself.

The general design

A multiple baseline design was used to analyze the intervention. The intervention was conducted across the three target storybooks. Target words and comprehension questions for these books were provided by the researcher. Once the baseline was established, an intervention with three sessions of coaching and feedback was applied to only one of the storybooks, over three weeks. When children's learning from the first storybook changed in the desired direction, the procedure was continued with the first storybook and also applied to the second book and similarly to the third storybook. If children's vocabulary and comprehension for those words in the target book and the comprehension of that book improved during applying the procedure, an argument for believing that the intervention was responsible for their changes would be made (Axelrod 1983). In this study, changes of the children's vocabulary and comprehension as well as of their family shared storybook reading practice were examined quantitatively and qualitatively through the three following phases: baseline, 10-week intervention (when children attended preschools), and 22-week maintenance (when children were on summer holiday and then went to primary school).

Outcomes

The parents

Comparison of the baseline with subsequent phases using qualitative and quantitative measures indicated that parents had increased awareness of the significance of shared reading at home, more informed selection of high quality storybooks, and greater articulation of reading goals for their child.

The parents now reported ways that their children could develop their language, memory, thought, imagination, and their cultural well-being through the activity. Reading books to their children provided the parents with chances to be close to their children and share with them thoughts and feelings. Two parents reported changing from being worried and blaming their sons for being slow, to being pleased that their sons could understand and remember the stories very well, and could give correct and thoughtful answers.

When selecting storybooks for their children, the parents now paid attention to factors such as the content, illustrations, and language used in the books, suitable for their own child's ability and interest. They thought about teaching new words and narrative meanings and when their children could not contribute a full response, they provided subquestions or subgoals presumed to be easier for their child to respond to. For instance, after reading a story to her son, one mother asked him to retell the story to her, but the child could not say anything. The mother scaffolded the task asking questions to support retelling small sections of the story. After that, her son could retell the whole story to her.

Furthermore, the parents improved their reading techniques. Before the intervention, most parents made pronunciation errors when reading aloud those words that are often affected by Hue accent (e.g. words ending with the letters 'n', 'nh', 't', 's', and words with the diacritic marks '~', '?'). After the intervention, they were better able to read aloud words of Vietnamese standard language using the ending letters and the diacritic marks. This ability helped their reading aloud to be more accurate, fluent and expressive, and also helped them to support their children when they learnt to read. Moreover, before the intervention many parents found it difficult to provide guidance to their children so that they could have a better understanding of the stories. After the intervention, their reading guidance was enhanced:

> *Mother One*: Before I did not know how I should read to my children, and how to start my reading to them. Now I know how to guide my children when listening to my reading, and how to make questions to develop their mind and emotion.
>
> (Conversation on 10 June 2006 at N.'s house)

They often combined verbal language, including their own dialect and accent, with their gestures or non-verbal language to provide clear and understandable explanations to their own child when teaching them new words or helping them to discover narrative meanings. For example, when explaining the meaning of the word 'hỏang hồn' [panic-stricken] from the storybook *Chơi dại* [Silly game] (Kim Khanh 2005) to her son, a mother made a link to how this word is often used in Hue dialect. Next, she described a specific situation in which this word was used correctly. Then, her son described another situation and tried to use the word. Their interactions were shown through the following discussion.

Mother Two:	'Panic-stricken' is understood in our dialect as 'unnerved.[2]
Child:	Panic-stricken.
Mother Two:	For example, when I visited my friend's house, suddenly a big dog jumped out and barked at me loudly woof . . . woof . . . woof . . . The dog made me panic-stricken. [Looking at her child]
Child:	[Smiling] When I was going out at night, my cousin stepped out quietly from a dark corner. He held my shoulders and said bo . . . h . . . At the time I was panic-stricken.
Mother Two:	Right! [Looking at her son and smiling].

(Observation on 20 April 2006 at K.'s house)

Changes the parents made in using the reading techniques to help their children develop vocabulary and narrative comprehension from baseline to intervention (over 12 weeks), across the three target books are shown in Table 15.2. The data are based on observations of 18 reading sessions at baseline (i.e. the six families read the three target books before the intervention) and 18 further reading sessions through the intervention (i.e. in each family, one reading session with each book was randomly selected to observe). The frequency of the reading techniques increased markedly from baseline to intervention for each book.

Table 15.2 Total frequencies of reading techniques used by the parents with three target books: baseline and intervention

Reading Techniques	Book 1		Book 2		Book 3		Total	
	Baseline	Intervention	Baseline	Intervention	Baseline	Intervention	N	Mean per cent
Warming up	6	6	5	5	5	6	33	5%
Identifying and labelling	11	18	11	14	12	4	70	10%
Explaining	20	17	28	23	15	20	123	16%
Recalling	25	31	17	32	35	34	174	25%
Inferring	4	11	5	4	13	14	51	7%
Relating	6	8	3	9	10	5	41	6%
Commenting	2	5	4	3	4	9	27	4%
Elaborating	0	4	3	4	3	4	18	3%
Praising and encouraging	2	18	11	32	19	36	118	17%
Having fun	6	7	6	12	10	8	49	7%
Total	**82**	**125**	**93**	**138**	**126**	**140**	**704**	**100%**

The frequency of different reading techniques varied (see Table 15.2). Two-thirds comprised 'recalling', 'explaining', 'praising and encouraging', and 'labelling and identifying', while the other techniques totalled 32 per cent. It appeared that the parents varied their use of the techniques according to their own child's ability and characteristics (e.g. attention and memory).

The effect on the parents of the shared reading activity is captured in the following comment from a mother who completed her education at Year Seven: 'I left school a long time ago. Since then I did not have contact with books, but now I really want to learn more so that I will be able to help my children study better' (conversation on 10 June 2006 at N's house).

The children

Through the joint reading activity, the children's habits of reading books were established and their vocabulary increased significantly, especially expressive words. Changes in narrative comprehension were also recorded. Their progress was sustained over a period of 22 weeks. The summary of their changes is shown in Table 15.3. Full details of the results and analysis in terms of the quasi-experimental design are shown elsewhere (Tran 2009).

Before the intervention, the children never asked their parents or other family members to share books with them. Of the three children who were read to occasionally, their parents often asked them to share books so that the children went to sleep easily or so they were kept quiet. After the intervention, all the six children were read to at least three times a week. They often asked their parents, siblings, other family members (e.g. aunt, cousin) and neighbours to read books to them. For example, one child whose parents were busy at work and whose older sister went to summer classes, often practised decoding and reading aloud texts in picture storybooks by herself. Then, she asked her parents or sister to listen to and check her reading. As a result of her practice, before going to primary school, she could read stories independently and quite fluently. She understood their narrative meaning and could retell them when required.

The vocabulary data gained from 14 testing sessions showed that both the children's expressive and receptive uses of the target words increased (see Table 15.3). Generally, their receptive vocabulary scores were higher than their scores of expressive vocabulary. However, the gap became smaller following the intervention. Both the children's mean scores of receptive vocabulary and expressive vocabulary nearly reached the ceiling level (i.e. 12 points for six fully correct answers or two points for each fully correct answer). Their vocabulary achievement was maintained over 22 weeks.

To avoid reactive responses by repeated measurements of the narrative comprehension test that required the children to listen to the stories before completing the comprehension tasks or questions, the children's narrative comprehension was probed just before the intervention (see Table 15.3).

Table 15.3 Mean scores of receptive and expressive vocabulary and comprehension all six children gained from three books across phases

Language Gains	Book One			Book Two			Book Three		
	Baseline	Intervention	Maintenance	Baseline	Intervention	Maintenance	Baseline	Intervention	Maintenance
Receptive vocabulary	9.00	10.72	11.70	8.47	11.83	12.00	8.67	11.43	11.85
Expressive vocabulary	2.67	10.08	11.70	3.93	11.50	12.00	4.31	10.87	11.40
Narrative comprehension	4.00	7.26	7.80	4.00	6.48	7.35	3.17	5.93	7.75

Note
– Ceiling level for receptive and expressive vocabulary is 12.00
– Ceiling level for narrative comprehension is 8.00

Similar to their outcomes of vocabulary tests, the children's mean scores of narrative comprehension increased significantly. Compared to the baseline data, the children's mean scores of narrative comprehension gained in the intervention were higher, with retelling scores increasing across each book, and this was maintained over 22 weeks (see Table 15.3).

In summary, associated with the parents' reading improvement, their children made significant gains of vocabulary and narrative comprehension on the target books. The children also showed increased love of reading and evidence of established reading habits. Moreover, their family members and neighbours were also involved enjoyably in this literacy activity.

Conclusion

The intervention described here is part of a research sequence of description and explanation, and planned interventions. The sequence draws on an existing descriptive base which has plotted the attributes of storybook reading. These attributes include the frequency and style of reading as well as how the activity is part of a family's and its community's language and literacy practices.

Experimental studies have confirmed that there are causal relationships between the attributes and developmental outcomes. The frequency and style of reading to preschoolers, as well as the features of story books themselves, influence children's emergent literacy knowledge of narrative schema, book concepts, and elemental items of decoding. They also influence aspects of expressive and receptive language, including vocabulary and comprehension (Jordan *et al.* 2000; Justice 2002; Whitehurst *et al.* 1988, 1994, 1999; Zevenbergen *et al.* 2003). This quasi-experimental study also showed that parent–child reading interactions were related to word learning and comprehension.

This study illustrates the critical steps in a programmatic sequence, from which we can better plan to ensure optimum results are achieved. One of the steps was the development and testing of a full model of the activity structure. The model was necessary to plan an initial demonstration of how to optimize language development for children from less well-educated Vietnamese families. A second step was evaluating the intervention programme operationalized from the model. These two steps contribute to both the explanation of the research sequence as well as the beginnings of the optimization of the sequence.

What follows next in an applied science which seeks to optimize developmental opportunities (Lerner *et al.* 2000) is perhaps more difficult than what has already been accomplished. The question of how to replicate the intervention systematically is an immediate concern. How dependent is the programme on the particular combination of personnel and events brought together in the quasi-experimental format? The issue of systematic replication requires further analysis of contextual constraints such as the availability of appropriate storybooks and resources for producing guidance and support for families. It requires developing procedures which are able to be reliably scaled up using personnel other than the original researchers. Optimization requires scaling up and further testing of the processes across families in different circumstances and with different needs for accessing resources. A full model requires consideration of the role of state policies and allocation of resources. Understanding each of these constraints is fundamental to the optimization sequence.

The study shows the programme could be effective with less well-educated families. It also provides evidence that significant effects on specific aspects of expressive and receptive language were long-lasting. But most interventions in education do not act like inoculations, and a gain in expressive words or comprehension needs to be examined further. Is this the limit and how much more strategic learning is possible that will increase the incidental acquisition, as well as the direct instruction of the children further? Researchers such as Biemiller (2006) have pointed out that learning a small sample of words provides a limited outcome when considered against long-term differences in trajectories of word learning by different groups.

The important effect of adding to the linguistic dexterity of the families was shown. The intervention was developed to add Vietnamese words to the Hue dialect and develop flexibility in control rather than replacing the Hue dialect. There are studies of book reading with families with a first language other than English that show the programme is effective in learning aspects of a second language (Roberts 2008). But how generative is this learning; what are the limits to the generalization to new words and new texts across languages?

Together with the questions about resources and training, systemic planning for scaling up the intervention and embedding the programme in early childhood education are questions yet to be addressed within the research sequence.

Notes

1 The comprehensive educational system in Vietnam consists of 12 years with three levels as follows: Primary: Years 1 to 5 (aged 6 to 11); Junior Secondary: Years 6 to 9 (aged 12 to 15); and Senior Secondary: Years 10 to 12 (aged 16 to 18).
2 Her own words in Vietnamese are 'Hỏang hồn' trong tiếng mìn [mình] là 'thắc kin' [thất kinh].'

References

Axelrod, S. (1983) *Behavior Modification for the Classroom Teacher*, New York: McGraw-Hill.

Baltes, P.B., Reese, H.W. and Lipsitt, L.B. (1980) 'Life-span developmental psychology', *Annual Review of Psychology*, 1: 65–110.

Biemiller, A. (2006) 'Vocabulary development and instruction: a prerequisite for school learning', in D. Dickinson and S. Neuman (eds) *Handbooks of Early Literacy Research* (vol. 2, pp. 41–51), New York: Guilford Press.

Bronfenbrenner, U. (1979) *The Ecology of Human Development*, Cambridge, MA: Harvard University Press.

Bruner, J.S. (1977) 'Early social interaction and language development', in H.R. Schaffer (ed.) *Studies in Mother-Child Interaction*, London: Academic Press.

Bus, A.G. van IJzendoorn, M.H. and Pellegrini, A.D. (1995) 'Joint book reading makes for success in learning to read: a meta-analysis on intergenerational transmission of literacy', *Review of Educational Research*, 65: 1–21.

Clay, M. (1972) *Reading: The Patterning of Complex Behaviour*, Auckland, New Zealand: Heinemann.

Clay, M. (2005) *Literacy Lessons Designed for Individuals Part One: Why? When? And How?* Portsmouth, NH: Heinemann.

Consortium for Longitudinal Studies (1983) *As the Twig is Bent: Lasting Effects of Preschool Programs*, Hillsdale, NJ: Erlbaum.

Dewey, J. ([1899] 1915) *The School and Society*, Chicago: The University of Chicago Press.

Durkin, D. (1966) *Children Who Read Early*, New York: Teacher College Press.

Gal'perin, P. Ia. (1969) 'Stages in the development of mental acts', in M. Cole and I. Maltzman (eds) *A Handbook of Contemporary Soviet Psychology* (pp. 249–73), New York: Basic Books.

Haden, C.A., Reese, E. and Fivush, R. (1996) 'Mothers' extratextual comments during storybook reading: stylistic differences over time and across texts', *Discourse Processes*, 21: 135–69.

Hayden, H. and Fagan, W. (1987) 'Keeping it in context: strategies for enhancing literacy awareness', *First Language*, 7: 159–71.

Heath, S.B. (1982) 'What no bedtime story means: narrative skills at home and school', *Language in Society*, 11: 49–76.

Heath, S.B. (1983) *Ways with Words: Language, Life and Work in Communities and Classrooms*, New York: Cambridge University Press.

Hoang, Thao Nguyen (2000) 'Phuong Phap Khac Phuc Loi Chinh Ta Phuong Ngu Cho Hoc Sinh Tieu Hoc Thua Thien Hue' [Strategies to Minimize Dialectal Spelling Errors for Primary Students in Thua Thien Hue Province], unpublished doctoral dissertation, Hanoi National University of Education, Hanoi, Vietnam.

Jordan, G.E., Snow, C.E. and Porche, M.V. (2000) 'Project EASE: the effect of a family literacy project on kindergarten students' early literacy skills', *Reading Research Quarterly*, 35: 524–46.

Justice, L.M. (2002) 'Word exposure conditions and preschoolers' novel word learning during shared storybook reading', *Reading Psychology*, 23: 87–106.

Justice, L.M. and Ezell, H.K. (2000) 'Enhancing children's print and word awareness through home-based parent intervention', *American Journal of Speech – Language Pathology*, 9: 257–69.

Kim Khanh (2005) *Cho'i Dai [Silly Game]*, Thanh Hoa, Vietnam: Thanh Hoa.

Kosonen, K. (2004) *Language in Education: Policy and Practice in Vietnam*, Hanoi, Vietnam: UNICEF.

Le, Nguyen Luu (2006) *Văn Hóa Huế Xưa – Đời Sống Gia Tộc* [Hue Traditional Culture – Family Life], Hue, Vietnam: Thuan Hoa.

Leont'ev, A.N. (1978) *Activity, Consciousness, and Personality*, Englewood Cliffs, NJ: Prentice Hall.

Leont'ev, A.N. (1981) 'The problem of activity in psychology', in J.V. Wertsch (ed.) *The Concept of Activity in Soviet Psychology* (pp. 37–71), New York: M.E. Sharpe.

Lerner, M.R., Fisher, C.B. and Weinberg. R.A. (2000) 'Toward a science for and of the people: promoting civil society through the application of developmental science', *Child Development*, 71: 11–20.

McDougall, W. ([1912] 1952) *Psychology: The Study of Behavior*, London: Oxford University Press.

McNaughton, S. (1995) *Patterns of Emergent Literacy*, Auckland, New Zealand: Oxford University Press.

Meyer, L.A., Stahl, S.A., Wardrop, J.L. and Linn, R.L. (1999) 'Reading to children or reading with children?', *Effective School Practices*, 17: 56–64.

Meyer, L.A., Wardrop, J.L., Stahl, S.A. and Linn, R.L. (1994) 'Effects of reading storybooks aloud to children', *Journal of Educational Research*, 88: 69–85.

Morrow, L.M. (1995) 'Family literacy: new perspectives, new practices', in L.M. Morrow (ed.) *Family Literacy: Connections in Schools and Communities* (pp. 5–10), Newark, DE: International Reading Association.

Ramey, C.T. and Ramey, S.L. (1998) 'Early intervention and early experience', *American Psychologist*, 53: 109–20.

Roberts, T.A. (2008) 'Home storybook reading in primary or second language with preschool children: Evidence of equal effectiveness for second-language vocabulary acquisition', *Reading Research Quarterly*, 43 (2), 103–130.

Rogoff, B. (2003) *The Cultural Nature of Human Development*, New York: Oxford University Press.

Schieffelin, B.B. and Cochran-Smith, M. (1984) 'Learning to read culturally: literacy before schooling', in H. Goelman, A. Oberg and F. Smith (eds) *Awakening to Literacy* (pp. 3–23), Portsmouth, NH: Heinemann.

Spielberger, J. and Halpern, R. (2002) *The Role of After-school Programs in Children's Literacy Development*, Chicago: Chapin Hall Center for Children at the University of Chicago.

Taylor, R.L. (1995) 'Functional uses of reading and shared literacy activities in Icelandic homes: a monograph in family literacy', *Reading Research Quarterly*, 30: 194–219.

Teale, W.H. (1984) 'Reading to young children: its significance for literacy development', in H. Goelman, A. Oberg and F. Smith (eds) *Awakening to Literacy* (pp. 110–21), Portsmouth, NH: Heinemann.

Tran, Thi Thanh Binh (2003) 'The storybook reading practices of first graders in Vietnamese families: six case studies', unpublished master's thesis, Dunedin College of Education, Dunedin, New Zealand.

Tran, Thi Thanh Binh (2009) 'Reading storybooks in Vietnamese families as a language intervention: an activity analysis', unpublished PhD thesis, the University of Auckland, Auckland, New Zealand.

Vygotsky, L.S. (1962) *Thought and Language*, Cambridge, MA: MIT Press.

Vygotsky, L.S. (1978) 'Mind in society: the development of higher psychological processes', in M. Cole, V. John-Steiner, S. Scribner and E. Souberman (eds) Cambridge, MA: Harvard University Press.

Wan, G. (2000) 'A Chinese girl's storybook experience at home', *Language Arts*, 77: 398–406.

Whitehurst, G.J., Epstein, J.N., Angell, A.L., Payne, A.C., Crone, D.A. and Fischel, J.F. (1994) 'Outcomes of an emergent literacy intervention in Head Start', *Journal of Educational Psychology*, 86: 542–55.

Whitehurst, G.J., Falco, F.L., Lonigan, C.J., Fischel, J.E., DeBaryshe, B.D., Valdez-Menchaca, M.C. and Caufied, M. (1988) 'Accelerating language development through picture book reading', *Developmental Psychology*, 24: 552–9.

Whitehurst, G.J., Zevenbergen, A.A., Crone, D.A., Schultz, M.D., Velting, O.N. and Fischel, J.E. (1999) 'Outcomes of an emergent literacy intervention from Head Start through second grade', *Journal of Educational Psychology*, 91: 261–72.

Zevenbergen, A.A. and Whitehurst, G.J. (2003) 'Dialogic reading: a shared picture book reading intervention for preschoolers', in A.V. Kleeck, Stahl, S.A. and Bauer, E.B (eds) *On Reading Books to Children: Parents and Teachers* (pp. 177–200), Mahwah, NJ: Lawrence Erlbaum Associates.

Zevenbergen, A.A., Whitehurst, G.J. and Zevenbergen, J.A. (2003) 'Effects of a shared-reading intervention on the inclusion of evaluative devices in narratives of children from low-income families', *Applied Developmental Psychology*, 24: 1–15.

Zigler, E. and Styfco, S.J. (1994) 'Head Start: criticisms in a constructive context', *American Psychologist*, 49: 127–32.

Chapter 16

Societal and cultural perspectives through a Te Kotahitanga lens

Mere Berryman and Russell Bishop

It has been clear for a long time just how poorly many indigenous students have fared in mainstream education systems (Shields *et al.* 2005). For example, Māori students in New Zealand have disproportionately higher levels of absences, early leaving certificates, stand downs, suspensions and expulsions and lower levels of qualifications on leaving school than do non-indigenous Pākehā students (Ministry of Education 2002). This chapter discusses the disparity in educational outcomes of indigenous Māori students, from both societal and cultural perspectives. It does this in relation to Te Kotahitanga, a New Zealand Ministry of Education funded research and development initiative designed to improve educational outcomes of Māori students and used in a number of New Zealand secondary schools since 2001 (Bishop *et al.* 2003; Bishop *et al.* 2007a; Bishop *et al.* 2007c). It begins by introducing some historical discourses and practices associated with the more common societal view of the underachievement of Māori students in schools, and that continue to pathologize Māori. It explains these discourses and practices from a sociological perspective associated with issues of power and control, and reflects on psychological viewpoints that are legitimized by these discourses. It continues by discussing how problems experienced by indigenous or minority ethnic peoples can most effectively be understood through the cultural lens of these people themselves. It suggests that cultural understandings such as these may well, as in the case of Te Kotahitanga, predispose to solutions that are effective given they fit with the group's own world view and cultural experiences, and are generated by that group, rather than being externally theorized and imposed.

The New Zealand situation

The historical signing of the Treaty of Waitangi in 1840 still influences, to varying degrees, the lives of all New Zealanders. While this Treaty promised power sharing and self-determination for both Pākehā and Māori, relations between these two groups have 'been one of political, social and economic domination by the Pākehā majority, and marginalisation of the Māori people' (Bishop and Glynn 1999: 50). Overpowering relationships of the dominant colonial group have been similarly experienced by many indigenous peoples in other parts of the world. In

New Zealand's formal education system, principles evolved from colonial images have served to guide teachers' actions and explain the basis for those actions. From this pattern of images and principles, education policies and rules of practice have been developed that required indigenous students to metaphorically leave their culture at the school gate in order to participate in education (Bishop *et al.* 2003; Bishop and Berryman 2006). Indigenous languages, values, beliefs and practices have not been represented and legitimized within New Zealand's classrooms and schools. This has resulted in the education provided by the state playing a major role in destroying Māori language and culture and replacing them with that of the colonizers (Bishop and Glynn 1999).

For Māori, a result of this domination continues to be an inequitable share in the benefits of education. Simultaneously, the suppression and belittlement of indigenous knowledge, language, and culture continue (Bishop and Glynn 1999). This situation has created the need to construct new metaphoric spaces in which people from indigenous or minority cultural backgrounds can feel safe to bring their own prior knowledge and experiences to mainstream educational contexts in order that they can more effectively relate to, interact with, and learn from each other.

Influence of discursive positioning

According to Burr (1995), one's actions and behaviours, how one relates to, defines, and interacts with others, are determined by one's discursive positioning. Burr asserts that a discourse refers to 'a set of meanings, metaphors, representations, images, stories, statements and so on that in some way together produce a particular version of events' (1995: 48). Claims as to what is reality, what is truth, 'lie at the heart of discussions of identity, power and change' (ibid.: 49). Burr suggests the meaning behind what we say 'rather depends upon the discursive context, the general conceptual framework in which our words are embedded' (ibid.: 50). For a number of reasons, within many mainstream settings, the dominant discourses associated with Māori continue to be as 'distanced others', or as 'junior' rather than 'autonomous' partners (Bishop 2005; Bishop and Glynn 1999; O'Sullivan 2007).

It is the contention of this chapter that this discourse is supported by Western psychological paradigms and practices that generally focus on the individual and their background rather than on the interactions between the participants in the primary relationship. The dominance of these discourses has meant that the low performance by Māori students in schools has largely been seen as the result of inadequacy on the part of the students themselves, or, more probably, their families and cultural backgrounds. Discourses such as these, within which one is metaphorically positioned and from which explanations for one's experiences are drawn and therefore how we understand and define other people with whom we relate, have generated the 'cultural deficit' explanation of poor educational achievement (Bishop *et al.* 2007c; Shields *et al.* 2005). If we see students as having deficiencies, our practices will address deficiencies. Alternatively, if we see them as having potential, our discourses and practices will focus on our own agency and responsibility to realize this potential. Fundamental to discourses is power (Burr 1995), given that within discursive positioning and in the development of relationships and interactions with others, some sets of discourses can be, and are, privileged over others.

Foucault (1972) argues that when metaphors from the language of the majority discourse are able to dominate, the minority discourse will be understood in deficit terms. Foucault suggests that discourses, rather than being understood as merely linguistic systems or texts, should be understood as discursive practices where power relations are developed into the sets of rules and conditions that are established between groups and institutions. These power relations become embedded and are explicit in economic and social practices and other patterns of behaviour (Bishop 2007c). Indeed, these assumptions of superiority are both explicit and implicit in metaphors and discourses of the colonizers, many of which have continued to theorize Māori in deficit terms to the present day. For example, aspects of Māori culture such as kapa haka (cultural songs and movement), prowess in warfare, and, today, prowess in sport, were and still are being used in wider society to reinforce the colonial metaphor of the 'savage other' (Hokowhitu 2001). The collective, collaborative decision-making processes preferred by Māori continue to be disparaged in the media and educational settings in favour of more individualized practices. Such assumptions have enabled dominant pedagogic practices to be maintained within mainstream schooling, often to the detriment of Māori students' educational engagement and achievement.

Influence of the traditional psychological paradigm

Education for New Zealand's children has been dominated by a Western system that has adopted a dominant transmission view of learning and a passive view of the mind. The curriculum for learning has been imposed by the majority group and served the majority group's agendas. Once education became compulsory for all children, the position of children who, for whatever reason, appeared to achieve less than their peers, and what to do about them, assumed a high focus. From the beginning of the twentieth century, educators began to turn to the new, growing profession of psychology for explanations of difference. Conventionally, from Western psychological paradigms, the blame for poor achievement could be laid at the door of the individual student or their family background.

One major response to these discrepancies by Māori has been the generation of a grass roots movement of resistance termed kaupapa Māori. As both a movement of resistance and of revitalisation, kaupapa Māori calls for new theories to be sourced from within te ao Māori (the Māori world) and a return to Māori theorizing and authority (G. Smith 1995): in short, an autonomous, self-determined Māori response requiring us to move beyond biculturalism (O'Sullivan

2007). O'Sullivan suggests that self-determination and biculturalism are underpinned by different assumptions of power, with biculturalism offering the role of junior partner, ongoing colonial dependence, and only limited progress towards self-determination. Self-determination asserts the right to determine one's own cultural, social, economic, and political destiny (Durie 2005), thus engaging and belonging with political status and rights at both a national and community level (O'Sullivan 2007). Such transformative action requires a movement away from previous policies of biculturalism to engagement with what is now being termed a politics of indigeneity (Tully 2000).

Despite the choice provided by Māori medium education in New Zealand, and decades of educational reforms and policies that have sought to address educational disparity, for the large proportion of Māori students, more than 90 per cent of whom attend mainstream schools (Ministry of Education 2002), there has been little if any shift in these disparities since they were first statistically identified 50 years ago (Hunn 1960).

It was the contention of the research and development project presented in this chapter, that answers to Māori educational achievement and disparities could lie within kaupapa Māori and within the sense-making and knowledge-generating processes of the culture that the system has historically succeeded in marginalizing. Accordingly, this project, known as Te Kotahitanga, offers a kaupapa Māori model based on an indigenous Māori response to the dominance of majority culture aspirations on Māori (Bishop 1996; G. Smith 1997; L. Smith 1999).

Te Kotahitanga

The Te Kotahitanga project (Bishop *et al.* 2003) aimed to develop a deeper understanding of Māori students' experiences, of what supports and hinders their classroom learning and achievement. The intention was to identify the kind of pedagogy that might lead to Māori students' increased education participation, engagement, and achievement at Years 9 and 10 (13 to 14 years old). This has traditionally been a time of crisis for Māori students, with disproportionately higher levels of non-engagement and non-participation in schools and lower levels of formal school qualifications (Ministry of Education 2002). This research, therefore, specifically sought to identify underlying education, structural responses and teacher attitudes and pedagogies that make a difference to engagement, participation, and achievement of Māori students during these two years.

This project began by talking with Year 9 and 10 Māori students about their experiences in classrooms. In so doing, the Te Kotahitanga research was predicated on an assumption that students have active agency in their own learning and, as such, researchers adopted a sociocultural constructivist (Bruner 1996; Vygotsky 1978), frame of reference. Researchers also talked with students' parents or caregivers, teachers, and principals. Out of these conversations, rich, collaborative narratives of educational experiences were developed (Bishop and Berryman 2006). Researchers identified factors from the narratives that the groups of people themselves believed would improve engagement and raise the achievement of Māori students in schools. These narratives have become the foundation upon which Te Kotahitanga was built.

Analysis of the narratives of experience

The analysis of each group's narratives identified three main discourses within which people interviewed were positioned when identifying both positive and negative influences on Māori students' educational achievement. These were discourses surrounding Māori students and their home communities, discourses related to structures and systems within schools, and finally discourses of classroom relationships and interaction patterns. These Māori students, their parents and caregivers, and their principals (and some teachers) saw that the most important influence on Māori students' educational achievement was the quality of the in-class face-to-face relationships and interactions between the teachers and Māori students. In contrast, the majority of teachers suggested the main influence on Māori students' educational achievement were deficiencies associated with the students themselves, or their home circumstances, or systemic and structural issues associated with schools.

This view aligns with the traditional psychological perspective discussed above, where understanding and responding to Māori students and their families may well be understood from the position that any deficits and causes of dysfunction reside in the individuals themselves, their families, and their cultural groups. This view is also consistent with discourses currently being perpetuated by some academics (Chapple *et al.* 1997; Harker and Nash 1990; Nash 1993). In contrast, sociocultural theories of human development (Bronfenbrenner 1979; Bruner 1996; Vygotsky 1978) point to the importance of a view of the mind as active in its search for meaning, and understandings of learning and behaviour as 'situated' in the contexts in which they occur. This highlights the need to better understand what the students themselves make of their relationships and interactions between themselves and teachers and subsequently between schools and home communities. Children communicate, understand, relate, interact and learn through active engagement with others in the social and cultural contexts of their own families and homes (Vygotsky 1978; Wearmouth *et al.* 2005). These social and cultural contexts support development of values and beliefs that will help them to understand and make sense of the new situations in which they will find themselves, and thus how they will respond in those situations. In these contexts, the range of other people with whom the learner is engaged can all help to mediate learning (Rogoff 1990; Vygotsky 1978).

The Effective Teaching Profile

On the basis of this analysis and specific suggestions from the narratives, the researchers developed an Effective Teaching Profile (Bishop *et al.* 2003). A group of Māori elders, who had actively contributed during the gathering of the narratives, provided their own cultural understandings and Māori metaphors to support this framework. This profile identified that effective teachers of Māori students were those who created culturally responsive and culturally appropriate contexts for learning in their classrooms (Gay 2000). The following definition of culture, from Quest Rapuara (1992), encapsulates what we mean by 'culturally responsive' (how we relate and interact), and 'culturally appropriate elements' (cultural iconography):

> Culture is what holds a community together, giving a common framework of meaning. It includes how people communicate with each other, how we make decisions, how we structure our families and who we think is important. It expresses our values towards land and time and our attitudes towards work and play, good and evil, reward and punishment.
>
> Culture is preserved in language, symbols and customs and celebrated in art, music, drama, literature, religion and social gatherings. It constitutes the collective memory of the people and the collective heritage which will be handed down to future generations.
>
> (Quest Rapuara 1992: 7)

Māori students suggested teachers who valued Māori iconography in classrooms (that is, were culturally appropriate) but who did not listen to or value the contributions and sense making of Māori students themselves (that is, were not culturally responsive), ran the risk of being viewed as tokenistic. As identified in Bishop *et al.* (2003), in the students' view, culturally responsive and appropriate teachers – their effective teachers – maintained the following understandings:

- Effective teachers positively rejected deficit discourses as explaining Māori students' educational achievement.
- Effective teachers knew and understood how to bring about change in Māori students' educational achievement. In this regard, the students' most effective teachers were professionally committed and demonstrated this in the following observable ways:

    - *manaakitanga* – the teachers cared for and respected Māori students as Māori (culturally-located)
    - *mana motuhake* – the teachers had high expectations for the participation and performance of Māori students
    - *whakapiringatanga* – the teachers had pedagogical knowledge and imagination and used this knowledge to create secure, meaningful, well-managed learning contexts
    - *wānanga* – the teachers engaged in a range of effective teaching interactions with Māori students so the students were able to bring prior experiences and sense making to the learning context

- *ako* – the teachers used strategies to promote effective reciprocal teaching and learning relationships and interactions with Māori students
- *kotahitanga* – the teachers promoted, monitored, and reflected on outcomes that in turn led to improvements in educational achievement for Māori students

Discursive repositioning

This Effective Teaching Profile provided the direction for working with schools participating in the Te Kotahitanga project. During professional development sessions, teachers would be challenged to 'reposition' within 'discourses of agency' or supported to maintain a position of agency. That is, the focus is clearly on teachers as active agents of change in their relationships and interactions with students inside their classrooms. This focus is not on things over which teachers have little or no agency (Māori students, and their homes and families). Thus, 'discursive repositioning' is the beginning of developing a new shared language for teachers, and also, importantly, it is the means for understanding the need to develop new relations with Māori students, and knowing how to do this (Bishop and Berryman 2006).

Teaching interactions

On account of new relationships with Māori students, Te Kotahitanga then supports teachers to use the wider range of specific pedagogical interactions identified by the original Māori students' narratives (Bishop and Berryman 2006). These pedagogical interactions extend from traditional instructional interactions where the learner is largely seen as the apprentice (Rogoff 1990) (instruction/modelling; monitoring; feedback/feed-forward on behaviour) and continue through to more interactive and dialogic interactions (prior knowledge; feedback/feed-forward on learning; co-construction). Interactions such as these acknowledge learners as active agents who come to know and understand the world in terms of their own engagement within it (Vygotsky 1978). Learning that occurs in contextualized social interactions with others is emphasized, as is the importance of learners having opportunities to interact with and construct knowledge themselves, with their peers and with teachers. Fundamental to approaches such as this, is that learners are seen to be assuming autonomy over their learning, and as entering into learning interactions, activities and routines, while developing social relationships with a range of other learners (Vygotsky 1978).

The professional development model

In order to change traditional classroom relationships, and to extend and develop pedagogical practices by introducing and embedding the Effective Teaching Profile in classrooms, members of the Te Kotahitanga team provide ongoing professional development to facilitation teams from the participating schools. In the main, Te

Kotahitanga school teams have comprised the principal, working with facilitators, both from within and external to the school. Once trained, the facilitation team provides all the professional development to participating teachers in their schools.

Hui whakarewa

The professional development in schools begins with the hui whakarewa (an initial three-day meeting to launch Te Kotahitanga) at which Te Kotahitanga and the Effective Teaching Profile are introduced to teachers through the use of the narratives of experience (Bishop and Berryman 2006). Facilitators and teachers begin the process of critically reflecting upon these experiences and the most commonly held discourse around Māori student disparity. Teachers' sense of themselves, as able to influence Māori students' learning and achievement in classrooms, is strongly promoted. Thus teachers are encouraged to focus on what they can do rather than pathologize Māori students and focus on factors over which they largely have little or no agency. The hui whakarewa is followed by a term-by-term ongoing cycle of individual classroom observations, follow-up feedback sessions, group co-construction meetings, and individual shadow coaching.

Observations and feedback

Observations involve the use of a timed sampling technique by a trained facilitator who observes in the classrooms of participating teachers, using a formal observation tool (Bishop *et al.* 2003). Facilitators are trained to systematically identify specific sets of evidence to show the extent to which teachers are implementing the Effective Teaching Profile in their classrooms (Bishop *et al.* 2007b). Teachers are consulted about when observations will take place and are fully aware of what the observation entails. The facilitator provides the lens through which the teacher can determine the degree to which they are implementing the Effective Teaching Profile. Observations are followed by feedback sessions based on the specific evidence gathered from the observation. In the feedback meeting, the facilitator provides the teacher with the completed observation sheet and targeted, evidence-based feedback from their classroom observation. Feedback concludes with the setting of an individual teacher goal.

Co-construction meetings and shadow coaching

Group co-construction meetings follow observation and feedback sessions. Co-construction meetings involve small groups of teachers from different curriculum areas who teach the same group of students. At these meetings, facilitators support teachers to reflect critically on their own evidence of Māori students' classroom achievement. Through examination of student evidence and linking this to their own practice, teachers continue to develop the shared language; they deepen their instructional knowledge; and they continue to challenge their own assumptions and practices about the effect they have had on Māori students' achievement. In the sharing of expertise and student evidence with colleagues, teachers are able to examine critically their own teaching practices and test their potential effect on the overall Te Kotahitanga goal of raising Māori students' achievement. Teachers are encouraged to use student achievement as the basis for engaging in regular, ongoing learning that often challenges their own pedagogical assumptions. These meetings include a clear focus on Māori students' educational achievement and provide an ongoing forum in which teachers reflect on evidence and show an increasing accountability of their role in contributing to these outcomes.

Co-construction meetings are followed by facilitators providing targeted shadow coaching. Shadow coaching occurs when the facilitator unobtrusively coaches and supports teachers to meet individual or group goals within an authentic teaching and learning context. This may be in the classroom or it may be in another setting where work towards the goal is naturally likely to occur. Shadow coaching provides a supportive environment in which teachers can plan new ideas and strategies, trial them in the classroom, then collaboratively process and reflect on the results with an informed colleague.

Shadow coaching seeks to build teacher capability rather than provide an extra pair of hands in the classroom. It may relate to any aspect of teaching. For example, shadow coaching could focus on lesson planning, use of resources, incorporating prior knowledge into lessons, modelling how to give academic feedback and feed-forward to students, developing relationships with students, or planning for providing culturally responsive learning contexts. Whatever the focus of shadow coaching, facilitators work to ensure there are direct links to classroom practice and that the shadow coaching supports teachers to achieve a goal which is focused on embedding the Effective Teaching Profile in their classroom.

Effect of Te Kotahitanga on students' achievement

In 2006, the first full cohort of students (including targeted Māori students) who had participated in Year 9 and 10 classrooms in Te Kotahitanga schools was in Year 11. In an important external evaluation of the project, Dr Michael Johnston from the New Zealand Qualifications Authority (NZQA) took the opportunity to investigate the effect of Te Kotahitanga on NCEA Level 1 (the first level on the national school qualification system), by using the results from the first full cohort of students in participating Te Kotahitanga schools. His analysis compared the increased rate of those gaining NCEA Level 1 from 2005 to 2006, with all data broken down by four ethnic groups (New Zealand Māori, European, Pacific Islands, and 'other', a group including Asian students), as shown in Table 16.1 (Johnston 2007). It is important to understand that in 2005, few Year 11 students were directly affected by Te Kotahitanga as teachers trained in Te Kotahitanga had only been working mainly with Year 9 and 10 students. However by 2006, most

Table 16.1 Numbers of students on Year 11 rolls and numbers and percentages of students on Year 11 rolls gaining NCEA level 1 at Te Kotahitanga schools in 2005 and 2006, with percentage-point and percentage increases between these years, by ethnicity

Ethnicity	Number of students on Year 11 roll		Year 11 students gaining NCEA Level 1		Percentage of Year 11 students attaining NCEA Level 1		Increase (percentage points)	Increase (absolute percentage)
	2005	2006	2005	2006	2005	2006		
NZ Māori	973	952	312	461	32.1	48.4	16.4	51.0
European	1210	1302	756	899	62.5	69.0	6.6	10.5
Pacific Islands	292	282	69	110	23.6	39.0	15.4	65.1
Other	263	231	181	175	68.8	75.8	6.9	10.1

Year 11 students had benefited from working with Te Kotahitanga teachers for two years and thus were directly affected by Te Kotahitanga.

Johnston's analysis, in Table 16.1, shows there was an increase in the rate of NCEA Level 1 achievement for all student groups from 2005 to 2006. Māori students had the highest percentage point gain (16.4) with Pacific Islands' students next (an increase of 15.4 percentage points). However, from these data it is clear students from all groups in these Te Kotahitanga classrooms benefited.

Next, Johnston undertook an analysis of a national comparison group to reflect the decile[1]-weighting and distribution of Te Kotahitanga schools. This comparison, of the percentage point increase for Year 11 students gaining NCEA Level 1 in the Te Kotahitanga schools with the national decile-weighted cohort of schools from 2005 to 2006, is shown in Table 16.2.

In the analysis of the national comparison group, Johnston identified significant increases in the rates of NCEA Level 1 achievement for all ethnic groups, and in both Te Kotahitanga school data and in the national decile-weighted comparison school data. As shown in Table 16.2, Māori students in Te Kotahitanga schools showed a 16.4 percentage points increase as compared to an 8.9 percentage points increase for Māori students in national comparison schools. Students from Pacific Islands' communities showed somewhat similar gains. Johnston also identified that compared to the national comparison schools, Māori students in Te Kotahitanga schools achieved at a significantly lower rate of gaining NCEA Level 1 in 2005 (32.1 as compared to 34.4 in the national comparison schools) but achieved at a significantly higher rate in 2006 (48.4 as compared to 43.3 in national comparison schools). These data were also highlighted in a Te Kotahitanga case study presented in the *Teacher Professional Learning and Development Best Evidence Synthesis* (Timperley *et al.* 2007: 259–64).

Table 16.2 The percentage point increase for Year 11 students by ethnicity, gaining NCEA level 1 in Te Kotahitanga schools compared with a national decile-weighted cohort of schools from 2005 to 2006

Ethnicity	Year 11 Students gaining NCEA Level 1	
	Te Kotahitanga schools	National decile weighted schools
	Increase (percentage points) 2005 to 2006	
NZ Māori	16.4	8.9
European	6.6	4.1
Pacific Islands	15.4	6.1
Other	6.9	8.1

Effect of Te Kotahitanga on Māori students' experiences

While Johnston's analysis provides quantitative evidence of effects of Te Kotahitanga on raising Māori students' achievement, there is also strong qualitative evidence to support these assertions.

Te Kotahitanga researchers asked facilitators from 12 schools to identify teachers who were high implementers of the Effective Teaching Profile. These teachers were then asked for names of Māori students whom they felt would be comfortable talking about their teachers' classroom practices. These students gave views about the teachers to the researchers. From these interviews, researchers learned that when Māori students have 'effective' teachers, they want to engage with learning and are able to thrive at school. Effective teachers embrace all aspects of the Te Kotahitanga Effective Teaching Profile, including teachers caring for the cultural location of Māori students, caring for their performance, and using a wide range of classroom interactions, strategies and student evidence to inform their practice.

In talking about these teachers, groups of Māori students from the identified schools said:

> You can tell he respects us, because when it comes to learning, big time he's always there, if we don't understand something he doesn't talk to us like little babies, he talks to us like young adults.
>
> And you can rely on him, he's there. Like some teachers are distant to you but he's always there.
>
> (School 1: Group 2, 2004)

> She is cool as, 'cause I go to her every morning.
>
> Yeah she jokes around too and she is cool.
>
> Yeah like and when I got in trouble she like knew what was wrong and stuff.

Yeah cause like you can talk to her like the counsellor. But she don't tell anyone like the counsellor does.

Yeah, that's lies [that they won't tell anyone], they tell.

(School 10: Group 3, 2005)

Effective teachers, they said, *'go that extra little bit':*

Mr H's always willing to go that extra little bit.

He also gets behind the class, like goes out of his way to make fun things for us, like ideas about going for a trip and fundraising for it, like sausage sizzles.

He makes an effort in everything we do, if he knows stuff is boring he tells us this is boring but if we get through it we can do something else.

(School 1: Group 2, 2004)

They act in a just and fair manner:

She wants to be like a good teacher. She doesn't want to be your friend or that sort of thing. She's like a friend, but not a friend.

She never ever picks her favourites.

She doesn't have favourites.

Like the whole class are her favourites. She treats everyone the same.

Then if you're good and if you still haven't done your homework that doesn't mean diddly, you're all in trouble. You gotta do it.

(School 10: Group 3, 2004)

Effective teachers consult with and listen to Māori students in order to ensure 'things' Māori are properly addressed:

Oh, do you know what I really like? She read the whole of *Whale Rider* out and she tried her hardest to say the Māori words. It was so cute.

Yeah, it was so cute . . . she was like 'kaaa huu' it was so cute.

Yeah, and she's like, guys how do you say this word? And then you would see her at the end of the day saying it.

Yeah, she just kept saying it and saying it and practising.

(School 11: Group 1, 2004)

Effective teachers want to teach Māori students and have high expectations of them:

She's dedicated to what we do in our class.

I think it's just her passion, that she likes seeing kids achieving instead of failing.

Feels cool, that we've got someone who's gonna help us get through school.

She thinks that we must be that brainy that we can do fifth form work.
She pushes us.
I think she believes in us.

(School 2: Group 3, 2005)

These teachers have a strong commitment to developing students as learners:

He'll be able to tell if something's wrong, and if we don't understand it he just explains it really detailed, or if we need him he'll be at his desk or something.

Or he'll make you think about it, sometimes you write something down and he says, are you sure that's right?, and you check it again.

Sometimes when you ask a question the teacher will slip out the answer but he doesn't do that, he's really careful about what he says, he makes us think hard.

(School 1: Group 2, 2004)

She makes us think, she doesn't give this one formula that we have to use throughout, so we don't remember. She makes us think about it and figure it out and then if we don't she'll like take a few of us away and like try and get it in their heads.

Yeah, it's better that way.

(School 10: Group 3, 2004)

They engage with students to critically reflect on their teaching:

At the end of every unit and the end of our test she gives out a piece of paper to the whole class and you have to write what's hot and what's not, with what you liked about the unit and what you didn't like about the unit.

(School 6: Group 1, 2004)

Like if we had a test and one of us got a real low mark, he will talk to you in private and he will pull you out of what you are doing and he will talk to you and he will say, like, this is your score, you only got this and this wrong, you need to go back and you have to think about what you have done wrong and then fix your mistakes and then I will re-mark your test.

(School 4: Group 1, 2005)

Effective teachers acknowledge student effort and learning:

And she congratulates you. She's like, well done on your test, you've got this much and this is the average of the class and. . . .

She encourages us.

'You're getting higher and higher every day' and. . . .
She just helps us understand it.
She helps us until we get it.

(School 4: Group 2, 2005)

She tells you if you've done good.
Like she sometimes rings your mum if you've done good.
Like if you've got 50 or 60 or 75 per cent.

(School 12: Group 3, 2004)

They are well organized and know how to teach:

She likes to be organized.
She understands our problems and tries to help us and stuff.
She always gets us to get our stuff out and do the work that's on the board, the 'do now'.
She likes to keep stuff planned; she doesn't like unorganized people.

(School 2: Group 3, 2005)

And for our exams we had last week she made us two sheets of just random questions of about two per unit for exams for revision and yeah that was really helpful because you had something to base your revision on rather than just opening your books and not knowing where to begin.
Yeah, that was really good.
And none of our other teachers did that.
So that was cool.

(School 6: Group 1, 2004)

When Māori students have teachers like this, they think about themselves differently:

I've got goals that I can achieve, that I can do, I'm one of the top in my class and not at the bottom and I can help people instead of them helping me. . . . I've never helped anyone at intermediate before, it's always been me getting helped but it's been a change that I'm helping my new mates this year.

(School 3: Group 1, 2005)

We just keep on getting higher and higher.
We are getting higher in our marks; 'cause last year none of us passed, none of us. And now this year we are getting like 87 per cent.
Yeah, it's good.

(School 7: Group 1, 2005)

Teacher interviews

The teacher interviews, undertaken at the same time as the student interviews, indicated the teachers had undergone a philosophical shift in the way they thought about teaching and learning. Teachers assuming a position of agency in regards to Māori students' participation and achievement, rather than blaming the students for any deficiencies, together with all elements of the Effective Teaching Profile, are the essential threads to bring about what this research is terming a 'culturally responsive pedagogy of relationships'. It is an approach that rests in the first instance on a commitment by teachers to develop strong caring and learning relationships and interactions with Māori students; in the second, for teachers to believe strongly that Māori students can improve their achievement; and third, that their students are able to take responsibility for their learning and performance.

Ongoing effect on teachers and schools

The iterative process of research and development within the Te Kotahitanga project has shown benefits from assisting and supporting teachers to develop what Gay (2000) terms a culturally responsive context for learning. These benefits include changes in teachers' classroom practice, their levels of satisfaction with teaching, and Māori students' participation and achievement outcomes. However, similar to Timperley *et al.* (2003), we have learned that professional communities of teachers who focus solely upon themselves and their development of specific contexts for learning will not necessarily bring about changes for Māori students. Rather it has been the development of communities that focus on the goal of improving Māori students' learning and achievement that have been instrumental in improving outcomes for these students.

As discussed, this is achieved in each school by the Te Kotahitanga research and development team providing specific support to the school facilitation team. This team manages a term-by-term cycle of teacher observation followed by feedback and individual goal setting that then feeds into collegial co-construction meetings and group goal setting. Teachers are supported to achieve their goals through in-class support provided by a facilitation team member. We have found that the co-construction meetings, as places where teachers from a variety of curriculum areas focus on and are responsive to Māori students whom they all teach, are essential. At these meetings, collegial reflection is based on student evidence with goal setting located within a 'pedagogy of relations' (Sidorkin 2002); that is, pedagogy based on one's relationships with learners and learning rather than just on curriculum expertise. In this way, teachers can critically reflect upon student data gathered in their classrooms, pertaining to student participation and achievement. They are then able to identify changes in practice necessary to ensure progress towards the collective goal of raising Māori student achievement.

The results from schools in Te Kotahitanga showed that where full professional development support was provided to teachers, changes occurred in teachers' relationships and interactions with Māori students, and these in turn had a positive effect on Māori students' participation and achievement. Changes for Māori students included increased on-task engagement; reduction in absenteeism; increases in work completion; and improvements in academic achievement.

Hence, teachers were able to increase the cognitive demands of the curriculum content of their classroom lessons (Bishop *et al.* 2003, Bishop *et al.* 2007b).

Conclusion

Research studies undertaken by Hattie (1999, 2003a, 2003b) and Alton-Lee (2003, 2006) identify that the most important systemic influence on students' educational achievement was the effectiveness of their teachers. While both Hattie and Alton-Lee had also considered traditionally perceived influences on learning and achievement, such as family, home community, pedagogy, teachers, school systems, and the students themselves, their analyses showed that with effective teachers, low socioeconomic settings were not immutable in terms of Māori students' achievement, as some others have asserted (Chapple *et al.* 1997; Harker and Nash 1990; Nash 1993). Findings from Te Kotahitanga support Hattie and Alton-Lee's findings. However, they also suggest that traditional initiatives are unlikely to make a difference unless there is also an attempt to address the dominant psychological discursive positioning inherent in many colonised societies, and that continues to pathologize and problematize the indigenous condition (Shields *et al.* 2005; Walker 1990).

The belittlement of indigenous knowledge, the maintenance of power imbalances, and explanations of low achievement that stem from Western psychological paradigms in educational contexts lead to the perpetuation of cultural deficit explanations (victim-blaming) of low performance. This in turn maintains ongoing mainstream discourses about the indigenous or cultural minority situation and continues maintenance of power over what is determined to be knowledge in classrooms and how relationships and interactions within pedagogy are played out (Bishop *et al.* 2003; Bishop *et al.* 2007b; Bishop and Berryman 2006).

Te Kotahitanga has highlighted solutions that come from within kaupapa Māori and from Māori students themselves. Raising Māori student achievement requires teachers to be ever mindful of the way 'power differentials' have contributed to inter-generational disparities for these students. This research has also identified that teacher effectiveness for Māori students has depended upon teachers' ability to form and maintain effective relationships with them. Further, it was the types of relationships developed between the teacher and Māori students that were the most crucial factor in mediating their engagement and learning in schools. Raising Māori student achievement requires a 'pedagogy of relations' that is where teachers improve or maintain respectful relationships with Māori students that are effective and positive for both student and teacher, as the basis for teaching and learning. In classrooms where this is modelled by teachers, all students stand to benefit.

Note

1   In New Zealand, schools are assigned a decile ranking between 1 (low) and 10 (high) based on the latest Census information about the education and income levels of the adults living in the households of students who attend the school.

References

Alton-Lee, A. (2003) *Quality Teaching for Diverse Students in Schooling: Best Evidence Synthesis*, Wellington: Ministry of Education.

Alton-Lee, A. (2006) 'How teaching influences learning: implications for educational researchers, teachers, teacher educators and policy makers', *Teaching and Teacher Education*, 22: 612–26.

Bishop, R. (1996) *Collaborative Research Stories: Whakawhanaungatanga*, Palmerston North, New Zealand: Dunmore Press.

Bishop, R. (2005) 'Freeing ourselves from neo-colonial domination in research: a kaupapa Māori approach to creating knowledge', in N. Denzin and Y. Lincoln (eds) *Handbook of Qualitative Research*, 3rd edn (pp. 109–38), Thousand Oaks, CA: Sage Publications.

Bishop, R., and Berryman, M. (2006) *Culture Speaks: Cultural Relationships and Classroom Learning*, Wellington, NZ: Huia Publishers.

Bishop, R., Berryman, M., Cavanagh, T. and Lamont, R. (2007a) 'The Te Kotahitanga Observation Tool: development, use, reliability and validity', paper presented at NZARE, Christchurch, New Zealand, December.

Bishop, R., Berryman, M., Cavanagh, T. and Teddy, L. (2007b) *Te Kotahitanga Phase 3 Whanaungatanga: Establishing a Culturally Responsive Pedagogy of Relations in Mainstream Secondary School Classrooms*, Wellington, New Zealand: Ministry of Education.

Bishop, R., Berryman, M., Powell, A. and Teddy, L. (2007c) *Te Kotahitanga: Improving the Educational Achievement of Māori Students in Mainstream Education Phase 2: Towards a Whole School Approach*, report to the Ministry of Education, Wellington, New Zealand: Ministry of Education.

Bishop, R., Berryman, M., Tiakiwai, S. and Richardson, C. (2003) *Te Kotahitanga: Experiences of Year 9 and 10 Māori Students in Mainstream Classrooms*, final report to the Ministry of Education, Wellington, New Zealand: Ministry of Education.

Bishop, R. and Glynn, T. (1999) *Culture Counts: Changing Power Relations in Education*, Palmerston North, New Zealand: Dunmore Press.

Bronfenbrenner, U. (1979) *The Ecology of Human Development*, Cambridge, MA: Harvard University Press.

Bruner, J. (1996) *The Culture of Education*, Cambridge, MA: Harvard University Press.

Burr, V. (1995) *An Introduction to Social Constructionism*, London: Routledge

Chapple, S., Jeffries, R. and Walker, R. (1997) *Māori Participation and Performance in Education: A Literature Review and Research Programme*, report for the Ministry of Education, Wellington, New Zealand.

Durie, M.H. (2005) 'Race and ethnicity in public policy: does it work?', *Social Policy Journal of New Zealand*, 24: 1–11.

Foucault, M. (1972) *The Archaeology of Knowledge*, New York: Pantheon.

Freire, P. (1996) *Pedagogy of the Oppressed*, London: Penguin Books.

Gay, G. (2000) *Culturally Responsive Teaching: Theory, Research and Practice*, New York: Teachers College Press.

Harker, R., and Nash, R. (1990) 'Cultural reproduction and school achievement: a case for kura kaupapa Māori', *ACCESS*, 9: 26–39.

Hattie, J. (1999) 'Influences on student learning', inaugural lecture, the University of Auckland, Auckland, New Zealand, available at: www.education.auckland.ac.nz/uoa/hattie (accessed 22 Aug. 2009).

Hattie, J. (2003a) 'Teachers make a difference: what is the research evidence?' paper presented at the Australian Council for Educational Research annual conference, October.

Hattie, J. (2003b) 'New Zealand Education Snapshot: with specific reference to the years 1–13', paper presented at the Knowledge Wave 2003, The Leadership Forum, Auckland, February.

Hokowhitu, B. (2001) 'Māori as the Savage Other: icons of racial representation', paper presented at the Tokyo Foundation International Forum on Social Equality, 31 October to 2 November, Howard University, Washington DC.

Hunn, J.K. (1960) *Report on the Department of Māori Affairs*, Wellington, NZ: Government Printer.

Johnston, M. (2007) 'The effect of Te Kotahitanga on success rates in NCEA Level 1', unpublished Research Note, Research and Knowledge Services, New Zealand Qualifications Authority, Wellington.

Ministry of Education (2002) *Monitoring the Achievement of Māori Students: in New Zealand Schools Ngā Kura o Aotearoa 2000*, a report to the Minister of Education on the compulsory schools sector in NZ 2001 [also known as the Schools Sector report 2001], Wellington, New Zealand: Ministry of Education.

Nash, R. (1993) *Succeeding Generations: Family Resources and Access to Education in New Zealand*, Auckland: Oxford University Press.

O'Sullivan, D. (2007) *Beyond Biculturalism: The Politics of an Indigenous Minority*, Wellington, NZ: Huia Publishers.

Quest Rapuara (1992) *Cultural Identity: A Resource for Educators: Whakamana Tangata*, Wellington: Quest Rapuara, the Career Development and Transition Education Service. [Out of print – available in libraries.]

Rogoff, B. (1990) *Apprenticeship in Thinking: Cognitive Development in Social Context*, New York: Oxford University Press.

Shields, C.M., Bishop, R. and Mazawi, A.E. (2005) *Pathologizing Practices: The Impact of Deficit Thinking on Education*, New York: Peter Lang Publishing.

Sidorkin, A.M. (2002) *Learning Relations: Impure Education, Deschooled Schools, and Dialogue with Evil*, New York: Peter Lang Publishing.

Smith, G. (1995) 'Whakaoho whānau: new formations of whānau as an innovative intervention into Māori cultural and educational crises', *He Pukenga Kōrero Koanga*, 1: 18–36.

Smith, G.H. (1997) 'Kaupapa Māori as transformative praxis', unpublished doctoral thesis, University of Auckland, New Zealand.

Smith, L.T. (1999) *Decolonizing Methodologies Research and Indigenous Peoples*, London: Zed Books Ltd. Dunedin, NZ: University of Otago Press.

Timperley, H., Phillips, G. and Wiseman, J. (2003) *The Sustainability of Professional Development in Literacy – Parts One and Two*, Auckland: the University of Auckland.

Timperley, H., Wilson, A., Barrar, H. and Fung, I. (2007) *Teacher professional learning and development: Best evidence synthesis iteration (BES)* Wellington: Ministry of Education.

Tully, J. (2000) 'The struggles of indigenous peoples for and of freedom', in D. Ivison, P. Patton and W. Sanders (eds) *Political Theory and the Rights of Indigenous Peoples* (pp. 36–59), Melbourne: Cambridge University Press.

Vygotsky, L.S. (1978) *Mind in Society: The Development of Higher Psychological Processes*, London: Harvard University Press.

Walker, R. (1990) *Ka Whawhai Tonu Matou Struggle Without End*, Auckland, New Zealand: Penguin Books.

Wearmouth, J., Glynn, T. and Berryman, M. (2005) *Perspectives on Student Behaviour in Schools: Exploring Theory and Developing Practice*, London: Routledge Falmer.

Chapter 17

Conclusion

Some potential influences of educational psychology on educational research

John Sweller and Christine M. Rubie-Davies

Educational psychology differs from most of the other subdisciplines of education. Some of the differences are to be expected of a psychology-based area. We expect that educational psychology might place a greater emphasis on human cognition and its consequences for learning and instruction than areas of education concerned with, for example, curriculum matters. The chapters of this book reflect that emphasis on the mind, its structures and functions and what those structures and functions mean for educational processes. In these relations we find the basic *raison d'être* of educational psychology.

There are other differences between educational psychology and at least some streams of endeavour in education that are more surprising and, to many educational psychologists, concerning. Those differences go to the very heart of research in education. Most educational psychologists use one or other version of a standard, scientific methodology when conducting their research. Frequently, they will use a theory to generate hypotheses, they will collect data to test the hypotheses and will determine whether the data support or contradict their theory and hypotheses. Sometimes, data may be collected in an exploratory fashion without strong theories or hypotheses. The data collected are often quantitative but can be qualitative depending on the nature of the questions under consideration. If the issue is whether a particular cognitive process exists, for example, qualitative data may be collected. In contrast, if the issue is whether a particular instructional procedure is better than another procedure, quantitative data will be required. In either case, most educational psychologists do not classify themselves as being qualitative or quantitative researchers. They are trained to be technically competent and carry out the type of research demanded of the questions being asked. Educational recommendations are made only after data have been collected, analysed and interpreted. In addition, educational recommendations frequently await partial or full replication of research findings. In the absence of these standard, scientific procedures, it can be argued that recommendations for educational change are rarely justified. Education should not be a discipline relying largely on changeable opinions and fashions. We should rely on theory-motivated data and only after such data have been collected and verified by replication should we recommend systemic changes in educational processes.

Perusal of any of the chapters of this book will provide case studies of scientific methodology as applied to education using an educational psychology framework. The importance of this methodology cannot be overestimated. It provides, in areas associated with educational psychology, at least in part, a barrier against the introduction of educational fads based on little more than opinion and advocacy. On occasions, some areas of education can run the risk of falling prey to fads. We do periodically see the introduction of novel procedures based on opinion alone with no discernible data supporting the introduction of the advocated procedures. There are several, well-known examples from both the more distant and recent past. In the more distant past, 'New Mathematics' provides an example. The procedures were hailed as a vastly superior technique for teaching mathematics. The new methodology required students to learn the basic rationale of mathematical procedures without explicitly learning how to carry out those procedures. It was introduced in the 1960s, only to be abandoned rapidly as it became apparent that knowing how mathematics worked was no substitute for being able to do mathematics. This debacle easily could have been avoided by running empirical studies comparing the effectiveness of the new against the old techniques.

In more recent times, whole-language learning was introduced to early readers in primary schools without testing its effectiveness against the traditional procedures associated with phonics-based procedures. An entire generation of students was taught to read and write a phonetically-based language such as English with no or only limited exposure to that phonetic base. It was only after randomized controlled experiments carried out by psychologists demonstrated the superiority of phonic-based instruction when young children learn to read English that the pendulum swung back to the inclusion of phonics. Those experiments should have been carried out by advocates prior to the introduction of whole-language procedures, not after the procedures had been introduced into educational systems. Having a hypothesis provides no justification for introducing radical educational change. Having a hypothesis associated with replicated data from properly designed, carried out and analysed research provides an appropriate foundation for advocacy leading to educational innovations. Merely stating 'the research indicates . . .' provides no substitute for actually having such research.

It has not only been young children who have been exposed to less than ideal educational procedures associated with data-free opinion along with insistent advocacy. Some of our best and brightest have similarly been exposed to new teaching procedures that were introduced prior to the required research being carried out. Problem-based learning provides an example. This technique has been used to dramatically alter the procedures used in training medical and other personnel without determining whether problem-based learning actually is superior to explicit instruction. Furthermore, the procedures associated with problem-based learning were introduced without reference to a human cognitive architecture that could support them. The theory on which hypotheses were based was missing. Little attempt was made to collect data that could provide evidence that the procedures were more effective than the explicit instruction that they replaced. Not surprisingly, most experiments that have been published testing the effectiveness of explicit instruction over instruction in which learners are expected to find the solution to problems themselves, with minimal guidance, demonstrate the superiority of explicit instruction.

It is of concern that once untested procedures are introduced into educational systems, if it becomes apparent that they are ineffective, rear-guard actions are taken to protect their continuation. That action sometimes consists of belated attempts to collect data, an action that, as indicated above, should have taken place prior to rather than after the introduction of the procedures into educational systems. More frequently, the major response is more advocacy. If the advocacy is successful, the procedure is retained. If another group has better advocates or just more numerous advocates, a new procedure is introduced. In this manner, educational procedures can be reduced to fads with the winner being whoever shouts loudest and longest. The consequence is a teaching profession that can happily ignore educational 'research' when it sees that some of the so-called research consists largely of opinions rather than data. A popular movement is no substitute for rigorous theory-building and data collection. It does not have to be this way. We can easily base our decisions on properly conducted research. Most research with an educational psychology base provides a template that could be used by other sub-areas of education. Providing examples of good educational psychology research is one of the best ways of accomplishing this aim. The exemplary work of our colleagues who have written chapters for this book provide excellent case studies of what can and should be done in terms of implementing rigorous research and providing sound, evidence-based outcomes.

This book is primarily aimed at academics researching in the various fields of educational psychology. However, it is hoped that it will provide an eclectic mix of topics for a new generation of postgraduate students and teachers coming back to study who will be inspired to follow a particular field in educational psychology and who will realize the necessity for combining change in education with an understanding of research-based outcomes. Conducting thorough and meticulous research in educational psychology can lead to the implementation of procedures in classrooms that, because they are evidence-based, will result in better academic and social outcomes for every child attending school.

Index

accountability 2, 3, 8, 11, 53, 103, 104, 107, 111, 112, 114, 185, 257
applied behaviour analysis 2, 5, 154; and behaviour management 167–9; and curriculum strategies 170–2, 173–4; dimensions of 167; and Project Early 168; research using 173–6; and self-management strategies 168, 169, 169–70; status of 174–6; 176–7; teacher education in 172–3, 176–7
assessment 102–14; for accountability 2, 53, 103, 104, 107, 111, 112, 114; asTTle tool for 108–11; and effective classroom teaching 18; high stakes 2, 107, 112; formative 18, 19, 32, 51, 54–5, 55–61, 104–8, 111; nature of 102–4; portfolio 53–4, 58; practices in 7; and quality of teacher judgements 108; reliability and validity of 2, 4, 52, 61, 102, 103, 108, 109, 110, 111, 114, 156; students' conceptions of 113; summative 2, 51–3, 61, 104–5, 107; teachers' conceptions of 111–13; see also writing assessment
Assessment Tools for Teaching and Learning (asTTle) 4, 7, 23, 60–1, 102; 104; 105, 108–11, 114; and writing assessment 23, 60–1; see also assessment
attention deficit hyperactivity disorder (ADHD) 203, 215, 216, 217, 222, 223; see also hyperactivity, preschool
atypical behaviour development 215–24; see also attention deficit hyperactivity disorder; autism; hyperactivity; atypical children 186, 208
autism 5; 167, 170, 175, 177

behaviour management 2, 5, 7, 144–5, 150–63, 173, 187, 194; and applied behaviour analysis 167–9; and behaviour continuum 152–3; and culturally responsive practices 157–61; and ethnicity 156–7; and inappropriate behaviour 151–2; and inclusive education 155–6; and Māori world view 161; and nature of classroom 150–3; and theoretical background 153–5; see also positive behaviour support

classroom environment
see socioemotional environment of classroom
classroom management see behaviour management
cognitive load theory 87–8, 92–3; and human cognitive architecture 87, 88–92; and instructional effects generated by 93–8; and long-term memory 88, 89, 91, 92, 93, 96, 98; and schemas 88–9, 89, 91, 92, 93, 94, 98; and working memory 89–90, 91–2, 92–3
community: classroom 2, 136, 139, 143, 145; involvement and learning 157–8, 235, 244, 264
cooperative learning 127, 129, 131, 188, 193, 204, 206
cultural deficit theorizing see deficit theorizing
culturally responsive instruction 150, 157–61; and deficit theorizing 250–2; 253; effective New Zealand practices in 159–61; and Māori world view 161; and teacher self-reflection 158–9;